EXPLAINING RISK ANALYSIS

Risk analysis is not a narrowly defined set of applications. Rather, it is widely used to assess and manage a plethora of hazards that threaten dire implications. However, too few people actually understand what risk analysis can help us accomplish and, even among experts, knowledge is often limited to one or two applications.

Explaining Risk Analysis frames risk analysis as a holistic planning process aimed at making better risk-informed decisions and emphasizing the connections between the parts. This framework requires an understanding of basic terms, including explanations of why there is no universal agreement about what risk means, much less risk assessment, risk management and risk analysis. Drawing on a wide range of case studies, the book illustrates the ways in which risk analysis can help lead to better decisions in a variety of scenarios, including the destruction of chemical weapons, management of nuclear waste and the response to passenger rail threats. The book demonstrates how the risk analysis process and the data, models and processes used in risk analysis will clarify, rather than obfuscate, decision-makers' options.

This book will be of great interest to students and scholars of risk assessment, risk management, public health, environmental science, environmental economics and environmental psychology.

Michael R. Greenberg is Distinguished Professor and Associate Dean of the Faculty at the Edward J. Bloustein School of Planning and Public Policy, Rutgers University, USA.

Earthscan Risk in Society series

Edited by Ragnar E. Löfstedt
King's College London, UK

Trust in Cooperative Risk Management
Uncertainty and scepticism in the public mind
Michael Siegrist, Timothy C. Earle and Heinz Gutscher

Trust in Risk Management
Uncertainty and scepticism in the public mind
Edited by Michael Siegrist, Timothy C. Earle and Heinz Gutscher

Uncertainty and Risk
Multidisciplinary perspectives
Edited by Gabriele Bammer and Michael Smithson

Judgment and Decision Making
Baruch Fischhoff

Risk Analysis and Human Behaviour
Baruch Fischhoff

The Spatial Dimension of Risk
How Geography shapes the emergence of riskscapes
Detlef Müller-Mahn

Effective Risk Communication
Edited by Joseph Arvai and Louie Rivers

Protecting Seniors Against Environmental Disasters
From hazards and vulnerability to prevention and resilience
Michael R. Greenberg

Anthropology and Risk
Åsa Boholm

Explaining Risk Analysis
Protecting health and the environment
Michael R. Greenberg

"Michael Greenberg's masterpiece book *Explaining Risk Analysis* is written in coherent terms, while guided by the Gestalt-holistic thinking. This combination makes the richness and complexity of risk analysis comprehensive to a broad readership. It is a gift to all of us—students, practitioners and scholars—in this ever-challenging and expanding field." – *Yacov Haimes, Lawrence Quarles Professor of Engineering, University of Virginia, former President of the Society for Risk Analysis, USA*

"Michael Greenberg, one of the world's foremost risk analysis scholars, authors, and practitioners, has written a delightful, thoroughly engaging and accessible introduction to the field of risk analysis, showing how it works, why it matters, and how individuals, organizations, and governments can apply risk assessment and risk management to make the world a better place. The tools introduced and vividly illustrated here with compelling case studies can help to make sense of, and to resolve with sanity and insight, some of the most contentious debates of our time. These include discussions of environmental justice, land use, climate change, responses to terrorism and saner and more effective individual, organizational, and governmental planning under risk and uncertainty. This lucid and fun exposition will benefit not only students, teachers, and practitioners of risk analysis, but also policy analysts and decision-makers who want to manage risks, uncertainties, complexities, and conflicts more effectively." – *Tony Cox, Editor-in-Chief,* Risk Analysis, *USA*.

EXPLAINING RISK ANALYSIS

Protecting health and the environment

Michael R. Greenberg

Routledge
Taylor & Francis Group

LONDON AND NEW YORK

earthscan
from Routledge

First published 2017
by Routledge
2 Park Square, Milton Park, Abingdon, Oxon OX14 4RN

and by Routledge
711 Third Avenue, New York, NY 10017

Routledge is an imprint of the Taylor & Francis Group, an informa business

© 2017 Michael R. Greenberg

British Library Cataloguing-in-Publication Data
A catalogue record for this book is available from the British Library

Library of Congress Cataloging-in-Publication Data
Names: Greenberg, Michael R., author.
Title: Explaining risk analysis protecting health and the environment /
Michael R. Greenberg.
Description: Abingdon, Oxon ; New York, NY : Routledge, 2017.
Identifiers: LCCN 2016013853| ISBN 9781138125339 (hb) | ISBN 9781138125346
(pb) | ISBN 9781315647579 (ebook)
Subjects: LCSH: Environmental risk assessment. | Health risk assessment. |
Risk management.
Classification: LCC GE145 .G75 2017 | DDC 333.71/4—dc23
LC record available at https://lccn.loc.gov/2016013853

ISBN: 978-1-138-12533-9 (hbk)
ISBN: 978-1-138-12534-6 (pbk)
ISBN: 978-1-315-64757-9 (ebk)

Typeset in Bembo
by FiSH Books Ltd, Enfield

DEDICATIONS

When I began writing this book, I realized how much I have learned by working with talented and caring people. Most of my best colleagues at Rutgers and Columbia universities are still here and will have an opportunity to see this book. Others have passed away and I dedicate this book to them. When I was a student and as a young professor at Columbia, I was privileged to have worked with George Carey and Leonard Zobler who were my adviser and co-adviser, respectively. I learned a great deal about history from Douglas McManis, economics from William Vickrey, quantitative methods in physical sciences from Arthur Strahler, and atmospheric science from John Oliver. At Rutgers, I learned a great deal about radiation science and risk management from Arthur Upton and exposure assessment from Paul Lioy. I owe a great deal to my colleague Ed Ortiz for speaking with me about environmental justice and Tayfur Altiok helped me understand some of the models used in industrial engineering. These colleagues were important to me in learning not only about risk analysis but about the larger challenges that life presents. I hope that they were aware of the important role they played in educating me.

CONTENTS

FIGURES

Boxes

TABLES

PREFACE

In 1951, I had an asthma attack and as a result subconsciously became a risk analyst. Our family physician, Dr. Goldberg, administered a shot of adrenaline, which helped. Bad pollen allergies primed the attack, and then something else triggered the reaction. I was scared, struggling to breathe, and was compliant when Dr. Goldberg later started me on allergy shots and gave me little green pills "Pyri Benzamine," which I took for many years, despite their bitter taste.

For over 60 years, I have been trying to prevent another asthma attack by studying what kind of events could precipitate one. I know what seasons of the year to be concerned about, what weather conditions increase the likelihood of a problem, and what foods to avoid during that season (e.g., carrots, walnuts). I try to get a little extra sleep. I stay as far away as I can from straw, goldenrod, and other pollens, and I avoid cats and horses during the Fall. Exercise has helped; so I exercise every day for at least an hour.

It is not possible to avoid every asthma trigger. If I feel a cold coming on, I have a protocol of using a nasal spray, and if I feel a fever coming on, I visit my physician. You will not be shocked to read that my physician specializes in allergy management. At this point, some of you are probably laughing. Maybe I overdo it, but I don't think so. I have managed to avoid another asthma attack, and four years ago, I stopped allergy shots because the literature shows that someone who has taken them for a long time should have a good internal sensor, and two-thirds of them no longer need the shots. I appear to be one of the fortunate two-thirds. In short, I have spent decades studying the hazard, estimating the likelihood of a reaction, and the consequences of not taking action. Then, I take steps to prevent the reaction and return to normal. My story is not unique. Many people who are vulnerable to a hazard learn how to reduce their risk.

In addition to individuals like me, many organizations use risk analysis to assess and manage a plethora of hazards that could have dire implications for their organization. Many of us who have been involved in risk analysis for decades support existing uses of the risk analysis, and we have advocated for expanding the boundaries of the discipline to new specific applications, as well as pressed for risk analysis to be incorporated into organizational planning. A major obstacle is that too few people understand what risk analysis can help us accomplish. Many university students, public and government audiences do not understand the definition of risk, risk assessment, risk management, risk analysis and allied concepts, and more generally do not know what risk assessors and risk managers can tell them that they are unlikely to learn from other approaches. Even among experts, knowledge is often limited to one or two applications. I flinch whenever someone gets up in front of an audience and describes the field through one application. Risk analysis is not a narrowly defined set of applications of a few tools. Risk analysis needs to be more effectively explained to a larger community than it has to date.

This book explains and illustrates risk analysis as both a set of tools and as a holistic planning process aimed at making more and better risk-informed decisions. This framework requires an understanding of basic terms, and I define the key terms, including explanations of why there is not universal agreement about what risk means, much less risk assessment, risk management and risk analysis. I begin to illustrate risk assessment and then risk management with brief examples that should be familiar to many of you, beginning with the development of chemical risk assessment and ending with factors that influence public perceptions, values and preferences about human and environmental risks.

I was a math major and teacher. I noticed that mathematical tools did not interest most students, until I started teaching with examples that brought the numbers to life. My students learn from engaging with examples that interest them, not by me teaching them methods. Hence, in this book I have written case studies about issues that you have likely read or heard about, been curious about and perhaps been part of. These case studies are about chemical weapons, environmental justice, passenger rail security, biological weapons, and freshwater supply. If I have done a good job picking and writing about them, then the reader should see the process and analytical tools come alive and help clarify rather than obfuscate risk-informed decision-making process.

During my more than half-century fascination with risk analysis, so much has changed. I discuss two major changes in this book. I know that some of us enjoy fiction, and so you will find a chapter that connects disaster science fiction books and movies to risk analysis. The link may seem irrelevant to explaining risk analysis, but when you read my characterization of how risk and risk analysts are treated in disaster science fiction, you may change your mind. A second major change is risk analysis online. You will find discussions in the book about using online tools to enhance your access to risk information. Lastly, I end the book by describing two externally imposed challenges to risk analysis and how I expect risk analysts to react.

If I have done a good job, especially with the cases, you will see that risk analysis can help lead to better risk-informed decisions. After you finish this book, I hope you have forged an emotional connection to some of the issues that will leave you intrigued, wanting more information and concerned about risks, rather than bored and ready to move on to your next activity.

Michael R. Greenberg
March 1, 2016

ACKNOWLEDGMENTS

I owe a debt of gratitude to many colleagues at Rutgers and Vanderbilt, where risk-related issues dominated conversations with Joanna Burger, Caron Chess, Jim Clarke, Michael Gallo, Mark Gilbertson, Bernard Goldstein, David Kosson, Steve Krahn, Henry Mayer, Charles Powers, Dona Schneider, and Dan Wartenberg. I worked for many years with outstanding experts in risk analysis through the Society of Risk Analysis (SRA). I know that interactions with the following SRA colleagues helped steer my path through risk analysis, especially Elizabeth Anderson, Terje Aven, Tony Cox, Michael Dourson, Charles Haas, Yacov Haimes, Sally Kane, Wayne Landis, Warner North, Michael Siegrist, Paul Slovic, Kimberly Thompson, Curtis Travis, and Rae Zimmerman.

Many of the studies I was involved in were funded by federal government agencies and private organizations, most notably the U.S. Environmental Protection Agency, the U.S. Departments of Energy and Homeland Security. While working on projects, I had the privilege of collaborating with risk scientists who were sometimes at universities and other times in government. I particularly want to acknowledge Tom Burke, Glenn Paulson, and Peter Preuss for collaborating when we all worked on cancer risks in New Jersey. The views, opinions, positions, conclusions, or strategies in this work are those of the author and do not necessarily reflect the views, opinions, positions, conclusions, strategies, or official policy or position of my colleagues and government agencies, and no implied official endorsement should be inferred from these acknowledgments.

I end these acknowledgments by thanking Jennifer Rovito Whytlaw for preparing the figures and maps included in the book, my wife Gwendolyn Greenberg for drawing the cartoon in Chapter 9, and I thank Wiley and Elsevier Publishers for allowing me to reuse materials I prepared for other publications in Chapters 3, 6 and 9.

1

RISK ANALYSIS

A start

Introduction

I introduce risk analysis to students and public audiences in three steps over 10 to 15 minutes. First, I ask them to:

1. Close their eyes, and think of the first three human health and environmental hazards, risks, and events that concern, worry and scare them the most;
2. After a minute, I ask them to open their eyes and write these three items on a piece of paper or their computer; and
3. We discuss the items on their list.

With rare exceptions, nuclear war tops their list, followed by a nuclear power plant accident, a virus or bug that causes a pandemic, and sometimes hurricanes, earthquakes, tornadoes and other natural hazards that they have lived through or much more likely seen on television. All of these hazard events are low probability but potentially high consequence. Few in the audience pick alcohol or drug abuse, tobacco, engaging in dangerous physical behaviors, living in a home with flaking lead or asbestos particles and without safe stairs, and other common and potentially consequential hazards. The point of this initial exercise is to get them to recognize that low probability and high consequence events rise to the top of the concern list.

My second step is to use the first discussion to motivate them to call for analytical and replicable approaches to assess risk and thoughtful, principled analysis to inform decision-making processes. This second step requires a commonly accepted language of key terms and concepts. The Society for Risk Analysis (SRA) (www.sra.org) has published several glossaries. One available through the website includes short definitions of more than 300 terms. The second produced by the

SRA Committee on Foundations of Risk Analysis divides the glossary into "basic concepts," "related concepts, methods, and procedures," and "risk management actions." It acknowledges that it is unrealistic to assume that there will be a single definition of these terms and concepts (Committee on Foundations 2015). The second glossary provides multiple definitions of the word risk and other terms, and I am a strong advocate of using it because of the depth it provides.

I have collected more than 20 definitions of risk written by individuals with backgrounds in public health, engineering, economics and others. In this book, I use the following definition of risk developed by William Lowrance (1976), and arguably the most widely cited: *Risk is a measure of the probability and severity of adverse events.*

In regard to the definition of risk analysis, as part of the celebration of the thirtieth year of the Society of Risk Analysis in the year 2010, a group of the editors of the society's journal, *Risk Analysis, An International Journal* summarized major accomplishments (Greenberg *et al.* 2012). Their effort was organized around the following six risk analysis questions:

1. What can go wrong? (hazard event);
2. What are the chances that something with serious consequences will go wrong? (likelihood);
3. What are the consequences if something does go wrong? (consequence);
4. How can consequences be prevented or reduced? (prevention);
5. How can recovery be enhanced, if the event occurs? (resilience); and
6. How can key local officials, expert staff, and the public organize and be informed to reduce risk and concern and increase trust and confidence? (organization).

The first three of these six questions are about *risk assessment*, the second set of three are *risk management* ones, and the six constitute *risk analysis*. There is nothing magical about two pairs of three questions each, that is, there are more nuanced versions of each of these six (Cox *et al.* 2008; Kaplan, Garrick 1981; Garrick 1984; Chankong, Haimes 2008; Greenberg *et al.* 2012). Whatever their imperfections may be, taken together the six questions constitute a systematic approach to try to understand risk and to use that knowledge to reduce vulnerability and potential harm.

Beginning with the first question, *hazard events* are naturally occurring and human actions that can occur and may trigger consequences. A slow leak of an underground gas line that no one sees, smells, or hears until a fire/explosion occurs is a hazard, as is a major earthquake that everyone in the area immediately feels and hears. *Likelihood* (e.g., probability, chance) is a measure of certainty of an event. Sometimes the likelihood numbers are precise, such as 6 percent percent with 95 percent confidence limits between 3 percent and 12 percent, and other times the estimates are in categories with subjective breaks in the classification (almost none, low, medium and high). *Consequences* of hazard events include impacts on human health, ecological systems, social organizations, and economies. Consequences range from not noticeable to catastrophic world-ending.

Prevention consists of risk management options to stop consequential events from happening. The main focus should be to reduce *vulnerability,* which is a state in which a person, an institution or a physical system is susceptible to damage that can lead to human health, economic, environmental, and social consequences. With regard to gas leaks, for example, monitoring and physically inspecting gas lines and replacing vulnerable ones are prevention policies; and not using equipment that causes sparks until you know where the gas line is a prudent step. Education is a key part of prevention. At least once or twice a week, I hear a radio announcement directing listeners to call 911 and evacuate if they see, hear or smell any signs of a gas leak. They may be wrong, perhaps there is no gas leak, but assuming that there is a gas leak, evacuating prevents deaths and injuries.

Resilience is the capacity of a system to continue operating under stress and restore normal functions or as close to normal as possible. Rerouting gas around a leak can help limit the damage to a small area, and fixing a leak can restore function. Sometimes, unfortunately, return to the previous normal is infeasible and a new normal emerges, which may mean displacement for a long period of time and inconvenience at a minimum. Many readers know at least one person who has lived through some of the massive hurricanes, earthquakes, and tornadoes during the twenty-first century and is still displaced from their previous residence (Greenberg 2014).

A successful *organizational* response requires high quality, dedicated personnel and budgetary resources. Cooperation among individuals and organizations is essential, including formal agreements among units and practice. Given trends that suggest pressure to reduce current levels of personnel and budgets, cooperation will become more critical (see Chapter 11).

As I indicated in the preface, agencies and companies have their own versions of the six risk analysis questions, and many of these are illustrated in this book. The major criticism I have heard about the six questions is from some government and private organization representatives. Their view is that risk assessment and risk analysis are part of risk management, not that risk assessment and risk management are part of risk analysis. For example, Reinschmidt *et al.* (2005), in a project for the U.S. Department of Energy (DOE), asserted that identification and analysis of project risks are part of risk management. (See also the International Organization for Standardization (ISO) in their ISO 31000:2009 ISO Guide 73:2009.)

Are these differences important? They should not be because a good risk analysis will include identification of possible events, likelihood, consequences, as well as prevention, resilience, and organizational capacity. Yet, these differences in the role of the elements of risk analysis could be important if managers direct that only hazards required by law to be studied are to be evaluated, and thereby hazards that scientists and the public believe might be a threat are ignored. It is important that risk assessment scientists maintain their capacity to explore an unlimited range of hazards. Also, differences in what is considered risk analysis practice can be important if those in charge mandate that analysts should automatically default to checklists and categorical risk categories, which may obscure important information and curtail opportunities for deep thinking about causes and effects.

Overall, I use the six risk analysis questions as the organizing framework for the book. I have included examples that were driven by risk assessor findings and others driven by risk manager necessities. The later group include challenges from public groups. While cases are primarily from the United States, I have introduced an international perspective in every instance, especially in regard to risk management perspectives, which can be quite different among and within countries.

Key probes, cause-and-effect and uncertainty in risk analysis

Understanding cause-and-effect and reducing uncertainty are the two most important academic challenges faced by risk analysts, and they are part of every chapter in this book and every risk analysis you will ever read. In order to sensitize you to their importance, I have provided several brief notes about them before you get deeply into the book. First, I provide a checklist (Table 1.1) that I use to manage my entry into every risk analysis case, and then a set of cause-and-effect questions (Table 1.2) that I have been applying to my work for many years (see Cox 2013 for a much longer discussion of cause-and-effect in risk analysis). Then, I briefly discuss how analysts deal with information gaps. Even though all the checklist and the cause-and-effect questions, as well as the suggestions about uncertainty are not discussed in every chapter of this book, they should be addressed in practice, where there are likely to be consequences for ignoring them. The checklist reminds me not to forget any key issues, and frankly I have (e.g., cascading effects), which is why I prepared the simple checklist, and each of these short checklist questions has additional follow-up probes as needed. Once I have some answers to the checklist questions, then I face, sometimes struggle with, the reality of the causes and effects implied in my initial answers to the checklist questions. Third, managing the risk analysis requires making decisions based on rules, guidelines and practice about managing uncertainty.

Answering these checklist, cause-and-effect and uncertainty issues is a challenge, in some cases a nightmare-causing one, and yet an opportunity to add clarity to the policy process. Tasked with providing support for decision-makers who are not necessarily very interested in science, cause-and-effect relationships, and have little patience for details, risk analysts try to deal with real issues in real time. They use rules or develop guidelines that help them choose the best data sets. They explore and choose mathematical models that fit the available data, typically beyond the range of the data, and they add conservative confidence limits in the name of coping with deep uncertainty and adding a margin of protection.

When the databases are too few and/or poor quality, outside experts are invited to participate. But even expert knowledge elicitation can produce arguable results about what are the primary and secondary causes, and about how much certainty we can have in relationships, and even what is most important to know. Based on

TABLE 1.1 Checklist for risk analysis

1. *What can go wrong? (hazard event)*
   1a. Human-initiated event? (equipment failure, accident, terrorism, etc.)
   1b. Natural hazard event? (earthquake, hurricane, landslide, etc.)
   1c. Biological, chemical, physical hazard event? Mixed human/natural event?
   1d. Cascading event? (localized, event spreads)

2. *What are the chances that something with serious consequences will go wrong? (likelihood)*
   2a. What do the individuals who brought up the hazard event believe the likelihood is? What is their evidence? What do the black and gray literatures, and experts report about likelihood? How persuasive is the evidence?
   2b. What specific vulnerabilities increase the likelihood of an event?
   2c. Is the information so uncertain that analysis should assume that the event will happen?

3. *What are the consequences if something does go wrong? (consequence)*
   3a. Who/what is at risk? (residents, vulnerable populations, workers, environment, infrastructure, property, social capital, legal compliance, economy, moral position, etc.?)
   3b. What are most important consequences? (death, injury, asset loss from cancer, epidemic diseases, explosions, fire, poisoning, other causes of death and injury, mental stress, loss of credibility, devaluation of assets, economic recession, political instability?)
   3c. What are the temporal and spatial extents of the hazard event?
   3d. What do the individuals who brought up the hazard event believe are the consequences? What do the black and gray literatures, and experts report about consequences? How persuasive is the evidence?

4. *How can consequences be prevented or reduced? (prevention)*
   4a. What can be done to eliminate the possibility of the worst consequences, cascading consequences? (legal measures, strategic investments, inspections, education, etc.?)
   4b. What can be done be eliminate the possibility of the less destructive consequences? (legal measures, strategic investments, inspections, education, etc.?)
   4c. What do the individuals who brought up the hazard event believe can be done to eliminate consequences? What do the black and gray literatures, and experts report about consequences? How persuasive is the evidence?

5. *How can recovery be enhanced, if the event occurs? (resilience)*
   5a. What needs to be in place to respond to an event? (in homes, businesses, in local and state government, in the form of training). What are key timing issues?
   5b. What do the individuals who brought up the hazard event believe can be done to increase resilience? What do the black and gray literatures, and experts report about resilience? How persuasive is the evidence?

6. *How can key local officials, expert staff, and the public organize and be informed to reduce risk and concern and increase trust and confidence? (organization)*
   6a. What legal and informal agreements exist among the key parties?
   6b. How often are these agreements discussed?

TABLE 1.1 continued

6c. How often do the parties practice their responsibilities?

6d. Are there striking problems with existing organizational capacity?

6e. What do the individuals who brought up the hazard event believe can be done to increase organizational capacity? What do the black and gray literatures, and experts report about organizational capacity? How persuasive is the evidence?

TABLE 1.2 Monitoring cause and effect

1. *Primary causes of effects being studied:*

- How confident are we that we understand the underlying causes and effects of what we are investigating? (biological, physical, chemical, economic, social, political?)
- Which of these do we think are primary causes?
- Do we have sufficient quality data to model the relationship between the primary cause(s) and the effects?
- Can we express the uncertainty in the cause-and-effect relationships to non-technical audiences in terms that they can understand?

2. *Other causes and contributing factors:*

- What other factor(s) directly or indirectly contribute to the consequences?
- How confident are we in bases of the models that tie together the primary and other causes and the effects?
- Do we have sufficient quality data to model the relationship between these factors and the consequences, between these factors and the primary causes, and between these factors and each other?
- Can we express the uncertainty to non-technical audiences in terms that they can understand?

3. *Following the chain of cause and effect:*

- Are the models explicit and have they been validated?
- Do the models express the consequences in a logical temporal order? If the models have a geographical component, do the events and consequences spread across the landscape in a logical order? Or do they spread across a hierarchy (e.g. large cities, rural areas, ports)?
- Do we have sufficient data to use appropriate tools to estimate the uncertainty in the primary model and the secondary ones? Can we at least bind the range of results?
- Can the models be replicated by others?

extensive empirical research, for example, Cooke (2015) recommends weighting responses based on knowledge and attributes of experts. Bolger and Rowe (2015a, b) disagree, calling for no weighting. Reflecting back on my days in school, my favorite regression analysis professor, if he were still alive, would shake his finger at me individually and risk analysts as a group for what he would call "making up data." On the other hand, he was a theoretician who specialized in proofs and never dealt with the need to try to protect human health, safety and the environment. Making these kinds of data-limited decisions is the art part of risk analysis.

An example: a nuclear power plant and radon gas

Cause-and-effect and uncertainty are major issues in my favorite example of a hazard event that few people know about, which is exposure to *radon*, a radioactive gas. I live in New Jersey, and much of the western part of the state (hilly old bedrock) has the potential for radon exposure. Yet, despite the fact home owners are required to have their homes tested for radon prior to sale, few of my undergraduate students know what radon is and the vast majority of residents had no knowledge, unless they were involved in selling or buying a home.

Below I introduce the six risk analysis questions by comparing nuclear power as a hazard with radon. In regard to *events (risk question 1)*, there is no denying that nuclear power plants have a large amount of very dangerous radioactive material in the reactor core and in the spent fuel pool. If nuclear power plants were ubiquitous and radioactive cores were in the open air, the results could be disastrous. The most famous, some would say infamous, study was so-called "WASH-740," "Theoretical Possibilities and Consequences of Major Accidents in Large Nuclear Power Plants," which estimated maximum possible damage from a nuclear reactor core meltdown. One of the scenarios in the report assumed that all of the fission products are emitted to the environment. The U.S. Atomic Energy Commission (U.S. Atomic Energy Commission [AEC] 1957) published the report in 1957. The consequences of this hypothetical event included 3400 deaths, 43,000 injuries and property damage of $7 billion (>$60 billion adjusted to the year 2014).

Compared to nuclear power plants, radon is a boring hazard. It is a radioactive gas that occurs naturally in bedrock that contains uranium. If I had to pick what to focus on solely on the basis of toxicity, I would be much more worried about nuclear power plants that discharged a large volume of the radioactive core to the environment than I would be about radon.

But now we need to consider *likelihood (risk question 2)* of something bad happening. WASH-740 was revised several times, and the risk assessment methods used in those reports have been replaced by new modeling techniques that allow analysis of reasonable events and their likelihoods. WASH-1400 (U.S. Nuclear Regulatory Commission 1975) concluded that the risk is small, that is, the likelihood of a core meltdown is 1 in 20,000 per reactor per year. Comparing its estimates to motor vehicle accidents, falls, fires, drowning and other kinds of accidents, the nuclear power failure case was far less risky. In essence, according to the authors of the study, you have a greater chance of being struck and killed by lightning and or killed by a tornado than of being killed in a nuclear power plant accident (U.S. Nuclear Regulatory Commission 1975).

This study was arguably the first risk assessment, and as such it has attracted considerable criticism and some praise (Lewis 1978; Office of Technology

Assessment 1984). The bottom line is how to interpret the results because they contain so much uncertainty. Under the worst conceivable conditions that reputable people could think of in the mid-1950s, the results are frightening, which is how the media portrayed them. Under more realistic assumptions about control of high level radioactive material in the reactor core and spent fuel, nuclear power even after TMI, Chernobyl and Fukushima events look less threatening to human health and safety than some other energy options. My point is not to support or condemn nuclear power. It is to show that nuclear power is an energy source that tends to attract polar opposite viewpoints and hence is known by many people.

In contrast, in regard to radon, large portions of the Earth are underlain by radioactive emitting substances. People have been exposed to radon for much of their lives. While the public was learning about nuclear power plant-related hazards, scientists were learning more about radon. In 1980, the Comptroller General of the United States submitted a report to the U.S. Congress, *Indoor Air Pollution: An Emerging Health Problem* (1980). The report identifies radon, carbon monoxide, formaldehyde, nitrogen dioxide and smoking as key concerns. Notably, radon is the first one identified in the report. The authors of the report to Congress indicated that there is a higher chance of lung cancer in areas, such as mining areas, with higher radon levels. In fact, lung cancer existed before smoking became common in the early twentieth century, although only about 10 percent of the rate in the late twentieth century. But even if tobacco is the bigger cause and radon the lesser one, radon cannot be ignored. Several papers (Mendez *et al.* 2011; Brooks 2012; McClellan 2014) discuss the interaction between radon and tobacco smoke in producing lung cancer. Using a simulation model, Mendez *et al.* (2011) estimate that the lifetime risk of radon-induced lung cancer death is 62 per 1,000 for ever smokers compared to 7 per 1,000 for never smokers. In other words, the odds of contracting lung cancer are enhanced by a combination of exposure to tobacco smoke and radon. The likelihood is 8.86 to 1 in the smoking/radon group vs. the radon group only one. This is an example of multiple major causes leading to an effect.

The public and many government officials tended to understate the importance of managing radon, except in uranium mines, until 1984 when a worker at the Limerick Nuclear Power Plant in Pennsylvania was found to have abnormally high levels of radiation when he reported for work (Centers for Disease Control 1985). His abnormal exposure occurred on several occasions, and managers of the nuclear power plant figured out that the problem was in his home in New Jersey. He was being exposed to over 50 times the annual dose for uranium mine workers. His home was on a slab, that is, no basement. This case triggered considerable concern in eastern Pennsylvania, adjacent western New Jersey and southwest New York State, and ultimately led to banks requiring testing for radon before houses could be sold. One of the most fascinating elements of this case is that less than 10 percent of the homes that were tested had levels that needed to be remediated. Literally some home owners were sitting on top of uranium deposits and yet their immediate neighbors were not, in other words, high uncertainty about extent of exposure.

Overall, estimating the probability of a major nuclear power plant release is both difficult and yet critical because of the geographically clustered consequences. Estimating the likelihood of a dangerous release of radon is not as difficult because the causes and effects are relatively well known, can be mapped and then investigated in detail.

The *consequences of exposure (risk question 3)* to radioactive emissions from a nuclear power plant accident are part of ongoing investigations. There has been considerable conjecture about whether there have been any human health effects from the Three Mile Island event in 1979. There were undeniably deaths and injuries from the Chernobyl and Fukushima events. The real question is how many injuries and deaths will ultimately be associated with these two events, and how many can be attributed to the nuclear power plant event compared to other causes. Exposure data are limited, making it difficult to know with a high degree of confidence.

Part of the nuclear power life cycle includes uranium mining, refining, and transportation. Each of these processes has risks, especially worker risk, and there is little public attention devoted to them, although they are major government issues. Part of the nuclear power plant challenge is closing plants, which is daunting and expensive, as well as potentially dangerous to workers. In other words, a nuclear power plant accident, the kind that we have all lived through, is not the sole potentially consequential hazard associated with nuclear power. There are causes and effects that are not commonly thought about, except by experts and responsible parties.

In the case of radon, a year 2009 report from the U.S. Environmental Protection Agency (2009) estimated that radon in the home is responsible for 21,000 lung cancer deaths in the United States, second only to tobacco smoking. The Centers for Disease Control and Prevention (1985) estimated the number at 5,000–30,000 deaths per year out of about 150,000 deaths from lung cancer during that decade. The radioactive material is in the rock, and some of it is in underground water. It slowly is emitted, and hence it follows that if we know where the underground radon is located and at what concentration, we should be able to know and prevent exposure. In principle this is a valid assertion. But case-by-case investigations find anomalies that depend on specific circumstances of the case. Also, unfortunately, radioactive radon and other naturally occurring forms of uranium have been incorporated into building products in some places, which adds a complication to keeping track of radon exposures.

At the end of the three stages of risk assessment, both nuclear power plants and radon are serious enough environmental health challenges to be worthy of risk management. Causes and effect relationships between the hazards and the consequences are apparent, but there is a great deal of uncertainty about the relative importance of each part of the chain leading to consequences.

The main risk management goal is to take steps to *prevent exposure (risk question 4)*. In the case, of nuclear power plants, a great deal has been learned about the causes of accidents. For example, pre-Three Mile Island (TMI), the major fear was loss of coolant water through the main sources of coolant water. But the failure at TMI, from which we were indeed fortunate to avoid a major disaster, led the industry to realize that smaller equipment failures could lead to devastating consequences, especially if the operators made the wrong risk management decisions. Two of the many major changes have been risk assessments for many of the world's nuclear power plants and training that requires operators to work with a mock-up of the reactor they are operating.

At Chernobyl, the industry learned that nuclear power plants need containments (the vast majority of them had them even before Chernobyl), and protocols for operations were drastically altered in some countries. Lessons learned from Fukushima are still being gathered. So far, we know that plant operators in some countries need a clearer set of instructions about how to react in a crisis, and spent fuel pools should be changed from liquid to solid as soon as possible. None of these lessons learned implies that everything that needs to be known about preventing nuclear-power related risk has been learned – far from it. But a great deal has been learned by the nuclear power industry from the major events and from other events, such as possible terrorist attacks. None of these risk management lessons is easy or inexpensive to apply, but the nuclear power industry is risking many billions of dollars in sunken investments, unless it can show that it is continually reducing risk.

In the case of radon, prevention is easy to describe but not so easy to implement. It means learning if you live or work in a building that has exposure. Then if the exposure is unacceptable, either exposure must be prevented by sealing the entry point and/or venting the gas. Also, behavioral changes can reduce the risk, such as not exercising in a basement with unacceptable levels of radon and not using building products with unacceptable levels of radioactive materials. Given the propensity of radon to show up in homes, banks routinely require radon testing before granting a mortgage, along with a test for termites and other possible problems.

Unfortunately, we know that hazard events do occur, and hence it is essential to have plans to return to normal or a new normal after the event, that is, to be *resilient (risk question 5) and recover*. Nuclear power plants with small problems can return to normal operations. In the case of Chernobyl, the new normal includes far fewer people in the area of the reactor and efforts to monitor the public and environment. In Japan, the public and the environment are being monitored, and the industry has been closed down, which means that Japan is spending tens of billions of dollars a year on other energy sources, which is a major challenge for their economy. They, I believe, will try to restart their nuclear industry, if they can rebuild confidence in the industry's safety culture.

In regard to radon, resilience means adapting to the realities of venting and preventing the gas from concentrating in buildings. Also, it may mean altering use of the building. The short-term solution is temporary relocation and retrofit of the home. I know dozens of people who have had their homes retrofitted to control radon. A number of them no longer ride exercise bikes, or use treadmills in their basements, even after their homes have been remediated. Some, with sufficient space, have moved a lot more of their activity upstairs.

The last of the six risk analysis question is about our ability to *create organizations and relationships* (risk question 6) that allow risk analysis to be implemented. This can be the most serious challenge. In the case of nuclear power, the nuclear industry understands that it has lost a great deal of its credibility because of major nuclear power events and now faces competition from natural gas, solar and wind power. Furthermore, nuclear power plant events do not respect political or institutional boundaries. For example, prior to the events in Fukushima, the U.S. Department of Energy (DOE) enjoyed moderate to high levels of trust among the two-thirds of people who lived near the DOE's major nuclear defense sites (Greenberg 2014). After the Fukushima events, levels of trust fell, on average 10 percent–15 percent, and even though these returned to pre-Fukushima levels in 2013, it was hard for DOE and U.S. Nuclear Regulatory Commission (NRC) managers to face the reality that they were guilty by association, an observation based on the author briefing them. Many readers know that Germany and Japan have opted out of nuclear energy entirely, at least right now. The world's nuclear industry has a lot to lose unless it makes good risk management decisions, and it must impose the best practices on every country. This requires strengthening large international organizations with considerable power to influence the owners and operators of every nuclear power plant. If they fail, the consequences can be ruin for the industry in every nation. They have a bottom-line incentive to organize.

In regard to radon, the burden has fallen on the housing industry and local governments to avoid the exposures. Communication with the public is critical, and failure to match words with deeds can be fatal to the credibility of the person delivering the message, and thereby undermine the program. For example, well over a decade ago, the State of New Jersey contacted the author and two colleagues to create a message to the public about their need to have their homes tested for radon. Unfortunately, none of us had had our homes tested. We realized that we would be sending a mixed message and that there was a good chance that our advice would be ignored. That flaw immediately was corrected because we would certainly have been asked by the media.

Organization of the book

This book has 11 chapters. This first chapter is followed by *Part I, Basics*, which consists of Chapter 2 about *risk assessment* and Chapter 3 about *risk management*. These are the longest chapters in the book and were written to provide the reader with sufficient background to understand what risk analysts do and the key challenges they face.

More specifically, Chapter 2 introduces risk assessment by explaining its evolution in response to the need to evaluate chemical carcinogenicity. It explains the stages of hazard identification, dose-response assessment, exposure assessment, and risk characterization, and considers the challenges of attempting to use human and animal studies, exposure analysis, and other approaches to characterize hazards. After beginning with cancer risk assessment, Chapter 2 offers examples of applying risk assessment to the nuclear power industry and to hazardous waste management. Then it moves on to risk assessment applications for food security, infrastructure, such as water and electric power, ecological systems, and terrorism. The chapter shows that risk assessors have broadened their thinking about how to assess risks and expanded analytical tools to accommodate these new issues.

Chapter 3 is about making decisions to protect human health, the environment, and assets. Common risk management issues, primarily those presented in Chapter 2, are used to illustrate tactical challenges presented by international and intra-agency differences in risk management and in resources to support risk programs. Chapter 3 also highlights the role of moral factors in risk management, especially when morality is evaluated differently by different groups. The chapter includes a presentation about how we learn from comparative risk analysis, optimization methods, and surveys as tools to gauge public perceptions and preferences that impact decisions. Each subsection highlights a point of tension for risk managers faced with making difficult risk management choices.

Part II, cases, include five risk analysis examples in Chapters 4–8. Several preliminary points are that every chapter in Part II begins with world-wide context, and then focuses on a case study. Each case was chosen to emphasize a different and I believe very interesting risk-related challenge. I have made a deliberate choice in these case studies to limit equations and tables and to emphasize pictures/maps, decision-assisting diagrams, and especially stories. For readers who want more details, I have provided the references, and I am sure that your instructors will provide supplementary reading from the literature suited to the subject areas. I would expect an engineering professor to emphasize different literature than a toxicology or law professor. Please note that these case studies are meant to be illustrative. For example, Chapter 8 focuses on anthrax but just as easily could have been Ebola, Cryptosporidium, smallpox, influenza, and other biological agents that pose serious threats if weaponized.

Chapter 4 focuses on managing one of the worst human-made hazards of the twentieth century – chemical weapons. I describe the history of these weapons of mass destruction, and what led the United States to decide to destroy their stockpile and for almost every nation to agree not to manufacture these weapons. Using an example of the Anniston, Alabama site, the chapter features the role of risk analysis in this process and emphasizes the risk to workers and surrounding communities, as well as strong public perceptions and preferences that arose during the destruction process that is more than 90 percent completed in the United States.

Chapter 5 is about environmental justice, a morally grounded policy, which arguably is the most important environmental management policy principle promulgated in the United States during the last quarter of century. The chapter describes the history, the U.S. political context, and the spread of environmental justice concepts to other nations. In the United States the U.S. EPA has been the major protagonist for environmental justice, and the chapter details issues related to hazardous waste siting, air pollution, lead removal and others and growing tension about the role of environmental justice in a political environment which has not necessarily been supportive.

Chapter 6 demonstrates three analytical tools that have been used to assess the consequences of events that could degrade a key infrastructure asset, the most widely used passenger rail asset of the U.S. Amtrak network located between Washington, D.C. and Boston. Focusing on a 60 mile segment between Trenton, NJ and Pennsylvania Station in New York City, the chapter features rail network, air pollution, and regional economic impact models. These demonstrate that the performance of the rail system can be replicated, and the consequences to human health and the economy can be estimated.

Chapter 7 examines the interconnected issues of freshwater, land use, and global climate change. Increasing development, population growth, land use changes, land grabbing, water mining and pollution, and the threat of climate change have led to freshwater problems on every continent and serious problems in some locations. Typically, the stressed areas are already semi-arid areas or rely on snowmelt. The chapter focuses on the normally neglected southern hemisphere, and uses Durban, South Africa, a moderately sized city in a poor part of the world to illustrate the development of a risk management approach that is sensitive to the needs of the poor.

Chapter 8, the last of the cases chapters, examines the threats of biological agents as a terrorist threat. Focusing on anthrax, the chapter highlights the difficulty of performing risk assessments and setting actionable exposure levels when little high dose human exposure data exits and nearly all the data are from animal studies. When anthrax was mailed through the postal service, the federal government spent hundreds of millions of dollars to try to kill every spore. Serious risk management consequences have followed from incidents during which federal agencies' handling of anthrax was not up to expectations

Chapters 9 and 10 constitute Part III, supplements. Reviewers, friends and students suggested disaster sci-fi and online risk analysis as ways of helping to explain risk and place it in perspective for younger audiences.

Chapter 9 explores risk analysis in disaster science fiction and movies. Disaster sci-fi stimulates emotions with attractive heroes and heroines; striking visual images; captivating music; and plots that resonate with public values or at least are tolerable to general audiences. The heroes and heroines' roles are stereotypical, for example, the ill-informed and self-absorbed elected official, the war mongering general, the greedy businessman, the nerdy scientist, and so on. I am concerned about the largely negative stereotypical image of risk scientists in disaster sci-fi, which if anything has worsened over the last half-century, and which I illustrate with a cartoon.

Chapter 10, risk analysis online, connects the reader to online glossaries, models and agencies and companies that use them. Ten U.S. Departments/Agencies sites that are high priority for risk analysts are briefly reviewed, and 40 other websites are added for follow-up. Twenty tools ranging from very simple to complex are described, and readers are cautioned to be skeptical about what these tools produce, especially when information is mapped or appears in charts. The chapter closes with a list of two suggested journals that focus entirely on risk analysis and ten other books for follow-up that go beyond what is presented in this book.

Chapter 11, the final chapter, focuses on two emerging externally imposed challenges for risk analysis in the early twenty-first century. These are globalizing risk and fewer resources. They increase political and economic pressure on risk analysts to promptly and unerringly assess threats and then manage them. In its worst form the pressure can distort the fundamental processes that legitimate risk scientists use to inform decisions and compromise protection of human health and the environment. Yet, this same pressure is an opportunity to improve risk analysis in ways that will lead to decision-making processes that are more risk-informed.

Use of book in courses

This book is intended to be basic reading in an introductory course in risk analysis that meets 36 to 48 hours during a single semester. The examples focus on human health and the environment, and to a lesser extent assets valued by humans.

Depending upon the background of the students, I add articles for students to read. I would consider another book, such as those listed at the end of Chapter 10. For example, the books by Cox (2013) and Silver (2012) would be good for students with backgrounds in math/operations research; Haimes's (2016) and Garrick (2008) for engineering students; Loftstedt (2008) and Renn (2008) for political science classes, Rosa *et al.* (2015), Slovic (2010) and Banerjee and Duflo (2011) for social science, planning and architecture classes, and Robson and Toscano (2007) for biology and chemistry courses. However, I recognize that many of these books are prohibitively expensive for some students. Hence, the second book option may not be feasible. Individual articles familiar to the professor and citations at the end of the chapters are a second option. The third is online special virtual issues prepared by the editors of the Society of Risk Analysis. These can be accessed via sra.org site and include terrorism risk analysis, ecological risk, influenza, economics, and foundations of risk analysis. The site also has links to webinars and talks by society members that may be suitable for students, depending upon their background.

I initially assess student understanding of the material by their ability to answer the questions at the end of each chapter. I have not provided any group assignments because of the diversity of student audiences and readers. However, these are possible. For example, my class in Fall 2015 did an online environmental justice exercise with EPA's *EJScreen* (Chapter 10). Each student entered their area code or drew a polygon, and then we compared the results by the end of the class or the next one. For chemistry and toxicology classes, students can pick a chemical(s) of interest and conduct a search of *IRIS* and other data bases and then report the results to class the following week. Training to use *HAZUS*, an economic modeling approach took a bit longer but groups of students were able to estimate the economic consequences of a major natural hazards event. *The Built Environment* is a recently released tool that could be applied to a neighborhood in a community, and should be particularly valuable for students in transportation planning, architecture and engineering. About 20 tools are described in Chapter 10, and each can be turned into a project for pairs of students, or a larger group.

What kind of group and class assignments at least partly depend not only on class size but also what the students are interested in and already know. I use the following table to help me set the class level, and it may be useful to you.

TABLE 1.3 Student profile

Name: _____

Contact information: email _____ Phone _____

Context: What is your current knowledge about …?	High	Medium	Low	Comments (experience, classes)
Risk assessment				
Risk management				
Anthropology				
Communications				
Economics				
Emergency management				
Engineering				
Epidemiology				
Environmental science				
Geography				
History				
Human health and safety				
Law				
Political science				
Security				
Sociology				
Statistics				
Urban planning				
Other: please list				
Other: please list				
Other: please list				
Other: please list				
Other: please list				
Other: please list				

References

Banerjee A, Duflo E. (2011) *Poverty and risk: a review of poor economics, a radical rethinking of the way to fight global poverty.* New York: Public Affairs Books.

Bolger F, Rowe G. (2015a) The aggregation of expert judgment: do good things come to those who weight? *Risk Analysis.* 351, 5–11.

Bolger F, Rowe G. (2015b) There is data, and then there is data: only experimental evidence will determine the utility of differential weighting of expert judgement. *Risk Analysis.* 35, 1, 21–26.

Brooks A. (2012) From the field to the laboratory and back: The what ifs, wows and who cares of radiation biology. *Health Physics.* 105, 5, 407–421.

Centers for Disease Control and Prevention. (1985) Health hazards associated with elevated levels of indoor radon – Pennsylvania, *MMWR.* 34, 43, 657–658.

Chankong V, Haimes Y. (2008) *Multiobjective decision making: theory and methodology.* New York: Dover.

Committee on Foundations of Risk Analysis. (2015) SRA glossary. www.sra.org/sites/default.files/pdf/SRA-glossary-approved22june2015-x.pdf. Accessed June 25, 2015.

Comptroller General of the United States. (1980) Report to Congress of the United States, indoor air pollution: an emerging health problem. Washington, D.C.: Superintendent of Documents, U.S. Government Printing Office.

Cooke R. (2015) The aggregation of expert judgement: Do good things come to those who weight? *Risk Analysis.* 35, 1, 12–18.

Cox, LA, Jr. (2013) *Improving risk analysis.* New York, Springer.

Cox LA, Jr., Greenberg M, Bostrom A, Haas C, Haimes Y, Landis W, Lowrie K, Moolgavakar S, North W. (2008) What is the scope of journal. *Risk Analysis.* 28, 5, 1135–1136.

Garrick BJ (1984) Recent case studies and advances in probabilistic risk assessments. *Risk Analysis.* 4, 4, 262–279.

Garrick BJ (2008). *Quantifying and controlling catastrophic risk.* Cambridge MA: Academic Press.

Greenberg M. (2014) *Protecting seniors against environmental disasters.* New York: Earthscan/Routledge.

Greenberg M, Weiner W, Kosson D, Powers C. (2014) Trust in the U.S. Department of Energy: a post-Fukushima rebound. *Energy Research & Social Science.* 2, 145–147.

Greenberg M, Haas C, Cox L. Jr, Lowrie K, McComas K, North W. (2012) Ten most important accomplishments in risk analysis, 1980–2010. *Risk Analysis.* 32, 5, 771–781.

Haimes Y. (2016) *Risk modeling, assessment, and management.* 4th edition. Hoboken, NJ: Wiley.

International Organization for Standardization. ISO 3100:2009. www.ownersmanual-download.net/iso-risk-management.pdf. Accessed December 31, 2014.

Kaplan S, Garrick BJ. (1981) On the quantitative definition of risk. *Risk Analysis.* 1, 1, 11–27.

Lewis H. (1978) *Risk assessment review group report to the U.S. nuclear regulatory commission.* Washington DC: NRC.

Loftstedt R. (2008) *Risk management in post-trust societies.* New York: Earthscan.

Lowrance W. (1976) *Of acceptable risk: science and determination of safety.* Menlo Park, CA: Wm. Kaufmann.

McClellan R. (2014) Radiation toxicity, Chapter 18, 883–995 in Hayes W, Kruger C., eds. *Hayes' principles and methods of toxicology.* Boca Raton, FL: CRC Press.

Mendez D, Alshanqeety O, Warner K, Lantz P, Courant P. (2011) The impact of declining smoking on radon-related lung cancer in the United States. *American Journal of Public Health.* 101, 2, 310–314.

Office of Technology Assessment. (1984) Nuclear power in an age of uncertainty. Chapter 8 *Public attitudes toward nuclear power.* Washington DC: OTA, 218–219.

Reinschmidt K, Committee for Oversight and Assessment of U.S. Department of Energy Project Management *et al.* (2005) *The owner's role in project risk management.* Washington, DC: National Academy Press.

Renn O. (2008) *Risk governance: coping with uncertainty in a complex world.* New York: Earthscan.

Robson M, Toscano T. eds. (2007) *Risk assessment for environmental health.* Hoboken, NJ: Wiley.

Rosa, E, Renn O, McCright A. (2015) *The risk society revisited: social theory and risk governance.* Philadelphia, PA: Temple University Press.

Silver N. (2012) *The signal and the noise: why so many predictions fail – but some don't.* London: Penguin Books.

Slovic P. (2010) *The feeling of risk.* New York: Earthscan.

U.S. Atomic Energy Commission. (1957) *Theoretical possibilities and consequences of major accidents in large nuclear power plants, WASH-740.* Washington, DC: AEC.

U.S. Environmental Protection Agency. (2009) A citizen's guide to radon. Washington, DC: USEPA.

U.S. Nuclear Regulatory Commission (1975). *Reactor safety study: an assessment of accident risks in U.S. commercial nuclear power plants. WASH-1400 (NUREG-75/014).* www.nrc.gov/reading-rm/doc-collections/nuregs/staff/sr75-014. Accessed October 31, 2009.

PART I
Basics

2
RISK ASSESSMENT

Introduction

The immediate impetus for health risk assessment was the challenge of carcinogenic chemicals, as well as radiation and hazardous waste sites. After focusing on these three, Chapter 2 reviews food hazards and infrastructure. Ecosystem-related risks, which are less studied than they should be, are the focus of the penultimate section. Terrorism risk analysis has attracted a great deal of attention and is the last focus.

Several caveats are in order. I have not tried to cover every type of risk assessment application, in other words, the chapter is not meant to be encyclopedic. Cyber-crime, sustainability and resilience, for example, are in the risk management chapter (Chapter 3). As noted in the preface, I have deliberately added examples from my experiences to add a flavor of the emotional as well as professional investment that risk analysts make assessing risk.

Chemicals: responding to a political emergency

The U.S. Environmental Protection Agency (EPA) began developing human health risk assessment in the 1970s in response to widespread fear that environmental cancers were epidemic in the United States. As a new agency, begun in 1970, it was under pressure to regulate public exposure to carcinogens in the air and water. The precedent was the Delaney clause, which was an amendment of 1958 to the Food, Drugs, and Cosmetic Act of 1938. The Delaney clause said that a substance that was found to cause cancer in people or animals could not be used as a food additive.

Adopting the Delaney clause for air and water was impractical because carcinogens are undeniably in the environment. A former colleague, for example, would use benzene, a ubiquitous carcinogen, to test his air samples. If low levels of benzene did not show up in the sample, he worried about the quality of the data.

Charged with developing water quality criteria for 64 contaminants, EPA asked the National Research Council to develop a defensible basis for regulating chemicals. The National Academy of Science Committee's (Committee on the Institutional Means for Assessment of Risk to Public Health, Risk Assessment in the Federal Government 1983) "red book" (the color of the cover was red), divided the assessment of chemicals into four parts:

- Hazard identification;
- Dose-response assessment;
- Exposure assessment; and
- Risk characterization.

Hazard identification

Hazard identification determines if a chemical is potentially a serious hazard (risk analysis question 1). Dose-response assessment examines the likelihood that a hazardous chemical will cause a problem at a particular dose (risk analysis question 2). Exposure assessment is determining how many are exposed to the chemical in question and for how long (part of risk analysis question 3). Risk characterization evaluates the severity of consequences. Is the substance a severe enough threat for risk managers to legally manage it, including banning it?

Each of these four steps represents an intellectual challenge, and I will illustrate each with a hypothetical chemical "dimethylchickenwire," or DMCW, created by my friend and former colleague toxicologist Michael Gallo. DMCW allows me highlight uncertainty at all four stages.

Let us assume that dimethylchickenwire is proposed to be used as part of a drug. How can I determine if it is a hazardous ingredient? Hazard identifications draw data from four sources. The first and most important, when available, are from human epidemiological studies. Let us assume that two epidemiological studies include DMCW data. One found human health impacts on the liver (positive results study) and the other no impacts. What weights should I attach to the one with positive results compared to the other one? Should I weight the positive ones more in order to be conservative and protective? Should I give more credence to the negative one because it included 500 people, whereas the positive one had only 50? What about the type of epidemiological study? Let us assume that the positive one was a retrospective study that used historical worker records, some of which are incomplete. The second is a prospective study in which the subjects have been followed for a decade. We prefer more cases and a prospective design, but can we afford to dismiss the results of the positive finding, even if the design is not the preferred one?

Here are some other factors need to be considered by analysts. Do the studies have to demonstrate statistically significant findings to be acceptable? If so, what level of statistical significance is required? Decades ago, for example, I was asked by a U.S. Senator to examine the quality of the data base underlying the U.S. ambient air quality standards. He had been told that some were not justified, and one of the major criticisms was that the results were not statistically significant at p<.05 (e.g., 5 percent or less probability that the results could have occurred by chance). When I read them, I learned that many did not report them; at that time it was common practice not to report statistical significance or provide confidence limits. Does that mean that they should be ignored? Nearly all the standards have remained the same.

A second factor that could change the interpretation of risk is the lack of a clearly defined control group (the group did not have the exposure to DMCW). How much does the absence of control group undermine the utility of a study? Yet another complication with epidemiological studies is that the route of exposure may not be the same as dimethylchickenwire used as a drug ingredient. For example, the proposed drug will be ingested, but the epidemiological studies investigated inhalation. The last complication is type of outcome, that is, for example, if one study focused on cancerous tumors and the second on benign ones. Overall, these study designs and data characteristics issues complicate interpretation of human epidemiological data. It is fair to say that interpreting results from contra-dictory human data sets is an anxiety-provoking task.

Anxiety-provoking is, however, preferable to having no human data, which is often the case, or the human data are poor quality. Analysts turn to animal data (see Chapter 8). Animal bioassays studies pose the same challenges as human epidemio-logical ones, in regard to sample size, statistical significance and type of design. But because humans do not have the same metabolic pathways as animals, animal studies present additional problems for analysts. It is difficult, and sometimes no longer possible, to use monkeys and dogs that are relatively close parallels to humans in animal tests. Instead, mice, rats, hamsters and guinea pigs are the test animals. How should differences in metabolism be included when interpreting consequences? How should we take into account that animal species bred because of their sensitivity are used for tests? Also, animals typically are given much higher doses and to locations that do not mimic human pathways. How should these differences be factored into drawing conclusions from the results? Let us further assume that the literature includes five animal studies. Only one shows toxicity and four do not. Should we assume that the one with health effects may be ignored because it was only 1 of 5?

Not every animal test has followed standard design practices, which means the quality of animal tests for dimethylchickenwire need to be checked in order to be certain that the prescribed dose was used, the animals were carefully observed and tested, that the data were properly recorded, and appropriate statistical analyses were used. There have been some cases where fraud was committed and the tests had to be redone.

Short-term tests such as in vitro (in test tubes) assays and bacterial mutagenicity tests are even further removed from humans than are standard animal bioassays. Let us assume that these tests show a potential human health problem with exposure to dimethylchickenwire. How much credence should be placed on these kinds of short-term tests?

The fourth option is to look at the chemical composition of DMCW compared to other chemicals with similar *structures*. Arguably, if chemicals with a structure similar to dimethylchickenwire were toxic, mutagenic, carcinogenic, then should there be an assumption that DMCW may also be problematic? If there is no such evidence, does that mean that dimethylchickenwire DMCW is not a problem?

At the conclusion of the hazard identification phase, the analyst should examine all the evidence and try to reach a conclusion about DMCW. However, sometimes there is a dearth of quality information and contradictory information. Sometimes the courts do not recognize the validity of animal studies, as was the case in the famous Agent Orange case argued before Judge Jack Weinstein in Brooklyn Federal Court (Schuck 1988). The judge did not value the animal data, which was a shock to some risk assessors who saw years of work dismissed.

Dose-response assessment

Dose-response assessment, the second part of this chemical risk assessment process, presents a different yet equally imposing challenge. Much of the data used in human and animal studies is based on high doses. Hence, a key question is how should high exposure data be extrapolated to low dose exposures, that is, the typical workplace, home and outdoor environments? If there is no threshold for harm, then should we assume that a single molecule of dimethylchickenwire can cause an effect (see radiation discussion below)? For some substances that assumption does not make sense. When I last had a colonoscopy, the doctor administered the proper dose of a sedative. A much lower dose would not even be noticeable, and yet a high enough dose could kill patients.

Analysts use mathematical curves (e.g., one-hit, multistage, Weibull, log-probit (see Box 2.1 and Motulsky, Christopoulos 2004) to fit existing data and extend the curve to estimate cancer likelihood. But curve fitting mathematical models implies cause and effect relationships between the agent and the exposed individuals. We know that some humans are much more sensitive than others to some agents. How can this human variability be taken into account? Health outcomes, most notably cancer, may not appear for decades. Most epidemiological studies and animal studies do not go back 20, 30 and more years. How should risk estimates be adjusted for what is typically a short follow-up time period? Ideally, when a study is conducted, the analyst begins with an expectation that certain parts of the body will be impacted because of human biology and chemistry. What should be done when other health outcomes, not part of the original study, show up in the data, and there is no obvious biological explanation?

Chemical agents can have an impact that is masked by other agents. One of the most famous is radiation and tobacco smoking (see Chapter 1 example). How should these interactive impacts be weighed in estimating the likelihood of health effects? Yet another complexity is how to integrate total exposure data in estimating likelihood of health outcomes. Arguably, total dose is the most important piece of information to have. Yet, when someone is exposed as a child that exposure may

BOX 2.1 Methylene chloride (MeCl) as a hazard

As a teenager, during the summer, I was a painter, wall paper hanger, and not a very skilled handyman. Painting was fun. Scraping old paint was not. One of my co-workers introduced me to paint strippers. I remember the substance had a sweet smell, and was happy to use it because the paint (including lead based paint) came off with less of a struggle. Years later, I learned that the paint stripper contained methylene chloride (dichloromethane, or MeCl), which is a solvent and a health hazard. MeCl (CH_2Cl_2) is colorless, but that sweet aroma gives it away.

Among the set of chlorohydrocarbons, MeCl is one of the least toxic, but high volatility means that it can be an acute inhalation hazard. In enclosed spaces, MeCl can lead to dizziness, nausea, headaches, and irritation of the eyes and upper parts of the respiratory tract. The worst cases have led to loss of consciousness and even death. In February 2013, the U.S Occupational Safety and Health Administration (OSHA) reported at that least 14 bathtub refinishers had died since 2000 from MeCl exposure (U.S. Occupational Safety and Health Administration 2013). The Occupational Safety and Health Administration set an occupational exposure standard, and EPA has set acute exposure guideline levels. The European Union banned its use in paint strippers available to the public and some workers.

MeCl is also considered to be a carcinogenic agent. Animal studies typically involve far less than 100 animals. Hence, in order not to miss a potent agent, as noted earlier, the animals receive high concentrations of agent. The animal data are high dose, far above what a human should be exposed to. Can a single molecule cause cancer, or is there a threshold of exposure that must be exceeded? Risk analysts developed mathematical models to extrapolate low-dose exposures based on high dose animal data. The models are based on different theories of carcinogenesis. The one-hit model is the most protective because it assumes that a single hit on DNA can eventually cause irreversible damage leading to cancer. The multi-stage model has many of the same conservative assumptions. The Weibull and Log-probit models assume a tolerance for exposures and hence a threshold before carcinogenesis.

Figure 2.1 visually shows the assumptions in the models. The 45-degree line is very conservative, whereas the other two lines assume increasingly larger thresholds.

U.S. Environmental Protection Agency (2015) Methylene Chloride Results – AEGL Programs. www2.epa.gov/aegl/methylene-chloride-results-aegl-program. Accessed November 15, 2015.

U.S. Occupational Safety and Health Administration. (2015) Methylene Chloride. www.OHSA.gov. Accessed November 15, 2015.

U.S. Occupational Safety and Health Administration. (2013) Methylene chloride hazards for bathtub refinishers. OSHA-NIOSH hazard alert 2013-110. OSHA and NIOSH. www.cdc.gov/niosh/docs/2013-110.pdf. Accessed November 16, 2015.

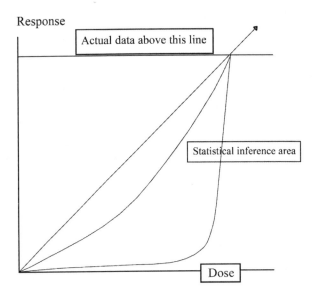

FIGURE 2.1 Hypothetical dose–response curves

EPA applied these kinds of models to MeCl and the results are shown below. The one-hit and multi-stage conservative models have higher probabilities at the 1 ug/m³ level than the other two, although the likelihoods are all very low. As the concentration increases, the differences narrow, and essentially are minimally different above 1,000 ug/m³.

Lifetime risk to humans from exposure to MeCl
(target is salivary gland sarcomas in male rats and 95% upper confidence limit)

Air concentration ug/m³	One-hit model	Multi-state model	Weibull model	Log-probit model
1	1.8×10^{-7}	2.0×10^{-7}	4.8×10^{-10}	3.5×10^{-31}
100	1.8×10^{-5}	2.0×10^{-5}	6.1×10^{-6}	2.5×10^{-15}
1,000	1.8×10^{-4}	2.0×10^{-4}	2.0×10^{-5}	1.3×10^{-9}

Source: U.S. Environmental Protection Agency, Health Assessment Document for Methylene Chloride, Final Report. February 1985. EPA-600-8-82-004F.

have more impact than an exposure much later in life. In other words, should recent doses be weighted less than earlier ones?

Animal bioassay studies face several other challenges, which are as much ethical as they are scientific. How does one interpolate from doses and impacts associated with transferring results from mice to humans? How will metabolic pathways and rates be weighed? If some species are more sensitive than others, how should the animal data be weighted when applied to humans?

Exposure assessment

Exposure assessment is the third part of the four part process, and it has markedly advanced during the last decade. Nevertheless, analysts face imposing scientific challenges. Much of the data used in hazard identification and dose-response studies comes from worker exposures and other heavily exposed populations. The literature shows that workers are typically healthier than non-workers, and hence how is that data to be used in judging the consequences to groups such as young children, seniors with pre-existing health conditions, pregnant women and other more vulnerable groups? How can the exposure assessment account for variations in diet, lifestyle, hobbies, and other behaviors? For example, if I want to estimate the consequences of inhaling pollutants driving to work every day on a road with many cars and buses in order to calculate the consequences, I should also know if the driver or people in the car with the driver smoke, or if they work in a bar where smoking is permitted and many people smoke.

Risk characterization

Risk characterization, the fourth part of the EPA's risk assessment process, is part science and part art. The bottom line is to determine which populations, if any, are to be protected against dimethylchickenwire. Toward that end, which dose-response assessments and exposure assessments are the bases for assessing the consequences? Why? What are the most important uncertainties in the risk assessment that should be acknowledged and how are they taken into account or at least acknowledged?

TaB – case study of saccharin

Dimethylchickenwire is a fictitious chemical; TaB, a soft drink, is real, and was marketed by the Coca-Cola Company in 1963 as a sugar free soda. I liked the metallic taste in TaB that came from a coal tar derivative. Animal bioassays of saccharin ($C_7H_5NO_3S$), the main ingredient in TaB showed saccharin to potentially be an animal carcinogen. A paper produced by the Chemical Carcinogenesis Program of the U.S. National Cancer Institute (Reuber 1978, p. 173) began with the following statement "Saccharin is carcinogenic for the urinary bladder in rats and mice, and most likely is carcinogenic in human beings." The results of multiple studies with about 20-50 animals with accompanying tables showed higher rates, especially among male rats and mice, but the dose-response curves were not linear. There seemed to be a threshold and then a pronounced jump in urinary bladder cancers at high doses. These studies led to a serious debate among scientists and in Congress, and ultimately all products containing saccharin were required to have a warning label to inform consumers that saccharin may cause bladder cancer. The label requirement was lifted in 2000, and in 2010 EPA removed saccharin from its hazardous substance list. TaB was replaced primarily by aspartame-containing diet drinks, which have been criticized by health researchers.

Scientists learned that rodents have a combination of high protein, high pH, and high calcium phosphate in their urine, which the literature suggests leads to the formation of small crystals that damage the bladder and ultimately lead to tumor formation. In other words, rats that drank a great deal of TaB had a high probability of developing urinary bladder cancer. You can now buy TaB in some stores, and the saccharin is mixed with aspartame.

Nuclear materials: coping with the nuclear war legacy and the peaceful atom

Thousands of chemicals and combinations of chemicals in the market and in waste represent a challenge to scientists and policy makers who prioritize risk reduction investments. Radioactive materials are another daunting challenge, as demonstrated by the $150 billion spent by the U.S. government to manage the hazards created by the manufacture of nuclear weapons (Craig 2014).

I begin by briefly describing ionizing radiation and associated risks. The periodic table of elements starts with hydrogen with an atomic number of 1. Everyone knows about hydrogen and simple chemical combinations of hydrogen and other elements, such as methane and hydrogen peroxide. At the bottom of the periodic table is Lawrencium (Lr) with an atomic number of 103. Named after the Ernest Lawrence, the inventor of the cyclotron, Lr is a synthetic radioactive substance produced by bombarding another radioactive element Californium with boron ions in an accelerator. I first learned about Lr and other actinides (synthetically produced radioactive elements with atomic numbers ranging from 89 to 103) in the early 1960s when a college professor discussed them in class because he was fascinated by their structures. He said nothing about their potential impact of these differences on human health; I learned about health impacts much later.

Hydrogen, Lawrencium and every other chemical substance can be characterized by its atomic structure, which includes neutrons, electrons, and protons, and even smaller particles (beyond the scope of this section). Electrons revolve around a nucleus that contains about the same number of neutrons and protons. If the relative number of neutrons to protons is out of balance or if the nucleus is disturbed by other particles, the nucleus will shift to a more stable state. A chemical in an unstable state is a radionuclide. As radionuclides rebalance their internal structure, they emit energy. Energy emitted can be in the form of particles (electrons, helium atoms), or they can be waves (light). This radioactive decay is called ionizing radiation. When ionizing radiation strikes iron, plastic, a human body, it creates ions, or electrically charged particles, and these particles can impact the object. Some radionuclides take a long time to rearrange their internal structure, others rearrange in fractions of a second, which is what fascinated my teacher when he drew chemical structures on the board, then erased them, and changed them again.

Electromagnetic waves, or gamma waves, are not charged, but are capable of penetrating most materials, including the human body, and can damage living cells, leading to alterations in DNA. Lead, concrete, or several feet of water can protect people against gamma radiation. Machines that produce gamma radiation are sealed with protective materials. Examples of gamma radiation that are brought to the attention of the public whenever there is threat of a nuclear event include Iodine-131, Cesium-137, radium-226, and cobalt-60. X-rays are less penetrating than gamma rays, but require shielding, as we find out when our dentist examines our teeth.

Alpha and Beta particles are charged and may be hazardous. For example, Beta particles are electrons removed from their orbits. Most do not penetrate the skin, yet prolonged exposure can cause damage. Strontium-90, carbon-14 and tritium H-3 are illustrations. Alpha particles, such as radium, radon, uranium, polonium, and thorium can be harmful if swallowed, inhaled or penetrate through an open wound. Their strong positive charge can cause serious damage, unless shielded by water, dust, or clothing.

A massive amount has been written about radiation, much more than can possibly be presented in this chapter (see McClellan 2014; Greenberg *et al.* 2009). Some key points are as follows. Radiation is ubiquitous in the environment, including from the Sun and from decay of radioactive materials in the ground (e.g., radon in Chapter 1). Human-initiated exposures are from medical procedures, detonations of nuclear weapons and from accidents at nuclear power plants. Compared to many chemicals, radiation, is relative easy to monitor, which is a major advantage in keeping track of it and avoiding exposures. The National Council on Radiation Protection and Measurements (2009) estimates the relative contribution of different radiation sources to U.S. population's exposure. Over a third was from naturally occurring radon and thoron, and about one-fourth from computer tomography (CT). Much of the rest is from cosmic radiation, nuclear medicine, and other medical interventions. This does not negate concern about nuclear power plants and nuclear waste management facilities, which under worst circumstances could deliver a very high and geographically concentrated dose.

A linear no-threshold model for radiation has been accepted by key government agencies, that is, the assumption is that a single hit can lead to a cancer. Others, however, have argued for a sigmoid-shaped model (see Box 2.1) with a no notable impact at lower doses and leveling off of impact at high doses. Hormesis is one of the most debatable issues in risk analysis. The hypothesis is that low level exposure to radiation and other agents actually stimulates a protective biological response, in other words, should reduce the rate of cancer and other health effects (McClellan 2014).

Nuclear power plants

George Apostolakis (2012), a former Commissioner of the U.S. Nuclear Regulatory Commission (USNRC), summarized the history of risk assessment and management in the nuclear industry. Noting that uncertainty was always a concern, he points out that the USNRC used safety margins and defense-in-depth written into regulations rather than risk assessment. The NRC required that plants be built to withstand postulated accidents without loss to critical safety systems and plants have multiple backups to make sure that a facility could withstand a failure. That philosophy is common to the USNRC and the DOE, that is, to design away uncertainty and risk.

As briefly noted in Chapter 1, reactor safety studies aimed at identifying and modeling uncertainty were initiated by WASH-1400 in 1975, and studies of each reactor began in 1988. In 1995, the USNRC noted that the use of probabilistic risk assessment (PRA) should be integrated into their defense-in-depth philosophy and should be used to reduce unnecessary conservative requirements. Using simulation tools, PRA allows analysts to estimate the likelihood of multiple problems occurring. Technical documents supporting the incorporation of PRA are imposing. In essence, the USNRC requires the owner/operator of a nuclear power plant to study the plant, the containment, and the surrounding site. In the case of a nuclear plant, the applicant is required to indicate the kinds of accident sequences that could lead to damaging the plant in operation, shutdown, and in a transition stage. An analysis is expected to be conducted on internal and external events that could cause public health effects outside the facility. In essence, there is a requirement for a plant model, a containment model, and a site/consequence model. Each begins with the USNRC's requirements and then the applicant is required to evaluate and model uncertainties that could compound effects.

The USNRC has committed to risk assessment and created many of the more valuable applications of probabilistic risk assessment in its efforts to evaluate reactor designs and to assess changes proposed by owners/operators of commercial plants, as well as to respond to new circumstances that had not been anticipated. For example, nuclear power plants were designed to withstand the crash of a jet liner, but jet liners have grown in size. More recently, the destruction of nuclear power plants by an earthquake, tsunami, and loss of energy in Japan has led the USNRC to ask questions of the many nuclear power plants located along the Atlantic Ocean and Gulf Coast of the United States, that is, to reassess their risk in light of events that could trigger other events.

Nuclear waste facilities

Like the USNRC, risk-informed decision-making is also at the core of the Department of Energy's environmental management programs that are responsible for the nuclear weapon legacy. And like the USNRC, DOE begins with defense-in-depth regulations. But unlike the USNRC, there have been few illustrations of the use of probabilistic risk assessment in the EM process. There is no prohibition by the DOE. A recent Omnibus Committee for the U.S. Congress (2015) observed that the DOE has not embraced probabilistic risk assessment compared to the USNRC, the National Aeronautics and Space Administration, and several other government agencies and industries. The DOE has emphasized that their use of PRA would be as a supplement qualitative/deterministic process for hazard assessments.

The West Valley PRA is one exception. The New York State Energy Research Development Authority (NYSERDA) commissioned a group of risk analysts to consider the case of a nuclear waste management facility in western New York near Buffalo (see Figure 2.2 for location) (Garrick *et al.* 2010). The site contains an estimated 2.4 million ft.³ of radioactive waste composed of 230 radionuclides that sit in seven trapezoidal-shaped trenches on a 15 acre site and on clay bedrock. The top of the trenches are covered by 10 feet of compacted clay and these caps are covered by a polyethylene cap that is water impermeable. The site has other engineered structures, such as French drains and slurry walls.

The reprocessing plant operated from 1963 to 1975, and was the only privately-owned nuclear fuel processing plant to operate in the United States. The plant was built as part of New York State Governor, Nelson Rockefeller's effort to build a nuclear industry in New York State. The former governor expected that fuel reprocessing would occur and 21 nuclear power plants are located in New York, and the nearby states of Connecticut, New Jersey, Pennsylvania, and Vermont, as well as others in Ontario and Quebec, which theoretically could have brought nuclear fuel rods to a site on the southern side of Lake Erie near Buffalo New York.

As part of the environmental impact statement to close the site, the preferred option was to manage the waste in place for 30 years as the radioactivity decayed and became less hazardous. NYSERDA asked the analysts, led by a researcher who led efforts to apply PRA to commercial nuclear reactors, to apply PRA to their site. Their objective was to better understand the risk of managing the nuclear waste in the same configuration for the next 30 years. This was the first application of PRA to shallow-land disposal of radioactive waste.

The authors of the West Valley study evaluated the three risk assessment questions presented in Chapter 1 (initiating events, likelihood, consequences). Their goal was to estimate human exposures resulting from possible events at the site. The analysts prepared 31 hazard event scenarios that represent possible triggering events, including flow of contaminants from the landfill latterly into the groundwater, breaches of the waste trenches, overflow of the trenches and airborne releases from the landfill. They used multiple quantitative models that estimated air and water emissions trench overflows, stream transport and deposition, erosion as well as failures of engineered facilities. Recognizing that each of these options individually as well as collectively have likelihoods associated with them, the authors used probabilistic analysis to develop aggregate and likelihood estimates of risk associated with each type of emission pathway. Specifically, the analysts are 95 percent confident that the frequency of release of 100 mrem in one year is less than

FIGURE 2.2 Locations of Love Canal, Kin Buc, Lipari, West Valley, Yonkers Reservoir and Water service area in New Jersey

0.02 during the next 30 years. The combination of events was simulated 10,000 times with the goal of determining the likelihood that 100 mrem is exceeded. They concluded that there is an exceedingly low probability of exposing the hypothetical individuals at risk to radioactivity above federal standards. The authors of the paper note that NYSERDA used these findings as part of their case for not substantively changing the management of these nuclear wastes. The analysts note that they did not consider worker and public exposure in the event that NYSERDA had chosen to alter the configuration of the site or even remove the nuclear waste from the site.

At the time of the writing of this chapter, DOE had issued an RFP for a phase 2 probabilistic analysis of four elements of the West Valley remediation in order to direct data collection, upgrade a deterministic analysis to a probabilistic one, develop a long-term probabilistic approach for federal and state EISs, and prepare materials for a supplemental environmental impact statement (EIS) (DOE 2015).

The future use of probabilistic risk assessment in the DOE is uncertain. A report to the U.S. Senate and House Appropriations Committees (Omnibus 2015) notes that risk assessments will continue to be done for site cleanups under the Comprehensive Environmental Response, Compensation, and Liability Act (CERCLA) and calls for a special committee to review PRA within the DOE context, offer recommendations and recommend applications.

Waste sites: the challenge of orphaned facilities

In 1977, I received an award from the U.S. Environmental Protection Agency for environmental research and education. I was proud, and my pride was heightened by the fact that Michael Brown, a reporter from the Buffalo Niagara Falls area, was seated next to me. While my research contributed, I was told, to better government decisions about water supply, Brown was at the forefront of an effort that raised hazardous waste sites to the top of the list of national priority issues. *Michael Brown was a 1970s version of a modern rock star, or so I thought. He was nominated for three Pulitzer Prize awards.* Using data produced by the EPA and cancer experts at the Roswell Park Memorial Institute in Buffalo, Brown asserted that Love Canal was poisoning people, and causing cancer and birth defects in a neighborhood outside of Buffalo, New York. He also interviewed local residents (see Figure 2.2). In 1979 Brown wrote:

> The Shroeder backyard, once featured in a local newspaper for its beauty, now had degenerated to the point where it was unfit even to walk upon.
>
> *(Brown, 1979, p. 12)*

Though the claims were challenged, hazardous waste became a major political issue and during the 1980s cleanup of abandoned hazardous waste sites became the largest budgetary item for the U.S. EPA. (See Chapter 3 for the implications of this priority on EPA). Love Canal scared people and government into determining how many Love Canal-like sites there were in the United States. President Jimmy Carter declared Love Canal a national disaster area. Congressman and later Governor of New Jersey, Jim Florio said:

> Improper hazardous waste management is the most serious environmental problem facing our nation today. It is the environmental issue of the 80's.
>
> *(In Greenberg and Anderson 1984, p. 84)*

The mass media figuratively feasted on the issue as more and more evidence accumulated that there were hazardous waste sites across the nation and some were a threat. With regard to threat, the U.S. EPA (1977) collected damage assessments The data from landfills, dumps, surface impoundments, waste storage facilities, slag and mine tailings sites and other waste sites showed few cases of fires, explosions, and direct contact poisoning. It did show many underground water pollution cases, requiring water purveyors and individual well owners to find a new fresh water supply.

Some of the sites were still operating, and government passed legislation, most notably the Resource Conservation and Recovery Act (RCRA) (1976) to control disposal of solid and hazardous waste, and emissions from these sites, and the Toxics Substances Control Act (TOSCA) (1976) that regulates new chemicals and some already existing ones (see Chapter 3).

The focus of EPA, especially its budget, was on so-called "orphaned sites," that is, abandoned facilities that were leaking, arguably jeopardizing health, markedly lowering property values, and especially burdening poor minority populations (United Church of Christ 1987). After several false starts yielded unreliable data and estimates ranging from 800 to 50,000 sites, EPA asked its regions to use their data bases to identify sites that had incidents or had the potential for events because of the types of materials handled at the sites. This so-called EPA "Quick Look" Data base found more than 11,000 sites. The Quick Look data base found over 600 sites in the following states: Texas, New York, Ohio, Michigan, and Illinois. All of these are urban industrial states, which surprised no one. What was surprising was that Florida, Louisiana, North Carolina and Tennessee, which had many chemical waste sources, had few sites on the list.

Overall, early efforts to estimate the number and extent of risk associated with hazardous waste sites was done in a near political emergency, and the results reflected a lack of data and transparent analytical process to assess the risk or even relative risk.

In 1980, the United States enacted the Comprehensive Environmental Response Compensation and Liability Act (CERCLA), otherwise known as Superfund. Having a systematic and replicable process became important because billions of taxpayer dollars were to be allocated to manage these orphaned sites. In 1981, 20 sites were picked for early engineering designs and early cleanups. Some of the sites were more than 100 acres and others were less than 20 acres. Some had been receiving waste for prior to 1940 and others were not opened until after 1970. In other words, there was variation in some of the attributes. But there was a clear pattern. The sites tended to be above-ground (60 percent), contained pesticides (70 percent), other organics (70 percent), inorganic wastes (70 percent), and threatened groundwater supplies (75 percent). The Northeast (40 percent) and Midwest (25 percent) contained most of the sites (Greenberg, Anderson 1984).

Two sites in New Jersey were among these 20 and illustrate why a more systematic risk-informed analysis was necessary. Located less than 5 miles from the author's home, Kin Buc was a 220-acre landfill located in Edison, New Jersey, in wetlands adjacent to the Raritan River, which drains into the Atlantic Ocean

(Figure 2.2). During the early 1970s, Kin Buc changed from a municipal landfill to an industrial waste site. The author was on-site trying to understand what was happening on the site, when a truck drove about 50 meters away and began dumping drums into a pit excavated from garbage. One of the drums split and light blue liquid poured out. Operations on the site proceeded uninterrupted by the spill.

On another occasion a bulldozer driver was killed when a drum he was moving caught on fire. Forty years after the closing of Kin Buc, the site sticks out of the flood plain as an eyesore. It is covered by vegetation so migration through the landfill into the adjacent site is limited. As part of the cleanup settlement, a walking, hiking and biking path allows residents to see the adjacent water and take their boats to a dock. Kin Buc was the second worst hazardous waste site that this author has ever seen. Kin Buc was frightening because it seemed out of control, that is, not managed for safety, much less than for human and environmental health. Fortunately, Kin Buc was not adjacent to homes and no underground drinking water supply is nearby.

In contrast, Lipari, located on southern New Jersey was a small 6–7 acre gravel pit that became a landfill, and did not look at all threatening until the specific attributes were studied (Figure 2.2). Lipari received liquid wastes from nearby chemical plants. This waste leaked through the porous site into drinking water supplies and affected adjacent orchards. Even more threatening, a pleasant middle-class neighborhood surrounded the site and a small college campus was nearby. These location attributes led to Lipari being ranked the most dangerous hazardous waste site in the United States. It was seen as an immediate threat, especially when children were observed playing on the site. Forty years later, after an expenditure of over $100 million, the site is controlled but water from the site continues to be pumped to a treatment plant for cleanup.

The author has visited many hazardous wastes, and the Kin Buc and Lipari sites illustrate that it is not necessarily obvious which sites are the most hazardous and hence deserving to be prioritized for government risk management resources.

While it continued to build its list of hazardous sites (the Emergency Remedial Response System), EPA was required by Congress under Section 105(8) of CERCLA to establish priorities for remedial action. The Mitre Corporation (1981) developed a hazard ranking model which relies on engineering judgment about what sites have the potential to inflict the most damage. This was a notably different kind of risk assessment from what was developed for individual chemicals and nuclear power plants because the outcomes and geographic scope of the assessments were much broader, and the tool was to be applied to thousands of sites that were eligible for remediation dollars.

The Mitre model, as adjusted by EPA, had routes and evidence of exposure:

Routes or pathways:

Groundwater
Surface water

Air
Fire and explosion
Direct contact

Rating factors:

Release
Waste attributes
Quantity
Targets

If a release has been observed, then the analyst needs no further evidence of possible exposure. If there is no evidence of release, then the analyst is challenged to demonstrate that the potential exists for a release through a pathway such as groundwater into a water supply. Waste characteristics include toxicity, persistence, reactivity, and reaction with other substances. The quantity is important, especially if it is not controlled. Targets are people and ecosystems through drinking water, boating and fishing. Beyond this level of generality, I found the model difficult to work with. Criticism has been directed at the model's ability to assess risk (Greenberg, Anderson 1984, Committee on Remedial Action 1994).

My criticism of the model is that it can be manipulated by clever analysts that want a higher priority rating in order to obtain government cleanup funds. An investment in a sampling program at the site of a spill or leak would likely find evidence of contamination and a path to groundwater. Some communities do not have the money to find the evidence, and therefore they did not have the chance to rise to the priority. States, most notably, New Jersey, New York and Massachusetts worked and invested resources to have their sites rise in the federal government's priority list. Other states did not.

An unintended negative outcome of variation in state efforts to get high scores with the Mitre model on the sites was that many people in states like New Jersey believed they had much higher exposure to chemical wastes than people in other states. The reality was that states that had more listed NPL sites were among the states with many abandoned waste sites and also among the states that wanted to reduce the exposure of their residents. Some states that had few sites on the NPL list were misleading their residents into believing that there was no exposure or potential exposure.

Any risk assessment process that prioritizes tens of thousands of sites has to balance the need for risk-related information against cost of obtaining the information. The National Research Council report *Ranking Hazardous Waste Sites* (Committee on Remedial Action 1994) compared federal and state approaches and divided the decision-making process into three tiers. The first tier is obtaining data for every site and using it to determine if there is sufficient evidence to eliminate the site from further analysis. Second, those sites that could be hazardous to human health and the environment require more data, an initial risk assessment and cost estimates, as well as consideration of future use of the site. The third tier places every site in a list of priorities.

The Committee listed eight features of the three-tiered multistage process:

- Should be applicable to every hazardous waste site;
- Should incorporate information regarding uncertainty when input parameters are not available or when there is a lack of confidence in the data;
- Should allow for tracking and updating;
- Should discriminate between immediate and long-term risks;
- Should include cost estimates of remediation alternatives;
- Should make sure that the structure of model is transparent;
- Should be user-friendly; and
- Should include appropriate security features to prevent unauthorized access.

This author was a member of that NRC committee, and I admit to have never seen a data base that includes all this information, including for the U.S. Departments of Energy and Defense, departments that have multi-billion dollar cleanup costs. Our criterion was a wish list.

With that caveat noted, I summarize one of the simpler screening risk assessment models, which has the virtue of addressing many of the attributes suggested by the Committee (1994) and at the same time seems transparent and replicable. Marsh and Day (1991) divided their screening risk assessment protocol into four stages that correspond comfortably with the three risk assessment questions. The following summarizes key elements of their checklist model, and I have modified their language in part:

Hazardous site determination (hazard identification question in risk assessment):

- Document that the site is hazardous;
- Determine the toxicity of the five most hazardous substances on site;
- Determine the quantity of these five most hazardous substances;
- Indicate the persistence of these five;
- Indicate the concentration of the five;
- Indicate the extent of site management and substance containment; and
- Indicate the potential for direct access to the site.

The second and third parts focus on likelihood of exposure.

Exposure potential of environmental pathways:

- Groundwater;
- Surface water;
- Air;
- Soil deposition on or in soil off site; and
- Presence in the food chain.

Potential for human exposure:

- Knowledge of a potentially exposed population;
- Evidence for human exposure/absorption; and
- Substances found through sampling.

The last set of metrics is for health consequences:

- Reports and allegations of exposure;
- Clinical or epidemiological studies;
- Expected current or acute or short-term;
- Expected chronic effects; and
- Severity of the expected effects.

Each question has four possible answers and a no data/information answer. For example, with regard to the potential for direct access to the site, respondents can answer as follows:

1. "no direct access" = 0
2. "occasional individual access" = 1
3. "small population (<100) with intermittent access" = 2
4. "large population with repeated direct access" = 3

The paper provides tables that help the user answer many of the questions. Analysts are able to assess any site with semi-quantitative metrics. For example, the Kin Buc landfill would be a serious hazardous waste site based on multiple sources of visual, record and monitoring data on multiple hazardous substances. In regard to exposure potential, surface and ground water contamination were demonstrable, air quality emissions were obvious, and off site deposition was measured, as well as present in the ecological food chain. The potential for human exposure had been demonstrated and there clearly were acute effects. The only issue for Kin Buc in this model was potential chronic effects to residents had not been demonstrated because of the latency period. Kin Buc would have a very high score for each question.

This small screening risk model has clear advantages. It includes six of the eight attributes suggested by the National Research Council Committee, but not an indicator of uncertainty or remediation cost estimates. These would need to be added in follow-up steps. Another issue is the break points in the metrics. A site becomes potentially more hazardous if a large population is exposed, and hence the 4-point scale makes sense. But do the breaks that separate the categories make sense? For example, some would argue that 50–100 people with intermittent access to the site is a serious problem if the substances are very toxic. Like any scale, the break points are critical. Nevertheless, this model is helpful and valuable when there are thousands of sites that must be screened across 50 states before detailed risk assessments are performed on some.

Like the Mitre model, this one could be used to separate and prioritize the most hazardous sites and it could be used in the case of much less threatening brownfield sites, where the comprehensive nature of the method and simplicity of use make it feasible for analysts without advanced science training (see Chapter 10 for a new online model intended for brownfield sites).

Food: the risk of overlooking the obvious

Before the public worried about risk associated with chemical agents, radioactivity, and waste, we knew that foodborne illnesses were a threat. When my son and youngest daughter were children they were fascinated by the story of Louis Pasteur, as told by Johnson and Pileggi's (1977) book for children *The Value of Believing in Yourself: the Story of Louis Pasteur*. The idea that bugs could kill people remains fascinating and scary for children, and I have read the same book to some of my grandchildren.

Bacteria, viruses, parasites and other organisms are a global challenge. In 2015, World Health Day highlighted food safety. The World Health Organization's (WHO) ten food safety facts include that over 200 diseases are caused by food contamination by bacteria, viruses, parasites and chemicals. The WHO estimates that 2 million deaths occur annually, and they explicitly link the risk to poverty, associated with unsafe water, lack of proper waste management, poor food production, inadequate handling and preparation (World Health Organization 2008).

In the United States, the Center for Disease Control and Prevention (CDC) 2011) estimates an annual average of 48 million U.S. residents (total U.S. population was 323 million in 2015) are sickened by foodborne illnesses, 128,000 are hospitalized and 3,000 die. Table 2.1 estimates the primary pathogens that cause hospitalization and death in the United States.

Risk management for food and beverages is different from that of single chemical agents, radioactivity and waste because food-related hazards are much

TABLE 2.1 Five primary pathogens contributing to death and hospitalization in the United States, 2011

Pathogen	Estimated deaths (rank)	Estimated hospitalizations (rank)
Salmonella (non-typhoidal)	378 (1)	19,336 (1)
Toxoplasma gondii (parasites/toxoplasmosis)	327 (2)	4, 428 (4)
Listeria monocytogenes	255 (3)	—
Norovirus	149 (4)	14,663 (2)
Campylobacter spp.	76 (5)	8,463 (3)
Ecoli	—	2,138 (5)

Source: Centers for Disease Control 2011.

more difficult to manage. Washing, cooking, and other parts in the home can only be improved through education. Hence, risk assessment is an important tool that allows government and industry to assess risk from the origin of the eventual food product to consumption, with the objective of identifying those stages with the greatest risk.

The list of food categories that can lead to human disease and death is long, including:

- Raw and smoked seafood, preserved fish, cooked and ready-to-eat crustaceans;
- Raw vegetables, and dried and raw fruits;
- Dairy products, including milk, various forms of cheese, ice cream and other frozen dairy products; and
- Meat, such as deli, spreads, frankfurters, hamburgers, meatballs, sausages, poultry and others.

Risk assessment for food is difficult and is becoming more complicated because of the globalizing world market. One recent example is importing meat from Australia to the United States in order to blend leaner Australian meat with higher fat U.S. meat. Kiermeier, Jenson, and Sumner (2015) estimated the risk associated with blending U.S. and Australian hamburger meat. They followed the food process from storage in 60 lb (27.2 kg) cartons, transport, grinding and mixing with U.S. beef, then retail storage, transport to homes, home storage, and cooking. They measured samples contaminated with *E. coli 0157*; and then traced the contamination through the following steps: effect of frozen storage and of grinding into patties; growth during retail storage, transport to home, and storage prior to cooking; cooking and inactivation of *E. coli 0157*; and consumption of the patties. The authors used a dose-response model (Haas, Rose, Gerba 1999) to derive the likelihood of illness from consuming a particular dose in a contaminated hamburger. The estimate was 49 cases in the United States, much lower than would be expected from native-United States meat sources. As in many of these cases, the authors made conservative assumptions protective of human health. In short, assuming a continuation of conditions, the 5 percent of the U.S. hamburgers that include Australian meat should not increase risk; it should reduce it, as well as introduce a leaner source of beef into meat-eaters' diets.

When the author visited France some years ago to deliver lectures about risk analysis, he was treated to some spectacular lunches that always included an amazing variety of cheeses. France is the leading exporter of cheese, and it would be a major blow to the cheese industry in France if there a serious disease outbreak traced to French cheese. Perrin *et al.* (2015) conducted a risk assessment associated with contamination of soft cheeses by the same E. coli strain studied in the above hamburger study. The authors built a model that includes the farm as a source, cheese production, and consumer elements. They estimate that the average risk per million servings (25 grams) is 4.2 cases of Haemolytic Uremic Syndrome (HUS, a severe outcome sometimes leading to renal failure in young children). This outcome can be reduced by vaccines, probiotics, milk sorting and exclusion, and all or a combination of these risk management steps can reduce the risk 76 percent to 98 percent, with the highest risk reduction achieved by vaccinations or treatments.

If I had to choose among the ghoulish list of foodborne illnesses that might be increased by the globalizing world economy, then I would focus on ready-to-eat foods (RTEF). RTEF foods are prepared in advance and can be eaten as sold. RTEF includes so-called "shelf stable" foods that can be eaten directly upon purchase. They also include frozen foods that only need to be heated. Canned olives, beans, carrots, mangos, and meats are among the popular shelf stable products that have been treated with preservatives to prevent microbial decomposition. Frozen foods that should be stored at temperatures of 40 degrees F or below include so-called "TV dinners" and French fries. Future Market Insights (2015) touted the RTEF industry as among the most promising with a forecast for substantial increases in North America, Europe, Russia and Asia. Their detailed report is grounded in some basic realities of the twenty-first century. In many developed countries people have more income, more people work, which reduces the time to prepare home-cooked meals, and overall the pace of living appears to be increasingly hectic, all of which lead to more purchase of convenience foods.

In 2001 and 2003, the U.S. Departments of Health and Human Services and the U.S. Department of Agriculture prepared quantitative risk assessments of the risk of listeria monocytogenes from RTEF (Center for Food Safety and Applied Nutrition 2003). The immediate context was that foodborne listeriosis had decreased from 0.5 to 0.3 cases per 100,000 people per year between 1996 and 2001. This decrease was attributed to improved surveillance, more effective outbreak responses, research and regulations. However, the study reported that further decrease was difficult to achieve, and notably the disease disproportionately impacted vulnerable populations causing approximately 500 deaths per year and 2,500 cases in total, or about one-third of total foodborne illness cases.

The U.S. study predicted median cases of listeriosis for 23 food categories. By far, the highest risk measured on a per serving basis and per annum basis was deli meats, which accounted for almost 1,600 of the 1,800 predicted cases. Pasteurized fluid milk, high fat and other dairy products, and frankfurters that were not reheated were estimated to be responsible for 178 more cases, and all other food for 20 more. The authors then explored the risk reduction associated with making sure that refrigerators operated below 41 degrees F, by labeling deli meat to warn buyers that it should be stored only for 14 days rather than 28, a similar recommendation for a reduction of seafood from 45 days to 30, and several others that would reduce the number of cases by up to 50 percent for certain food types. For deli meats the authors' simulations suggest growth inhibitors, and reducing the time and temperature of refrigerated storage.

The interested reader will find many more risk assessments to try to better understand the options for food products, their transportation and storage, and preparation for consumption in an outstanding book *Quantitative Microbial Risk*

Assessment (Haas, Rose, Gerba 1999). The key agents being scrutinized are *Salmonella, Campylobacter jejuni, E. coli 0157:H7*, and *Listeria monocytogenes*.

Serious food-related illnesses and deaths are concentrated in vulnerable populations. For example, Pouillot *et al.* (2015) adopted the U.S. RTEF risk assessment model published in 2003 in order to analyze demographic variations in vulnerability. The authors gathered animal data and used five dose-response models (exponential, gompertz-log, logistic, multi-hit, and probit) to fit the data. They also examined recorded human outbreak data.

Table 2.2 shows the relative risk of French subpopulations. The reference group is less than 65 year old people with no pre-existing conditions. These remarkable data underscore the importance of surveillance and risk assessment of data because they offer the opportunity for targeting risk prevention and response efforts among the most vulnerable.

Infrastructure and other community assets: protecting critical facilities

The logic and needs that led to applications of risk analysis for chemicals, hazardous waste, and nuclear facilities is increasingly applied to assets such as airports, bridges, energy, water and other human infrastructure systems. I summarize three non-terrorist-related asset examples: public potable water supply, electrical transmission and a university community.

TABLE 2.2 Relative risk of invasive listeriosis by age group in France, 2001–2008 data*

Population	Relative risk (95% confidence limits)
Reference group (<65 years old and no pre-existing conditions)	1.0
Hematological cancer	373.6 (217.3, 648.9)
Solid organ transplant	163.7 (26.3, 551.5)
Renal or liver failure	149.4 (82,270.1)
Pregnancy	116 (71,194.4)
Inflammatory diseases (rheumatoid arthritis, ulcerative colitis, Crohn's disease)	58.5 (25.2,123.4)
Nonhematological cancer	54.8 (34.2,90.3)
HIV/AIDS	47.4 (10.5,140.4)
65+ years old and a pre-existing condition	13.9 (8.6,23.1)

Source: *Data for table from Pouillot *et al.* 2015, from Table I, p. 96

Water supply system: risk assessment and risk management combinations

Urban civilization will not exist for long without a dependable supply of potable water. In an emergency, water can be trucked into an area, but not for an indefinite period. Given growing concern about terrorism, protecting water supplies is important. The author lived in southeast Yonkers, NY for eight years, about half a mile from the Hillview Reservoir, which is the pass through point for a billion gallons a day of water from upstate New York to New York City (see Figure 2.2). As a teenager my friends and I ran around the 90 acre site for exercise (it is about 10,000 feet around the oval), and we had picnics and could watch the trotters (horse races) at the adjacent Yonkers Raceway. Today, because of a fear of terrorism, the reservoir is not open to the public and is surrounded by high fences, and guarded by police who will not let anyone near it.

Long before there was widespread fear of terrorists dropping poison into a water supply or blowing up facilities, there was fear of poisoning by sea gulls (now dealt with at the site), and there was drought. When a drought occurs, there will be water rationing. If it continues, closing of unessential facilities and search for additional water sources follow. Communities cannot let the problem get to the point where there is a lack of water pressure that will increase the risk of major fires. The ultimate risk from drought is friction and war (Gleick 1993, Greenberg, Ferrer 2012, see also Chapter 7).

Before that field of risk analysis started, my first experience with risk analysis was about potable water in the greater New York City-New Jersey region. From a precipitation perspective, this is a well-endowed region averaging 45 inches of precipitation a year with a typical range from 40 inches to 50 inches. However this region is one of the most densely populated areas in the world. New Jersey is the only state in the United States with a population density of more than 1,000 people per square mile and the population density of New York City and its immediate suburbs exceeds 20,000 per square mile. Consequently, the region, despite major water resource assets, is vulnerable to short-term reductions in precipitation.

I first witnessed this vulnerability as a young boy when my father, grandfather, and uncle expressed frustration at not being able to shave and bathe because of a drought, and no one was allowed to water their lawns. They showed me a photograph from the newspaper with men growing beards because the reservoirs were only a third full and as a result water use was being restricted, even for shaving. That drought was superseded by a much more severe drought from 1962 through 1966. Water companies lowered their so-called "safe yield" of freshwater from 9 percent to 28 percent (Greenberg, Hordon 1976). Massive reservoir systems, such as those serving the City of New York began to look like bathtubs without any water in them. There was a cause and effect relationship between drought as a hazard event and the consequences that followed, or so we were told by the media and elected officials – in other words, the problem could not be controlled.

As a skeptical student, I was able to obtain the water supply records, and I was able to prove to myself that this was an unprecedented drought for this region, worse than the previous record drought between 1929 and 1932. I fitted the historical precipitation data to a curve and estimated that the probability of such an extended drought was very rare (less than 1 percent a year) but that a loss of 5 inches (about 10 percent) in any one year could be expected about every decade. In other words, applying my math major skills and using my slide rule and pieces of semi-logarithmic graph paper, I was able to crudely estimate the likelihood of a drought in this area.

However, my simplistic cause and effect deterministic relationship between drought and the need to suppress water demand quickly broke down. I learned that there were other cause and effect relationships that were impacting the ability of the system to supply the water. One was that demand was increasing. To avoid a plethora of detail, I will focus on northern and central New Jersey, a 10-county area with 4.5 million residents at that time (Figure 2.2). Water demand in that region more than doubled from the mid-1940s through the late 1960s as people moved from cities to suburbs and more people moved into the region, many to suburban areas with single family homes with large lots and lawns that needed watering. I also learned that the network of pipes, pumps, and valves linking different sources of water with areas of demand did not exist in many places. The 4.5 million people lived in 166 local government jurisdictions and their water supply was delivered by water companies that served as few as 45 people and as many as 767,000. The smaller systems were, with few exceptions, unable to adjust to the drought, even if they had sufficient groundwater because of their engineering shortcomings.

During the height of the drought, seven major reservoirs had less than 10 percent of their normal supply, but others had 18 percent to 46 percent and had groundwater, but that supply could not be transferred to other areas that literally did not have enough water to suppress fires. Pipelines did not exist where they should have, and there was little confidence that the pumps, valves, and pipes actually worked, even if they existed. Yet another issue was the quality of the remaining water. Was it safe to drink? In some rivers, most of the flow was wastewater that had been treated in sewage plants.

In short, while it is clear that the drought was the proximate cause of the effect, in reality the region was seriously vulnerable because of a lack of appropriate analysis of the risk to the region and risk management planning. We were able to estimate the likelihood of dropping below specified precipitation levels, and then build an optimization model for risk management predicated on the assumption that we wanted to minimize the cost to consumers across the region subject to constraints on supply, demand for potable water, and especially on the network that links the supplies with the demand.

Chapter 3 uses this water system case to illustrate optimization models. Chapter 3 also overviews uses of optimization models for other water-related risks such as emissions into water bodies used for drinking water and fishing. In those cases, too many emissions can contaminate a water body, driving down oxygen and killing fish and other species, and requiring water companies to add expensive chemicals to remove the contamination. Another important water-related example is the regulation of releases from reservoirs used for recreation, irrigation, and electricity generation. The risk is that a large release can cause serious erosion and flooding. Insufficient release can mean loss of other uses. Reservoir cases demand extraordinarily careful analysis of historical data and simulation for wet and dry periods of the year. Managers are always balancing among needs. Summarizing, drought, demand increase, network failure, water pollution, and competing demands for water are causes of water supply problems with potentially serious human health, safety and environmental consequences. Each of these causes is subject to analysis using risk assessment processes and tools, and each of them can be modeled as stochastic variables. The result should lead to a planning effort by risk managers, as has been the case in New Jersey where the state organized a master plan water supply commission.

Electric power

Electric power energy sources and networks are necessary to meet growing demand and to transfer electricity in the case of emergencies. These have their dark side. For example, dams will sometimes fail leading to cascading water. Oil and gas pipelines can fail. Oil tankers run aground and discharge oil, and nuclear power plants have periodically had accidents. People recognize these that these hazardous events can happen. But electromagnetic fields created by high-voltage transmission lines (HVTLs) as a cause or promotor of cancer came as a surprise to the vast majority of people and experts.

Above-ground transmission lines are unsightly, sometimes make noise, but HVTL as a cause of cancer only started when Wertheimer and Leeper (1979) published an article that observed that childhood leukemia was higher in neighborhoods of Denver, Colorado near to electric power lines. They added that children who spent their entire lives in their neighborhood had elevated rates compared to those that did not, and the two authors could not attribute the findings to auto traffic, family attributes, economic status or other factors. A few studies had found a relationship but typically only in homes with extremely high exposures (Mezei *et al.*, 2008; Greenland *et al.*, 2000). The clear majority of studies have found no relationship (Tynes, Haldorsen 1997; World Health Organization 2002; Kleinerman *et al.* 2000; Kroll *et al.* 2010; Wünsch-Filho 2011; Sermage-Faure 2013 *et al.*). Paul Brodeur (1989, 1993), a gifted writer for the *New Yorker,* seized upon the newly proposed hazard and made it accessible to influential members of the public and elected officials who made the case understandable to the public and decision-makers.

Low frequency electromagnetic fields (EMF) are produced by home electric appliances (hair driers, computers, televisions, electric razors, etc.), wiring, and power lines. These fields are a form of non-ionizing radiation caused by the movement of electrons through wires. As the voltage increases, the strength of the electric field increases. As the current increases, the strength of the magnetic field increases. Power lines are always operating, hence they have ongoing electronic and magnetic fields, whereas home appliances do not have a magnetic field, which is only created when the appliance is on. Magnetic fields are focus of the health concern. Animal studies have shown little evidence of a cause and effect. EMFs are non-ionizing and low energy, and so do not pose a direct threat to DNA. But some have suggested that they reduce melatonin (a hormone made by the pineal gland in the brain that is involved in various bodily functions). Scientists continue to investigate the proposed link between EMF and childhood leukemia and brain cancer, adult breast cancer, and worker cancers. Foster, Erdreich, and Moulder (1997) conclude that the data show that the exposed population is so large that even if the individual risk is small the collective risk across the many millions living near such facilities make it a significant risk issue that will continue indefinitely. In other words, it is hard to prove that there is no risk across the billions of people who are exposed. If there is a cause and effect relationship, the delivery of electricity through large power lines would need to be entirely rethought. The economic impacts of such a reconfiguration would be substantial.

I am much more sanguine about a relationship between distance from high-voltage lines and property values. Even before the EMF and cancer link made headlines, there were a few studies showing property values near high-voltage transmission lines (HVTC) were up to 30 percent lower. But other studies showed no effect (see reviews by Bottemiller, Wolverston 2013; Gregory, von Winterfeldt 1996). The causes were attributed to unsightly appearance of the lines, noise from the lines, and home disturbance because of utility right-a-way access.

After the Wertheimer and Leeper paper was published, appraisers and social scientists had incentives to investigate the relationship and include location near a tower as a variable. Researchers found values lowered 5 percent to 10 percent, and court cases show awards to some plaintiffs but no award to others. A major source of uncertainty is the small number of studies that adequately control for the main effect and other factors, including type of transmission lines, and the surrounding housing market. Bottemiller and Wolverston's (2013) study in Portland (OR) and Seattle (WA) is illustrative. They followed approximately 1,100 transactions over a two-and-a-half year period, matching cases (sales near HVTLs) with those not near sites. In what these appraisers characterized as a "sellers" market, they found a -1.65 percent effect of location near HVTLs, which in meant an average $4,884 lower price. The presence of a pool, a landscape rated as "fair" quality and several neighborhoods were more detrimental to sales price than was distance from a HVTL.

In the Seattle area, the loss was -2.429 percent, or $12,504 less on an average sale. Several stronger negatives were a moderate slope, a landscape that was characterized as rural, a visible cell phone tower, a torch down roof (roof made of sheets of polyester and bitumen added to regular gravel and tar, which is then burned down in specific areas by torches that melt the asphalt concrete at seams), and location in several less desirable neighborhoods. The most interesting part of this study is that the authors compared the HVTL effect of the 25 percent most expensive homes against the other 75 percent. The HVTL effect was about markedly higher in the expensive homes (-11.2 percent). Overall, HVTLs are one of a number of factors that influence property sales that are not internal to the housing unit. If researchers continue these types of risk assessment studies, they should be able to reduce the uncertainty about the impact of HVTLs on property values.

Some assert that the proposed relationship between EMF and cancer is junk science influencing public perceptions and public officials. That may be true, but does not matter. Risk assessors can and should help clarify the importance of this issue for decision-makers through rigorous studies.

A university

A university is a major community asset, and some are national and international assets. The Massachusetts Institute of Technology (MIT) is surely among the best universities in the world. With a campus of 168 acres located in Cambridge, Massachusetts, MIT has over 11,000 students and almost 12,000 staff. Opened in 1861, it also has many famous older buildings and accompanying infrastructure to manage. Li *et al.* (2009) focused on the MIT campus and built an interesting risk assessment process model for campus risk managers.

In regard to potential hazard events, the authors used historical data and experts to list potential hazards.

- Natural hazards included earthquakes, freezes, heavy rain, hurricanes, and storms during the winter, and tornadoes; and
- Human-caused hazards included cyber/IT attacks, explosions, fires, infectious disease outbreaks, internal flooding, and vandalism.

MIT and other universities, hospitals, prisons, and other large institutions need a process that leads to a process for risk assessment linked to risk management. The MIT authors gathered data on six specific criteria to assess the extent to which these potential hazards were a concern:

(1) Frequency – number of events;
(2) Severity – assessed as consequences;
(3) Detectability – warning that the event is occurring;
(4) Awareness – cognizance of MIT managers of the issue and work already completed to mitigate the event;
(5) Importance – necessity of addressing the threat; and
(6) Satisfaction – MIT's current efforts to prevent or respond to the event.

Each of the six criteria were rated along a five point scale, (4=high to 0=extremely low). University managers chose the following hazard events to include in analyses:

- Internal flooding;
- Fires;

- Explosions;
- Winter storms;
- Rain associated flooding; and
- Vandalism.

Earthquakes, infectious diseases outbreaks, and cyber-attacks were not included. The latter two are subject of another study, and a severe earthquake was not considered a threat for this campus.

The authors classified the university's assets into mission related (academic and research); support and service (administrative offices, athletic centers, residential facilities, medical center); and other key assets (central utility plant, hospital, and others). As part of this analysis, the group determined the physical, cyber, geographical and organizational dependencies of these assets.

Consistent with risk assessment practice, the authors created hazard event scenarios and built event trees, which are sequences, some of which can lead to damage (see Chapter 4 for an illustration). For example, a winter storm could impact the entire campus, whereas internal flooding is more likely to impact a building. With over 150 buildings on campus and a large amount of infrastructure, the researchers studied historical records of these events, reviewed the literature, and asked experts for their judgments. The latter process involved designing protocols, holding workshops and eliciting information. The results of the expert inputs were compared to historical and literature-based data.

Up to this point in the analysis, their risk assessment process was similar to many others in the literature. Beyond this point, the authors added other process and analytical tools. They acknowledged that events could impact human health and safety, economic assets, and hard to value research information and other assets valuable to the university. Hence, they used the analytical hierarchy process (AHP) to weight a variety of impacts. AHP is a systematic process for comparing a list of alternatives or objectives (Saaty 1980). I last used it to help a large company evaluate the strengths and weaknesses of 16 international headquarter options. In this university risk case, the authors used it to create impact weights.

The initial AHP-based weights were reviewed and modified by decision-makers. The four highest final weights are listed below:

Impact category*	Global weight
Impact on people	0.295
Impact on the environment	0.196
Programs affected	0.138
Intellectual property damage	0.128
All other categories	0.243
Total weight	1.000

Source: *adapted from larger table in Li *et al.* 2009, Table IV, pp. 446–447.

Impacts on people and the environment accounted for almost half of the weight. With a total of 270 scenarios in play, these weights allowed the analysts to consider a variety of risk management options and introduce stochastic elements into their analysis. The authors grouped events into categories, for example, high risk and high probability hazard, moderate risk and high probability, and low probability but high consequences. Also, the authors estimated the 5 percent and 95 percent likelihood risk cases so that risk managers would see the impact of uncertainty on the results.

Both the process and results are valuable for major institutions. For example, internal flooding may seem less significant than an earthquake, but the analysis showed that internal flooding is important because it is ten times as likely to occur as any other event. The causes are plumbing failures, drains that overflow, poor design, condensation, and failures in sprinkler systems. The consequences of an internal flood at an older university like MIT can be quite serious, including destruction of equipment that is both expensive and difficult to replace, and loss of irreplaceable records.

The author has experienced three internal floods in over 45 years at universities. The most recent one was caused by an overflow of chiller condensation in the system on top of a five-story building. The personnel that regularly checked the system had been moved to work on something else, and without warning, a cascade of water began to flow into a room about 70 feet from the author's office. Fortunately, a faculty member alerted the author, and we, along with the custodial staff, inserted trash barrels to catch much of the water. We then rigged a hose and pumped the water into a sink. Had the building been unoccupied, the damage could have been over $100,000, whereas the actual damage was about $10,000, including destruction of some computers, paper supplies, walls, rugs, floors and ceilings, all of which had to be replaced. Another negative outcome was considerable angst between the author's school and the university building and grounds staff, which carried over to management of other infrastructure. Frankly, we lost trust in their capacity to manage those systems, keep us informed, and to include us in the decision-making process.

With a student body of over 67,000, about 10,000 staff, spread over three major campuses, and almost 800 buildings, Rutgers can benefit from this type of asset risk assessment process. Looking across the set of hazard events that can impact universities and small cities, the MIT risk assessment process can be a powerful planning tool, one that helps managers determine what events have the most severe consequences, rather than managers reacting to pressure from influential individuals who do not know what is behind the walls, under the floors and above the ceilings.

Ecology: a major gap to fill

The National Environmental Policy Act (NEPA) became a U.S. law on January 1, 1970. NEPA is the most emulated U.S. law in the world and the author has often heard it referred to as the "environmental Magna Carta." The preamble asserts that the main emphasis is on balancing ecological systems and human needs. The first ecological risk paper that this author found in *Risk Analysis* is about the Exxon Valdez oil spill (Stewart, Leschine 1986). Despite the legal driver of NEPA and versions of it in over 100 nations, ecological risk assessment has lagged in government and private support.

Some of the most interesting treatments of uncertainty appear in this literature. In risk analysis, the examples began with major oil spills and contaminated sites, and have grown to embrace aspects of global climate change and species change. Invasive species is a major focus. Risk assessors must isolate pathways by which the pests are introduced and move, and they must understand the susceptibility of different hosts. Two papers (Yemshanov *et al.* 2009; Koch *et al.* 2009) are illustrative. The authors studied *sirex noctilio,* a wasp which migrated from Europe, western Asia and northern Africa to Ontario, Canada, and New York State. The threat is to native pines in those areas and eventually to southern pines. Total projected losses in the U.S. and Canada are over $1.5 billion.

The authors' approach was to create and map scenarios that show high risk, low risk and medium risk invasions. They mapped the geographical spread of the invading species and the uncertainty in their results, which visually shows a high degree of uncertainty. They add that they do not have data that will allow them to measure the impact of quarantine or inspection efforts. The papers focus risk manager attention on intercepting and inspecting all wood packages and raw materials to reduce the probability of survival of the invading species. Packages are supposed to be fumigated or heat treated, which means inspecting boxes, crates, packing cases, pallets, drums, spools and reels, and other packages.

Burgman *et al.* (2010) examined the invasion of southern Queensland, Australia, by red fire ants. The ants damage crops, animals, and farm infrastructure, the environment, and injure people who intrude on the fire ants' space. In Australia, the fire ants found a niche in disturbed and open ecosystems. Risk management options include aerial spraying and injecting nests. The authors note a lack of data, and the need to rely on expert judgment. To include uncertainty, they used Bayesian nets, which are trees showing intersections of probabilities, and the authors use these to show how far the existing data and models can be taken to generate reliable results.

Another illustration that emphasizes uncertainty is from a series of studies by Landis and Bryant (2010). The authors note that there has been a decline in Cherry Point Pacific herring in the Puget Sound of the State of Washington. They show that Pacific herring has also been declining in the remainder of the Puget Sound region. Average age of herring was estimated to have fallen from 8–9 years to 4 years and abnormalities were found in many larvae.

Landis and Bryant acknowledge the high degree of uncertainty and turn to weight of evidence (WOE) processes to assess the proposed causes. WOE assessments are based on strength, consistency and specificity of the information, as well as biological plausibility of possible causes, experimental evidence, and sequencing of the decline. They assess three explanations of the decline in the herring. One is that global climate change has warmed the waters and invasive pests are attacking the herring. Second, contamination by polychlorinated biphenyls, DDT, and hexachlorobenzene has undermined the immune systems of the herring. Viral disease is a third plausible explanation.

After weighting all the evidence, the authors posit that as the water warmed invasive species moved into the Puget Sound and undermined the herring population, already weakened by pollution and disease. Landis and Bryant offer an explanation with a caveat that a great deal more is required to explain the Cherry Point Pacific herring decline. These authors acknowledge the need for the discipline to confirm risk assessment models and risk management decisions by field studies and by using historical data to predict current states.

I would be disingenuous, if I led the reader to believe that all ecological risk assessments are transparent about uncertainty and that risk assessment findings drive risk management. There are several prominent cases where they have not been. The oil platform blowout in the Gulf of Mexico is such a case. Written for the U.S. Department of the Interior (2007), the 69 page report presents an oil spill risk analysis. The analysts estimate the number of spills of >1,000 and >10,000 barrels during the estimated life of the facility (2007–2046). The authors indicate that they examined every spill in U.S. federal waters during the period 1964–1999 and every tanker spill for the period 1974–1999 according to their relevance. Perhaps the justification is presented in the document and I did not see it, but I could not replicate what was done based on the description and data in the paper.

What is at issue here is that U.S. EPA risk assessments for chemicals, U.S. NRC protocols for nuclear energy plants, and EPA requirements for ecological risk assessment at Superfund sites are based on relatively rigid process protocols. Perhaps they are too rigid, but at least a reader can follow what was done and normally can see the data or at least some of the data. In this case, what I find is that the authors had a great deal of latitude on what to do and how to do it, maybe too much latitude. Furthermore, what happened with their findings, which is part of risk management, is hard to understand. Assuming that their estimates are appropriate, and I have no way of assessing that for the reasons just noted, the estimated likelihood of one or more oil spills of >10,000 barrels for the central area from platforms are 4 percent to 6 percent (U.S. Department of the Interior 2007, Table 1b, p. 52). These estimates in my experience are remarkably high and merited a second level of risk assessment with an objective of lowering these likelihoods. This would have involved detailed engineering analysis of the planned structure and review of human factors to determine how the risk could be reduced far below these estimates.

I did not find any such consideration in the environmental impact statements that preceded the drilling. The April 2007 document refers to stipulations on the lease and regulations to minimize loss, and discusses mitigation measures and monitoring requirements specifically for whales, polar bears, sea turtles, permafrost and many other conditions. How these measures are related to the risk assessment is not clear. Nor can I find evidence that the risk assessment evaluated a worst case scenario and that risk managers instructed engineers and designers to adjust the drilling and mining plan.

Could the ecological disaster have been avoided with a more detailed preliminary risk assessment, with a follow-up to these preliminary probabilities that acknowledged that probabilities as unacceptably high and required a second stage of proposed risk management followed by a more refined risk assessment? I am not certain that reasonable changes in the design would have prevented the blowout in the Gulf of Mexico that occurred on August 20, 2010 leading to the release of between 150 and 200 million gallons, and created a slick of about 25,000 square miles, which cost the lives of 11 people, cost BP, the company, over $50 billion, and killed many animals, fish and birds in the Gulf of Mexico, and the states of Louisiana, Alabama Mississippi and Florida. I do not know enough about oil drilling and recovery to say that this ecological and human disaster could have been avoided. But I suspect that it could have been had there been redundant systems that I would expect with the risk levels reported in the risk study. Some of the questions I raised here, in fact, have been addressed after the event. But I cannot find a definitive set of documents in the pre-event black or grey literatures prior to it.

Terrorism: a major new concern

Natural hazards, equipment failures, human errors, worker and public exposure to hazardous chemicals in the environment, food poisoning, and other non-deliberate human failures are assumed to be random acts that can be estimated by consulting historical experiences and/or experts. Terrorism is a deliberate, non-random act, which raises the question of the validity of the normal methods for estimating likelihood.

Considerable debate has focused on this issue, which I will briefly summarize by highlighting a few papers. Rosoff and Winterfeldt (2007) examined the risk of a dirty bomb attack on the ports of Los Angeles and Long Beach. A dirty bomb is nuclear material detonated by conventional explosives. Based on expert opinion, the authors created 36 possible terrorist attack scenarios. The authors concluded that the impacts would largely be economic and psychological because while the massive ports would close and people would be frightened, human health effects would be minimal because the detonation would take place in a sparsely populated non-residential area, and there would be no fission (see longer discussion of CREATE in Chapter 3).

I was editor of *Risk Analysis*, which published this paper, and was pleased to see the publicity it received. In fact, it became the most consulted paper for about a year. Yet, as much as it was a compelling paper, the results rest on the assumption that a counterintelligence expert could recreate the logic, values, design and implementation of a terrorist. People with bad intentions do not always do what experts think that they should. Keeney (2007) speaks to the need to try to model the values of terrorists and defenders in order to try to prioritize investments, which is certainly a worthy and remarkably difficult challenge.

Cox (2008) presented a detailed critique of using standard risk assessment, focusing on the capacity of intelligent adversaries to learn and adjust. Hall (2009) and others suggest that natural and random events should be studied by risk analysts but that events created by deliberate choice should be addressed by game theory and other approaches (see also Ezell *et al.* 2010, Brown, Cox 2011). Game theory is a normative tool that instructs the analyst how to play the game. Players' objectives must be known and describable. A terrorist might want to damage the economy, scare people, destroy a strategic asset, and a symbol of a country, such as a famous art museum. Indeed, the list of worthy targets is remarkably long. Defenders cannot equally defend everything. But we need to know what assets they prioritize to play a game. Running many combinations of even simple games and using sensitivity analysis can take a great deal of time and distress managers who think that some of the games are entirely unrealistic, of course until they happen. There is no substitute for the insights that one can gain by using game theory.

While agent-based models, like game theory, can be informative, they also can misdirect risk managers. Taken literally, the results will tend to steer investments toward protecting assets that defenders think are important, which can increase vulnerability to a terrorist without the resources to attack a large target and planning on attacking a small one. If analysts are clear about the limitations of game theory, it can be a good tool to understand what actions to take against attackers with different kinds of objectives and resources.

I have a strong preference for starting with simple approaches to even complex problems like anti-terrorism; specifically I use influence diagrams, which show the relationships between decisions, events and outcomes as graphs (Pate-Cornell 2007). Assume for example, a hypothetical case of a medium-sized city that has heard rumors that a two or three former town residents with limited skills but a great deal of knowledge of town and hate for the town are planning to attack the town. The response is a small security unit with the objective of determining if the threat is real, and if so, how to stop it. They will try to infiltrate the group. They have access to electronic eavesdropping, and the local police and, if required, and could call upon federal security agents. They would like to know what the terrorists are planning. For example, are they planning an attack on several bridges that are vulnerable because of age and lack of security? Would they attack a local city hall during a meeting, a local school with only a single security guard, the police department itself? Influence diagrams allow the defenders (attackers can also use them) to list and assess their options, and isolate additional information that they need to make decisions. Figure 2.3 illustrates a simple influence diagram.

One choice is whether to continue with regular patrols around sites or to randomize those patrols so that the attackers cannot plan their attack with the knowledge of where police patrols will be. However, the attackers could determine that the patrols had been changed and withdraw before they could be arrested. The

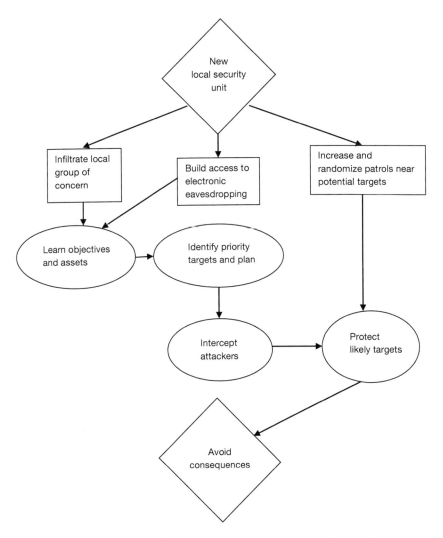

FIGURE 2.3 Influence diagram for a local security group in a small to medium-sized city

police team could choose to infiltrate the group, and/or listen in on conversations in order to learn more about what the attackers are planning to do. However, these efforts could be discovered. The influence diagram highlights the choices, leading to debate.

Trying to defend against adversaries is more likely to succeed if their motives, resources, and plans can be discovered. But societies cannot depend on the success of those efforts. It needs a clear prioritization of what assets are the most valuable and must be protected. Of course, this is not a simple task, because it involves making difficult choices. No one wants to be part of the set of assets that are not essential. Internationally, efforts have been underway to identify the most critical infrastructure. For those hazard events that do not make the short list of critical facilities, I would start with influence diagrams to indicate what we know and do not know about relationships between decisions, events and outcomes.

Before leaving this section, I will say that we need to push past the ongoing debate about how to view terrorism risk analysis. While this ongoing debate is important and stimulating, we need to deal with specific threats ranging from detonating nuclear weapons to attacks aimed at food and water supplies, the electric grid, airports and ports for ocean-going vessels (Hartnett *et al.* 2009, Atkinson *et al.* 2008). These events could be initiated by nation states or disgruntled individuals. For example, Wein, Choi and Denuit (2010) studied the impact of a 10-kt improvised nuclear device detonated in the Mall in Washington, D.C. at 10 a.m. on a weekday. Their assessment focused on the impact of the decision to shelter in place or to evacuate. The first step focused on calculating the immediate effects of heat, blast, and radiation. The authors made assumptions about how many people are indoors, and what types of places they are in when the event occurs. Their model estimates close to 80,000 deaths and another 10,000 serious injuries. Then they make assumptions about what people do after the initial effects have passed. They estimate 360,000 survivors without access to vehicles and 42,600 would die if they self-evacuated by foot. Sheltering above-ground would save several thousand and sheltering in the basement for 12–14 hours would save about a third of those that would otherwise die. This study is far from perfect because so many assumptions are used to build the risk assessment model. However, the authors are clear about what these are, and analysts can question and change these assumptions. This kind of risk assessment work is critical for risk managers because it forces us to consider the implications of conventional wisdom about risks and risk management options.

What did Chapter 2 explain about risk analysis? Summary and learning objectives

Chapter 2 introduced risk assessment by explaining its evolution in response to the need to evaluate the carcinogenicity of chemicals. The chapter presents the stages of hazard identification, dose-response assessment, exposure assessment, and risk characterization, and it considers the challenges of attempting to use human and animal studies, exposure analysis, and other approaches to characterize hazards. With that beginning as context, the chapter reviews two other early applications of risk assessment to the nuclear industry and to hazardous waste management with emphasis on the modifications of existing lines of thought and introduction of additional ways of thinking about and analyzing risk. Then, the chapter shifts to food, infrastructure systems, ecological risk, and terrorism, describing the efforts made by risk analysts to further broaden ways of thinking about and estimating risk. Each of the sections includes case studies, and the author as described in the preface uses personal experience to highlight some challenges of producing risk assessments that will inform risk management options.

At the end of this chapter readers should be able to answer the following seven questions:

1. What hazards and human health outcomes initiated risk assessment?
2. What are the four steps commonly used in risk assessment of chemicals?
3. What are some of the challenges in using human, animal, and other approaches to hazard identification?
4. How have risk assessors used a variety of models to estimate the relationship between dose and response?
5. How has risk assessment been used in the nuclear, hazardous waste, water supply, electric power, and other infrastructure systems, and in university settings to assess risks and link risks to risk management?
6. What are some of the reasons why ecological risk assessments are difficult to conduct?
7. What are the reasons why some think that standard risk assessment methods can be applied to terrorism and others think that such applications are problematic?

References

Apostolakis G. (2012) Application of risk assessment and management to nuclear safety. cmrapostolakis@nrc.gov. Accessed February 25, 2015

Atkinson M, Cao Z, Wein L. (2008) Optimal stopping analysis of a radiation detection system to protect cities from a nuclear terrorist attack. *Risk Analysis.* 28, 2, 353–371.

Bottemiller S, Wolverston M. (2013) The price effects of HVTLs on abutting homes. *The Appraisal Journal.* Winter, 45–62.

Brodeur P. (1989) *Currents of death: power lines, computer terminals, and the attempt to cover up the threat to your health.* New York: Simon and Schuster.

Brodeur P. (1993) *The great power line cover-up: how the utilities and government are trying to hide the cancer hazard posed by electromagnetic fields.* Boston, MA: Little-Brown.

Brown G, Cox LA Jr. (2011) How probabilistic risk assessment can mislead terrorism risk analysis. *Risk Analysis.* 31, 2, 196–204.

Brown M. (1979) *Laying waste: poisoning of America by toxic chemicals,* New York: Pantheon Books.

Burgman M, Wintle B, Thompson C, Moilanen A, Runge M, Ben-Hiam Y. (2010) Reconciling uncertain costs and benefits in Bayes networks for invasive species management. *Risk Analysis.* 30, 2, 277–284.

Center for Food Safety and Applied Nutrition, Food and Drug Administration, USDHSS, and Food Safety and Inspection Service, USDA. (2003) *Quantitative risk assessment of the relative risk to public health for foodborne Listeria monocytogenes among selected categories of ready-to-eat foods.* Washington, DC: USDA.

Centers for Disease Control and Prevention. (2011) Estimates of foodborne illness in the United States. 2011. www.cdc.gov/foodborneburden-estimates.html. Accessed April 3, 2015.

Committee on the institutional means for assessment of risk to public health, *Risk assessment in the federal government: managing the process.* (1983) Washington, DC: National Academy Press. Available at: www.nap.edu/catalog/366/risk-assessment-in-the-federal-government-managing-the-process.

Committee on Remedial Action. (1994) *Ranking hazardous waste sites.* Washington, DC: National Academy Press.

Cox LA, Jr. (2008) Some limitations of "risk = threat × vulnerability × consequence" for risk analysis of terrorist attacks. *Risk Analysis.* 28, 6, 1749–1761.

Cox LA, Jr. (2013) *Improving risk analysis.* New York: Springer.

Craig J. (2014) Acting Associate Principal Deputy Assistant Secretary for Environmental Management, *EM Program Update and FY 15 Budget Overview*, April 23, 2014.

Ezell B, Bennett S, von Winterfeldt D, Sokolowski J, Collins A. (2010) Probabilistic risk analysis and terrorism risk. *Risk Analysis.* 30, 4, 575–589.

Foster K, Erdreich L, Moulder J. (1997) Weak electromagnetic fields and cancer in the context of risk assessment. *Proceedings of the IEEE*, 85, 5, 733–746.

Future Market Insights (2015) Read-to-eat market – global industry analysis, size and forecast, 2014–2020. www.digitaljournal.com/pre/2501154. Accessed March 23, 2015.

Garrick BJ, Stetkar J, Bembia P. (2010) Quantitative risk assessment of the New York State Operated West Valley radioactive waste disposal area. *Risk Analysis.* 30, 8, 1219–1230.

Gleick P. (1993) Water and conflict: fresh water resources and international security. *International Security.* 18, 1, 79–112.

Greenberg M, Anderson R. (1984) *Hazardous waste sites: the credibility gap.* New Brunswick, NJ: Center for Urban Policy Research. Reprinted by Transaction Press, 2012.

Greenberg M, Ferrer J. (2012) Global availability of water, *The Praeger handbook of environmental health*, Robert Friis, Editor. Volume 3, Chapter 1, 1–20. Santa Barbara, CA: Praeger.

Greenberg M, Hordon R. (1976) *Water supply planning.* New Brunswick, NJ: Center for Urban Policy Research.

Greenberg M, West B, Lowrie K, Mayer H. (2009) *The reporter's handbook on nuclear materials, energy, and waste management.* Nashville, TN: Vanderbilt University Press.

Greenland S, Sheppard AR, Kaune WT, Poole C, Kelsh MA. (2000) A pooled analysis of magnetic fields, wire codes, and childhood leukemia. Childhood leukemia-EMF study group. *Epidemiology.* 11, 6, 624–634.

Gregory R, von Winterfeldt D. (1996) The effects of electromagnetic fields from transmission lines on public fears and property values. *Journal of Environmental Management.* 48, 201–214.

Haas C, Rose J, Gerba C. (1999) *Quantitative microbial risk assessment.* New York: John Wiley & Sons, Inc.

Hall J. (2009) The elephant in the room is called game theory. *Risk Analysis*, 29, 8, 1061.

Hartnett E, Paoli G, Schaffer D. (2009) Modeling the public health system response to a terrorist event in the food supply. *Risk Analysis.* 29, 11,1506–1520.

Johnson S, Pileggi S. (1977) *The value of believing in yourself: the story of Louis Pasteur.* New York: Value Communications.

Keeney R. (2007) Modeling values for anti-terrorism analysis. *Risk Analysis.* 27, 3, 585–596.

Kiermeier A, Jenson I, Sumner J (2015) Risk assessment of Escherichia coli 0157 illness from consumption of hamburgers in the United States made from Australian manufacturing beef. *Risk Analysis.* 35, 1, 77–89.

Kleinerman RA, Kaune WT, Hatch EE, Wacholder S, Linet MS, Robison LL, Niwa S, Tarone R. (2000) Are children living near high-voltage power lines at increased risk of acute lymphoblastic leukemia? *American Journal of Epidemiology.* 151, 5, 512–515.

Koch F, Yemshanov, McKenney D, Smith W. (2009) Evaluating critical uncertainty thresholds in a spatial model of forest pest invasion risk. *Risk Analysis*, 29, 9, 1227–1241.

Kroll ME, Swanson J, Vincent TJ, Draper GJ. (2010) Childhood cancer and magnetic fields from high-voltage power lines in England and Wales: a case–control study. *British Journal of Cancer.* 103, 7, 1122–1127.

Landis W, Bryant P. (2010) Using weight of evidence characterization and modeling to investigate the cause of changes in Pacific herring (*Clupea pallasi*) population dynamics in Puget Sound and at Cherry Point, Washington. Risk Analysis. 30, 2, 183–202.

Li H, Apostolakis G, Gifun J, VanSchalkwyk W, Leite S, Barber D. (2009). Ranking the risks from multiple hazards in a small community. *Risk Analysis*, 29, 3, 438–456.

Marsh G, Day R. (1991) A model standardized risk assessment protocol for use with hazardous waste sites. *Environmental Health Perspectives.* 90, 199–208.

McClellan R. (2014). Radiation toxicology, in A. Wallace Hayes, Claire Kruger, eds. *Hayes' principles and methods of toxicology*, 6th edition, New York: CRC Press, 884–948.

Mezei G, Gadallah M, Kheifets L. (2008) Residential magnetic field exposure and childhood brain cancer: a meta-analysis. *Epidemiology.* 19, 3, 424–430.

Mitre Corporation. (1981). *Site ranking model for determining remedial action priorities among uncontrolled hazardous substances facilities.* Working paper for the U.S. Environmental Protection Agency, Washington D.C.

Motulsky H, Christopoulos A. (2004). Fitting models to biological data using linear and nonlinear regression. New York: Oxford University Press.

National Council on Radiation Protection and Measurements (2009) *Report 160. Ionizing Radiation Exposure of the Population of the United States.* Bethesda, MD: National Council on Radiation Protection and Measurements.

Omnibus Risk Review Panel. (2015) A Review of the use of risk-informed management in the cleanup program for former defense nuclear sites. Report presented to the Appropriations Committees of the U.S. House of Representatives and U.S. Senate. Washington, D.C., U.S. Congress, August.

Pate-Cornell ME. (2007) The engineering risk analysis method and some applications. In W Edwards, R Miles Jr., D von Winterfeldt, eds. *Advances in decision analysis.* Cambridge: Cambridge University Press.

Perrin F, Tenenhaus-Aziza F, Michael V, Miszczycha S, Bel N, Sanaa M. (2015) Quantitative risk assessment of haemolytic and uremic syndrome linked to 0157:H7 and non-0157:H7 shiga-toxin producing *Escherichia coli* strains in raw milk soft cheeses. *Risk Analysis.* 35, 1, 109–128.

Pouillot R, Hoelzer K, Chen Y, Dennis S. (2015) *Listeria monocytogenes* dose response revisited – incorporating adjustments for variability in strain virulence and host susceptibility. *Risk Analysis.* 35, 1, 90–108.

Reuber M. (1978) Carcinogenicity of saccharin. *Environmental Health Perspectives.* 25, 173–200.

Rosoff H, von Winterfeldt D. (2007) A risk and economic analysis of dirty bomb attacks on the ports of Los Angeles and Long Beach. *Risk Analysis.* 27, 3, 533–546.

Saaty T. (1980) *The analytic hierarchy process.* New York: McGraw-Hill.

Schuck P. (1988) *Agent orange on trial: mass toxic disasters in the courts.* Cambridge, MA: Belknap Press.

Sermage-Faure C, Demoury C, Rudant J, Goujon-Bellec S., Guyot-Goubin A, Deschamps F, Hemon D, Clavel J. (2013) Childhood leukaemia close to high-voltage power lines – the Geocap study, 2002–2007. *British Journal of Cancer.* 108, 9, 1899–1906.

Stewart T, Leschine T. (1986) Judgment and analysis in oil spill risk assessment. *Risk Analysis.* 6, 3, 305–315.

Tynes T, Haldorsen T. (1997) Electromagnetic fields and cancer in children residing near Norwegian high-voltage power lines. *American Journal of Epidemiology.* 145, 3, 219–226.

United Church of Christ. (1987) *Toxic waste and race.* Washington, D.C.: United Church of Christ.

U.S. Department of Energy (2015) *DOE issues RFP for West Valley demonstration project probabilistic performance assessment.* http://energy.gov/em/articles.doe-issues-rfp-west-valley-demonstration-project-probabilistic-performance-assessment.pdf. Accessed April 3, 2015.

U.S. Department of the Interior. (2007) *Oil-spill risk analysis: Gulf of Mexico Outer Continental Shelf (OCS) lease sales, central planning area and western planning area, 2007–2012 and Gulfwide OCS program, 2007–2046. MMS 2007-040.* Washington, D.C.: U.S. Department of Interior.

U.S. Environmental Protection Agency (1977) *Wastes disposal practices and their effects on groundwater: report to Congress.* Washington, D.C.: US Government Printing Office.

Wein L, Choi Y, Denuit S. (2010) Analyzing evacuation versus shelter-in-place strategies after a terrorist nuclear detonation. *Risk Analysis.* 30, 9, 1315–1327.

Wertheimer N, Leeper E. (1979) Electrical wiring configurations and childhood cancer. *American Journal of Epidemiology.* 109, 3, 273–284.

World Health Organization, International Agency for Research on Cancer. (2002) Non-ionizing radiation, Part 1: static and extremely low-frequency (ELF) electric and magnetic fields. *IARC Monographs on the Evaluation of Carcinogenic Risks to Humans.* 80, 1–395.

World Health Organization. (2008) *First formal meeting of the foodborne disease burden epidemiology reference group (FERG).* Geneva: WHO. www.who.int/foodsafety/publications/foodborne_disease/FERG_Nov07.pdf. Accessed April 3, 2015.

Wünsch-Filho V, Pelissari DM, Barbieri FE, Sant Anna L, de Oliveira C, de Mata J, Tone L, de M. Lee M, de Andrea M, Bruniera P, Epelman S, Filhovc V, Kheifets L. (2011) Exposure to magnetic fields and childhood acute lymphocytic leukemia in São Paulo, Brazil. *Cancer Epidemiology.* 35, 6, 534–539.

Yemshanov D, Koch F, McKenney D, Downing M, Sapio F. (2009) Mapping invasive species risks with stochastic meddles: a cross-border United States-Canada application of *sirex noctilio* fabricius. *Risk Analysis.* 29, 6, 868–884.

3

RISK MANAGEMENT

Introduction

Risk managers use human and financial assets to achieve societal, organizational, and individual goals. In this book, the goals are protecting human health and safety, the environment and human assets. The three risk management questions identified in Chapter 1 are a terse reminder of what needs to be accomplished by risk managers:

1. How can consequences be prevented or reduced? (Prevention)
2. How can recovery be enhanced, if the event occurs? (Resilience)
3. How can key local officials, expert staff, and the public organize and be informed to reduce risk and concern and increase trust and confidence? (Organization)

I begin with a small example of the interaction of these three. Suppose I am owner of an organization that houses and cares for senior citizens. We want to build a new assisted living facility in a coastal area that has seen substantial growth in numbers of seniors. My risk prevention goal is to build it in a safe location. At a minimum, I should look for a site out of the 100-year floodplain and away from areas that have experienced storm surge. I want the site to be far enough away from forest-fire prone areas and other natural hazard events or human ones. The bottom line is that I want to avoid having to evacuate my clients.

But bad things do happen, even in seemingly safe locations. Hence, I must consider investing to reduce the probability of needing to evacuate and rebuild the structure. I will invest in water and wind resistant materials, add drains, pumps, the best roof possible, water absorbent plants, and a generator(s) that will immediately activate, if electricity goes off. If the facility is damaged, but I have invested in these kinds of assets, then painters, carpenters, and others who repair after the event should have less wet furniture and rugs to remove, and fewer walls with mold to replace. All of these investments should speed recovery back to normal operations.

The organization question, the last of the three risk management ones, is critical because investments in structures are necessary but not sufficient to protect people and assets. The organization must be sure that personnel understand their role in managing risk. Who communicates with the fire and police departments? Who removes the medications so that they are available to the residents? Who maintains the assets? Who communicates with the residents, and who does other essential tasks? When I visited some assisted living facilities, I was impressed by the ability of the staff to explain exactly what they would do if an event occurred, including who they would replace in the event another staff member could not come to the facility.

Factors that influence organizations and individual risk management decisions are listed in Table 3.1. Human health and safety would be at the top of the list for an assisted living facility. Legal mandates, budgets, politics, and technical assets would be other major considerations. Some individuals and organizations that manage senior facilities are more attuned to hazards than are others, and have organizational protocols to guide on-site managers (Greenberg 2014).

Individual risk-related decisions are associated with personal attributes, such as sex, race/ethnicity/nationality, income, and education. Perceptions, trust, values and other experiential-based factors add to these. People create mental heuristics, which are rules of thumb, that guide them to decisions.

This chapter illustrates how these risk management influences play out in real cases. The reader will see how optimization and heuristic tools, public surveys, and comparative risk analysis have been used to better understand how to manage risk-informed priorities. In general, I tried to focus on the topics in Chapter 2. A final preliminary contextual point is that each sub-section ends by identifying a point of tension for risk managers.

Chemical risk management: how much influence can powerful nation-states have?

This section focuses on the United States and the European Union's efforts to manage chemicals. Global chemical sales were over $3 trillion in 2011 and approximately doubled between 2001 and 2011. In 2001, 57 percent of chemical sales were attributable to the United States and the EU, in 2011 this proportion was 37 percent, reflecting larger increase in Asia (European Chemical Industry Council 2013).

The United States

Chapter 2 summarized the evolution of risk assessment in the United States, beginning with the need of the Environmental Protection Agency to base regulation of chemical agents on credible science. This chapter summarizes how risk management of chemicals evolved during the 1970s when risk assessment as

TABLE 3.1 Factors influencing priorities for risk management

Organizations	Individuals
Human health and safety	Risk perception
Public	Trust of organizations
Employees	Values (distribution of wealth, optimism
Environmental protection	about the future, sustainability)
Water (surface, underground)	Personal experiences/history
Air	Knowledge
Land (geology, soils)	Importance attached to financial resources
Endangered species	Socioeconomic status
Cultural Assets	Race/ethnicity/nationality
Historical	Age
Other significant	Sex
Legal Mandates and Regulations	Political identification
National	
Tribal Nations	
State	
Local	
Budget Resources	
Short-term	
Long-term	
Political Issues	
Federal	
State and Local	
Public Concerns	
Regional economic impact (jobs, income)	
Community social effects	
Environmental justice	
Local values and preferences	
Infrastructure impacts	
Technical Concerns	
Ability of current or near term	
technology to accomplish the objective	
Availability of labor force to apply	
the technology	

we know it today was just beginning and became a key part of the regulatory apparatus.

Prior to the mid-1970s, the lack of information about chemical toxicity and ability to manage chemicals led the chemical industry to try to determine on its own how to manage hazards. They were producing and marketing chemicals in states with no or limited legal guidance. Some states, even local governments had regulations, but these were inconsistent, which made it difficult for industry (Kraft, Vig 2010). Tens of thousands of possibly toxic chemicals were in the market and contaminants were emitted into the environment. However, there was little understating about the impact of the vast majority of them. The author, for example, was asked to estimate the emissions of a chemical plant in a densely populated area and then determine where plumes would go. The company would not provide the information, and my effort to extrapolate data from similar plants in other locations produced results that were too uncertain to be valuable to policy makers.

The massive data gap began to close in 1970. The EPA was able to regulate some air and water pollutants and pesticides under provisions of the Clean Air Act of 1970, the Federal Insecticide, Fungicide, and Rodenticide Act of 1972, and Federal Water Pollution Control Act Amendments of 1972. The Occupational Health and Safety Act of 1970 (OHSA) had exposure limits for some chemicals used in workplaces.

The chemical industry had a dilemma. As the example above indicated, some companies did not want to provide any data to those of us who might link their emissions to exposures. Yet, the chemical industry wanted consistency among states, which required providing some information. Environmental organizations worked with the industry and the EPA to support a set of new laws to regulate chemicals and their waste products. The Resource Conservation and Recovery Act of 1976 (RCRA) focused on facilities that produced chemicals; and the Comprehensive Environmental Response, Compensation, and Liability Act of 1980 (CERCLA) addressed abandoned hazardous waste facilities, so-called "orphan sites," which mostly had chemical substances (Chapter 2). The Safe Drinking Water Act of 1974 was intended to reduce emissions to drinking water bodies, and the Pollution Prevention Act of 1990 created legal incentives to orient chemical producers away from creating chemical wastes.

This period from 1970 to 1990 marked the halcyon days of environmental protection in the United States. The new laws and regulations gave government the opportunity to markedly reduce public exposure to toxic chemicals. The new field of risk assessment, which would tell us which chemicals needed strong regulation and which did not, strengthened this feeling that protecting human health and safety, as well as the environment was a political priority.

I believed that the Toxic Substances Control Act of 1976 (TSCA) was supposed to be the crown legislative jewel. It was intended, I thought, to collect information about chemicals and then manage risks to the public and the environment from new and existing chemicals. Excluded, I assumed reasonably so, were drugs, food, pesticides and other substances covered under the other 1970s environmental laws. The first disappointing surprise for the author and many like me was when 62,000 chemicals in use when the law was passed were "grandfathered," which means that they did not need to be screened for toxicity. I read but did not believe that they were safe just because they were already in use. Next, post-TSCA chemicals were not required to generate or to provide to EPA information about their toxicity (U.S. Government Accountability Office 2005, 2009; Wilson, Schwarzman 2009). Also, industry was able to claim as confidential most of the data that it provided to EPA. In essence, U.S. taxpayers through EPA had to conduct tests of substances that they considered suspicious rather than obtain information from industry. Wilson and Schwarzman (2009) point to three gaps as a result of the limitations of TSCA:

- Data Gap – lack of information on over 80,000 chemicals in commerce;
- Safety Gap – lack of government legal and regulatory tools to protect the public; and
- Technology gap – lack of industry incentive to invest in safer chemicals.

Under Lisa Jackson (2010), EPA administrator from 2009 to 2013, considerable discussion focused on TSCA reform. The EPA created voluntary programs to collect data that it could not obtain through its legal powers. A particularly interesting program is Design for Environment (DfE), which encourages partnerships around green chemistry and offers and a Green Chemistry Challenge Award (U.S. Environment Protection Agency 2010a, b; Taylor 2010).

While it may appear that every chemical company wants TSCA powers limited, that conclusion is false. Companies with a large consumer market worry about their stock prices and have been trying to learn on their own what substances are in their products in order to find substitutes because they feared public backlash (Seuring, Muller 2008; Guth *et al.* 2007; U.S. EPA 2010c). To illustrate, one of the author's doctoral students was hired by a major pharmaceutical company to study their drugs, prioritize them for reformulation, and then begin the process of finding less hazardous materials as building products. He was an in-house "green" chemical engineer, and he told me that his boss's job depended upon removing the company from the list of "biggest toxic polluters."

Another challenge to TSCA's shortcomings has come from several states. California, Maine, Massachusetts, and Washington passed their own regulations with the goal of filing in the three gaps identified earlier (data, safety, technology). California, if it was a country, would rank after the U.S. as a whole, China, Japan, Germany, France, the UK, and Brazil, as the world's eighth largest economy. Its risk management decisions make a difference.

It took time and major investments for these states to take action that should have been in the purview of the national government. For example, in the early 1980s, New Jersey launched a data gathering program that eventually turned into the Toxics Release Inventory (TRI) to obtain some of the data needed to manage chemical risks. The New Jersey design, as developed by this author, faced two years of litigation. For example, a major soft drink company argued successfully that its trade secret ingredients and formulas would be disclosed. As part of a compromise, New Jersey agreed to eliminate some of the data points, and the author was required to keep all of the data in a locked office in locked file cabinets and return all of the data to the state after entry into the data base. To prevent stealing information from the data base, the author and his chief computer analyst had multiple key codes that would unlock the data base. These were periodically changed to prevent theft of the data. A version of the New Jersey work became the basis for national TRI data base, which I am pleased to say is publicly available and which arguably has been a valuable risk management tool by making data available to community groups that thought the worst of business because they had no access to data.

The International Council for Chemical Associations (2010) started a voluntary Responsible Care program shortly after the year 1984 Bhopal Chemical event. Since participation was voluntary, many companies did not participate and those that did have not necessarily adopted the ICCA suggestions (King, Lenox 2000). In 2010, the American Chemistry Council (ACS) called for a "risk-based" approach for risk management of chemicals (American Chemistry Council 2010). Frankly, I have been disappointed by the response of many U.S. companies and by government, and I believe that efforts in Europe have pressured United States-based and all other chemical industry to reconsider their resistance to publicly available data as long as it does not disclose real trade secrets.

European Union

The European Union's Registration, Evaluation, Authorization, and Restriction of Chemical's (REACH) legislation in 2006 requires all chemicals produced in or imported into the EU in quantities above one tonne a year to report information on the properties of the products and chemicals in those products (European Union 2007; European Commission 2003; Ruden, Hansson 2010). The REACH regulations are close to 900 pages and took about seven years to develop and pass. I believe it to be the most thorough set of regulations in the world, by far. It is to be phased in over a decade, and part of that time involves building a European Chemicals Agency (ECHA) to manage REACH.

Any company that produces or imports one tonne or more per year must register their substances with ECHA. About 150,000 substances were registered by 2008. Substances that are considered very high concern (SVHC) receive additional attention. U.S. companies who do business in Europe must comply with REACH, which is an incentive to companies that want to do business in the large EU market. REACH is a massive program detailed in a massive document, but for me, it boils down to requiring unprecedented cooperation and honestly sharing information, which has been an uncommon practice in the past. The EU distributes a software package (IUCLID), which guides companies on how to submit data.

Another important part of the REACH program is to inform every user in the life cycle of the substance about chemicals in their products, especially about safety data. Digging into the rationale, I believe that Europe, even more than the United States, had a hodgepodge of country-specific laws that were hurting business and were adamantly attacked by Green parties. Public pressure in many parts of Europe is to have the power to phase out toxic chemicals. With well over 100,000 chemicals in commerce, it is infeasible to eliminate the most toxic of these when adequate knowledge exists for only 1 percent of those in commerce. REACH places the burden on companies to prove that their chemicals are safe, which was not the author's experience while developing the data system that ultimately led to TRI. In New Jersey, 35 years ago, government was expected to go through the data on the forms and prove that there was a risk, which was not feasible with a state government budget. By doing it centrally, the EU is trying to become more transparent about the thousands of chemicals in commerce.

REACH has been criticized for its implementation cost and to some extent its ongoing management costs. It is difficult to calculate the number of cancers, toxic poisonings, and other impacts avoided. A legitimate major concern is the impact on international commerce. Other issues not covered are non-isolated chemical intermediates, the transportation of chemical toxins, wastes, and radioactivity is excluded. REACH is not perfect.

Yet, REACH is a provocative legal step that closes the data gap. The United States Government Accountability Office (2007) pointed to three differences between TSCA and REACH. TSCA does not require companies to develop data on chemical effects on human health and environment unless EPA requires them via a rule, which does not often happen (see Chapters 5 and 11), whereas REACH does require that information. TSCA requires EPA to choose the least burdensome regulatory path, REACH does not. REACH limits the amount of information that chemical companies can claim to be confidential. The key difference is that the burden of proof in REACH is on the companies to prove that their chemical substances are safe.

In short, risk management of chemicals is in a transition period, and the point of tension focuses on whether REACH will pressure companies in the United States, China, Japan, Russia, and other major consumers of chemicals to be more forthcoming with research and information. Given the tension over this risk management option, I expect the emphasis to be on designing safer products followed by pressure to demonstrate safety. Other options include labelling through the life cycle and modeling pathways leading to upstream and downstream protection of consumers. It remains to be seen how the United States, Japan, China and others will conform to REACH. Other nations with strong trade relations with Europe already are conforming as the legislative regulations are phased in.

Readers of this book should follow the news for stories indicating reactions to REACH and other programs. How this tension between the EU and other nations is resolved will have important world-wide implications for many years to come.

Managing nuclear and chemical wastes at former nuclear weapons sites: how influential are human health and safety in risk management?

I begin one of my classes with the following question: How much larger is the budget of the U.S. EPA than the environmental management branch of the U.S. DOE? The mostly masters-level students will normally guess 5 to 10 times as large because EPA is responsible for dozens of programs in every state and territory whereas EM currently focuses on the cleanup of 16 sites in the continental United States. The answer is that the average budget for EPA for all of its activities is only slightly larger than that of the DOE's environmental management program.

The risk management challenge summarized in this section is how should risk management decisions be made when budgets are stable or shrinking?

One reason that the EM program has had a large cleanup budget is that it has a moral commitment. In 1995, then Secretary Hazel O'Leary stated:

> *The United States built the world's first atomic bomb to help win World War II and developed a nuclear arsenal to fight the Cold War. How we unleashed the fundamental power of the universe is one of the greatest stories of our era. It is a story of extraordinary challenges brilliantly met, a story of genius, teamwork, industry, and courage.*
>
> *We are now embarked on another great challenge and a new national priority: refocusing the commitment to build the most powerful weapons on Earth toward the widespread environmental and safety problems at thousands of contaminated sites across the lands. We have a moral obligation to do no less, and we are committed to producing meaningful results. This is the honorable and challenging task of the Department's Environmental Management Program.*
>
> *(U.S. Department of Energy, 1995, p. vii)*

The former Secretary's candid remarks follow from the Manhattan project that literally built a nuclear factory across the United States during World War II that carried over into the Cold War. The factory mined, refined, transported, and tested uranium products containing nuclear materials at over one hundred specific sites across the nation. The DOE and its predecessor agency remediated contaminated parts of the nuclear factory (Department of Energy 1995), including massive cleanup and decommissioning in Hanford (WA), Savannah River, (SC), Oak Ridge (TN), Idaho (ID), Portsmouth (OH) and Paducah (KY) sites (see Table 3.2). The number of sites the DOE-EM focuses on for active cleanup has decreased from 107 to 16. However, these 16 sites not only are a challenge for nuclear and chemical waste management, but also have been a major economic ingredient of their regions, sometimes the most important creator of income, jobs and taxes (Greenberg et al. 2003). For a governor and a mayor, a declining DOE budget means fewer taxes, more unemployment, and tighter budgets, as well as unhappy constituents.

During the period 1989–2014, the DOE spent over $150 billion (about $6 billion a year). The estimated life cycle cost of remediating the 16 sites is $290 billion (see Table 3.2). On a per site basis, these anticipated costs dwarf the costs of government and private business sites across the United States by a factor of ten or more times. Some of these DOE sites are massive, hundreds of square miles in size, and contain multiple contaminated sources. About 36 million gallons of so-called high level nuclear waste sits in 49 tanks at the Savannah River site in Aiken, South Carolina. Many of these are below the water table. At Hanford about 55 million gallons are in 177 tanks.

Under the American Recovery and Reinvestment Act of 2009, the U.S. federal government substantially increased budgets to DOE-EM sites in order to complete as many projects as possible and to stimulate the economy. But that extra spending

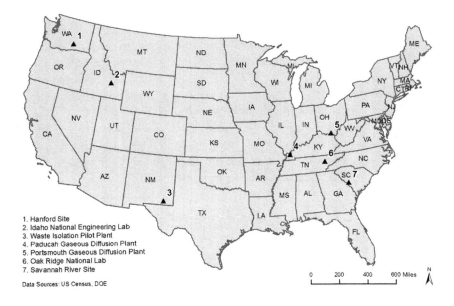

1. Hanford Site
2. Idaho National Engineering Lab
3. Waste Isolation Pilot Plant
4. Paducah Gaseous Diffusion Plant
5. Portsmouth Gaseous Diffusion Plant
6. Oak Ridge National Lab
7. Savannah River Site

Data Sources: US Census, DOE

FIGURE 3.1 Location of major DOE cleanup sites

has ended, and Table 3.2 shows estimated costs associated with the 16 major sites and recent annual budgets.

The author chaired a Committee for the Appropriations Committees of the U.S. Senate and House that examined the remediation needs across the DOE-EM comples (Omnibus 2015). The cost of moving forward as had been planned is about $8 billion a year compared to $5.3–$5.8 billion that is likely to be available in the near future. Everyone of the 16 sites has good reason to want no reduction in their budget. How can the DOE make risk management choices?

Protecting human health and safety has been a key priority of the DOE (Omnibus 2015). Health and safety are not the only considerations. In 1992, as part of an effort to understand how limited federal resources should be used to remediate federal sites managed not only by DOE, but also the U.S. Department of Defense, and several others, the U.S. EPA organized the Federal Facilities Environmental Restoration Dialogue Committee (1996), or FFERDC, which issued its recommendations, which have been used by federal agencies, including the DOE, to guide their allocations. FFERDC concluded that risk plus other factors should be considered in priority setting, that is, human health was the primary consideration, but that other factors should be considered. These other factors are as follows:

TABLE 3.2 Environmental management costs by nuclear waste site, 2015, $ billions

Site	Life cycle costs, 50% confidence level	FY 2015 Enacted	FY 2016 Requested
Savannah River	65.88	1.260	1.337
Hanford, ORP★	65.77	1.212	1.414
Hanford, RL★	58.12	1.007	0.914
Idaho National Laboratory	19.61	0.405	0.367
Paducah Gaseous Diffusion Plant	11.23	0.270	0.232
Oak Ridge	10.75	0.431	0.366
Portsmouth Gaseous Diffusion Plant	9.21	0.276	0.227
Waste Isolation Pilot Plant	7.03	0.324	0.248
All other sites and headquarters	42.73	0.682	0.713
Total EM★★ program	290.33	5.861	5.818

Notes: ★The Office of River Protection and the Richland Site Office each manage a distinct set of cleanup activities at the Hanford site. ★★Totals may not add to total program due to rounding.

Sources: U.S. DOE, 2014; Department of Energy, FY 2015 Congressional Budget Request, Environmental Management; U.S. DOE, April 2013; Whitney, EM FY 2016 Budget rollout Presentation, February 2, 2015; Omnibus 2015.

- Cultural, social, and economic factors, notably environmental justice;
- Long and short-term ecological impacts, especially degradation of resource value and hence use;
- Land use decisions, especially as these impact the economic health of the area:
- Acceptability of the proposed action to regulators, and the public;
- Incorporation of the views of Tribal Nations into project designs;
- Life cycle costs;
- Importance of reducing infrastructure and operation-maintenance costs;
- Availability of new technologies;
- Legal and statutory requirements;
- Cost and effectiveness of proposed actions;
- Availability of funding; and
- Practical considerations, such as accomplishing projects and working on remediation projects without hindering other activities.

This list of considerations substantially overlaps the list for organizations in Table 3.1. The complexity of trying to make risk management decisions, given this broad set of factors, is daunting. Every site has a good set of arguments for more money and against budget reductions. For example, Savannah River has emptied some of its tanks, blended nuclear waste with molten glass, and buried these in massive 8-feet high stainless logs enclosed in stainless steel in a building. This multi-billion dollar effort has immobilized nuclear waste that theoretically could leak into the groundwater or under the worst circumstances become airborne. Savannah River wants more money to move its successful tank program along, it needs resources to keep its deteriorating infrastructure from further deterioration, and it has other needs.

Hanford, the site with the largest EM budget, has the largest number of underground tanks. Currently, the DOE Hanford site has committed many billions of dollars to waste treatment plants that are not operational and will not be operational in the near term future. The State of Washington has argued for more resources to move forward on these projects and other problems rather than defer because DOE-EM resources have decreased. The problem is where should these dollars come from? Is it a higher priority to move the program at Hanford forward faster than the one at Savannah River? This is not a question that is comfortable to ask, but when budgets are limited, it has to be asked.

I could make compelling arguments for all the other 14 sites, although not quite as compelling as for these two. Much of DOE-EM's remediation program is governed by the Resource Conservation and Recovery Act (RCRA) and the Comprehensive Environmental Response, Compensation and Liability Act (CERCLA), as well as their accompanying policies, regulations and guidance. While these laws as noted under the chemicals section above are intended to protect human health and safety, as well as other media, full adherence to laws that were originally designated for chemical contamination cases of limited scope are hard to apply to the DOE sites because the scale of the sites and cost of remediation is so much larger. For example, when the author visited the Hanford site in the Summer of 2014, he toured the newly opened groundwater treatment plant that was remarkable for its cleanliness compared to what he had seen elsewhere. When I returned home, I remarked to my colleagues that I could have sat on the floor of the water plant and eaten my lunch – that is how clean it appeared to be. That single facility cost several hundred million dollars and was paid for by American Recovery and Reinvestment Act of 2009.

The DOE, EPA and the State of Washington as do some other states have a federal facilities agreement (FFA), which codifies what risk management actions are to be taken and when. When the DOE seeks to cut back the plan because of financial limitations, the State of Washington exerts pressure through its power under the Resource Conservation and Recovery Act and its role with DOE and EPA to take DOE to court to force the DOE to meet those agreements. The implication is that in a zero sum budget environment, the resources could come from Savannah River or other DOE sites.

Part of the Washington case for major DOE resource commitments is strengthened by a strong environmental culture in the state as a whole. Tribal Nations add to the political pressure because the nations located in the State of Washington consider the Columbia River part of their heritage and they have claims to some of the Hanford site. Washington east of the Cascade mountains is quite different physically, demographically, socially and with regard to values than is South Carolina near the Savannah River site, or Tennessee near the Oak Ridge sites.

DOE-EM has other important federal partners. DOE-EM's human health and safety programs are reviewed by the Defense Nuclear Facilities Safety Board

(DNFSB), which has a group in its Washington, D.C. headquarters but has personnel on-site to overview day-to-day actions. DNFSB has played a significant role in pushing DOE-EM toward protecting human health and safety, whereas the states and the EPA, while clearly in support of these priorities, often concentrate on environmental media and cultural assets. The DOE-EM also consults with the Nuclear Waste Technical Review Board, with the Nuclear Regulatory Commission (U.S. NRC), and the National Academy of Sciences on selected topics. Each of these parties has their own specified objectives and talents that they bring to bear on risk management decisions.

The White House Office of Management and Budget (OMB) is a relatively silent partner, but not when it comes to budget amount and direction. OMB plays a budget management role with every federal government department/agency, and their views of risk assessment and management are quite important to the DOE-EM program as they are to every federal body. DOE-EM is guided by risk principles that were developed by OMB (Dudley, Hays 2007). Their memo urges DOE to prepare its own risk analysis guidelines. The OMB has the following thoughts about the distinction between risk assessment and management.

> In undertaking risk analyses, agencies would establish and maintain a clear distinction between the identification, quantification, and characterization of risks, and the selection of methods or mechanisms for managing risk. Such a distinction, however, does not mean separation. Risk management policies may induce changes in human behaviors that can alter risk.
>
> *(Dudley, Hays 2007, p. 4)*

The OMB paper states that "the depth or extent of analysis of risks, benefits and costs associated with decisions should be commensurate with the nature and significance of the decision" (p. 4). Another principle is to seek peer review of risk assessments and to obtain input from key parties.

Each of the 16 sites under DOE's purview are unique entities, and yet DOE's national mission implies a national rather than solely a local perspective. A national perspective implies consistency in risk management decisions across the complex. For example, should the DOE allow inconsistencies in cleanup standards among the Hanford, Savannah River, and Oak Ridge sites? Should it allow different land use policies at each site? Each of these is a major risk management decision posed by the Omnibus Committee (2015).

Yet another risk management issue is the reality of scheduling the work. It is foolish to start a major project and stop work because of budget and technical limitations. At some of these massive sites, the most experienced workers will resign if work is stopped and then not come back.

In other words, sequencing of work, cost effectiveness, as well as regulatory compliance, the availability of skilled workers, DOE Headquarters budget restrictions, and input from local, state and national stakeholders, as well as Tribal Nations are all in play at the national scale and at each site. As the team that wrote the FFERDC report understood, risk management decisions are not risk-based, that is, driven solely by risk assessment results, but are risk-informed.

The risk information is quite extensive. In the case of DOE-EM, several risk analysis processes and tools are prominently featured at the DOE sites. Documented Safety Analysis (DSA) is required by DOE as part of their nuclear safety analysis. These detailed documents present the life cycle hazards of a facility during design, construction, operation, and cleanup phases. The DSAs form the basis for engineering and operating controls that are meant to eliminate any chances of an event (U.S. Department of Energy 2014).

EPA's (U.S. EPA 2014) risk assessment guidance under CERCLA requires DOE and facility managers of these hazardous waste sites to follow specific protocols, procedures and training before preparing a risk assessment. The basis of the approach is human exposure through pre-specified pathways. Each of these pathways has to be examined.

Even though formal risk analysis tools enter into risk management decisions, risk management decisions are a combination of analysis and deliberation. The analysis part "uses rigorous, replicable methods, evaluated under the agreed protocols of an expert community – such as those of disciplines in the natural, social, or decision sciences, as well as mathematics, logic, and law-to arrive at answers to factual questions." Deliberation, on the other hand, is "any formal or informal process for communication and collective consideration of issues. Participants in deliberation discuss, ponder, exchange observations and views, reflect upon information and judgments concerning matters of mutual interest and attempt to persuade each other." The U.S. NRC's categorization is a good way of describing how DOE-EM and many other governmental organizations make decisions about risk. Figure 3.2 summarizes the process that goes from analysis to deliberation and then back again as many times as is required to render a decision. In short, every item in Table 3.1 and the FFERDC (1996) report is involved in risk management decisions made by DOE-EM, especially at the major sites (Hanford, Savannah River, Oak Ridge, Idaho, etc.).

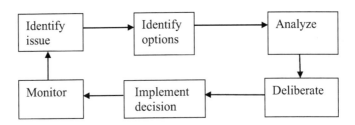

FIGURE 3.2 Risk informed decision-making process

Source: U.S. Nuclear Regulatory Commission 2012, Figure 3.1, page 3.1.

The tension point in risk management decision-making for the Department of Energy is how much emphasis to place on human health and safety risk information in priority setting compared to other legitimate factors that influence decisions, including legal agreements stipulating that certain risk management steps are to be accomplished by specific times. When budgets are high, few of these points of tension arise, and when they do the parties typically will negotiate a reasonable compromise. But when budgets are lowered and yet expectations are not, there will be winning and losing sites and the postponement of worthwhile projects for reasons that are not necessarily part of risk assessments.

Critical infrastructure: can invisible assets be protected against bad intentions?

Twenty-first century attacks on the United States, France, the United Kingdom, Germany, Russia, and many other nations have not only created a new lexicon about terrorism (domestic vs. international, individual vs. group, ideological vs. personal, for example) but have also changed our view of infrastructure. As a boy, I remember seeing a geyser-like eruption of a water main in New York City and blackouts. Actually, I recall them with a smile. It was fun. Today, if the same event occurred, we would be thinking about them as possible terrorist events. Did an old pipe break, circuit fail, or was it a deliberate attack?

New businesses have grown around terrorism. The entertainment business includes fictional books and movies (see Chapter 9). Instead of chasing local thieves and members of the underworld motivated by money, emphasis seems to have shifted to people from other countries or unhappy locals with ideological and revenge motives. The United States has a Department of Homeland Security (DHS) that merged many other departments and agencies, but interestingly not the Federal Bureau of Investigation (FBI).

DHS focuses on stopping terrorists from killing people. A second key objective is to protect water, electrical, and other so-called "critical infrastructure." It defines critical infrastructure as:

> Critical infrastructure is the backbone of our nation's economy, security and health. We know it as the power we use in our homes, the water we drink, the transportation that moves us, and the communication systems we rely on to stay in touch with friends and family. Critical infrastructure are the assets, systems, and networks, whether physical or virtual, so vital to the United States that their incapacitation or destruction would have a debilitating effect on security, national economic security, national public health or safety, or any combination thereof.
>
> *(U.S. Department of Homeland Security 2013)*

Protecting infrastructure is assumed to be a good public investment. The Multihazard Mitigation Council (2005) examined many case studies and concluded that $3.5 billion spent on hazard mitigation in the United States during the years 1993 and $2003 saved 14 billion in estimated losses. However, they also observed that some investments were more beneficial and others.

The National Infrastructure Protection Center (2013) described the following risk management process:

- Set security goals;
- Identify assets, systems, networks, and their functions;
- Assess risks (consequences, vulnerabilities and threats);
- Prioritize;
- Implement protective programs; and
- Measure effectiveness.

The idea is to connect these six objectives and build feedback loops for continuous improvement of infrastructure protection. The federal government was to allocate money to states and local government, and in turn they were to allocate the resources to specific facilities and assets. It is up to the facility and owners/managers to implement the programs.

California examples

The Center of Risk and Economic Analysis of Terrorism Events (CREATE) was the first of a dozen university-based DHS centers of excellence. CREATE has an online library of papers, reports and selected talks (http://reserach/create/usc.edu). Their work focuses on risk management, especially on economic costs and benefits of risk management decisions. Critical infrastructure has been a major focus of their work. For instance, Kleinmutz *et al.* (2006) presented and illustrated an approach for allocating resources to protect infrastructure in California. The group built and operationalized models that chose optimal places to invest limited resources. Risk management options were evaluated in regard to four consequences: (1) health, (2) economics, (3) mission and (4) psychological.

Assessments included consideration of threat, vulnerability, consequence, and how much consequences could be reduced by investments as well as the cost effectiveness of the projects. The scores for each of the four consequences were added to produce a consequence index for each proposed investment.

For example, the researchers worked with the California Office of Homeland Security to assess a Buffer Zone Protection Program (BZPP) to prevent terrorists from conducting surveillance or launching attacks near key infrastructure sites. The CREATE group reported that 90–100 sites were eligible for funding and that resources could be made available for only about 10 percent.

They investigated chemical and hazmat facilities, dams, commercial buildings, oil refineries, the electric grid, transportation systems, water treatment plants, nuclear power plants, defense industry bases, and postal and shipping facilities. The team concluded that dams, chemical plants and some commercial facilities were the highest priorities. For chemical plants, the analysts chose facilities with many nearby residents that would be affected by a major release. In regard to dams, the priority was on large areas that would be inundated by a dam failure, leaving many people and jobs at risk.

In later papers, Kleinmutz and colleagues described multi-objective decision models, heuristics based on ratios of risk reduction to cost. As part of their work, the CREATE group was clear about the difficulty of assembling data about threat probability, attack vulnerability, and consequences, including indirect economic costs (see Chapter 6 for an example). Given these limitations, they suggest that high-risk sectors be identified by order of magnitude differences in risk exposure (see also Liesio, Mild, Salo 2007; Kleinmutz 2008; Kleinmutz Willis 2009).

These papers and reports were some of the early products of CREATE. The group's work on critical infrastructure and terrorism has continued, but as the U.S. Department of Homeland Security has become more involved in natural hazards, CREATE has ventured into studying the impacts of natural hazard events on infrastructure. For example, in 2009, more than 300 engineers and scientists from the United States Geological Survey and its California equivalent created a hypothetical MW 7.8 earthquake event on the southern San Andreas Fault (Jones *et al.* 2008). The hypothetical had 13 m offsets. The research group generated maps featuring shaking intensities with peak ground velocities of 3 m/s near the fault and velocities greater than 0.5 m/s over an area of 10,000 km². The hypothetical produced 1,800 deaths and 53,000 injuries that would require emergency room care. Part of the event included 1,600 fires resulting in the destruction of 200 million ft².

The estimated economic cost of the event was $213 billion (Rose, Wei, Wein 2011). Rose, Wei, and Wein estimated $79 billion in business losses and $113 billion in in property damage in the eight-county Southern California region. Fire and water were expected to be the most damaging components with impacts of $40 billion, followed by ordinary building damage of $32.7 and content damage of $25 billion. The authors assert that they had anticipated higher losses but that the region has gradually become more able to withstand natural hazard events and be more resilient when they do occur. They asserted that that the most important risk management improvement is to prevent fire and business loss by improving the water network, and that this region needs to have interim solutions for repairing and restoring water service.

Cyber terrorism

In 2015, my university's Internet systems failed, first for a day, and later a week. We have had computer system failures in the past, but this one was different because it was deliberate, and as of this writing the FBI, Department of Homeland Security, and the university are still trying to find the individual(s) who disrupted the ability of students to use certain library materials, our ability to record and issue grades, and in general reduced the capability of the university to function normally. The attack on my university's computer network is cyber terrorism. But not everyone would agree that it is as important as other forms of terrorism. James Lewis (2002) recognized the growth of a new form of cyber terrorism. Yet he argued that critical communications infrastructure is less vulnerable than the common computer network. Lewis views computer network vulnerabilities as an increasing threat to business, but these business vulnerabilities are the focus of a great deal of thought and investment and are not a threat to national security, he argued. Lewis discussed historical and current efforts to bring systems back from physical attacks and cyber ones, and characterizes many cyber attacks as no worse than routine failures, and that it would take a massive number of cyber attacks on water, power, air traffic and other systems to raise the threat to a level of national security. Natural hazard events like hurricanes, tornadoes, he considers to be more costly threats, and he characterizes cyberattacks as a weapon of "mass annoyance" (Lewis, 2002, p. 4) He recommends that government needs to increase redundancy, better monitor normal rates of failure, and systematically implement polices to more effectively control cyber access. Lewis is not the only one to assert that the term cybercrime needs to be used more selectively than it has been (see also National Infrastructure Protection Center 2013).

Lewis's paper was published in 2002, and the last decade has shown that cyber attacks have increased and become more costly. For example, in October 2013, Singapore, one of the most connected nations, had been attacked often enough to invest in a 24-hour-a-day, seven-day-a-week surveillance program. The 2013 attack, which led to arrests, was alleged to be due to censorship regulations. Was this a national security threat, or a democratic protest? Lewis's point is there is a tendency to tell the public and business that the sky is falling and this amounts to over-marketing this issue, which can lead to misallocation of resources and alarm. Will people be responsive when there is a cyber attack that truly threatens national security?

Deciding how to distribute anti-terrorism funds

How should government decide where to invest limited funds to prevent and recover from terrorist attacks? I might want to start by assuming that risk management decisions are risk-based, or at least risk-informed (see nuclear waste management example above). That would be a naïve assumption in a country that has diverse political interests, 50 states, and thousands of local governments. The Congress of the United States reflects this political diversity. The Senate has two representatives for each state, in other words, 100 senators, and hence the Senate represents an equity-based distribution of political power. The United States House of Representatives is population-based. States with the most people, California, Texas, New York, and Florida have the most members. Given the history of federal government allocations for housing, environmental protection, commerce and federal aid for a variety of other programs, we should not be surprised to find equity and population size reflected in DHS allocations for risk management.

The DHS has multiple grant programs that dispersed several billion dollars a year to states and local governments. The expectation that the distribution of these resources would be risk-based was reviewed by Greenberg, Irving, and Zimmerman (2009). Under the Patriot Act every state, Washington, D.C and Puerto Rico, received 0.75 percent and the four territories of American Samoa, Guam, the Northern Marianas Islands, and the Virgin Islands each received 0.25 percent. Hence, 40 percent ([52 × 0.0075) + 4 (0.0025)]=0.39 + 0.01=0.40). The remaining 60 percent was said to be allocated based on risk and expected effectiveness of the investment.

At the state scale, the correlation between fiscal 2006 and 2007 funding and population size was r=0.92. But the macro scale relationship could be misleading, that is, population size could be a strong correlate of risk to people and assets. Greenberg, Irving, and Zimmerman (2009) used electricity kilowatt hours produced as a surrogate for critical infrastructure as a U.S.-wide pilot test of the relationship between critical infrastructure and distribution of resources as risk management at the country scale (n=3140). For example, a county that created 2 percent of the national electrical energy would get 2 percent of the resources. In this case, kilowatt production is surrogate for water, sewer, communications, rail, road and many other infrastructure systems. The authors built a linear programming optimization model that maximized the distribution of resources to counties with critical infrastructure subject to a series of constraints.

One of these is an equity constraint, similar to the one in the Patriot Act. A second constraint was an allocation based on population size. In other words, the more populous states would receive more money. The equity and population size constraints were varied. A third constraint set an upper limit to what a state as a whole could receive. In other words, if no state could receive more than 10 percent of the national total, then the sum of resources that all of the counties in New Mexico could receive was set at 10 percent, even if New Mexico had half of the electrical generation production (see below for an illustration of a linear optimization model).

The results showed clear winners and losers. For example, when the minimum for each states as whole is set high, then states with few residents, such as North Dakota and Montana, for example, were winners, but Georgia, Illinois, South Carolina, and Texas with counties that generate a great deal of electricity lose tens of millions of dollars. This model allows users to assess the trade-offs between risk management based on equity, population size, and risk. Other infrastructure sectors would need to be included in order to make this approach a more realistic way of assessing the distribution of risk management resources against critical infrastructure at the macro and meso geographical scales.

Overall, risk analysts must try to avoid the temptation of believing that investments are risk-based; they are risk-informed. The tension point is between suggestions that emanate from risk assessment and the political realities that anti-terrorism funds are dollars that mean jobs and taxes. Elected officials want as many anti-terrorism funds as they can get, irrespective of the risk in their jurisdictions.

Animal factory farming: can a moral challenge make a difference?

Humans have been eating beef, duck, chicken, pork, fish and many other kinds of meat for as long as the human race has existed. There are those who adamantly oppose eating meat for health reasons and others for ethical reasons, and their voices have been growing and are being heard.

I deliberately chose animal factory farming because of the complexity of the risk management challenges, especially the moral ones. With the context that the demand for animal meat continues and is rapidly growing in some nations, decision-makers must deal with three issues:

- Human health effects;
- Ecological impacts; and
- Ethical/moral challenges associated with treatment of animals in food factories.

Human health risk analysis

European Union members have experienced serious outbreaks of animal disease that sometimes have caused human health effects. An outbreak of foot-and-mouth disease (FMD) occurred in in Great Britain in 2001 and in the Netherlands a month later. Bouma *et al.* (2003) described the event and risk management responses in Netherlands. The Netherlands instituted the UK's risk management programs, that is, herds within a kilometer of each outbreak were culled. Nevertheless, additional outbreaks occurred. It became necessary to vaccinate herds in one area to prevent reproduction, amounting to vaccinating all susceptible animals on 1,800 farms. In aggregate, 26 outbreaks occurred. Over 260,000 animals were slaughtered.

Based on the Dutch experience, Velthuis and Mourits (2007) used a simulation model to study the impact of controlling movements among Dutch farms to reduce the spread of the virus and hence FMD. With less animal movement, the number of epidemics in rural locations was estimated to have fallen from 31 infected farms in 65 days to eight in 53 days. The policy did not work as well in more densely farm populated areas, but there nevertheless was a decrease of over 20 percent in number of infected farms and an 8 percent decrease in length of infection period.

Denmark experienced a Salmonella outbreak in 1993 related to pork. Hurd *et al.* (2008) note that a decade later after the expenditure of €95 million, there has been a substantial reduction in the risk. The issue is what strategic investments should be made to further reduce the risk. Using descriptive data and models, the authors concluded that it makes little sense to invest in in-farm improvements. The next biggest reduction would be at the abattoir process level, most notably decontaminating hides and carcasses with water or water and acid, which is standard practice in the United States.

Bollaerts *et al.* (2009) studied the life cycle of human salmonellosis in freshly minced pork meat in Belgium. Their risk assessment shows that undercooking is the major problem and secondarily inadequate hand-cleaning by cooks. They urge more focus on risk management at these two stages.

Vos *et al.* (2010) examined the risk management policy of waiting six months before exporting pigs from an area that had foot-and-mouth disease (FMD) versus screening the animals and then exporting them. The authors built a risk model around FMD prevalence in the herd, within-herd prevalence, and the probability of detection of FMD at slaughter. They estimated very small differences between the options. They recommend further reducing the risk by heat treating the pork. Given the economic benefit of exporting pigs, they conclude that the risk does not support waiting six months for exports.

Ireland has experienced pig-related Salmonella problems. Soumpasis and Butler (2011) built a simulation model to try to better understand high and low Salmonella conditions in pig pens. Using data from prior studies, they modeled high and low-risk conditions, but have no concrete results to report other than the need for more data to try to better understand why in two holding places one may be ten times or more likely to have Salmonella than another.

Simons *et al.* (2015) built models to understand what happens during transport and short-term retention of pigs. The found that environmental contamination and animal stress are major sources of infection. Experts emphasized stress, however, the authors had no empirical data to support that hypothesis.

Hill *et al.* (2016) focused on on-site farm policies that could control the spread of Salmonella in pigs. They studied the impact of keeping pigs on site versus transferring them before slaughter to another farm. The same idea was tested on an individual farm, that is, confining the pigs to a single herd versus allowing them to mingle. They examined if food type (wet vs. dry and pellet vs. not pelleted) made a difference in infections, and whether a slated floor would reduce risk more than straw, wood and other options. An important finding was that it is essential that pigs showing any symptoms of shedding virus be isolated and cleaning the areas that the pigs inhabit was critical.

While much of the risk-related literature focuses on the health of nearby residents, the occupational health literature highlights a long list of worker impacts. Langley (1995) listed the following worker hazards: needlesticks, infections from contact with swine, nose, mechanical and electrical injuries, weather extremes, repetitive motion disorders, and respiratory problems (see also National Institute for Occupational Safety 1990; Donham *et al.* 1995). Genoways (2014) observed that farm factory workers are disproportionately migrants and not well treated by their bosses. Indeed, he asserts that there is more support for humane treatment of the animals than of the farm workers.

Environmental impact

Pig-related viruses and other diseases in factory farms are the major threat to humans. Historically, much less risk management effort has been focused on by odors and other air pollutant contaminants, and by water and land contamination (Schinasi *et al.* 2011; Horton *et al.* 2009). Livestock farms have long been a target of those concerned about water quality and its potential impact on public health. But, more recently, well known media outlets have been featuring the issue.

The Natural Resources Defense Council (NRDC) is a strong environmental organization and among the most outspoken advocates of reducing environmental impacts of livestock farms. The Natural Resources Defense Council (2013) summarized its major concerns, some of which I have noted below:

- The number of hog operations in the U.S. fell from 666,000 to 69,000 between 1980 and 2011, although production remained the same, which means that emissions are more spatially concentrated than in the past;
- Massive open-air waste lagoons, the size of multiple football fields, leak and spill concentrated untreated waste. Spills and ruptures in North Carolina, Illinois and in other livestock-producing areas caused by natural failure and tropical storms (e.g., Irene in 2011) killed tens of millions of fish;
- Nutrients from runoff from these livestock factories introduced massive amounts of nutrients that cause dead zones downstream;
- Ammonia can be released from the waste disposal facilities and drift with the wind settling on and polluting land and causing intolerable odors in populated areas;
- Antibiotics used to induce rapid growth among livestock are placed in feed, which increases the likelihood of resistant bacteria as they diffuse through the water and other environments; and
- Large hog farms emit hydrogen sulfide (rotten egg smell) and high concentrations from manure pits can kill people.

Major news networks cover environmental events that they consider disasters. Animal farm pollution is not usually among those. An exception occurred on February 2105, when CNBC (2015) broadcast a story called "Water, air quality fears conflict with pig farms." Supported with strong images and language, the story explained the growth of large animal farms (pigs featured), and while noting that these factory farms had proven to be profitable, they were creating problems, most notably phosphorous, nitrates and bacteria from fertilized and accumulated manure in water bodies, as well as air pollution. The story featured the views of several farmers who had installed grass strips, tilled less and otherwise tried to reduce the risk. The reporters examined the basis of law suits filed in Iowa and North Carolina (two major hog producing states) to try to shift the focus back from profits to clean water and air. While activist groups were involved in these law suits as part of their efforts to try to promote small farms, one of the parties to a law case featured in the story was the Des Moines, Iowa water utility, which has had to pay for a special water treatment system so that the potable water it sends to water lines could meet drinking water quality standards.

Near the end of the story, reporters highlighted the viewpoints of farmers who said that they are willing to reduce the impact, but it will cost time and money, and several irate residents, one of whom is quoted as saying "It just stinks like the devil." The story ends with the following quote from a local professor at Iowa State University: "Society needs to be engaged in a conversation about what trade-offs we are willing to make and who is going to bear the cost." This statement underscores the dilemma of risk management with regard to animal farm factories. This hazard gradually appeared across the landscape, and unlike the problems of chemicals, nuclear waste and terrorism, has not had a single major event that has persuaded decision-makers to take stronger steps.

The *National Geographic*, a popular magazine with pro-environmental protection leanings, wrote a story about pig farms and water pollution story. With North Carolina as the focus, Peach (2014) reported the following facts: sales of $2.9 billion worth of swine in 2012, and the presence of 8.9 million hogs (almost as many hogs as people). Reporting from a small airplane flying over the rural landscape, she graphically points to the telltale signs of hog waste in North Carolina (pink ponds). Even with the state of North Carolina engaged in more enforcement, closing some waste lagoons and buying some hog farms, the problem is far from under control. Powerful odors saturate the area when there is a strong wind, and the problem is compounded by the increasing demand for pork in the United States, as well as Mexico, Japan and China (see Genoways 2014 for a description of the change from family to large company owned farms).

The *Economist* covers a wide variety of public policy stories with an economics orientation. In March 2015, it published a story in a section called water pollution with the following title: "Bay of Pigs Movement." The story (Songjiang 2013) was not about problems in the European Union or the United States. It was about dead pigs found in a branch of the Shanghai's Huangpu River, a major water source for over 2 million people. The story attributes the dead floating pigs to famers who dumped dead pigs into the water. The story then focused on other major water pollution issues in China and the challenge of delivering a clean water supply in the nation (see Chapter 7). Notably, the story lead and the photos are of dead pigs.

The *Atlantic* magazine (formerly the *Atlantic Monthly*) is an over 150-year-old publication that focuses on world affairs and thought leaders. On March 11, 2013, Kuo (2013) summarized the dead pig and water supply story with the following title and subtitle: "2,800 Dead Pigs in a Shanghai River: How Did this Happen? And What does it say about China's water supply?" Accompanied by very powerful photos of floating dead pigs, the last paragraph of the story begins as follows:

> Residents are already worrying about what they're not being told – hardly surprising, given the utter lack of credibility the government inspires in protecting its people from sometimes lethal contamination of food and drink sources.
>
> *(Kuo 2013, p. 3)*

The dead pig-water supply story received a great deal more media coverage. *The Guardian* (Davison 2013) led with an observation that there were more dead pigs in the Jiapingtang River than live fish. This story reported 16,000 dead pigs and the visual images are indescribably powerful. The information is not at all comforting. The story reports that 7.7 million pigs are raised in the province and with a mortality rate of 2–4 percent, that translates to 300,000 pig carcasses a year in need of disposal. While some farmers are said to throw dead pigs into the water for convenience, others are said to take the dead pigs and butcher them. When the government arrested and jailed some of these butchers, farmers began throwing them into the water. The story continues by noting that China has laws to protect the water but that they are not enforced. It ends by pointing to protests that were "quashed." The story reiterates in several places that China consumes about half of the world's pig products and that the dilemma of having enough food and protecting at-risk water supplies will not go away any time soon.

Moral outrage and response

Business and government agencies have been facing strong and growing protests from animal rights activists about animal farm factories. These challenges are exacerbated by media stories and images of brutal treatment of animals.

The EU nations and the United Kingdom as an EU member (although they have voted to withdraw from the EU) have taken legal positions that send a message to the rest of the world and business. Pigs are omnivorous, eating both plant and small animals. Pigs have been domesticated for centuries and have been a source of food and other products. The presence of factory farms is the major source of moral outrage. Among the practices that distress people are killing animals without rendering them unconscious; forcing pregnant sows to live in tiny crates on cement floors; mutilation of tiny pigs; and others that I will not describe.

EU directive 2001/120/EC (European Union Council 2008) joined several earlier ones and began to address the moral outrage issues. These include sections about farming, holding of the animals, transportation, slaughtering and other parts of the life cycle. For example, animals are to be rendered unconscious before slaughter, pregnant pigs are to be housed in larger pens that allow them to lie down on their sides with their legs stretched out, and then they are to be released to larger pens. The EU regulations call for less risky surfaces that will be less likely to injure the pigs, protecting against infestations of parasites, no tethering and many other manifestations of more humane treatment. They also call for more scientific investigations of the animals and better education. These may not seem like much, but they are an improvement in humane treatment, if enforced.

Within the EU, the United Kingdom has a strong program that was formalized as the Animal Welfare Act of 2006. The law notes that it is an offense to cause or to allow unnecessary suffering of animals, and there is a duty to care for animals. The law and its regulations discuss shelter, diet, protection from pain, suffering, injury, and disease (Department of Environment, Food and Rural Affairs 2012).

Stevenson (2012) published an excellent report on the EU legislation that discusses the history, legal basis, and intent. While applauding what has been accomplished, he criticizes them for permitting long trips and allowing animals to be slaughtered without stunning for religious practices. All of the EU humane regulations were phased in and hence the industry has been able to postpone implementing them. Furthermore, without enforcement resources, some of the regulations will not be followed. Hunt and O'Leary (2012) assert that only the UK, Luxembourg, and Sweden are compliant with the requirements. The authors argue that when the rules become fully enforced the EU pig farming industry will decline 5 percent to 10 percent. The article points to a $6 billion industry with major imports to Russia, Hong Kong, and China, and the decline of that industry.

Pressure will continue to build for more humane treatment and elimination of brutal treatment, as well as dealing with human health and safety, and environmental risks. For risk managers, the issue is who is going to be in charge (federal, state, local levels), how much money is going to be spent on enforcing the requirements, and can the agricultural industry hold back the growing pressure against their practices. Market forces are paramount, and the Chinese market is the biggest and growing. EU and U.S. practices to a lesser extent are pushing in the direction of more humane treatment and safer environmental and occupational practices. The tension point is a moral challenge against a growing business opportunity.

Balancing priorities: can we make better decisions by comparing apples and oranges?

As noted in Table 3.1 a host of forces push and pull on risk managers. What can we learn about setting risk management priorities by comparing risks?

Comparative risk analysis

The U.S. EPA was created in 1970 under President Nixon. As Chapter 2 demonstrated, it had little time for deep contemplation about how to use its resources. EPA had to react to perception and sometimes the reality of chemical contamination, hazardous waste sites, and cancer clusters. The word reactive is an apt description of where it stood. Enormous pressure was placed on the U.S. EPA to deal with problems, not think about whether the right problems were being addressed.

I was working on hazardous waste sites and was pleased to see that more of EPA's budget was being focused on the CERCLA (Superfund cleanup program). However, the United States had many other kinds of issues, and hence we were pleased to hear that EPA administrator Lee Thomas had established an agency task force to assess and compare the risks associated with a larger number of environmental problems. EPA asked 75 senior staff members to prioritize environmental problems, which in the case of the senior EPA staff meant integrating their knowledge of science, engineering, economics and policy. The group (U.S. EPA 1987) divided the problems in 31 areas, and they further subdivided their focus into four separate areas:

- Human cancer risk;
- Human non-cancer health risk;
- Ecological risk; and
- Welfare risk.

The group was asked not to take into account whether EPA was mandated to deal with the risk, the economic benefits of the actions that cause the impacts, and difficulty of controlling the risks.

The EPA committees used available data and their judgment because there were major data gaps. In about nine months they produced relative ranks of the 31 problems for each of the four types of risk. The major results were that EPA's priorities were not a good match for the problems that the staff compiled.

The staff produced four lists, one for each of the four categories. The problems that ranked high in three out of four categories or medium or higher in all four categories were as follows:

- Criteria air pollutants (carbon monoxide, lead, nitrogen dioxide, ground-level ozone, particulate matter, sulfur dioxide);
- Stratospheric ozone depletion;
- Pesticide residues in food; and
- Pesticide runoff into surface water and air contamination by pesticides.

Problems that were high in cancer and non-cancer health effects but low in ecological damage and welfare risk were:

- Hazardous air pollutants;
- Indoor radon gas;
- Indoor air pollution, other than radon;
- Pesticide applications;
- Exposure to some consumer products (e.g. sprays and hair dyes); and
- Worker exposure to chemicals.

The gap in EPA's risk management priorities is found in the list of problems that were high on EPA's agenda but low in risk and vice versa:

- High-priority, low risk (treatment storage and disposal facilities, abandoned hazardous waste sites, leaking underground storage tanks, municipal nonhazardous waste sites).
- Low priority, high risk (indoor radon, indoor air pollution in addition to radon, global warming, stratospheric ozone depletion, nonpoint source pollution, pesticides, accident releases of toxins, consumer products, and worker exposure to chemicals).

The 100 page report also notes that the Agency's list of priorities seem to reflect public perceptions and sentiments more than they do risks.

In 1989, EPA asked its Science Advisory Board (SAB) to review the 1987 report, evaluate its findings and to develop options for reducing risk. The SAB review included three working sessions, 12 public meetings, and document reviews. The ranked results are not markedly different from those in the 1987 report (U.S. Environmental Protection Agency 1990). The SAB offered recommendations to EPA. I have collapsed several of them into two:

- EPA should focus its efforts on the opportunities for greatest risk reduction, and it should reflect these priorities in its strategic planning and budgeting; and
- EPA should attach as much attention to ecological risk as to human health risk, and should develop improved methods for value natural resources and account for long-term economic effects.

Recognizing that states have different circumstances, values and issues, EPA followed up their national-scale projects by launching and funding similar projects at the state scale. EPA's goals were promoting a consensus on statewide agenda and priorities, assembling data on the risks, promoting coordination among agencies, and formulating strategies to address the priority ones. They certainly accomplished some of these. For example, Vermont's committee ranked 16 different risks and compared them to a survey (Minard 1991). The survey ranked drinking water contamination, pollution of lakes, and streams, air pollution, hazardous waste and solid waste as 1–5, respectively. The Committee ranking had indoor air pollution, loss of wildlife habitat, global warming, ozone depletion and air pollution as 1–5, respectively. The only overlap in the two lists was air pollution. The Spearman rank correlation coefficient between the Committee and survey data was 0.17, essentially no relationship. Green (2004) studied 20 state comparative risk reports, finding a lack of relationship between resource allocation and risks. At a minimum a comparative risk analysis can wake up not only government officials but also challenge the public's collective risk priorities.

A later EPA Science Advisory Board Committee that I had the privilege to serve on used comparative risk analysis as part of its overall effort to integrate environmental decision-making (U.S. Environmental Protection Agency 2000). The recommendations from these reports drove home the need to try to meld science and non-science based agendas. Comparative risk analysis clearly has limitations. One is that environmental problems are so broad that it is difficult to know exactly what a category means. Second, data sets on some of these issues are inadequate and the EPA and state staff used their judgment in lieu of data (see Chapter 2). A major gap is not only in the biological, physical and chemical sciences but in the economic ones. Our ability to assess economic impacts is hindered by a lack of basic data (see Chapter 6 for efforts to overcome some of those limitations. In the end the major criticism of comparative risk analysis is that it is a crude tool for setting environmental priorities and requires balancing of apples, oranges and watermelons. The greatest strength is that a minimum comparative risk analysis forces government and other stakeholder to confront the uncomfortable reality that they need to avoid narrow thinking about how to use limited resources to reduce risk.

Balancing among multiple objectives

Balancing among competing billion plus dollar programs is an undeniable challenge, leading to strong public passion when different groups look at the same information and options and see different outcomes. A vacant lot in a city can be turned into a park for children and residents, a parking lot, houses, and other land uses. Each option has implications for human health, safety and the environment.

In my experience, water resources are the most difficult balancing act for managers. The contending parties include boaters, fishermen, electric utility managers, farmers, flood control managers, water supply and quality managers.

No issue in my experience raises more risk management related issues than building a dam and regulating its use. At one extreme, the electrical utility wants to build a dam to regulate the flow of water so that there will be sufficient water for cooling. On the opposite side are white-water rafters who do not want new dams and want existing ones removed.

Risk managers can conduct surveys (see below), hold focus groups and meet with individuals to determine preferences. They also have used optimization models to guide their thinking. The goal of many models is to maximize the benefits across the set of contending preferences. Models started to appear in the literature over 60 years ago, including managing reservoirs for multiple uses (Mannos 1955; Manne 1962; Thomas, Revelle 1966 Revelle *et al.* 1969; Loucks 1968) and controlling emissions into water environments (Thomann 1965; Sobel 1965). The ability to use these models is vastly improved because of high-speed computers, and it is possible to conduct multi-objective decision-making analyses to inform decision-makers about options. Nevertheless, whatever the computer program and software packages, the challenge is to obtain data and formulate objectives and constraints that will be accepted by decision-makers (Chankong, Haimes 1983).

In Chapter 2, I briefly reviewed a water supply network case study that contributed to water supply planning in New Jersey. We were able to map the system of sources of water, places where water was needed, and the network linking them. We were able to obtain prices for water purchase from the wholesalers and water retailers and enter them into the optimization model. When the model ran, we showed decision-makers the cost of operating the system under various conditions. When the supply was insufficient, we were able to show them precisely where investments were needed. Some of those investments required building new links and enlarging existing ones. Emphasizing uncertainty, we used so-called "chance constrained programing" where we would estimate the probability of the need for supply increasing to a certain level, and then we would combine that with expected supply. Decision-makers could see what combinations of supply, demand and network completeness made the system work and what combinations lead to failure.

The actual system had 97 entities supplying and consuming water and over 150 links. Box 3.1 provides a simple representation of the model.

One of the less endearing policy lessons learned from this life experience was about the politics of water supply. A rational decision-maker assumes that local governments would cooperate during a water crisis. Some refused, until the then Governor of New Jersey, Richard Hughes used his public health powers to require them to transfer water. Several insisted that the price to transfer the water needed to be much higher, and in this author's opinion some water purveyors proposed outrageously high rates. Again the state government was required to intervene to keep the prices within reason. The lessons learned for risk analysis were as follows:

- Precipitation varies, a historical record exists, and even if does not reach back to biblical times, it can be used to estimate credible probability-based precipitation levels for risk assessment;
- Demand for water can be modeled as a stochastic variable. Specifically, population change can be modeled in regard to size and location, and per capita water use can be changed by altering price and through education. In large and growing regions there is no reason not to be doing state-of-the-art water demand analyses;
- Older regions have water systems that leak because of antiquated transfer systems, and there is a record of system failures that can be modeled as a stochastic process, which will guide risk managers to where they need to make repairs and expand their systems; and
- While not discussed in the above example, some regions have serious water quality problems that effectively lower the available supply. The quality-quantity relationship is subject to the same kinds of risk assessment analysis.

The tension point raised by comparative risk comparisons and optimization models is that both tools offer transparent comparisons of options, which may not be what some decision-makers want the public to see.

The public factor in risk management: what does survey data tell decision-makers?

In countries that monitor public opinion and meaningful elections occur, leaders would commit political suicide by not listening, or at least appear to be listening. The case study in Chapter 5 (environmental justice) is primarily about the public factor, and every case study in part 2 of this book has a public component. The risk perception literature tells us that humans in every country tend to fear many of the same things, such as war, nuclear weapons, for example. The reasons for high

---

BOX 3.1 Water resources linear programming illustration

This simple model illustrates the water supply network model discussed above and in Chapter 2.

Node of supply and demand	Supply, mgd*	Demand, mgd
N1	20	10
N2	10	8
N3	0	10
N4	10	5
Total	40	33

Note: *mgd is millions of gallons of water a day. Nodes could be a town and/or a water source.

The four locations of demand and supply have a capacity of 40 mgd and a need for 33 mgd. Nodes 1, 2, and 4 have excess capacity, whereas node 3 depends on the others The capacity in mgd to transfer water among the four nodes and the cost of supplying the water through that link is as follows.

Link	Cost $/mg	Capacity, mgd
X1	250	5
X2	300	3
X3	270	10
X4	270	15
X5	340	10
X6	325	5
X7	200	20
X8	175	10
X9	225	10

The model below is composed of four parts. Equation 1 is the objective function, which minimizes the cost of supplying water. In other words, the model looks for a solution to meeting demands, and then looks for the least expensive one. The least expensive water is X8, which is node 2 supplying water to its own town.

The first four equations are demand constraints for nodes 1, 2, 3 and 4, respectively. In other words, 10 mgd has to supplied to node 1 through three connections [equation 1]. Equations 4–6 are supply constraints, that is, water can only transferred up to the capacity of the source. For example, equation 5 indicates that the amount transferred through links 4 and 7 must be less than or equal to 20 mgd. Equations 8–16 are individual capacity for transfers. For instance, link X1 must be 5 mgd or less. The last listed equation [17] is actually nine more constraints, which require that all of the options to be used must be 0 or some positive number.

Minimize: Z= 250X1 + 300X2 + 270X3 + 270X4 + 340X5 + 325X6 + 200X7 + 175X8+ 225X9

X1	X2	X3	X4	X5	X6	X7	X8	X9		
X1 +	X2 +					X7			=10	[1]
							X8		=8	[2]
	X2 +		X4 +	X5 +					=10	[3]
					X6 +			X9	=5	[4]
			X4 +			X7			≤20	[5]
X1 +	X2				X6 +		X8		≤10	[6]
		X3 +		X5				X9	≤10	[7]
X1									≤5	[8]
	X2								≤3	[9]
		X3							≤10	[10]
			X4						≤15	[11]
				X5					≤10	[12]
					X6				≤5	[13]
						X7			≤20	[14]
							X8		≤10	[15}
								X9	≤10	[16]
X1 ,	X2 ,	....							≥0	[17]

Solution: Z=$7225, X4=10; X7=10; C8=8; X9=5.

Source: Greenberg 1978, pp. 187–188.The solution sends 33 mgd through four system links. The analyst would want to test many options to provide multiple back up plans for meeting the demands, not drawing more water than is available and only transferring the amount of water up to the system capacity. In reality a water network would have many more options and analysts would want to explore all of them to be prepared for variations in precipitation, changes in demand, transfer system capacity, and variations in water prices.

concern tend to be intuition and affect. Feeling of lack of personal control, dread based on lack of knowledge, personal vulnerability, lack of trust, presence of children, new kinds of hazards, and other factors contribute to people fearing what scientists would consider to be small risks and ignoring larger risks (Slovic 2000, 2010; Sandman 2003).

In this chapter, I use a 2013 survey to try to interpret messages people send to risk managers. Michel-Kerjan and Kunreuther (2012) calculated that 20 of the 30 most damaging disasters during the period 1970 and 2011 happened after 2001 and that 13 were in the United States. Nearly all of these were natural disasters and almost all hit the Atlantic and Gulf Coasts. In 2005, tropical storm Katrina, struck the Gulf Coast, devastating New Orleans and surrounding areas. Katrina was the single most destructive hurricane in United States history; costs were estimated at well over $100 billion (Knabb, Rhome, Brown 2006; Burton, Hicks 2005). Prior to Katrina, Florida was generally considered the most vulnerable in the United States (Wang, Kapucu 2007). In 2011 and 2012, tropical storms Irene and Sandy substantially damaged large areas along the Atlantic Coast of the United States, with estimates of about $50 billion compared to over $100 billion for Katrina when it hit New Orleans.

Governments and companies have taken these two events seriously and have been focusing on making prudent investments, despite a clear change in government that leans to less spending (Jordan 2012; Spivey 2013; Higgs 2013; Bates 2012; Pollack 2012; Larsen 2013). But even if the state and federal governments are willing to support risk management plans that will reduce collective risk, is the public as a whole willing to support the plans and their implementation? For example, if government offers to buy out homes located in vulnerable areas, how much of the public will accept the offers? If the government wants to rebuild devastated areas or reinforce structures in its state, what can they accomplish if the residents are unwilling to pay for these efforts and resist the changes?

The author and colleagues collected data in four months after tropical storms Sandy and 19 months after Irene struck New Jersey. We wanted to know the following:

1. How much support is there for government-led programs that will reduce the number of housing units in high flood risk areas?
2. What factors are most strongly associated with willingness to support these policies?

A special issue of on "Climate Change Risk Perceptions and Communication" in *Risk Analysis* (Pidgeon 2012) emphasized that those that have not experienced a major flood hazard would not be supportive of altering government policies or their habits (Spence, Poortinga, Pidgeon 2012; Johnson 2012; Kahan *et al.* 2012; Malka, Krosnick, Langer 2009). In 2011 and 2012, the two massive tropical storms caused unprecedented damage, leading local pollsters to conclude that the public had been surprised by the severity of the events and were worried about others in the near future (Watson 2013; Spoto, 2013a, b; Murray 2012, 2013). Even local elected officials seemed to temporarily cease bickering and cooperate in formulating ideas and listening to expert views about rebuilding, public health, infrastructure, and other ideas that would prevent risk and increase resilience (Schoonejongen 2012; Schwab *et al.* 1998, Condon, Cavens, Miller 2009; Landesman 2011).

One would expect considerable support for protective risk management policies and investments after such a massive pair of storms. To use a well-worn expression, four months after a historically unprecedented storm would be the "educable moment." However, do people care enough to be willing to support the program by paying for some of it? There are good reasons to support the ideas, but paying for them through taxes is another step in the process to gauge how seriously they support the challenge.

The world is increasingly committed to cell phones and now about half of U.S. residents only receive calls on their cell phones. This survey was 65 percent land-line and 35 percent cell phone to capture the increasing number of cell phone only users. The sample of 875 was of persons 18 years and older who were not institu-tionalized (see Greenberg *et al.* 2014 for full survey details).

The survey asked residents the extent to which they personally support state and local action to prevent rebuilding on vulnerable properties, for example, (1) prohibition of housing in some areas, (2) requirement that homes built in some areas be constructed to resist natural disasters, and five other risk-reducing options (Table 3.3).

Table 3.3 shows that 53 percent to 63 percent of respondents strongly favored having the federal and state governments identify areas to not be redeveloped, permitting local governments to require housing in some areas to be built in ways highly resistant to natural disasters, and relocating water and other infrastructure away from the flood prone areas. Forty-two and 49 percent supported allowing the government to provide financial incentives to rebuild in ways that reduce future

TABLE 3.3 Proportion of respondents who supported land use, design and financial changes, NJ residents, 2013

Summary data	Strongly agree, %	Somewhat agree, %	Neutral, somewhat or strongly disagree %
Allow local governments to require housing in some areas to be built in ways highly resistant to natural disasters (n=864)	62.5	22.4	15.0
Have the federal and state government identify the areas to not be developed to provide natural buffers in the event of storms (n=855)	61.3	22.3	16.3
Relocate water, sewers, natural gas, roads, and other infrastructure away from the most vulnerable areas of the state (n=857)	53.0	25.8	21.2
Have the government give financial incentives to rebuild in ways that reduce future risks (n= 866)	49.1	30.8	20.1
Allow local governments to prohibit housing in some areas (n= 859)	42.5	26.6	30.9
Limit the number of times homeowners in high risk areas may receive federal disaster relief (n= 859)	38.2	21.5	40.4
Have the federal and state government purchase property in vulnerable areas and turn it into open space (n= 862)	35.0	25.8	39.2

Source: Adapted from Greenberg *et al.* 2014.

risk, and prohibiting housing in some areas, respectively. Over 35 percent strongly favored limiting the number of times homeowners in high-risk areas may receive federal disaster relief, and allowing the federal and state government to buy property in vulnerable areas and convert it to open space. Across the set of options in Table 3.3, 49 percent "strongly favored" four or more of the seven risk-reducing policy options, and the proportion strongly and somewhat favoring each of the options ranged from 61 percent to 85 percent. These results are remarkable for a state that had normally spurned any effort by state and even local government to interfere in homeowner use of their property.

Willingness to sacrifice can be measured as giving time, going to meetings, and in other ways supporting the common good. However, as many of us were told by our parents, a bottom line metric of a high priority is willingness to pay for it. The context is that New Jersey, New York and other areas impacted by these and other storms have received funds after a presidential disaster declaration for rebuilding, buy-outs and other efforts to prevent damage and speed recovery from the events. However, federal funds are not sufficient to implement a risk management flood disaster plan in this state (Greenberg, Weiner *et al.* 2014). Hence, we asked respondents to consider five ideas for raising revenue for a dedicated fund for risk management in response to the storm and future ones. Four of these (Table 3.4) asked for tax increases that would last only five years, and the fifth was buying bonds to be paid over 30 years. Public support was weak. Few were willing to pay a small gasoline tax, raise state income or sales taxes. A slightly larger proportion was willing to approve a dedicated bond issue, and over half favored an additional tax on hotels, motels, airports, and recreational facilities. A cynical interpretation of these results is that less than 1 in 5 would pay out of their own pocket. Two in five

TABLE 3.4 Willingness to support revenue-generating policies in support of protecting vulnerable areas

Policy	Agree or strongly agree, %	Neutral, %	Disagree or strongly disagree, %
Add a special additional tax of 1% on hotels, motels, airports, and recreational facilities for five years	52.5	14.3	33.2
Approve a multi-billion dollar bond issue to be paid out over 30 years	42.0	29.5	28.5
Raise state sales tax by 1% for five years	24.2	11.3	64.4
Raise state income taxes across the board by 5% for five years	19.0	12.4	68.6
Add a 5-cents-per-gallon tax on gasoline sales for five years	14.4	7.8	77.8

Source: Adapted from Greenberg *et al.* 2014.

would support a bond issue that would kick the cost down the road for them and their children. One in two would support a revenue source that would be at least partly paid by tourists and travelers.

What might explain these results? Table 3.5 summarizes a series of statistical analyses that separated survey questions into three categories. One set of variables contributes to factors that increased support for the policy options to reduce vulnerability. These include personal risk concern and concern to the state, as well as belief that global climate change is occurring. A second set contributing to support is trust of scientists, the media, and in the capabilities of the federal, state and local governments. Worldviews, including views that society would be better off if wealth were more equally distributed (an egalitarian world view), and self-identification with the Democratic Party were associated with more support for the land use policies.

In follow-up discussions, we learned that the public is accustomed to the federal government paying quite a bit toward redevelopment. If the public strongly supported a special fund to rebuild and buy vulnerable lands, some think the federal government would have an excuse to provide less money. A second reason is that the public and many other areas does not trust money dedicated to one task to be used for that purpose. In New Jersey, reallocation of targeted funds has happened and reduced the government credibility to follow through on promises. Third, many people do not believe that government, even their local government, has the expertise to make major competent decisions, even if their values are in the right place.

Looking beyond the numbers, there are several mixed messages for risk managers. The two events woke up the population about the potential impacts of storm events. About half of the respondents "strongly" supported at least four of the seven policies, and 30 percent favored five of the seven. If somewhat supported is included along with strongly supported, the proportion favoring four of seven of the options is about four out of five respondents, a remarkable finding in a state, as noted earlier, with a history of opposing government instruction in personal behavior and especially property rights. For those who believed that the public was disconnected from the issue of global climate change, this survey found that 64 percent of respondents agreed that global climate change is a risk to them, their family and friends. Whether tropical storms Irene and Sandy are proof of global climate change is neither the point, nor have the author and his colleagues made that assertion. What is notable is that most of the public believes that to be the case. I consider that belief to be current conventional wisdom.

However, favoring a policy does not mean a willingness to support it financially. The remarkably low rates of support for the taxes and bond we proposed were described by one individual at a public meeting at which the author presented these results as embarrassing and many shook their heads in dismay. This low rate of support cannot be explained by socioeconomic status. Poor people did not disproportionately reject paying for this dedicated program. Trust continually came up in one-on-one and group discussions, as well as the survey. More than half of

TABLE 3.5 Linear regression analysis results of support for policy options to reduce vulnerability#

Variable	B-value (Standard error)	Beta value	t-value
Perceptions and values associated with concern about global climate change:	.293 (.037)	.289	7.86★
Personal risk			
Global climate change is risk to me, my family and my friends			
Global climate change is a risk to NJ			
I believe that global climate change is occurring			
Trust			
I trust the scientific community to honestly report their findings related to climate change			
The international scientific community understands the science behind global climate change			
The media I rely on communicates to us honestly			
Our state and local officials understand the implications of global climate change for our region			
I trust federal government to manage redevelopment			
Worldviews:			
Society better off if distribution of wealth was more equal			
Self-identify as Democrat			
Local environment will be worse in 25 years			
Willingness to contribute to a special fund	.208 (.038)	.203	5.53★
Raise state sales tax by 1% for 5 years			
Raise state income taxes across the board by 1% for 5 years			
Add a 5-cents per gallon tax on gasoline sales in NJ for 5 years			
Add a special additional tax of 1% on hotels, motels, airports and recreation facilities for 5 years			
Approve a multi-billion dollars bond issue to be paid out over 30 years			
Shore resident (1 or 0)	.080 (.070)	.039	1.14
Constant	.108 (.106)		1.03

Notes: #F-value was 47.6, adjusted r^2 was 0.167, and degrees of freedom were 709.
★Statistically significant relationship at $p<.01$.

Source: Adapted from Greenberg *et al*. 2014.

respondents did not believe that state and local government officials understand the implications of global climate change for their region, and about two-thirds did not even not trust their local media to inform them about events. Along with a generic lack of trust of the U.S. federal government in many places, a large proportion of the population believes that government will divert the money to other projects, which this author has seen too often.

While the state collects money from the United States government and slowly disperses, a small collection of not-for-profit groups are carrying the torch forward in the absence of a strong and ongoing state effort. These groups are trying to build a social movement around storm-related risk management. Meanwhile public support will attenuate, unless there is another event that will cause state officials to take on this issue as a major priority (Wang, Kapucu 2007; Dillon, Tinsley Cronin 2011; Lindell, Arlikatti, Prater 2009; Lindell, Perry 2012; Paton, Johnston 2001). More recent surveys show ongoing distress, especially among those who lost their homes and have not been able to return (Greenberg 2014).

If I was the governor of New Jersey, this is what these data would tell me. Unless another event occurs, at which point there will be considerable finger pointing and a call for accountability, the public wants many of these risk management policies. However, these risk-reducing steps are not enough of a priority for them to be willing to step up and fund a program that goes beyond what can be done with funds from the federal government, insurance companies and well intentioned groups (Spoto 2013 a, b). In 2015, about four years after Irene and three years after Sandy, I do not feel a strong tension point for action. Frankly, the public, with some exceptions has moved on to other issues, at least until there is another event. If there is a tension point, it is between those who know that there will be more storms and action needs to be taken to limit the consequences and others, the vast majority, who have lost interest.

What did Chapter 3 explain about risk analysis? Summary and learning objectives

This chapter is about making choices about protecting human and ecological health, as well as assets. Examples are used to highlight six common challenges. One is resolving international differences in risk management, which is illustrated by comparing the efforts in the United States (TSCA) and the European Union (REACH) to gather information about potential chemical hazards and to manage them. A second is choosing among priorities within a single government program. This challenge is illustrated by the U.S. Department of Energy's efforts to protect human health and safety at the U.S. legacy nuclear weapons facilities during a period of budget restrictions. The third section is about the options available to protect critical infrastructure when there are so many needs in so many places and limited resources. Section four highlights the multiplicity of risk-related challenges, including moral ones in managing factory farms. The last sections introduce comparative risk analysis, optimization methods, and surveys as tools to inform decisions.

At the end of this chapter readers should be able to answer the following seven questions:

1. What legal processes are used in the U.S. to gather information about chemicals in commerce and how do these compare with the EU's?
2. What factors does the U.S. Department of Energy consider when it prioritizes risk reduction resources at former nuclear weapons sites?
3. What is critical infrastructure, and what processes are used to allocate resources to protect them?
4. How does cyber terrorism fit as a critical infrastructure concern?
5. What are factory animal farms and what special risk-related environmental, social and economic challenges are associated with them?
6. What are comparative risk analysis and mathematical optimization models, and how can they be used to help us better evaluate priorities?
7. How can survey data help us understand public risk management priorities?

References

American Chemistry Council (2010) www.americanchemistry.com/s_acc/sec_about.asp?CID=6&DID=9. Accessed June 19, 2015.

Bates T. (2012) Is retreating best option for the state? *Home News Tribune*. December 26.

Bollaerts K, Messens W, Delhalle L, Aerts M, Van der Stede Y, Dewulf J, Quoilin S, Maes D, Mintiens K, Grijspeerdt K. (2009) Development of a quantitative microbial risk assessment for human salmonellosis through household consumption of fresh minced pork meat in Belgium, *Risk Analysis*. 29, 6, 820–840.

Bouma A, Elbers A, Dekker A, de Koeijer A, Bartels C, Vellema P, van der Wal P, van Rooij E, Pluimers F, de Jong M. (2003) The foot-and-mouth disease epidemic in the Netherlands in 2001. *Preventive Veterinary Medicine*. 57, 155–166.

Burton L, Hicks M. (2005) Hurricane Katrina: preliminary estimates of commercial and public sector damages. Huntington, WV: Marshall University Center for Economics and Business Research. www.Marshall.edu/cber/research/katrina/Katrina-Estimates.pdf. Accessed May 3, 2013.

Chankong V, Haimes Y. (1983) *Multiobjective decisionmaking: theory and methodology*. Mineola, NY: Dover Publications.

CNBC. (2015) Water, air quality fears conflict with pig farms, www.cnbc.com/id/102428720. Accessed June 24, 2015.

Condon P, Cavens D, Miller N. (2009) *Urban planning tools for climate change mitigation*. Cambridge, MA: Lincoln Land Institute.

Davison N. (2013) Rivers of blood: the dead pigs rotting in China's water supply. *The Guardian*. www.theguardian.com/world/2013/mar/29/dead-pigs-china-water-supply. March 29. Accessed June 24, 2015

Department of Environment, Food and Rural Affairs. (2012) Pig farming, welfare regulation – detailed guidance. August 24. www.gov/uk/pig-welfare-regulations. Accessed June 24, 2015.

Dillon RL, Tinsley CH, Cronin M. (2011) Why near-miss events can decrease an individual's protective response to hurricanes. *Risk Analysis*. 31, 3, 440–449.

Donham K, Reynolds S, Whitten P, Merchant J, Burmeister L, Popperndorf W. (1995) Respiratory dysfunction in swine production facility workers: dose-response relationship of environmental exposures and pulmonary function. *American Journal of Industrial Medicine*. 27, 3, 405–418.

Dudley, S, Hays, S (2007) *Memorandum for the Heads of Executive Departments and Agencies*.

M-07-24, September 19.

European Chemical Industry Council (2013) *The chemical industry.* www.environmental-chemicalindustry.org/the-chemical-industry/the-chemical-industry.html. Accessed July 2, 2015.

European Commission (2003) Regulation of the European Parliament and of the Council concerning REACH, establishing a European Chemicals Agency and amending Directive 1999/45/EC and Regulation (EC) on persistent organic pollutants: extended impact assessment. Brussels. http://ec.europa.eu/s,art-regulations/impact/.../sec_2003_1171/en.pdf. Accessed November 28, 2015

European Union Council (2008) Directive 2008/120/EC. December 18, 2008. http://europa.eu/legislation_summaries/food_safety/animal_welfare/sa0009_em.htm. Accessed June 25, 2015.

European Union (2006) Regulation (EC) No 1907/2006 of the European Parliament and of the Council of 18 December 2006 concerning the registration, evaluation, authorization and restriction of chemicals (REACH), establishing a European Chemicals Agency. www.enisa.europa.eu/activities/risk-management/current-risk/laws-regulation/national-security/regulation-ec-no-1907-2006. Accessed May 4, 2016.

European Union. (2007) REACH: evaluation, authorization, and restriction of chemicals. *Official Journal of the European Union.* http://ec.europa.eu/environment/chemicals/reach/reach/_intro.htm. Accessed June 19, 2015.

Federal Facilities Environmental Restoration Dialogue Committee, U.S. EPA. (1996) *Final report of the federal facilities environmental restoration dialogue committee: consensus principles and recommendations for improving federal facilities cleanup,* EPA/540/R-96/493, April. www.epa.gov/swerffrr/fferdc.htm. Accessed May 13, 2014.

Genoways T. (2014) *The chain.* New York: Harper.

Green M. (2004) *State-level environmental risk perception: an analysis of 20 comparative risk reports.* Lafayette, LA: University of Louisiana.

Greenberg M. (1978) *Applied linear programming for the socioeconomic and environmental sciences.* New York: Academic Press.

Greenberg M. (2014) *Protecting seniors against environmental disasters: from hazards and vulnerability to prevention and resilience.* New York: Routledge.

Greenberg M, Irving W, Zimmerman R. (2009) Allocating U.S. Department of Homeland Security funds to states with explicit equity, population and energy facility security criteria. *Socio-Economic Planning Sciences.* 43, 229–239.

Greenberg M, Miller KT, Frisch M, Lewis D. (2003) Facing an uncertain economic future: environmental management spending and rural regions surrounding the U.S. DOE's nuclear weapons facilities, *Defence and Peace Economics,* 14, 1, 85–97.

Greenberg M, Weiner M, Noland R, Herb J, Kaplan M, Broccoli T. (2014) Public support for policies to reduce risk after Hurricane Sandy, *Risk Analysis.* 34, 6, 997–1012.

Guth J, Denison R, Sass J. (2007) Require comprehensive safety data for all chemicals. *New Solutions.* 17, 233–258.

Higgs L. (2013) NJ Transit eyes 2 new train yards. *Home News Tribune.* January 28, pp. 1.

Hill A, Simons R, Kelly L, Snary E. (2016) A farm transmission model of Salmonella in pigs, Applicable to EU Member States. *Risk Analysis.* 36(3), 461–481.

Horton RA, Wing S, Marshall S, Brownley K. (2009). Malodor as a trigger of stress and negative mood in neighbors of industrial hog operations. *American Journal of Public Health* 99, S610–S615.

Hunt N, O'Leary N. (2012) EU welfare rules to trigger exodus of pig farmers. www.reuters.com/article/2012/05/02/pigs-europe-/dUSL5E862EZ320120502. Accessed June 24, 2015.

Hurd HS, Esoe C, Sorensen L, Wachman H, Corns S, Bryden K, Grenier M. (2008) Risk-based analysis of the Danish pork *Salmonella* program: past and future. *Risk Analysis*. 28, 2, 341–351.

International Council of Chemical Associations. (2010) Responsible care. www.responsible.org/page.asp?n=whatwedo&I. Accessed June 19, 2015.

Jackson L. (2010) The U.S. Environmental Protection Agency's international priorities. A memorandum to all EPA employees. EPA. http://blog.ep.gov/administrator/2010/08/17/the-us-environmental-protection-agency%E2%80%99s-international-priorities/#me-895. Accessed June 19, 2015

Johnson B. (2012) Change communications: a provocative inquiry into motives, meanings, and means. *Risk Analysis*. 32, 5, 973–991.

Jones LM, Bernknopf R, Cox D, Goltz J, Hudnut K, Mileti D, Perry S, Ponti D, Porter K, Reichle M, Seligson H, Shoaf K, Treiman J, and Wein A. (2008) The ShakeOut Scenario: USGS Open File Report 2008–1150 and California Geological Survey Preliminary Report 25, http://pubs.usgs.gov/of2008/1150 and http://conservation.ca.gov/cgs, Sacramento, CA. Accessed May 22, 2015.

Jordan B. (2012) State will rethink its development plan. *Home News Tribune*. November 14, 2.

Kahan D, Peters E, Braman D, Slovic P, Wittlin M, Larrimore Oulette L, Mandel G. (2012) Tragedy of the risk-perception commons: culture conflict, rationality conflict, and climate change, *Nature Climate Change*. 2, 732–735.

King A, Lenox M. (2000) Industry self-regulation without sanctions: the chemical industry's responsible care program. *The Academy of Management Journal*. 43, 698–716.

Kleinmutz D. (2008) Resource Allocation Models for Terrorism Risk Management. Seminar, Finnish Operations Research, November 13.

Kleinmutz D, von Winterfeldt D, Willis H, Bowman H. (2006) Risk-based multiobjective resource allocation for infrastructure protection. Paper presented at Society of Risk Analysis annual meeting, December 2006, Baltimore, MD, December 4, 2006.

Kleinmutz D, Willis H. (2009) Prioritizing terrorism vulnerability analyses for critical infrastructure sectors. Indianapolis, In, Decision Analysis Affinity Group Meeting, May 18.

Knabb R, Rhome J, Brown D. (2006) Tropical cyclone report: Hurricane Katrina, 23–30 August 2005. Miami, Florida: National Hurricane Center, 2006. www.nhc.noaa.govpdf/TCR-AL12205.Katrina.pdf. Accessed May 3, 2013.

Kraft M, Vig N. (2010) Environmental policy over four decades: achievements and new directions. In NM. Vig and ME Kraft, eds. *Environmental policy*. 7th edition, Washington, D.C.: CQ Press, 1–26.

Kuo L. (2013) 2,800 Dead pigs in a Shanghai river: how did this happen? *The Atlantic*. www.theatlantic.com/china/archive/2013/03/2-800-dead-pigs-in-a-shanghai-river-how-did-this-happen/273892/. Accessed June 24, 2015.

Landesman L. (2011) *Public health management of disasters: the practice guide*. Washington, D.C.: APHA.

Langley R. (1995) Occupational hazards on swine farms, http://ncsu.edu/project/swine_extension/healthy/hogs/book1995/langely.htm. Accessed June 25, 2015

Larsen E. (2013) Line in the sand. *Home News and Tribune*. January 17, 9.

Lewis J. (2002) Assessing the risks of cyber terrorism, cyber war and other cyber threats. http://csis.org.files/media/csis.pub/021101_risks_of_cyberterror.pdf. Accessed March 24, 2015.

Liesio J, Mild P, Salo A. (2007) Preference programming for robust portfolio modeling and project selection. *European Journal of Operational Research*. 181, 1481–1505.

Lindell MK, Arlikatti S, Prater CS. (2009) Why people do what they do to protect against earthquake risk: perceptions of hazard adjustment attributes. *Risk Analysis.* 29, 8, 1072–1088.

Lindell MK, Perry RW. (2012) The protective action decision model: theoretical modifications and additional evidence. *Risk Analysis.* 32, 4, 616–632.

Loucks D. (1968) Computer models for reservoir regulation. *Journal of Sanitary Engineering, American Society of Civil Engineers.* 94, SA 4, 657–669.

Malka A, Krosnick JA, Langer G. (2009) The association of knowledge with concern about global warming: trusted information sources shape public thinking. *Risk Analysis.* 29, 5, 633–647.

Manne A. (1962) Product-mix alternatives: flood control, electric power and irrigation. *International Economic Review.* 3, 1, 30–59.

Mannos M. (1955) An application of linear programming to efficiency in operation for a system of dams. *Econometrica.* 33, 3, 335–336.

Michel-Kerjan E, Kunreuther H. (2012) Paying for future catastrophes. *The New York Times.* Opinion. November 25, SR7.

Minard R. (1991) A focus on risk: states reconsider their environmental priorities. *Maine Policy Review.* 1, 1, 13–27.

Multihazard Mitigation Council. (2005) National hazard mitigation saves: an independent study to assess the future savings from mitigation activities. Washington, D.C.: National Institute of Building Sciences.

Murray P. (2012) Sandy's impact on New Jersey. Press release, Monmouth University. www.monmouth.edu/polling. Accessed December 10, 2012.

Murray P. (2013) Sandy recovery slow but steady in Jersey. Press release, Monmouth University. www.monmouth.edu/polling. Accessed February 20, 2013.

National Infrastructure Protection Center, DHS. (2013) National infrastructure protection plan: partnering for critical infrastructure security and resilience. Washington, D.C.: USDHS. www.dhs.gov/publication/nipp-2013-partnering-critical-infrastructure-security-and-resilience. Accessed June 29, 2015.

National Institute for Occupational Safety and Health (NIOSH). (1990) Preventing death of farm workers in manure pits. NIOSH Alert. Cincinnati, OH, May 1990.

Natural Resources Defense Council (2013) Facts about pollution from livestock farms. www.nrdc.org/water/pollution/ffarms.asp. Accessed June 24, 2015.

Omnibus Risk Review Committee. (2015) A review of the use of risk-informed management in the cleanup program for former defense nuclear sites, report presented to Appropriations Committee of U.S. House of Representatives and U.S. Senate, Nashville, TN, Vanderbilt University, August.

Paton D, Johnston D. (2001) Disasters and communities: vulnerability, resilience and preparedness. *Disaster Prevention and Management.* 10, 4, 270–277.

Peach S. (2014) What to do about pig poop? North Carolina fights a rising tide. *National Geographic.* October 30. http://news.nationalgeographic.com/news/2014/10/141028-hog-farms-waste-pollution-methane-north-carolina-environment. Accessed June 24, 2015.

Pidgeon N. (2012) Climate change risk perceptions and communication. *Risk Analysis.* Special Issue. 32, 6, 951–956.

Pollack W. (2012) After Sandy, just rebuilding won't be enough. December 19, www.rpa.org/2012/12afer-sandy-just-rebuilding-wont-be enough. Accessed December 19, 2012.

Revelle R, Joeres E, Kirby W. (1969) The linear decision rule in reservoir management and design, 1, development of the stochastic model. *Water Resources Research.* 5, 4, 767–777.

Rose A, Wei D, Wein A. (2011) Economic impacts of the shakeout scenario. *Earthquake Spectra*. 27, 2, 539–557.

Ruden C, Hansson S. (2010) Registration, evaluation, and authorization of chemicals (REACH) is but the first step – how far will it take us? Six further steps to improve the European chemicals legislation. *Environmental Health Perspectives*. 118, 6–10.

Sandman P. (2003) Four kinds of risk communication. *The Synergist*, 26–27.

Schinasi L, Horton R, Guidry V, Wing S, Marshall S, Morland K. (2011) Air pollution, function, and physical symptoms in communities near concentrated swine-feeding operations. *Epidemiology*. 20, 208–215.

Schoonejongen J. (2012) In Trenton, Sandy proving to be a bipartisan storm. *Home New Tribune*. December 2, F1.

Schwab J, Topping K, Eadie C, Deyle R, Smith R. (1998) Advisory Service Report number 483/484, Chicago, IL, American Planning Association, Planning for Post-Disaster Recovery and Reconstruction. Planning 1998.

Seuring S, Muller M. (2008) From a literature review to a conceptual framework for sustainable supply chain management. *Journal of Cleaner Production*. 16, 15), 1699–1710.

Simons R, Hill A, Kelly S, Snary E. (2016) A transport and lairage model for Salmonella transmission between pigs applicable to EU member states. *Risk Analysis*, 36(3), 482–497.

Slovic P. (2000) *Perception of risk*. London: Earthscan.

Slovic P. (2010) *The feeling of risk*. London: Earthscan.

Sobel M. (1965) Water quality improvement programming problems. *Water Resources Research*. 1, 4, 477–487.

Songjiang N. (2013) A bay of pigs movement. *The Economist*. March 12. www.econmist.con/blogs.analects/2013/03/water-pollution. Accessed June 24, 2015.

Soumpasis I, Butler F. (2011) Development of a self-regulated dynamic model for the propagation of Salmonella Typhimurium in pig farms. *Risk Analysis*. 31, 1, 63–77.

Spence A, Poortinga W, Pidgeon N. (2012) The psychological distance of climate change. *Risk Analysis*. 32, 6, 957–972.

Spivey M. (2013) N.J. orders utilities to better prepare for big storms. *Home News Tribune*. 2013; January 27, 1, 6.

Spoto MA. (2013a) New Jersey will get $20b to $25b in federal aid, Christie says. *Messenger-Gazette*. May 20, 2013.

Spoto MA. (2013b) Jerseysans say Hurricane Sandy victims should follow FEMA rules or return aid. *The Star Ledger*. March 19, 2013.

Stevenson P. (2012) European welfare legislation on the welfare of farm animals. London, Compassion in World Farming.

Taylor D. (2010) Principles into practice: setting the bar for green chemistry. *Environmental Health Perspectives*. 119, A254–A257.

Thomann R. (1965) Recent results from a mathematical model of water pollution control in the Delaware River estuary. *Water Resources Research*. 1, 3, 349–359.

Thomas H, Revelle R. (1966) On the efficient use of the High Aswan Dam for hydropower and irrigation. *Management Science*. 12, 8, B296–B311.

U.S. Department of Energy. (1995) *Closing the circle on the splitting of the atom*. Washington, D.C.: U.S. Department of Energy.

U.S. Department of Energy. (2014) [DOE STD-3009.94 http://energy.gov/sites/prod/files/2013/12/15/documented-safety-analysis.pdf. Accessed December 4, 2014.

U.S. Department of Homeland Security (2013) What is critical infrastructure? www.dhs.gov/topic/what-critical-infratrcuture? Accessed June 29, 2015.

U.S. Environmental Protection Agency (2010a) Green chemistry. www.epa.gov/gcc. Accessed June 19, 2015.

U.S. Environmental Protection Agency (2010b) Design for the environment: an EPA Partnership program. www.epa.gov/dfe. Accessed June 19, 2015.

U.S. Environmental Protection Agency (2010c) Laws and regulations. www.epa.gov/lawsregs. Accessed June 19, 2015

U.S. Environmental Protection Agency (U.S. EPA). (1987) Unfinished business: a comparative assessment of environmental problems. Washington, D.C.: Office of Policy, Planning and Evaluation.

U.S. Environmental Protection Agency (U.S. EPA). (1990) Reducing risk: setting priorities and strategies for environmental protection. SAB-EC-90-021, Washington, D.C.: Science Advisory Board.

U.S. Environmental Protection Agency (U.S. EPA). (2000) Toward integrated environmental decision-making. SAB-EC-00-011, Washington, D.C.: Science Advisory Board.

U.S. Environmental Protection Agency (U.S. EPA). (2014) Radiation risk assessment guidance, Chapter 10. www.epa.gov/oswer/riskasessment/rags/ch10.pdf. Accessed December 4, 2014.

U.S. Government Accountability Office. (2005) Chemical regulation: options exist to improve EPA's ability to assess health risks and manage its chemical review program. Washington, D.C.

U.S. Government Accountability Office (2009) High-risk series: an update. Washington, DC.

U.S. Government Accountability Office (2007) Chemical regulation: comparison of U.S. and recently enacted European Union approaches to protect against the risks of toxic chemicals. GAO-07-825. www.gao.products.GAO-07-825. Accessed June 22, 2015.

U.S. Nuclear Regulatory Commission. (2012) A proposed risk management regulatory framework. Washington, D.C.: USNRC, Figure 3-1, page 3-1.

Velthuis A, Mourits M. (2007) Effectiveness of movement-prevention regulations to reduce the spread of foot-an-mouth disease in the Netherlands. *Preventive Veterinary Medicine.* 82, 262–281.

Vos C, Nielen M, Lopez E, Elbers A, Kekker A. (2010) Probability of exporting infected carcasses from vaccinated pigs following a foot-and-mouth disease epidemic. *Risk Analysis.* 30, 4, 605–618.

Wang X, Kapucu N. (2007) Public complacency under repeated emergency threats: some empirical evidence. *Journal of Public Administration Research and Theory.* 18, 57–78.

Watson S. (2013) Post-Sandy poll shows New Jersey residents favor assessing future flood risks over rebuilding. *Press of Atlantic City.* www/pressofatlanticcity.com/news/breaking/post-sandy-poll-shows. Accessed February 18, 2013.

Wilson M, Schwarzman M. (2009) Toward a new U.S. chemicals policy: rebuilding the foundation to advance new science, green chemistry and environmental health. *Environmental Health Perspectives.* 117, 1202.

PART II
Cases

4

DESTROYING CHEMICAL WEAPONS

Introduction

If I had to pick one case study that I was both personally involved in and that illustrates the utility, challenges and fascination of risk analysis, I would pick the destruction of the U.S. chemical weapon stockpile. I served for six years on the National Research Council's so-called "Stockpile" Committee, one of the overseers of the United States Army's program to destroy its unitary chemical weapon stockpile.

I know from personal experiences and surveys that the public has been concerned about chemical weapons – somewhere between frightened by what they have heard and yet subtly attracted by the exotic nature of these agents. For example, I have spoken to local high school chemistry classes about weapons, and each time the talks were switched to larger rooms to accommodate more students, faculty and staff. On one occasion, the audience asked questions well into their lunch hour. As far as I could see, no one even looked at their cell phone. The most frequently asked question is if chemical weapons really look like those green beads in Sean Connery's action movie *The Rock* (1996).

This chapter is an opportunity to dig into a multiple-stage interaction between risk assessment and risk management. The chapter begins by briefly recounting the first major use of chemical weapons during World War I. Then it summarizes the world-wide effort to destroy the weapons. Most of the chapter is devoted to efforts to destroy the weapons in the United States, focusing on whether to use incineration, which was the baseline method, suggested by the Stockpile committee, including this author, and other methods, some of which were bad ideas that would have increased risk, and several others that have been deployed at four of the nine stockpile sites.

The Army used standard risk assessment tools (Chapter 2), which are described in this chapter. It also reached out to community groups, using typical and innovative risk communication approaches, which many thought that it would not do. The bottom line is that in 2015, all the weapons at the five incineration sites were destroyed. Smaller stockpiles were destroyed with hydrolysis (heated water) at two other sites, and two with smaller stockpiles remain to be destroyed. By now, I believe that the entire stockpile would have been destroyed had the Army used incineration. It chose not to for reasons described and highlighted in the chapter. I was in the middle of a great deal of this risk analysis activity, and I have deliberately introduced personal experiences in this chapter because some of the interactions between risk assessment and risk management would only be known to those that were personally involved, and I believe some of these interactions were among the most interesting.

Chemical weapons: historical and international contexts

Arsenic was used against soldiers in Europe and China well over a thousand years ago (Tucker 2006). Conventional killing and maiming weapons were more effective. Inability to control chemical weapons (wind directions can suddenly change) posed a threat to the attackers. Some argued that chemical weapons are unethical, an interesting notion. Chemical weapons were located near the bottom of the killer list because they were relatively less effective than other options.

World War I brought them back, with a cost of about 100,000 deaths, and about a million casualties. A key niche was attacking soldiers in trenches or mountain locations that had protected them against conventional bombs and bullets. For example, about a decade ago, I visited the northwestern border of Italy and Slovenia where the River Isonzo drains south and empties into the Adriatic Sea separating Italy and Slovenia (see Figure 4.1). A beautiful area of steep mountains and winding rivers, during World War I, soldiers from the Italian and Austro-Hungarian armies fought in the Soca and Isonzo river valleys and mountains at elevations of 2,000+ meters (6,500+ feet). The armies clashed more than a dozen times between 1915 and 1917. Both sides had a difficult time killing their opponents with conventional weapons because the troops would duck into caves. The warring parties tried several innovative methods to kill entrenched troops. They fired over entrenched mountain positions in order to cause avalanches that would trap their opponents. The attackers also fired chemical-laden rounds that would kill or maim troops that were otherwise protected.

The Kobarid Museum and several others, located in the western part of Slovenia, contain exhibits from many of these river valley and mountain battles, including some particularly gruesome ones that show suffocated soldiers. For first lieutenant Erwin Rommel, a famous general in World War II who commanded the Afrika Korps, and his counterparts in other armies, these deadly battles were an opportunity to understand mountain warfare, for instance, the need to use water or urine-soaked garments to prevent inhalation of the gas, to stand up (nearly all the chemical weapons were heavier than air), to recognize that the winds could

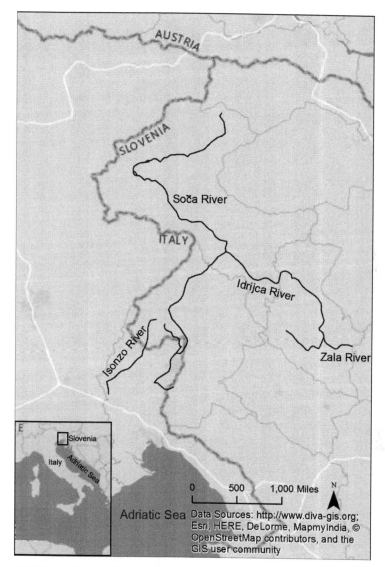

FIGURE 4.1 Soca and Isonzo River Valleys: Area Where Chemical Weapons Were Used During WWI

carry the gas back to the attacker's troops, and to improve the lethality of chemical weapons by introducing phosgene and mustard gas.

Not everyone's takeaway from these battles was to try improve killing. The photos in these museums make a compelling case for not using chemical weapons. An ambulance driver, Ernest Hemingway (1929), used his experiences as a Red Cross volunteer in this area as the basis for *A Farewell to Arms*.

The use of chemical weapons was a war crime in these World War I battles, as defined by The Hague Declaration of 1899 against using asphyxiating gases and The Hague convention of 1907. After the end of World War I, the 1925 Geneva Protocol forbade the use of chemical weapons, but not stockpiling them. The Protocol was signed by nearly all nations within a decade. The United States was reluctant to immediately sign. Opponents of the agreement persuaded elected officials that dying from poisoning was not worse than dying from bombs, machine guns, knives, and drowning in a destroyed ship. The prevailing political argument for a short time was that the United States should not be swept up by irrational emotions and agree not to use chemical weapons.

The United States and Russia, concerned by potential use of these weapons against their troops built massive chemical weapons arsenals during World War I, and their stockpiles increased for decades. Table 4.1 lists the major types of chemical warfare agents and summarizes their health effects.

Fast-forward a century from the first major uses of chemical weapons in World War I to 2015. The supply of acknowledged chemical weapons has declined, especially during the last two decades. In 1997, the Chemical Weapons Convention (CWC) outlawed the production, stockpiling, and use of chemical weapons and many of their precursors. The treaty is administered by the Organization for the Prohibition of Chemical Weapons (OPCW), located in The Hague. The 190 states that have agreed to the convention requirements are prohibited from developing a stockpile, using chemical weapons, and obligated to destroy their existing stockpiles. As of late 2014, over 80 percent of the existing acknowledged world stockpiles had been destroyed. In addition, members recognize that facilities can be inspected. (I have stayed in facilities in the United States refurbished for inspectors.)

According to OPCW's data, about 13,000 tons of chemical weapons remain to be destroyed. This compared to over 71,000 when signatory nations disclosed their stockpiles. In reality, the vast majority of the destroyed and remaining chemical weapons belong to the United States and Russia. Albania and India have destroyed chemical weapons. Iraq and Syria have used them, a few other nations have not signed the agreement, and private organizations like the Japanese Aum Shinrikyo group is held responsible for the March 20, 1995 subway attack that killed 12 and injured thousands of passengers. Overall, the destruction of the world's known chemical weapons arsenals and the means to manufacture them has steadily reduced the risk. However, there are no guarantees that nations and persons with bad intentions are not manufacturing and storing the chemicals and acquiring the means to use them.

When I served on the Stockpile Committee, we were briefed about proactive efforts to offer financial and technical assistance to support destruction of chemical weapons outside the United States. The United States, the United Kingdom, Germany and several other North American and European nations have provided financial assistance.

TABLE 4.1 Major chemical warfare agents

Type of agent	Signs of health effects and health effects
Blistering (vesicant) H (mustard with impurities) HD (mustard) HN (nitrogen mustard) Lewisite	Initial symptoms are development of blisters in hours to a few days; eyes and lungs rapidly affected; vapors-related symptoms appear in 4 to 6 hours; skin effects in 2 to 48 hours
Blood AC (hydrogen cyanide) CK (cyanogen chloride) CN (sodium, potassium, calcium salts)	Immediate effects are rapid breathing, then convulsions, and coma; death at high dose
Nerve GA (tabun) GB (sarin) GD (soman) GF (cyclosarin) VX	This cholinesterase inhibitor causes breathing difficulty, convulsions, dimming of vision drooling, and sweating; at high concentrations it can cause death; vapor-related symptoms appear in seconds to minutes; skin effects at 2 to 18 hours
Respiratory agents Chlorine Phosgene	Initial symptoms include breathing difficulties, tearing of the eyes, damage to lungs causing suffocation and death; gas-related symptoms may appear immediately or be delayed for 3 or more hours

Notes: GA (tabun) = N,N-dimethyl phosphoroamidocyanidate; GB (sarin) = methylphosphonofluoridate isopropyl ester; GD = pinacolyl methyl phosphonofluoridate; H/HD (mustard) = Bis (2-chloroethyl) sulfide; HT (mustard) = Bis 2(2-chloroethylthio)ethyl ether; VX = S (diisopropylaminoethyl) methylphosphonothiolate o-ethyl ester.

Sources: Table modified from Greenberg 2003; U.S. Army Center 1999.

The United States

Background

The U.S. stockpile was primarily blistering agents and nerve agents (U.S. Army 1988; Munro et al. 1999; National Research Council 2001; U.S. Army 1999). The United States stopped building these weapons in 1968, and based on conversations I estimate the total U.S. stockpile was about 36,000–40,000 tons during the late 1960s. The U.S. unilaterally began destroying its stockpile under the cut holes and sink 'em program (CHASE) by sinking ships with chemical weapons in the Atlantic Ocean. I do not know how many tons were destroyed between 1967 and 1970. Using personal sources, I was able to estimate that it was probably between 4,000 and 6,000 tons.

Next, in 1986, Public Law 99-145 required the Army to destroy its aging chemical weapons. The U.S. government had multiple motivations. One of the most powerful was that the weapons were stored at United States military facilities and posed an increasing threat to U.S. troops and operations at those sites as they aged in storage sheds. The case study for this chapter, Anniston, Alabama, illustrates the Army's challenge.

After the CHASE program ended in 1970, the United States indicated that it had 31,500 metric tons of weapons stored at eight locations on the continental United States and at Johnston Island, an atoll about 600 miles (970 km) from Hawaii (Figure 4.2 and Table 4.2).

Taken at face value, the data in Table 4.2 can be misleading about risk for two reasons. These are old data and nearly all those weapons have since been destroyed. Second, the data imply that that Toole (Utah) was the most dangerous site because it had the most munitions by far. But before summarizing the multi-stage risk analyses conducted at these sites, I will briefly explain why more tonnage does not necessarily mean more risk. About 60 percent of the original chemical stockpile had been stored in large bulk containers (the kind of containers that are used to store propane and other chemicals). No explosive device or energy were part of the bulk storage. These chemicals were less hazardous than those in munitions, such as artillery projectiles, bombs, cartridges, land mines, mortar rounds, and spray tanks.

Chemicals with attached explosives and fuel are riskier. X-rays of a sample of these weapons showed that the chemical agent inside some of the weapons had decomposed into liquid, solid and gas. In addition, the surface between the gas and the fuel could be vulnerable to failure. The reaction of aging rounds to a disturbance was unpredictable. Also, because of manufacturing failures, a small

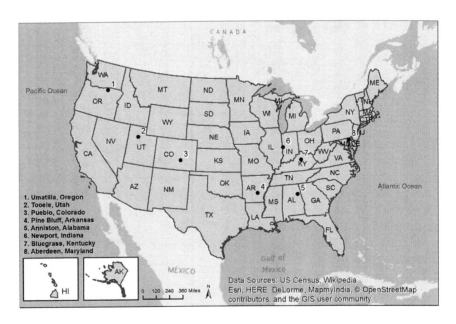

FIGURE 4.2 Location of continental U.S. chemical weapon storage sites

TABLE 4.2 Distribution of unitary chemical weapon stockpile, by storage location prior to the major demilitarization program and status in 2015

Site	Tons	Agent	Munition	Disposal method	Status
Tooele, Utah	13.6	H/HD/HT, GB, VX	C, P, TC, R, B, M, ST	Incineration	Completed
Pine Bluff, Ark	3.9	HT/HD, GB, VX	TC, R, M	Incineration	Completed
Umatilla, Ore	3.7	HD, GB, VX	TC, P, R, B, M, ST	Incineration	Completed
Pueblo, Colo	2.6	HT/HD	C, P	Hydrolysis/ biotreatment	Party completed by summer of 2016
Anniston, Ala	2.3	HT/HD, GB, VX	C, P, TC, R, M	Incineration	Completed
Johnston Atoll	2.0	HD, GB, VX	C, P, M, TC	Incineration	Completed
Aberdeen, Md	1.6	HD	TC	Hydrolysis	Completed
Newport, Ind	1.3	VX	TC	Hydrolysis	Completed
Blue Grass, Ky	0.5	HD, GB, VX	P, R	Hydrolysis/ supercritical water oxidation	In progress
Total	31.5	...	...	...	

Notes: See Table 4.1 for description of warfare agents. TC = ton containers; R = rockets; M = mines; ST = spray tanks; B = bombs; C = cartridges, mortars; P = projectiles.

Source: Updated and modified from Greenberg 2003.

portion leaked, and these "leakers" as they were not affectionately called, had to be stored in another container to prevent a serious leak. Furthermore, when the Army tried to remove the explosives, the front end was supposed to unscrew, but in some cases did not. A new device to remove the explosives had to be designed, and meanwhile these weapons had to be stored. A good deal of the aging chemical stockpile was stored in earth-covered bunkers. These so-called "igloos" could, under some conditions, be compromised. The age of these weapons made storage a major concern.

The number of people near the sites was another important risk-related factor. The vast majority of the weapons fortunately were stored in remote locations. Johnston Island, the first of the sites where the new incineration technology was used is about 800 miles from Hawaii (Figure 4.3), and only soldiers and contractors lived on the site. It truly is a remote site, albeit some residents of surrounding islands were extremely distressed at what they perceived as a deliberate racist effort to move chemical weapons from Europe, where the population is predominantly white to an island in the middle of the ocean where the population is non-white (Greenberg 2011).

Tooele, the site that had the largest number of weapons, has mostly farms and homes within 10 miles (16 km) of the site. The nearest population center is Salt Lake City, which is more than 50 miles away (Figure 4.2). Hence, Tooele was shown by the risk assessment not to be the riskiest location from the human health and safety perspectives. That distinction fell to Pine Bluff, Arkansas site, where people lived within a mile of the site in a small community that might have been difficult to evacuate under the worst air quality and transportation scenarios. In other words, population distribution and egress are key risk-related drivers (see below).

On one trip to the Pine Bluff site that I attended, prior to the destruction of the weapons, a resident of the Pine Bluff area became agitated about terrorism, and he called for an attack helicopter to constantly fly over the area. Pine Bluff and the other sites were surrounded by multiple fences topped with razor wire, and armed guards searched everyone entering the sites and patrolled it. The helicopter suggestion was rejected. The military did not disclose any other measures regarding security against air attacks to our committee. We did not need to know, and the Army did not offer to tell us.

At Pine Bluff, the probability of a release was low, but there was a concern because there was only one public road out of the area. The Army provided

FIGURE 4.3 Johnston Island, former chemical weapon storage site

communications and alternative air handling capacity for the population in a local school. The idea of relocating residents during the destruction period was summarily and aggressively rejected by a local elected official as unacceptable (Talbott 1996a, b). Throughout this multi-year process at this site and several others, conversations between outsiders like the author and his colleagues, and representatives of local communities were challenging because we were starting in such different places with regard to the technical issues and local policy concerns. These difficult exchanges between representatives of federal, state, and local organizations which went on for several hours illustrate why the sixth risk analysis question (see organization question Chapter 1) is so difficult to answer.

Risk also depends upon the fate and transport characteristics of the chemicals. The Army set stringent protocols to limit risk. Starting from the inside out, employees were not allowed to enter rooms with chemical agents unless they were in pairs, and they entered in sealed impervious suits. Their shifts were strictly limited because the suits were stressful to work in and dehydration was a risk. Before workers were permitted to enter a chemical weapons storage shed, the air quality inside had to be measured, and a specially designed truck for treating exposed workers stood ready outside the shed.

The author heard of cases where workers were fired for violating worker procedures. I personally observed one, a civilian contractor was discharged because he could not find his gas mask and borrowed another worker's mask. In the case of outsiders, such as the author, facial hair was not permitted (concern about the seal on the gas mask). We were required to be able to fit a gas mask, and we had to run in place for ten minutes, after which our blood pressure was taken.

With regard to the facilities themselves, they were built with a design that we normally associate with submarines, that is, rooms with separate air handling systems. The facilities had indoor and outdoor air quality and stack exhaust monitoring, had liquid decontamination solutions on hand, and proactive management of equipment was expected (National Research Council 2001; U.S Army 1999). The level of risk management expected at these nine sites was expensive, much more expensive than had been anticipated. In 1985, the estimated cost of destroying the stockpile was $1.7 billion (Lambright et al. 1998). The costs have grown and estimates range from $30 to $40 billion (Shepherd 2013; Lewis 2013). The destruction of the U.S. chemical weapons stockpile has been an expensive investment to protect worker and public health, and the U.S. Army's credibility.

The United States' risk management decisions were affected by international relations. As noted above, the United States had been skeptical of arms treaties involving chemicals, and it did not immediately sign on to all the Chemical Weapons Convention requirements, which went into place in 1997. Some high ranking members of the U.S. Congress argued that some nations would sign and violate the treaty and others would not sign it. Yet, U.S. Presidents were also operating under the so-called "overwhelming and devastating" nuclear response to a nuclear or chemical weapon attack (Conley 2001), which implied that a chemical weapon stockpile was no longer necessary.

The Chemical Weapons Convention required inspection. Congress paid to have some older barracks upgraded for visits and demonstrations. Industrial espionage during inspections in the United States was a concern (Committee on Foreign Relations 1996; General Assembly 1992; Rotunda 1998; Yoo 1998). In my opinion, the United States was primarily focused on protecting our own troops from these weapons and about its relationships with the Soviet Union. The United States and the Soviet Union signed a treaty in 1990 that required 80 percent of their stockpiles to be destroyed, as well as production of chemical weapons to cease. This agreement, I believe was very important to President Reagan and President George H.W. Bush as part of their strategy to reduce chemical and nuclear weapons and to work constructively with Mikhail Gorbachev (Gorbachev 2000). In short, before any formal serious risk assessment studies were conducted, the United States government already had made risk management decisions to destroy the weapons.

Risk assessment and risk management of the U.S. chemical weapon stockpile

The U.S. government not only mandated that the weapons be destroyed but that there be considerable oversight by parties, including the following:

- National Research Council;
- Centers for Disease Control and Prevention (CDC);
- Environmental Protection Agency (EPA);
- U.S. Department of Health and Human Services;
- Council on Environmental Quality;
- Occupational Safety and Health Administration;
- Office of the Secretary of the Defense; and
- State and local government agencies.

Citizen advisory commissions were organized to bring local and state concerns to the table. The governor of each of the host states appointed one group of representatives and the NRC appointed the Stockpile Committee (National Research Council 2000a). This oversight and especially public meetings attracted large crowds and community residents expressed strong feelings and opinions. The issue of trust in government authority, including the Army, the governor of the state, and the Academy of Sciences was called into question on multiple occasions. Below I will illustrate this statement with the Anniston, Alabama case.

In 1987, within a year of being ordered by Congress to begin to destroy the weapons, the Mitre Corporation conducted a risk assessment about the Army's first major decision: where to destroy the weapons (U.S. Army 1988; Mitre 1987). Mitre was called upon to make quantitative comparisons of accidental chemical-related risks associated with a single national site, several regional sites, and on-site disposal. The risk assessment was simplified to focus only on transportation by assuming the same weapons disassembly process would be used at every site and that incineration would be used to burn the chemicals. Another simplification is that Mitre focused on health risk to the public outside the site, not on workers. In other words, residents near the site and along transportation routes were the focus. Third, only accidents that could cause lethal concentrations to be released were to be considered. Last, and certainly, not least, chronic effects of low-level long-term exposure to storage and incineration were not included in this initial risk assessment.

This section does not present details of the methods used in that analysis, however, they will be familiar to many practitioners and are similar to those presented as part of the Anniston study. Mitre's national study examined five options:

1. *On-site disposal.* The stockpile would be incinerated at current locations. The risk was handling the chemicals on–site, moving them from the sheds or other storage locations to the incinerator and destroying them in a facility.
2. *Two regional disposal sites.* All the weapons would be shipped by rail to Anniston (AL) or Tooele (UT). Compared to the on–site option, the risk related to transportation would be higher but local risks associated with incinerator would not exist at most of the sites.
3. *Several relocations.* The stockpiles at Aberdeen Proving Ground (MD) and Lexington-Blue Grass Army Depot (KY) are relatively small. Hence, this option would move both of these stockpiles by air to Tooele (UT).
4. *National disposal.* All the chemical weapons in the United States (not including Johnston Island) would be moved to Tooele (UT).
5. *No-action alternative.* Every environmental impact statement (EIS) must have a no-action alternative. This one would continue to store the chemical rounds for at least 25 years.

Earlier, I noted that Mitre studied acute human health effects. Seven metrics were specified:

*   Maximum individual risk;
*   Maximum lethal plume distance, or minimum distance of an individual from a given site or transportation corridor with no risk of lethal exposure;
*   Maximum total time at risk for an individual;
*   Probability of one or more fatalities;
*   Maximum number of fatalities;
*   Expected fatalities; and
*   Total person-years at risk and expected plume area.

This first risk analysis strongly supported on-site disposal. For example, with mitigation measures in place, on–site disposal had the lowest likelihood of causing one or more fatalities, and the four other options described above were five to 11 times more likely to experience one or more fatalities. Movement of weapons meant greater likelihood of airplane and rail accidents in areas with relatively dense populations. Indeed, in regard to total number of fatalities, the comparative risks associated with moving long distance were 10 to 30 times higher. Looking at on-site storage and on-site destruction, 25 year storage was by far the worst choice because of the unlikely but possible catastrophic events that could discharge a large lethal dose while the chemicals were in sheds. Given these results, it is not surprising that the Army and the Congress chose on-site disposal.

This set of risk assessments, albeit limited in scope, were valuable because they focused on basic issues of risk trade-offs between on-site destruction and shipment before destruction.

Anniston Alabama, risk assessment and risk management under duress

Background

I chose Anniston as the case study for this section of the chapter, despite the fact that risk assessment showed Pine Bluff to have a higher risk profile because I found risk management more challenging in Anniston, by far. Groups at the Anniston site were organized, highly motivated and worked hard to present points that they considered to be critical to the Army and others that might influence the decision.

Now that the weapons have been destroyed, I am able to say that my perception was that there was a major gap in trust between some residents of the Anniston region and the United States government, including the U.S. Army and the Federal Emergency Management Agency (FEMA), and this lack of trust extended to the Stockpile committee, including this author. At every site, I observed and read records (the Army clipped and provided local media stories to our committee) that showed public concern with the Army's disposal program. At Anniston, I found the levels of concern and distrust were the highest across the sites. In order to explain this perception, I will briefly summarize the regional context.

The Anniston chemical weapon stockpile is in Calhoun County, Alabama, and the City of Anniston is the main urban center and the county seat. With a population of 22,000, the City of Anniston lies at the southern tip of Appalachian mountain chain (Figure 4.4). Anniston's population is split almost evenly between Caucasians and African Americans. Alabama as a whole ranks forty-second in per capita income, and Calhoun County and Anniston are in the top third in income in Alabama (U.S. Bureau of the Census 2014). In other words, the site is in a relatively affluent part of a relatively poor state.

Anniston itself has a cultural heritage and sections of the city have lovely well maintained Victorian-style homes and beautiful religious-affiliated structures representing multiple denominations, including Christian and Jewish. Anniston's sense of self was partly defined by the presence of the *Anniston Star* a local newspaper. Unlike many small newspapers in the twenty-first-century United States, this local newspaper was seriously invested in the community and had a strong, smart and experienced editor and reporters. The editor-in-chief, for

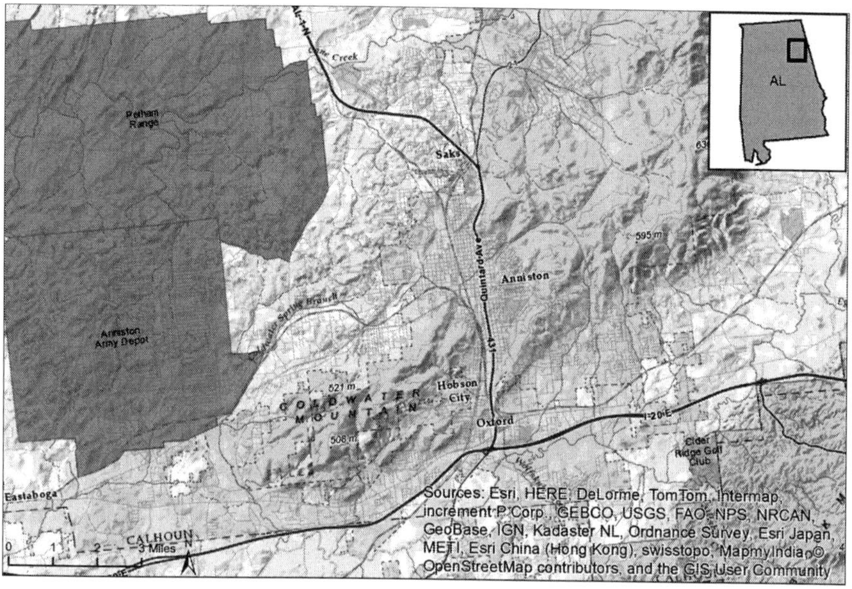

FIGURE 4.4 Anniston Alabama area

example, requested dinner with members of the Stockpile Committee, during which he asked some excellent and pointed questions of Committee members. Based on his questions, the newspaper had done its homework about the issues and the Committee members. Local radio and television stations were present at meetings and seemed to me to be interested in what a group of scientists and engineers from outside the area had to say. That is, they did not, I believe, come with preconceived ideas about what we would say, nor dismiss the Committee because we did not live in the area. Other sites the author visited had reporters at meetings, but not all of them, and they appeared to me to be much less prepared than Anniston's.

Before visiting sites, I would check the newspapers to determine if there were any issues in the area that might confound the Army's stockpile destruction. There was an important one at Anniston. In 2002, the television show *60 Minutes* (WCBS 2002) had classified this small city as one of the most toxic United States cities. Solutia Inc.'s plant located about a mile from downtown produced polychlorinated biphenyls (PCBs) for decades, and even though that site had not been made a Superfund site under CERCLA, individuals at the public meeting about the chemical weapons depot were angry at the Company for causing the problem. That anger, I perceived, carried over to the federal EPA, the regional EPA office (located in Atlanta), and the state environmental protection agency. The public was angry because they believed that government agencies had not taken control of the situation and were allowing residents to potentially be exposed.

Frankly, some of the public remarks at public meetings were ugly. One particularly distressed woman with her baby in hand stood up and asserted that she had trusted the company, EPA, and the state, and now she would not trust the Army, even if it had nothing to do with the PCB contamination. In fact, this was one of the more gentle slaps taken at the Army, the Committee, and other outside parties. Several of the exchanges that were aimed directly at the Army are described below. They illustrate a priming effect that seriously hampered the Army's decision to use incineration. Whether risk managers wanted to acknowledge public priming effects or not, they existed and impacted risk management.

Fort McClellan was a second priming effect. The War Department established Camp McClellan 1917 (named after a former general and former governor of New Jersey) to respond to World War I, which it did by sending over 20,000 troops to the European theater. After World War I ended, the camp remained open, grew in size and was designated Fort McClellan and added an airfield, hospital, storage bunkers, and infrastructure for 50,000 persons, as well as new missions, including a prisoner of war camp, National Guard training, a military police school, and a Chemical Corps training.

During the 1950s, the Army used the Anniston site to test decontamination methods, a point which distressed many residents when they found out, which led to the call for a registry to monitor the health of troops exposed at Fort McClellan. Part of the site is being reused for residential, commercial, industrial, retail, education, research, and technology developments. Another part became the Mountain Longleaf National Wildlife Refuge. Many of these activities and others I have not listed were ended by the BRAC recommendation to close the site, which residents had not forgotten when the Army was planning to destroy its stockpile. Losing the base was not welcomed, nor was the history of testing chemicals.

The focus of the stockpile destruction activity was the Anniston Army Depot (ANAD), which is a major Army facility. The Depot produces and repairs combat vehicles, repairs and upgrades small arms weapons technology, and had about 7 percent of the national chemical weapon stockpile. The ANAD section maintains the M1 Abrams Tank and other critical heavy-tracked combat vehicles. The author watched vehicles being upgraded and remanufactured. The depot also repairs, restores and upgrades infantry pistols, rifles, and machine guns. The Army has employed over 5,000 people, an important economic benefit to a stressed region. There was a great deal of history, good and bad as far as vocal members of the public were concerned, that primed public perception in regard to the destruction of the chemical weapon stockpile. With this context, the remainder of the section reviews the Anniston risk assessment.

Risk assessment methods

The methods used for the Anniston chemical weapons risk assessment are standard for risk assessors, and the same design was used for all eight continental United

States chemical weapons sites. A few changes were made from the national analysis that was briefly described above.

The sequences of events stemming from each initiator and leading to agent release were identified and modeled. This involves an evaluation of systems, operations, and physical phenomena. The analysts identified events that could cause serious consequences for the stockpile. For example, I visited a storage shed "called igloo" and was briefed that the Army had been removing the detonators on artillery rounds. That makes sense, but it does require moving a munition, which we did not think was a good idea. The analysts worked on this option. Other event initiators in the risk assessment were human failure, equipment failures, and depending upon the site tornadoes, earthquakes, lightning and even airplane crashes.

Before reviewing what SAIC's approach in the first set of site-specific risk assessments (SAICa, b), I note that other deterministic analyses and probabilistic risk assessments were also completed. The risk assessment described below was followed by one that drilled deeper into unresolved options and these follow-ups allowed for the use of probabilistic methods. In other words, the Phase I risk assessment, which is illustrated below, is followed by a Phase 2 assessment, which also includes worker risk and more explicit acknowledgment and analyses of uncertainty. As part of the permit to operate the incinerator, health risk analyses were conducted (Alabama Department of Environmental Management 2007).

The list of internal events (e.g., human failure) or external event (e.g., tornado) was lengthy. For internal events, analysts would examine diagrams of the engineered systems and the operations or equipment looking for failures that could upset the processing, for example, a munition to fall. Drop of a munition could lead to no agent release, a spill or leak, or even to an explosion of a single round or trigger a major cascade of explosions.

The analysts tested single event and combinations that could cause a serious release. As they worked through these events, they noted measures to prevent the event or to lessen the consequences if it occurred. For example, a simple solution for forklifts was to set stringent requirements on how munitions were to be handled to prevent a fall. The SAIC group used tree diagrams to identify serious events. Figure 4.5 is one for dropping a munition from a forklift. This is a simple event. There could be a combination of a dropped munition and a munition dented by a forklift.

Using the tree diagrams, analysts reviewed the literature and/or collected data to estimate the probability of the events. In some cases, there were data, in other cases, there were not. Some sequences of events were so consequential that the chain of events were followed back from failure to find at what place a risk management step can prevent it, such as the mandating how forklifts would handle munitions. Analysts examined weather, earthquake and human reliability data sets. They used mechanistic analyses and blended these with expert judgments.

Assuming the event occurs, the objective is to estimate the probabilistic distribution of the spread of agent in regard to magnitude and concentration of the

(Begins with a munition in a shed holding several thousands rounds)

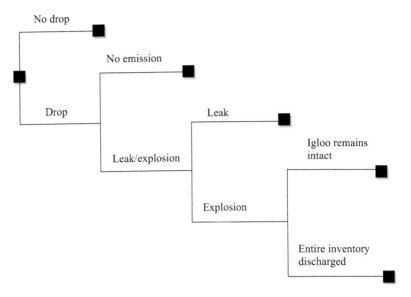

FIGURE 4.5 Accident progression for a forklift drop of a munition in an igloo

agent and direction of its movement (see Chapter 6 for an illustration of chlorine). This requires information about the following six variables:

1. Type(s) of agent released;
2. Quantity of each type;
3. Physical state of the released agents (vapor or liquid aerosol);
4. Rate, timing, and duration of the release;
5. Elevation of the release; and
6. Time of day at which the release is possible.

The SAIC analysts used a dispersion model calibrated for chemical agents to estimate a probabilistic distribution of exposures that could lead to acute deaths and excess cancers. All of the SAIC risk assessments for the chemical weapons sites followed the same processes and expressed the results in the same format. They presented the numeric results as the product of the frequency of an accident (expected number of times the accident would occur in a set of repeated trials of the chemical destruction process) and the severity of the consequences (e.g., how many fatalities could be expected). The risk was presented as acute public fatalities over the life of the destruction of the stockpile (typically about four years) compared to continued storage (assumed 20 years). The Army used 100 kilometers as the maximum credible distance from the facility storage yard to estimate population at risk, a conservative estimate.

Table 4.3 summarizes the probability of at least one death over the time period and Figure 4.6 is a diagram of the risk assessment process.

These risk estimates are low, and hence some stakeholders suggested that it was safer to leave the weapons in place until "safer" methods of destruction could be developed. However, the Army was not going to make that decision, especially for the riskier configuration weapons, that is, those not in bulk storage containers. One reason is international treaties required destruction. Furthermore, one death for 39 years of storage at Anniston seems extremely low. But in fact, the most feared risk at this and almost all the others sites is a major natural hazard event that could vent the entire stockpile and kill and injure many people. The U.S. government would be in untenable ethical and legal positions if the very improbable occurred and many civilians as well as its soldiers were the victims.

Behind these analyses were several key risk management drivers. One was that storage is the major concern because of natural hazard events that could cause an entire igloo of weapons to be ignited. Lightning in particular was a major concern (estimated 62 percent of risk at Anniston by SAIC 1997a). The Army was concerned that electromagnetic fields could be created in igloos struck by lightning, even with lightning protection equipment, and that the M55 rockets were particularly vulnerable to ignition from electromagnetic fields. To respond to this low risk, but one with potentially very serious consequences for the U.S. government, no processing was permitted as lightning approached and when winds reached a specified level. Furthermore, the base commander would be apprised of the expected weather every day and that information along with the work for the day would be sent to the nearest local government in order to keep the most vulnerable communities apprised.

TABLE 4.3 Comparison of likelihood of at least one acute death at the continental U.S. stockpile sites

Site	Twenty years of continued stockpile storage with no destruction of the stockpile	Stockpile storage during destruction of weapons	Destruction of weapons
Anniston	1 in 100 (or 1 death in 39 years)	1 in 1,890 over 3.8 years	1 in 435,000 (or 1 death 56,700 years), or 2.3×10^{-6} for the disposal process over 3.8 years
Blue Grass	1 in 64	1 in 1,400 over 2 years	1 in 83,000 over 2 years
Pine Bluff	1 in 33	1 in 500 over 3 years	1 in 20,000 over 3 years
Pueblo	1 in 1 million	1 in 10 million over 2.4 years	1 in 1 billion over 2.4 years
Tooele	1 in 220	1 in 9,600 over 7.1 years of processing	1 in 100,000 over 7.1 years of processing
Umatilla	1 in 400	1 in 6,000 over 3 years	1 in 300,000 over 3 years

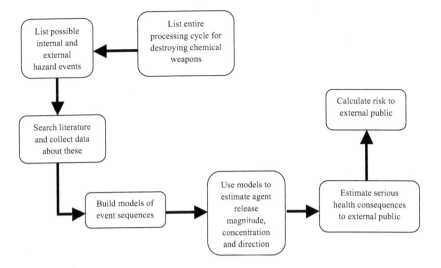

FIGURE 4.6 Quantitative risk assessment process for chemical hazards: initial site risk assessment

At several stockpile sites, there was concern about earthquakes and other natural hazards. In the case of earthquakes, the concern was that munitions might fall from their stacks and leak or explode, which could detonate others in the igloos. There was also the possibility of earthquake-related fires.

The risk management process started with the munitions that were most dangerous and systematically proceeded to lower risk ones. The first campaign targeted rockets with GB because these were by far the most dangerous munitions at Anniston. Next the VX rockets were destroyed, and then the GB rounds were incinerated. By the end of the third year, the site was left with VX mines to eliminate. After each campaign, the storage risk was notably reduced, especially when the GB rockets were incinerated.

In regard to on-site processing at Anniston, the major concern was handling of rockets when they were removed from igloos (about 74 percent of the risk). The Army had an extremely strict risk management protocol for handling ordinance in igloos, moving it outside and loading it into massive on-site containers (ONC) and then onto a specially built truck. The ONCs are 142 inches long and 102 inches high, constructed of layers of stainless steel, polyurethane foam, and they contain ceramic fiber insulation blankets. The ONCs can carry two pallets of m-55 rockets, and various other amounts of ordinance. Trucks with ONCs made more than 20,000 trips from storage sheds to destruction facilities. To prevent possible problems transportation was not permitted in the dark. Once the truck arrived at the processing facility, the pallets were loaded from the ONC on the truck onto a conveyor belt that would carry them through the facility for processing.

The author observed scores of engineering innovations responding to the original risk assessments for Johnston Island and then the Tooele site (U.S. Army 1990a, b). Nearly all of these were incorporated into the risk management designs when newer plants were built. For example, it was determined that someone could accidentally send a rocket or mine to the dunnage incinerator (DUN) that treats secondary process wastes from the incinerator destruction. That recognition resulted in a design to prevent the entrance of these to a DUN.

As noted earlier and repeated for emphasis, the focus in this chapter is on the interaction between risk assessment and risk management about acute risk events caused by equipment failure, human error or natural events. I do not discuss terrorism or ecological impacts, which were considered later in the process.

Public reactions and risk management

The Army's Anniston plan to use incineration to destroy chemical weapons was controversial. Earlier I noted that the closing of Fort McClellan and the PCB problem associated with the Monsanto facility contributed to concern about the Army program. The Army's program was also burdened with trust issues. Trust is divided into competence, communications and values (Greenberg 2014). At Anniston my experiences were that the Army's trust-related problems were not related to competence, but were related to communications problems and the feeling of some people that the Army did not share their values, as several examples will demonstrate.

Everyone has experienced waiting for someone who has set up a meeting and then does not come. An Army officer in charge of a major part of the Anniston program did not attend a public meeting, and residents were angry (Pezzullo 1997a). The reader may think that failure to attend a meeting or being late to a meeting are not important, but it was to people who felt like they were being treated as unimportant.

A major concern of the local public was a rumor that the Army was going to destroy the stockpile chemical weapons and then use the incinerators to destroy non-stockpile munitions. This military officer had been instructed not to come to the meeting in order to prepare a plan to destroy non-stockpile ordinance (Pezzullo 1997a, b). When the Committee came to hear the public's concerns about stockpile disposal, the potential incineration of non-stockpile weapons undermined the Army's plan. While the Stockpile committee tried to persuade the Anniston region population to trust the Army's program, that is, the part we were focusing on, the large audience questioned the communications and values of the Army and its representatives. Rather than agree to the program to incinerate, individuals who attended the meetings questioned everything about the program, including technical competence. Over many years of experience, I have learned that when the public does not trust the communications and values, they lose trust in the science.

At Anniston, they asserted that the Army should take economic impact into account and presented evidence to argue that their property values would decline when an incinerator was used. Indeed, they appealed to the Stockpile committee for suggestions on how to prevent the Army from using incineration, from accepting non-stockpile materials, and asked this author to provide them with references about the economic impact of incinerators on property values. Despite the Committee's efforts to explain that the then $575 million incinerator was built for specific types of waste, many members of the audience did not accept incineration or trust the incineration program not to bring non-stockpile chemicals to the site for incineration (Pezzullo 1997b).

Also, people at the meetings accused the Army of testing a variety of chemical agents, including hallucinating agents like BZ (3-Quinuclidinyl benzilate) at the Anniston site and then burning these agents in the open air. While no evidence was produced at the meeting, the impact on the audience was to further undermine trust (Chisholm, Chisholm, Kilpatrick 2013).

As part of their mistrust, the audience aggressively criticized the composition of the NRC Stockpile Committee and the community committee appointed by the Governor of Alabama to represent the Anniston area. The Stockpile committee was criticized for lacking younger female and Afro-American scientists and engineers. The local community committee was criticized for not representing the racial, age, or gender groups in the Anniston area. One person sitting in the audience was the chief engineer in charge of building the facility. When he represented himself as a member of the community, the audience identified him as an outsider and shouted at him that he already had too much influence, and would leave the area when the project was completed. Several people insisted that building the incinerator would lower property values, and they produced a local survey that suggested that would be the outcome. At one of the meetings, the anger was so blatant that the local chair suggested suspending the proceedings. In an effort to restore civil dialogue, a local member of the public and this author spoke to public about what they were hearing from the public and what their respective roles were in addressing some of the concerns in the future.

The ability of authorities to evacuate should there be an accident was also questioned. The Federal Emergency Management Agency (FEMA), not the Army, was responsible for emergency planning, and I would characterize their efforts to work with some state and local government officials as difficult. The U.S. General Accounting Office (GAO) reported that the site was not prepared to respond, that two-thirds of the money already allocated had not even been spent, and that the Army, FEMA, and the state and local governments were in disagreement regarding fund amounts and allocation (U.S. General Accounting Office 1996). These issues were not immediately solved (U.S. General Accounting Office 1997, 2001). Community members were aware of these issues, and used this to argue that no further progress should be made on the incineration facility until this problem was fixed. Their anger boiled over at one of the meetings, and markedly compromised the Army's plans in the short run. Frankly, while the Army had a good technical plan, their plan to deal with value and communication elements of trust was inadequate.

Given the Anniston and several other similar experiences, members of the Stockpile committee (Committee on Review 2000) organized a subgroup to review the Army's community involvement efforts, which led to suggestions to upgrade the effectiveness of the Army's efforts. Several of these are paraphrased below:

• A clearly stated mission and vision and a strong commitment from senior management;
• A clear strategy, with metrics, funds, personnel, and strategic thinking about even routine activities;
• A lessons learned program connecting all the sites; and
• A capability to anticipate serious problems and the ability to address them.

Had these four suggestions been implemented a decade earlier, I believe that the Army's program across the eight sites would have been completed earlier. Nevertheless, on September 22, 2011, the Army announced that the last of the munitions at Anniston were destroyed (661,000 nerve and mustard agent munitions and 2,200 tons of chemical agent) (U.S. Army 2011). Munition storage began in 1963 and destruction in 2003. The Army summary contained the following quote from a local community official: "Today, we can pause with confidence, take a deep breath and know we no longer have to worry about chemical weapons" (U.S. Army 2011, p. 1).

Non-incineration technologies: risk management challenges

The Anniston and other initial risk assessments assumed that the Army would use incineration. However, other methods were never explicitly ruled out. The Army's plan was to build incinerators for liquid agents and burn the stockpile at temperatures exceeding 2,000 °F (1,093 °C). But incineration is one of the last steps. Liquid agent in bombs, mortars, artillery shells and other weaponized forms had to be safely moved from the storage shed, carried in pallets and placed in an ONC, then placed onto a truck for delivery to the destruction facility. Once reaching the incinerator, the ONCs were unloaded onto a conveyor belt, and then moved into rooms for unloading and preliminary processing. The first set of steps for shells were unscrewing the front end of the munition to remove the explosive, then holes were made in the energy pack to drain the energetics and in the main body of weapon to drain the chemicals, which in some cases had partly solidified. As noted earlier, these steps do not always work and some weapons were set aside for later processing. The liquid agent is directed to the liquid incinerator. The weapon parts went on conveyor belts and into a metal furnace where they were melted at close to 1,500 °F (816 °C) to make sure that any residual toxic material was destroyed. This process was first built and used at Johnston Island to destroy all the weapons on that atoll and was part of the plan for the other incineration sites. Each proposed risk management option was preceded by a risk assessment.

Neutralization

Neutralization was an alternative proposed for chemicals stored in large bulk storage containers (Committee of Review and Evaluation 1995; National Research Council 1998; U.S. Army 1995; Chemical Materials Agency 2010). Without an explosive device or energetics, and the need to remove them, neutralization was chosen for Edgewood and Newport (Figure 4.2), where the volume of munitions is small and in bulk containers. What was at issue was that the process needed a chamber that could manage highly corrosive and erosive materials, and while the overseers were convinced that the process would work, the only metal container that was found suitable for the reactor was made of platinum! The industrial wastewater produced by the process, known as hydrolysate, was sent to a permitted commercial hazardous waste storage, treatment and disposal facility for treatment and disposal.

Neutralization was the selected method for the facilities in Pueblo, Colorado, and Richmond, Kentucky. The problem at these sites is that the technology was not proven and before it could be used it had to be evaluated, which meant that the United States would not be able to complete destruction until after 2020, which is related to its treaty obligations.

Why was there such adamant opposition to the use of incineration at several sites? The decision to use alternative technologies means more storage time and more risk. In the case of two sites where the weapons were in bulk containers, the added risk is very small. But at Pueblo and Richmond, the small risk would have been eliminated by the time this chapter was written had the community trusted the Army to find another approach.

Part of the explanation, I believe, is the word "incinerator." My parents lived in New York City. Their building had an old incinerator and a nearby municipal incinerator. Those incinerators meant fly ash that can only be controlled by not opening windows or by placing a fine meshed screen in the window. My grandmother's preferred term for incinerators was something that produced "schmutz" (Yiddish word for dirt) and provoked some people to find a new residence. Modern municipal incinerators are nothing like those of 65 years ago, but the reputation lingers (Luloff et al., 1998; McAvoy 1998; Smith, Marquez 2000). The author has observed the same anti-incinerator perceptions appear in various locations (Greenberg 1999). Thermal destruction units might be a better choice, which would include all the other methods used by the Army to destroy the chemical weapons at high temperatures.

The Army faced major pressure for government and industry to choose technologies that some members of the public and some interest groups considered smaller scale and overall more friendly to the environment than incinerators (Berry 1999; Norberg-Bohm 1999; Schwepker, Cornwell 1991). However, in reality as we said to several audiences, none of these technologies was risk free and all required some form of thermal destruction.

Independently of the author's anecdotal observations, the Army conducted surveys at the eight continental U.S. sites. These surveys support the observations made at the public meetings. Williams *et al.* (2003) conducted phone surveys of 2600 residents living in officially designated emergency response zones near the eight continental U.S. sites, including 629 samples from the Anniston area. The study showed that those who favored incineration disproportionately had the following attributes (all statistically significant at p<.05):

- Trusted the Army;
- Aware of Army's chemical weapons program;
- Perceived that the site was negatively impacting the community;
- Were male; and
- Had higher income.

Pro-incineration respondents disproportionately had the following perceptions of incineration:

- Cost-effective;
- Economically beneficial;
- Best disposal method;
- Better than storage;
- Favored by the community as a whole;
- Process used at other sites;
- Fastest disposal method; and
- Understandable method.

In contrast, those that favored neutralization were likely to be:

- Women;
- College-educated;
- Relatively young;
- Ready to participate in decision-making about the issue; and
- Influenced by media attention to the subject in their area.

Notably, these surveys showed that those who lived in Anniston, Tooele, and other locations with an operating or nearly completed incinerator, such as Anniston, disproportionately favored that approach. But those in Blue Grass, Aberdeen and several others have been reading and hearing about other options tended to favor those alternative technologies.

The Chemical Weapons Working Group, in particular, was vociferous in its opposition to incineration. Marshall (1996) wrote a historical and sociological paper that charged the Army with environmental injustice for using incineration. Located at Jacksonville State University and north of the Anniston Depot, the history professor asserted that the Army built facilities and provided jobs at these locations, and, in essence, did what it chose to do on the sites. She continued that local officials did not fight back because of the economic consequences of opposing the military. Marshall presented summary evidence of the disproportionate number of poor and African American or Native American people living in the vicinity of these chemical stockpile sites. I have heard these same arguments at public meetings at some other chemical weapons stockpile sites. The conclusion of Marshall's paper was that the Army should stop incineration at Johnston Atoll, Tooele, and not start it at any other site. She proposed alternative technologies that are non–combustion, closed-loop, produce no or only low levels of emissions and other steps built around President Clinton's environmental justice executive order 12894.

It would be an understatement to say that a shift from one technology to another as proposed by the Chemical Weapons Working Group in Marshall's paper was a challenge for the U.S. Army. Table 4.4 lists the laws that the stockpile destruction program was subject to. Had the Army been required to go back to other technologies at all the sites, the United States would not now have destroyed nearly all of the weapons, and it would have been compromised the health and safety of the residents and facility workers.

TABLE 4.4 List of Federal Acts requiring compliance

Archeological and Historic Preservation Act
Clean Air Act
Clean Water Act
CERCLA (Super Fund)
Coastal Zone Management Act
Endangered Species Act
Estuaries Protection Act
Federal Water Project Recreation Act
Federal Wildlife Refuge System Administration Act
Fish and Wildlife Coordination Act.
Hazardous Materials Transportation Act
Land and Water Conservation Act
Marine Mammal Protection Act
Marine Protection, Research and Sanctuaries Act (including the Ocean Dumping Ban Act of 1988)
Migratory Bird Treaty Act
National Environmental Policy Act
National Historic Preservation Act
Resource Conservation and Recovery Act
Rivers and Harbors Act
Toxic Substances Control Act
Watershed Protection and Flood Prevention Act
Wild and Scenic Rivets Act
Presidential Executive Order 11990 (1977)
Protection of Wetlands
Presidential Executive Order 12088 (1978)

Congressional intervention, public involvement, and alternative technologies

The problem with "friendlier" technologies is that some are not so friendly to workers, community health and legal agreements. In order to respond to building pressure for not using incineration as the choice of record, Public Law 102-483 (October 23, 1992) mandated that the Secretary of the Army establish a citizens' commission for each state with a low volume of chemical wastes. One of the most interesting provisions was that each state commission should have nine members appointed by the governor of that state, with the constraint that seven of the nine should be from the local affected areas and the other two should be representative of the state government with direct responsibility related to chemical weapon destruction.

A Committee on Alternative Chemical Demilitarization Technologies of the National Research Council was appointed to evaluate and compare the baseline demilitarization program (incineration) with alternatives focusing on safety, environmental protection, and cost-effectiveness. The so-called "Alternatives" committee evaluated about two dozen alternative technologies. I did not serve on that committee, however I read their work and spoke with several colleagues that did. My assessment is that several of the proposals imposed considerably greater human health risk than incineration. Others could be made to work, but would require careful investigation. The Stockpile Committee confirmed its support of the safety and effectiveness of incineration-grounded technology, and it recommended that the Army focus on four neutralization-related technologies. One of these was stand-alone neutralization, which means hydrolysis of chemical agents to less toxic wastes, followed by burning the neutralization products in an incinerator. A second was neutralization followed by supercritical water oxidation; a third was neutralization followed by wet air oxidation and subsequent biotreatment; and the fourth was neutralization followed by biodegradation.

Human health and safety risk was the primary concern, although not the only concern of Congress, the Army, state and local officials, and those who pushed for alternative technologies. Consequently the Army drafted criteria for assessing alternative technologies. The Army created ten broad assessment criteria categories, which they divided into 55 evaluation factors and then further subdivided into 169 specific assessment criteria. The latter were expressed as questions. In other words, the Army developed a checklist tool. I have listed several illustrations from the Army report in Table 4.5. These questions illustrate the breadth of concerns, including legal, human health and safety, and public acceptance.

The Stockpile Committee was charged with evaluating the Army criteria, which we did by examining the criteria and by soliciting written input from the Army, environmental organizations, state regulators, community groups and interested individuals.

This preliminary review using the checklist, however, only takes the risk management process to the pilot testing scale. Consequently, the Stockpile Committee of Review (1995) suggested four important steps:

TABLE 4.5 Illustrative probes from the U.S. army assessment criteria to aid in selection of alternative technologies

Evaluation factor	Assessment criteria
3.1 Public law	
3.1.1 Significantly safer	Is the alternative technology significantly safer than the baseline technology?
3.1.2 Equally or more cost-effective	Is the alternative technology equally or more cost-effective than the baseline process?
3.1.3 Meets the schedule for complete stockpile destruction	Does the alternative technology meet the schedule for completion of stockpile destruction?
3.2 Regulatory legal	
3.2.1 International Agreements	Does this technology achieve irreversible destruction?
	Does this technology enable inspectors to sample and analyze any part of an item in the storage and destruction facility?
	Can the technology achieve the destruction level specified by the treaty?
...	.....
3.4 Worker safety	
3.4.1 Agent release outside of engineering controls	What is the probability of stockpile release over the duration of the disposal program?
	What is the expected rate of stockpile handling errors based on the process demands?
	What is the probability of facility release due to external events over the duration of the disposal program?
	What is the probability of process upsets due to equipment failure over the duration of disposal program? Which if unmitigated have the potential for agent release?
	What is the probability of process upsets due to human error over the duration of the disposal program? Which if unmitigated have the potential for agent release?
	What is the probability of agent release outside engineering controls given that a process upset has occurred?
	What evaluation operations indicated the use of local exhaust ventilation (LEV)?
	What local exhaust ventilation is best suited to contain exposure to Chemical Surety Material (CSM), non-CSM?

TABLE 4.5 continued

Evaluation factor	Assessment criteria
	What heating, ventilation and air-conditioning system is best suited for these operations?
	Do the LEVs and HVAC control exposure in accordance with federal and Department of the Army regulations and guidelines?
3.5 Public acceptance	
3.5.2 Public perception of risk	How difficult is it to communicate the magnitude of the public risk from the technology?
	What is the perceived level of public risk from the technology?

Source: U.S. Army Chemical Demilitarization and Remediation Activity. (1995) Assessment Criteria to Aid in Selection of Alternative Technologies for Chemical Demilitarization. Department of the Army, Alternative Technology Branch. Aberdeen Providing Ground, MD, April 26.

- Laboratory-scale research to narrow down the most promising combination of technologies;
- Bench-scale tests (20 to 30 gallon reactors) for preliminary evaluation and for generating data for large-scale facility;
- Analyses to identify the products of these neutralization and biodegradation technologies, which is needed to obtain regulatory approval; and
- Design a pilot plant (500–20,000 gallon reactors) to demonstrate the best available technology choices.

In evaluating each of the four technologies, the Stockpile Committee of Review (1995) focused on four critical factors:

- Process efficacy, for example, detoxification of the chemical agent; meeting treaty requirements; meeting environmental and other regulatory requirements; management of process residuals; process stability, reliability, and robustness; process monitoring; natural resource requirements; scale up requirements; and applicability to other wastes.
- Process Safety: specifically, risk of catastrophic failure leading to agent release; risk of exposing plant workers to agent and other hazardous substances; risk from latent health effects (cancer and non-cancer endpoints); risk from release during transport; potential impact from natural resources; and others.
- Schedule: impact of the use of alternative technologies on meeting pre-existing agreements, and
- Costs: these include cost of extending the storage period; process development, implementation and operation; plant disassembly; and discounting of the technologies.

Lastly, the Committee noted that evaluating the options with these criteria did not constitute a risk assessment, although some of the questions would be those in risk assessments (see Figure 4.6), and that the criteria do not easily lead to a total integrated risk assessment.

With clear messages and steps taken to include public involvement in risk management, the Project Manager for Chemical Stockpile Disposal (1998) sent an even more unambiguous message about including public input. It conducted public meetings at three sites. I am liberally quoting the exact language to emphasize the increasing importance that the U.S. Army attached to public input as the process evolved:

> Over the last decade, public scrutiny of and input to the program have increased, in part because of changes in legislation that require public input and involvement during environmental reviews. ... The public has expressed the sentiment that the Army does not adequately consider the views of citizens who could be impacted by the disposal program.
>
> *(p. 2)*

> Community viewpoints will play a vital role in shaping decisions, particularly in instances where issues involve trade-offs between potentially competing factors. For example, what would be the correct decision if a change could either greatly reduce worker risk or reduce risk to the public by a somewhat lesser amount, but not both? And what does it mean if these workers are also members of that same community? These types of value judgments extend beyond the realm of science and into the arena of public policy, where community involvement is absolutely essential.
>
> *(p. 3)*

> All of these risks lie in a continuum between a definite outcome (for example, a 100 percent chance that an individual would have a specific health problem) down to very rare occurrences (for example, one chance in 1 billion that the person would have that problem). As described previously, there are analysis tools (QRAs and HRAs) that help identify risks and how great they are. These tools have their own limitations that also factor into decision-making. The estimated risks are uncertain due to limitations of knowledge concerning both the likelihood and consequences of events. They may also be uncertain due to randomness involved in the risk phenomena (for example, lightning may strike someone at a golf course with a probability that may be fairly well-known, but there is an element of randomness as to which golfer might get struck). These uncertainties must also be considered by the decision-makers.
>
> *(p. 9)*

However, none of these analysis tools can ultimately determine the best risk management decisions. Individuals, elected officials and other decision-makers all determine acceptability. ... Hence wide public involvement is needed when the PMCD must make a decision regarding issues that could affect the community.

(p. 9)

These statements are among the clearest statements that this writer has heard from a government-sponsored group about the role of risk analysis tools and public input into the process.

In this 1998 report, the Army not only articulated a policy of public involvement, but also recognized the limitations of the audience. The report notes that the public does not want to be inundated with insignificant changes to plant operations, and they feel uncomfortable in public meetings that are heavily populated by experts (I have heard the word "intimidated" used to describe the feeling.). The public also suggested:

- World Wide Web pages;
- Draw down phone menus;
- 800-number response/inquiry lines; and
- Direct and mass mailings.

Indeed, earlier, I had suggested several of these ideas to the Army, and they had implemented several of them. For example, having an 800-number inquiry line is a great idea but only if the inquiries are answered within a reasonable period of time, which takes resources (Committee of Review 2000). The community meetings also suggested that the public was not enamored of standard public meetings. Instead they suggested the development of ad hoc committees for specific issues and focus groups to focus on specific topics.

The Army had to balance between wearing out the public with information that the public did not want to know and being criticized for ignoring the public regarding important decisions. Consequently, they developed the following list of potentially significant issues that warranted public input:

- Significant modifications to the furnace or pollution abatement systems;
- Proposed increase in stack emission limits that are included in the RCRA permits;
- Significant changes to chemical agent and explosive material handling;
- Significant changes to incineration, pollution abatement explosive handling, or other major processing technologies; and
- Any physical or operational modification that could increase risk, as assessed by the quantitative risk assessment or health risk assessment.

What did Chapter 4 explain about risk analysis? Summary and learning objectives

The destruction of the U.S. chemical weapon stockpile (90 percent complete as of this writing) is already a success and could have been completed on time had the baseline incineration been used. Yet, two communities that argued against the baseline technology and for alternative technologies prevailed. Personally, I will continue to be slightly nervous until the last bit of the stockpile has been eliminated. But local preferences prevailed. Furthermore, Russia, the second nation with a massive stockpile, has destroyed much of its stockpile, as have many other nations. Countries headed by leaders with bad intentions and terrorist groups can try and probably succeed in building these weapons. I would not advise it. They are likely to kill or injure themselves in the process, if they manufacture them.

The chapter featured multiple applications of risk assessment. One, at an early stage, used risk assessment to better understand the location and transportation choices. A second was used to highlight the difference between storage and destruction. Site-specific risk assessments were also done at later stages to make decisions about very specific options and as part of facility permitting. The chapter showed a simple event tree and part of a checklist to assess risks. Perhaps the most interesting part of the chemical weapons stockpile destruction for risk analysts was not the quantitative tools, but rather the Army's small and then large steps to involve in the public in appropriate parts of the process, even though such involvement slowed down the destruction of the chemicals at two sites.

At the end of this chapter readers should be able to answer the following seven questions:

1. What are the major types of chemical weapons?
2. When were chemical weapons first used in large-scale warfare?
3. What treaties and other agreements have attempted to control the production and use of chemical weapons?
4. Where were chemical weapons stored in the United States, and why were these locations important in the decision to destroy the weapons?
5. How was risk assessment used to determine where to destroy the weapons?
6. What technologies have been used to destroy the weapons, and why were these selected?
7. What role did state, not-for-profit organizations and local community groups play in selecting the destruction technologies?

References

Alabama Department of Environmental Management. (2007) Hazardous waste facility permit. AL3 210 020 027. Issued to the United States Department of the Army, Anniston Army Depot. November 13. www.epa.gov/epawaste/hazard/tsd/permit/tsd-regs/sub-x/anniston.pdf. Accessed April 29, 2015.

Berry J. (1999) *The new liberalism: the rising power of citizen groups.* Washington, D.C.: Brookings Institution Press.

Chemical Materials Agency. (2010) Creating a safer tomorrow. www.cma.army.mil.html. Accessed February 14, 2010.

Chisholm, Chisholm, & Kilpatrick, Ltd. (2013) Combined environmental exposure report for Fort McClellan Alabama. Providence, RI, Chisholm, Chisholm, & Kilpatrick, Ltd.

Committee on Foreign Relations. (1996) Executive report 104-33. Washington, D.C.: U.S. Senate.

Committee of Review and Evaluation of the Army Chemical Stockpile Disposal Program, NRC. (1995) Evaluation of the armies draft assessment criteria to aid in the selection of alternative technologies for chemical demilitarization. Washington, D.C.: NRC.

Committee of Review and Evaluation of the Army Chemical Stockpile Disposal Program, NRC. (2000) A review of the Army's public affairs efforts in support of the chemical stockpile disposal programs. Washington, D.C.: NRC.

Conley H. (2001) Not with impunity: assessing U.S. policy for retaliating to a chemical or biological attack. Maxwell Air Force Base, AL, Air War College. www.dtic.mil/dtic/tr/fulltext/u2/a408805.pdf. Accessed April 25, 2015.

General Assembly of the United Nations. (1992) *Convention on the prohibition of the development, production, stockpiling and use of chemical weapons and on their destruction.* New York: United Nations.

Gorbachev M. (2000) Russia deserves US help in disposing of weapons. *Houston Chronicle* [serial on-line]. Oct 22; Available at: www.communications-network.net/CNS/web. Accessed November 1, 2000.

Greenberg M. (1999) *Restoring America's neighborhoods: how local people make a difference.* New Brunswick, NJ: Rutgers University Press.

Greenberg M. (2003) Public health, law, and local control: destruction of the US chemical weapons stockpile. *American Journal of Public Health,* 93, 8, 1222–1225.

Greenberg M. (2011) *The environmental impact statement after two generations: managing environmental power.* New York: Routledge.

Greenberg M. (2014) Energy policy and research: the underappreciation of trust. *Energy Research and Social Science,* 1, 152–160.

Hemingway E. (1929) *A farewell to arms.* New York: Scribner.

Lambright W, Gereben A, Cerveny L. (1998) The army and chemical weapons destruction: implementation in a changing context. *Policy Studies Journal.* 26, 703–718.

Lewis P. (2013) US struggles show hazards of chemical weapons destruction. *The Guardian.* September 11. www.theguardian/world/2013/sept/11/us. Accessed May 2, 2015.

Luloff A, Albrecht S, Bourke L. (1998) NIMBY and the hazardous and toxic waste siting dilemma: the need for concept clarification. *Society & Natural Resources.* 11, 1, 81–89.

Marshall S. (1996) Chemical weapons disposal and environmental justice. Chemical Weapons Working Group. www.cwwg.org/EJ.HTML Accessed April 28, 2015.

McAvoy G. (1998) Partisan probing and democratic decision-making: rethinking the Nimby. *Policy Studies Journal.* 26, 2, 274–292.

Mitre Corp., McLean, VA. (1987) Risk analysis supporting the chemical stockpile disposal program (CSDP), prepared for the Office of the Program Manager for Chemical Demilitarization, U.S. Army, Aberdeen Proving Ground, MD, December.

Munro N, Talmage S, Griffin G, Waters L, Watson A, King J, Hauschild V. (1999) The sources, fate, and toxicity of chemical warfare agent degradation products. *Environmental Health Perspectives.* 107, 933–974.

National Research Council, Committee on Review and Evaluation of the Chemical Stockpile Disposal Program. (1998). Using supercritical water oxidation to treat hydrolysate from VX neutralization. Washington, D.C.: National Academy Press.

National Research Council, Committee on Review and Evaluation of the Chemical Stockpile Disposal Program. (2000a) A review of the army's public affairs efforts in support of the chemical stockpile disposal program. Washington, DC: National Academy Press.

National Research Council, Committee on Review and Evaluation of the Chemical Stockpile Disposal Program. (2000b) Integrated design of alternative technologies for bulk-only chemical agent disposal facilities. Washington, D.C.: National Academy Press.

National Research Council, Committee on Review and Evaluation of the Chemical Stockpile Disposal Program. (2001) *Occupational health and monitoring at chemical agent disposal facilities.* Washington, D.C.: National Academy Press.

Norberg-Bohm V. (1999) Stimulating "green" technological innovation: an analysis of alternative policy mechanisms. *Policy Sciences.* 32, 13–38.

Pezzullo E. (1997a) Review panel talks of need to "trust" in weapons disposal. *Anniston Star.* December 13, 2a.

Pezzullo E. (1997b) Army seeks to defuse weapons queries. *Anniston Star.* December 14, 1, 4a.

Rotunda R. (1998) The chemical weapons convention: political and constitutional issues. *Constitutional Commentary* [serial on-line]. 1998; 15:131. Available at: http://web.Lexis-nexis.com/universe. Accessed March 2002.

SAIC for US Army. (1997a) Anniston chemical agent disposal facility phase I quantitative risk assessment. Aberdeen Proving Ground, MD, SAIC.

SAIC for U.S. Army. (1997b) Pine Bluff chemical agent disposal facility phase I quantitative risk assessment. Aberdeen Proving Ground, MD, SAIC.

Schwepker C, Cornwell B. (1991) An examination of ecologically concerned consumers and their intention to purchase ecologically packaged products. *Journal of Public Policy & Marketing.* 10, 2, 77–101.

Shepherd K. (2013) Time Magazine notes high cost of destroying chemical weapons. www.newsbusters.org/blogs//ken-shepherd/2013/09/11/time-magazine. Accessed June 15, 2014.

Smith E, Marquez M. (2000) The other side of NIMBY syndrome. *Society & Natural Resources.* 13, 3, 273–280.

Talbott G. (1996a) NRC: Burn stockpile. *Pine Bluff Commercial.* October 30, 1, 2a.

Talbott G. (1996b) NRC panel visits arsenal neighbor. *Pine Bluff Commercial.* October 31, 1, 2a.

Tucker J. (2006) *War of nerves: chemical warfare from World War I to Al-Qaeda.* New York: Pantheon Books.

U.S. Army. (1988) Chemical stockpile disposal program full programmatic environmental impact statement, Vol. 1, 2, and 3, Program Executive Officer-Program Manager for Chemical Demilitarization. Aberdeen Proving Ground, MD, US Army.

U.S. Army Program Manager for Chemical Demilitarization (1998) Change Management process Plan. Aberdeen Proving Ground, MD, US Army.

U.S. Army. (1990a) Johnston Atoll chemical agent disposal system, final second supplemental environmental impact statement for the storage and ultimate disposal of the European chemical munition stockpile, Volume 1. June 1990.

U.S. Army. (1990b) Comments on Johnston Atoll chemical agent disposal system, final second supplemental environmental impact statement, Volume 2. June 1990.

U.S. Army. (1995) Assessment criteria to aid in the selection of alternative technologies for chemical demilitarization. Aberdeen Proving Ground, MD: Alternative Technology Branch.

U.S. Army. (2011) Exceptional accomplishment: Anniston chemical weapons stockpile end of operations. CMA News. www.army.mil/article/68503. Accessed April 4, 2015.

U.S. Army Center for Health Promotion and Preventive Medicine. (1999) Derivation of health-based environmental screening levels for chemical warfare agents. Aberdeen Proving Ground, MD, U.S. Army.

U.S. Bureau of the Census. (2014) *Selected economic characteristics 2006–2010.* American Community Survey, 5-yerar estimates. Accessed April 25, 2015.

U.S. General Accounting Office. (1996) *Chemical weapons stockpile, emergency preparedness in Alabama is hampered by management weakness.* Washington, DC: GAO/NSAID Publication 96-150.

U.S. General Accounting Office. (1997) *Chemical weapons stockpile: changes needed in the management of the emergency preparedness program.* Washington, D.C.: GAO/NSAID Publication 97-91.

U.S. General Accounting Office (2001) *FEMA and army must be proactive in preparing states for emergencies.* Washington, DC: GAO Publication 01-850.

WCBS. (2002) Toxic secret. *60 Minutes.* www.cbsnews.com/stories/2002/11/07/60minutes/main528581.shtml. Accessed April 25, 2015.

Williams B, Suen H, Zappe S, Pennock-Roman M. (2003) Diffusion of U.S. Army chemical weapons disposal technologies: public perception of technology attributes. *Journal of Environmental Planning and Management.* 4, 499–522.

Yoo J. The new sovereignty and the old constitution: the chemical weapons convention and the appointments clause. *Constitutional Commentary* [serial on-line]. 1998; 15:87. http://web.Lexis-nexis.com/universe. Accessed March 2002.

5

ENVIRONMENTAL JUSTICE

Introduction

Environmental justice is a world-wide social and political movement, a slogan for many across the globe who seek risk management decisions that are more informed by equity considerations, more accessible and transparent to the public, and more protective of not only disadvantaged population but also the environment that supports life. I believe it to be among the most powerful forces for global change, a counterforce to unfettered globalization with implications for the kinds of risk assessments that are done and how risk-informed decisions are made.

While inequities are not new, during the 1980s, some U.S. scholars recognized that a disproportionate burden of the environmental risk was being borne by poor and several minority populations. The U.S. government's formal response was a Presidential Executive Order in 1994 (see below for more details). The U.S. program is the focus of this chapter beginning with the first steps taken by the United Church of Christ and leading up to the EPA's ongoing efforts, several of which are discussed in this chapter. Around the world, other nations were slower to formally acknowledge the issue, but as this chapter will show some are moving forward.

Two caveats are in order about this chapter. One is that it is difficult to keep up with environmental justice activities at the global level. One reason is that so much about environmental justice never appears in the black or even gray literatures, although web releases by organizations and blogs are sources to be routinely scanned. Much of what appears in the black literature misses the subtle behind-the-scenes efforts made by thousands of people to assemble coalitions to pressure government and business to be cognizant of environmental justice. Second, I have been involved in parts of this story, and make no pretense that I can separate myself from what I have done.

I decided to focus this chapter on U.S. efforts, and especially the efforts of the U.S. EPA. This decision allows me to focus on the government agency that I believe to have received more environmental justice-related praise and criticism than other government body. EPA was active in environmental justice before President Clinton's environmental justice presidential order in 1994. Yet, as the chapter will demonstrate, EPA walks around with bullseye on it and has been criticized by some parties for not doing enough and others for doing more than it should. While the chapter focuses on the EPA, other U.S. government bodies and other nations are discussed, albeit in less detail.

Growing global recognition

The start: hazardous waste sites in the U.S.

When scholars first noticed that environmental hazards, such as landfills and other waste sites were disproportionately found in communities with many poor, African American and Latino Americans, little of what they learned reached government departments or made media headlines. At the national scale, little happened in regard to environmental justice until an incident in North Carolina provoked a national response. In the early 1980s, the State of North Carolina chose a site in rural Warren County to place soil contaminated with polychlorinated biphenyls in a landfill (see description of the role of Charles Lee in Greenberg 1999). Warren, with a population of 16,232 in 1980 (now over 20,000), has been one of the poorest counties in the state. In 1980, it ranked 97 out of 100 in per capita income in North Carolina, second in percent below the poverty level, and second in housing units with lack of complete plumbing facilities. About 60 percent of the 1980 population was African American, the highest in North Carolina. The areas immediately adjacent to the waste site were rural and the population was over 75 percent African American.

The local population was angry and asked for assistance from the United Church of Christ (UCC), a relatively small Protestant church headquartered in Cleveland, but one with a strong history in the civil rights movement. Unlike many others, UCC's interest in civil rights had not ebbed. As the process evolved in North Carolina, over 500 people were arrested for lying down in front of dump trucks in protests against the Warren County site.

Charles Lee, along with colleagues Benjamin Chavis and Dr. Charles Cobb of the UCC, assumed that hazardous waste sites across the United States, not just North Carolina, were disproportionately located in areas with many poor and racial/ethnic minorities. In 1987, they published *Toxic Waste and Race* (Commission for Racial Justice 1987). I was adviser to the UCC study, which used simple statistical comparisons and multivariate analyses to make the results independent of the specific statistical test.

The United States had 415 commercial hazardous waste sites. The 36,000 five-digit zip codes were divided into four groups with the following results (Commission for Racial Justice 1987, p. 41):

- Group 1 (without an operating commercial hazardous waste facility)– 12.3 percent minority, or so-called "nonwhite";
- Group 2 (with one operating commercial hazardous waste treatment, storage, or disposal facility that is not a landfill) – 23.7 percent minority;
- Group 3 (with one operating commercial hazardous waste landfill that is not one of the five largest) – 22.0 percent minority;
- Group 4 (with one of the five largest or two or more operating commercial hazardous waste facilities that are not a landfill) – 37.6 percent minority.

These results were not subtle. This race/ethnicity finding was confirmed by discriminant analysis, a multivariate statistical tool, which found race/ethnicity as the single strongest discriminating indicator among the zip codes at the national scale. Mean household income ranked second. In other words, race/ethnicity was a stronger correlate than various measures of socioeconomic status.

The aggregate national results, however, mask some interesting regional differences. Table 5.1 compares the mean incomes and proportion that is minority in the host zip code compared to the host county. In every EPA region the income is lower and in nine of the ten regions (the exception is Region 2, NY-NJ), the minority proportion is higher. However, the results are more consistently different by income than by race/ethnicity.

TABLE 5.1 Summary national and U.S. EPA regional statistics for environmental justice

Area, EPA region	Number of commercial hazardous waste facilities (n=415)	Difference in minority %, 1980	Difference in mean income, 1980, $
United States	415	5.0★	–2,745★
1 Boston, New England	21	4.7	–4,638★
2 New York City-NY, NJ, and Puerto Rico, U.S. Virgin Islands, and 8 tribal nations	41	–1.5	–2,239★
3 Philadelphia-Mid-Atlantic	25	1.5	–3,740★
4 Atlanta-Southeast	70	5.5★	–1,922★
5 Chicago-Great Lakes	122	3.9★	–2,302★
6 Dallas-South Central	38	1.6	–1,905★
7 Lenexa, KS-Midwest	25	7.4	–2,677★
8 Denver-Mountains and Plains	11	15.8★	–5,876
9 San Francisco-Pacific Southwest	46	13.9★	–4,228★
10 Seattle-Pacific Northwest	13	4.0	–2,262

Notes: Total does not add up to 415 because several sites are located elsewhere.

★Statistically significant result using zip code vs. matched pairs test at P<.05.

Source: Commission for Racial Justice, Toxic Waste and Race, 1987, selected data from Table B-3, p. 43.

This report was widely publicized. For example, the *New York Times* story was "Race Bias in Location of Toxic Dumps" (Williams 1987, see also Weisskopf 1987). Speaking for the United Church of Christ, Benjamin Chavis expressed concern about the human health effects of this inequitable distribution of waste sites, a position that the UCC has emphasized in its continuing work on environmental justice. Chavis's comments were entirely reasonable, given the very limited amount of exposure data available at that time.

EPA's response was product of the pre-environmental justice era. Speaking for the EPA, Dr. J. Winston Porter, assistant administration for hazardous waste for EPA, said that EPA does not decide where sites go, states make the decisions and EPA approves. A critical part of his statement, made in 1987 was: "*We primarily look at technical factors, emissions, ground water monitoring. Sociological factors are not a part of our review.*" (in Williams 1987, p. 1) This type of statement was common during the 1980s and early 1990s. I personally heard similar remarks by EPA, other federal government and state officials in response to my own presentations. Prior to 1990, EPA was not yet ready to consider equity.

Several other studies followed, which led to meetings between the EPA, the Congressional Black Caucus and selected analysts. The Congressional Black Caucus had sufficient political power to put pressure on EPA to no longer ignore these findings. In response, EPA created an "Environmental Equity Workshop" to formally investigate the hypothesis that racial minorities and low-income people disproportionately bear a higher environmental risk burden. The report *Environmental Equity: Reducing Risk in All Communities* (U.S. EPA 1992) offered multiple recommendations, including the creation of an office within EPA to address environmental justice. This became the Office of Environmental Justice in 1994.

The EPA hired Charles Lee, a force behind the 1987 *Toxic Waste and Race* UCC report, for an environmental justice leadership position. On February 11, 1994, the most important legal step occurred when President Clinton issued Executive Order 12898, requiring federal agencies to be compliant with Title VI of the Civil Rights Act of 1964. The key objectives of President Clinton's declaration were to define environmental justice as fair treatment of people of all races, cultures, and incomes with respect to the creation, implementation, and enforcement of environmental regulations, laws, and policies and move toward a reality that no group would disproportionately bear the negative consequences of risky industrial, personal and government actions. I summarize the five-page executive order highlighting several provisions in Box 5.1:

The chapter will return to the story of how EPA became and continues to be the federal government leader in environmental justice, following a review of environmental justice issues outside the United States.

Environmental justice in Europe

Environmental justice in Europe should not duplicate the United States experience because the U.S. programs, as illustrated above, emanated from the struggles for

---

BOX 5.1 Highlights of Executive Order 12898, 1994

Section 1.1 Implementation

1.101 *Agency Responsibilities*: To the greatest extent practicable and permitted by law, and consistent with the principles set forth in the report on the National Performance Review, each Federal agency shall make achieving environmental justice part of its mission by identifying and addressing, as appropriate, disproportionately high and adverse human health or environmental effects of its programs, policies, and activities on minority populations and low income populations in the United States and its territories and possessions, the District of Columbia, the Commonwealth of Puerto Rico, and the Commonwealth of the Mariana Islands.

Section 1.101 ordered the EPA Administrator to create an *Interagency Working Group on Environmental Justice,* and it names members of the working group, including the Department of Defense; Department of Health and Human Services; Department of Housing and Urban Development; Department of Labor; Department of Agriculture; Department of Transportation; Department of Justice; Department of the Interior; Department of Commerce; Department of Energy; Environmental Protection Agency; Office of Management and Budget; and others.

The role of the Working Group is to provide guidance to Federal agencies about criteria for identifying environmental justice, be a clearing house for agency strategies, coordinate data and research among agencies and departments, hold public meetings, and develop model projects to demonstrate interagency cooperation.

Sections 1.103 and 1.104 call for each agency/department to develop an environmental justice strategy and sets timelines for their development and reporting out to 24 months.

Section 2.6 include actions for data collection, research and analysis, on subsistence consumption of fish and wildlife; public participation and access to information.

Source: Executive Order 12898 of February 11, 1994. Federal Actions to Address Environmental Justice in Minority Populations and Low Income Populations, *Federal Register* 59, 32, February 16, 1994.

---

racial equality, and that influence remains. In the EU, Laurent (2011) attributes the formal introduction of environmental justice in the EU to a Ministerial Conference in Aarhus, Denmark, on June 25, 1998. Laurent states that every person now alive and future generations should have the right to:

- Access information;
- Participate in decision-making; and
- Access to justice in environmental issues.

The United Kingdom was the original focus and the issues were distributive, procedural, and policy justice. The first asks if environmental threats (factories, waste sites, etc.) and benefits (parks) are distributed equitably, in other words, do some people and places face more threats and receive fewer benefits. Procedural justice questions if equity exists in regard to decision-making processes and the laws. Policy justice asks the question of how do policy decisions focus on different groups.

Laurent (2011) argues that the EU should:

- Adopt environmental justice as a principle for policy development;
- Include environmental justice as part of the impact assessment process; and
- Improve its data bases so that geographical-specific information can be produced that will allow for better environmental assessments.

If the UK represents the leading EU program, then central and eastern Europe have perhaps faced the most challenges. Varga, Kiss, and Ember (2002) assert that they cannot conduct environmental justice studies in eastern Europe because of a lack moral, political, and financial support. Steger (2007) reporting for the Center for Environmental Policy and Law (CEPL), examined environmental justice in central and eastern Europe, focusing on the Roma (Gypsies). The exact size of the Roma population is not known, however, over 2 million are estimated to live in Romania, Bulgaria, the Czech Republic, Hungary, Slovakia, Albania, Poland and Croatia, where they comprise 0.2 percent to 4.5 percent of the national population. Steger notes that the Roma are more exposed to hazardous pollutants, as well as poor housing, lack of sanitation, flooding, and suffer from many other deprivations, leading to low-life expectancy. Steger also reported on occupational exposures in central and eastern Europe. The last paragraph of the report begins as follows, and notably includes the word racism:

> A safe and healthy place to live, work, and play is important for all Europeans. It is most egregious and disconcerting when such fundamental needs are denied due to discrimination, prejudice, and racism.
>
> *(Steger 2007, p. 55)*

Much of what I find in the EU is found in U.S. and vice versa. Laurent (2011) says the Scottish and British experiences are grounded in social conditions. I agree that the U.S. focused on race, and that legacy remains. Yet I believe the U.S. and EU policies are closer than most believe and will become closer in regard to environmental justice because of world events. As noted above, while not emphasized in the published U.S. literature, in fact, income differences and indeed age differences are also apparent even in the original 1987 *Toxic Waste and Race* report. As noted in Table 5.1, the income differences by U.S. EPA region are more consistent than the racial/ethnic ones. When the case was made before the U.S. public, race was emphasized and the political coalition that initially pressed the U.S. EPA to adopt an environmental justice agenda focused on race. However, EPA's environmental justice efforts also include low-income people and indigenous people (see below).

The U.S. is rapidly becoming a very diverse nation in regard to race and ethnicity. It is going to be difficult to maintain a strong environmental justice program unless recent large minority groups in the United States are involved or are at least sympathetic. Ignoring demographic reality is perilous. The latest long-term series by the U.S. Bureau of the Census (Colby, Ortman 2014) estimates the U.S. population will grow to 417 million by the year 2060. This compares to 227 million in 1980 (the data upon which the first toxic waste and race report was based), and then to 319 million in 2014. In 1980, 86 percent of the population was reported as White, and the African American population was almost double that of so-called Hispanics origin. In 2014, Colby and Ortman report that 17.4 percent of the population was Hispanic (Latino American) and 14.3 percent African American. Also 6.3 percent was Asian American. Assuming moderate increases in immigration, and a moderate birth rate, they project that the country will add almost 100 million people and reach 417 million in 2060. The vast majority of the additional people will be the so-called "nonwhites." By 2060, the Hispanic/Latino population is expected to constitute 29 percent of the population, the African American 18 percent, and the Asian American one 12 percent. Political support for environmental justice in the United States will falter if the racial groups that brought the issue to the attention to government do not make a strategic decision to be more inclusive, especially in regard to poor people of every racial/ethnic group, a mistake I do not believe that they will make.

On the other side of the Atlantic Ocean, I believe that the EU will be pressed to have more of a nationality basis, if not racial/ethnic, for its environmental justice programs as its native population shrinks because of historically low birth rates and rapid growth of immigrant populations. Europa (2015) reported continued growth of immigrant working age populations in EU states. In some states, the proportion from outside EU nations exceeds those from inside the EU. In Luxembourg, Cyprus, Latvia, Estonia, Austria, Ireland, Belgium and Spain more than 10 percent of the national population was born outside the country, and almost half of Luxembourg's population was foreign born. Massive immigration from Syria in 2015 further increases the immigrant population and associated challenges.

While Europe has historically categorized differences by socioeconomic group, it will be pressed to disaggregate by at least nation of origin. Europe, like the U.S., is being challenged to deal not only with human health and environmental justice issues, but education, housing and many others.

Also, I would urge both sides of the Atlantic to pay more attention to the role of age and disabilities in the environmental justice issues. The data clearly demonstrate that older seniors (who disproportionately vote) and disabled people, as well as children, are far more at risk of death and injury from natural hazard events (Greenberg 2014).

Globalization and environmental justice in the southern hemisphere

Globalization is the process of increasing the movement of goods, services, and capital across the world, having the effect of making national boundaries more porous and making it difficult for national and local governments to manage decisions in their regions (see also Chapter 11). Weakening of unions, diminution of worker benefits, environmental and human health degradation sometimes follow from globalization. Drawn to places where they can find employment, people are cut off from their traditional cultures and family structures, and they frequently face inadequate housing, lack of fresh water and inadequate waste management, limited access to schools and health services, and many other health and safety-related issues. Some face occupational exposures that would not be tolerated in North America or the EU. It is typical for conflicts to erupt over land use changes when traditional cultures and practices collide with the needs of globalization, for example, farming for export, conversion of water bodies for hydroelectric power and for agricultural use, clearing of forest, and overall disruption of the indigenous communities (see Chapter 7).

The impacts of globalization, especially in regard to mining, agriculture, forest removal, and hunting are motivation for environmental justice movements in Africa, southern Asia, the Pacific Islands, and South and Latin America. South Africa's challenges are illustrative. Kearney (2012) estimates that South Africa has the world's fifth largest mining sector as measured by gross domestic product compared to ranking twenty-seventh in the world in population (48 million in 2014). South Africa exports manganese, platinum, gold, diamonds, chromite ore and vanadium among others, and other mineral deposits are expected to be found and mined. The other side of the coin is the Mining and Environmental Justice Community Network of South Africa (MEJCON-SA), which posts cases of human and environmental problems related to mining (see also McDonald's 2002; Carruthers 2008; Greider 1997; Singh 1999; United Nations 1999).

Fields (2013) posted the following statement made in 2002 by Nelson Mandela who remarked on what it felt like to return to the rural village where he spent his youth:

> the poverty of the people and the devastation of the natural environment painfully strike me. And in that impoverishment of the natural environment, it is the absence of access to clean water that strikes most starkly.
>
> *(Fields 2013, p. 1)*

Using South Africa as an illustration, Williams (2012) raises the north–south issue as an environmental justice issue, noting that the U.S., Europe, Canada, Japan, and now increasingly China are causing global climate change, and while they have the resources to respond, vulnerable Southern Hemisphere nations do not.

Pope Francis's May 24, 2015 encyclical addressed global environmental degradation. Born in Argentina (the first Pope to be born in the Southern Hemisphere), Francis's lengthy encyclical (teaching document) touches on global climate change, drinking water, loss of biodiversity, and points to the impact of rich countries on poor ones. Other Popes have touched on environmental issues, this one focuses on it. On July 2, 2015, U.S. EPA administrator Gina McCarthy during an encyclical panel in Washington, D.C. stated that the EPA's environmental justice mission is a moral obligation to protect our children and their children's children (Georgetown 2015). The EPA administrator directly linked EPA's mission to the Pope's encyclical.

The U.S. EPA: old battles and new battlegrounds over environmental justice

The analysis of hazardous waste sites certainly did not end with the United Church of Christ's (1987) Toxic Waste and Race report. Several important arguments have emerged. One stipulates that the largest number and most noxious sites are in poor, African American, Hispanic and American Indian areas and this was done on purpose because these populations have little political power or resources to fight siting. The counterargument is that the pattern is not consistent and when it does exist is caused by historical patterns of industrial development in the United States, so-called "outcome inequity," as opposed to "process" inequity in which a process was used to deliberately steer the site to a poor and powerless area (see Anderton et al. 1994; Been 1994; Bullard 1983; Bullard et al. 2007; Cutter 1995; Greenberg 1993; Zimmerman 1993) The argument is unresolvable because the results can change depending on scale, time period, and facility type. For example, Greenberg (1993) demonstrated that depending upon what statistic was used (mean, population-weighted mean, proportion, geometric mean, and other) and the scale of the analysis (town or zip codes) the results would support a case for environmental justice or reject it.

In 2007, the UCC published an updated version of *Toxic Waste and Race at Twenty Years, 1987–2007* (Bullard et al. 2007), which argues that environmental injustice is at least as prevalent or even more prevalent in 2007 as it was 1987. Pointing to government response to Hurricane Katrina and other situations, and using more precise and better defined data about hazardous waste sites than were available for the 1987 report, the authors severely criticize government and business for a lack of a strong response and for allowing inequitable conditions to continue. An extension of this environmental justice concern discussed in the twentieth year anniversary report is that companies should not be dumping their hazardous waste in poorer nations in Africa, Latin America or elsewhere. Whatever the merits of the arguments, I believe that commercial hazardous waste and government waste management decision makers are wary of siting a facility without considerable planning and consultation, and they have been driven to recycle and to use less waste producing raw materials to reduce costs and avoid charges that might upset their stockholders.

Chester and Camden

Another severe test is the U.S. courts. What would the U.S. courts do in response to a suit brought against a company or a government agency to site a facility or grant a permit to an applicant? The first major test was in Chester, Pennsylvania. I note that I was involved in the case, and hence I have access to the logic of the arguments.

Chester is a small city of 34,000 and 7.4 square miles located less than 20 miles (32 km) south of Philadelphia. The population was 75 percent African American and 9 percent Latino. Chester is one of the poorest small cities in the United States, with about one-third below the poverty level, and the city's population has been steadily declining since it reached a high of 66,000 in 1950. It was a location for escaped slaves and where African Americans settled and worked in the factories and other industries located along the Delaware River waterfront.

This small city has had serious financial problems, and has many waste management facilities, including a large county incinerator, a sewage plant that treats almost all the county sewage, and six other waste management facilities. Nearly all of these facilities are located in one census tract (#4056) that is 0.4

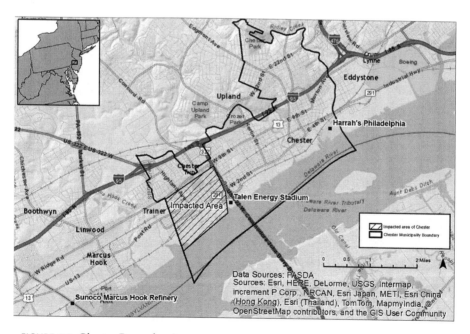

FIGURE 5.1 Chester Pennsylvania area

square miles in size and a population that was 74 percent African American when the civil case was filed (Chester Residents 1996).

No one can demonstrate that these facilities are responsible for health-related problems in Chester as a whole, but certainly the following data show a disproportionate burden in the city. Research showed that the city had higher rates of the following compared to Delaware County within which Chester city sits:

- A 40 percent higher age-adjusted mortality rate;
- A 37 percent higher age-adjusted cancer mortality rate;
- A 97 percent higher infant mortality rate;
- An 82 percent higher proportion of low birth weight babies; and
- 75 percent of the air pollution complaints (nearly all from facilities in tract #4056).

In 1995, Region 3 of the U.S. EPA (1995) released a study that they called an "Environmental Risk Study for City of Chester, Pennsylvania." In order to conduct this study, they gathered data from a variety of EPA and state sources. In the preface, the authors state that this study is "to provide general guidance as a 'model protocol' related to methods of performing aggregated risk studies at other locations. It is generally accepted that cumulative risk studies are needed to provide technical information and a framework for decision-making related to proposed and/or current sources of pollution" (U.S. EPA 1995, p. ii).

The study presents five conclusions and six recommendations. I quote two conclusions and two recommendations that were most critical to the law suit that followed:

Two conclusions were:

1. Both cancer and non-cancer risks ... from the pollution sources at locations in the city of Chester exceed levels which EPA believes are acceptable.
2. Air emission from facilities in and around Chester provide a large component of the cancer and non-cancer risk to the citizens of Chester.

Two recommendations were:

1. Sources of air emissions which impact the areas of the city with unacceptably high risk should be targeted for compliance inspections and any necessary enforcement actions.
2. A voluntary emission reduction program should be instituted to obtain emissions reductions from facilities which provide the most emissions in the areas of highest risk.

(U.S. EPA 1995, p. 1)

To place this case in the larger literature, Chester was the first effort by EPA to model cumulative risk and was the first law suit based on Title VI violations that went to the courts. The EPA clearly was concerned about air pollution in the city. However, the State of Pennsylvania granted a permit to an applicant to Soil Remediation Services, Inc. (SRS) to build a facility in census tract #4056 that would treat about 900 tons of oil contaminated soil a day. Tract #4056 is located next to the Delaware River (Figure 5.1).

On May 28, 1996, 18 plaintiffs (14 were residents of tract #4056) filed a law suit against the State of Pennsylvania. They asserted that the Pennsylvania DEP violated the Civil Rights Act of 1964 (42U.S.C. §2000d et seq.). The suit quotes from the Civil Rights Act of 1964:

> No person ... shall on the grounds of race, color or national origin ... be subjected to discrimination under any program or activity receiving federal financial assistance.
>
> *(Chester Residents 1996, p. 7)*

They asked the court to order the Pennsylvania DEP to rescind the SRS permit, and that the Pennsylvania environmental organization should receive no federal funding because of this violation.

> A recipient (of federal financial assistance) shall not use criteria or methods of administering the program which have the effect of subjecting individuals to discrimination because of their race, color, or national origin, or sex ...
>
> *(Chester Residents 1996, p. 7)*

The district court dismissed the case, but then the Third Circuit Court of Appeals restored it, ruling that private individuals can bring discrimination claims to enforce Title VI regulations. While this was a major legal victory for the environmental justice claims, and the case was going to be heard by the U.S. Supreme Court until it learned that the project developer abandoned the project. Hence, the Chester case became moot.

Camden, New Jersey is on the other side of the Delaware River about 19 miles from Chester (Figure 5.1). In this case, the St. Lawrence manufacturing company proposed a cement plant in Camden's Waterfront area, where 91 percent of the residents were Afro- or Latino American. Like Chester tract #4056 this area has a sewage treatment plant, a garbage burning facility, a cogeneration plant, and some brownfield sites. The cement plant was to grind and process granulate blast furnace slag, and the material would be added to cement. The area would also be impacted by an average of about 200 trucks into and out of the site on a daily basis. A suit was filed by local residents again charging violation of Title VI. The district court ruled that the NJ DEP violated Title VI by not considering the facility's adverse disparate impacts. The developer did not pull the permit request, and courts vacated the air permits, and the court remanded the case to the NJ DEP. Ultimately, the plant was built in 2002 and remains a point of heated debate, and was characterized by the New Jersey Director of the Sierra Club as a "national disgrace. Not only does it symbolize environmental racism, it proves its existence" (In Williams 2009, p. 1).

Yet another case was filed in Alabama. In that case, the U.S. Supreme Court in a five to four decision ruled against the plaintiffs. I quote some of the text of the decision. Justice Scalia, now deceased, for the majority (Rehnquist, O'Connor, Kennedy, and Thomas) wrote:

> Neither as originally enacted nor as later amended does Title VI display an intent to create a freestanding private right of action to enforce regulations promulgated under §602. We therefore hold that no such right of action exists.

Justice Stevens writing for the minority (Souter, Ginsburg, and Breyer) offered the following comments about the majority:

> [It] couples its flawed analysis of the structure of Title VI with an uncharitable understanding of the substance of the divide between those on this Court who are reluctant to interpret statutes to allow for private rights of action.
> *(Quoted in Goldshore, Wolf 2001, p. 2)*

While this ruling was a setback for environmental justice cases, Goldshore and Wolf (2001) argued that the plaintiffs could argue their case for disparate impacts discrimination in violation of EPA's implementation regulations to Title VI (42 U.S.C. § 1983). Overall, these cases show that some judges were persuaded that environmental justice cases could be brought, but the time and cost involved is significant, and the chances of prevailing not high based more on legal precedent rather than on merit of the risk.

When is environmental injustice inappropriate?

I present two illustrations of why environmental injustice may be appropriate. The first concerns hazardous waste sites.

Chapter 2 briefly described EPA's approach to choosing the most dangerous sites, which involved designation by states and by application of the HRS model. I noted some of my concerns about HRS in that chapter. However, absent any other system to rank the sites, the HRS model was used and produced scores for all the nominated sites. Table 5.2 is based on the 928 highest ranked sites (most dangerous) at that time. Please note that any site included in the table is a hazard, but the table divides the hazards into five equal sized groups from group 1 which has the most dangerous to group 5, which has the least dangerous sites.

Column 2 lists the average proportion of the population in the host census tract (if there was one, or municipality if there was not). The table literally indicates that

TABLE 5.2 Priority ratings for hazardous waste NPL (Superfund) sites in the United States, *c.* 1995

Ranking, National Priority List (NPL) sites (1=most dangerous, 928= least dangerous)	Average % of population, African and Latino American in the Census Tract, 2000 (95% confidence limits)
20% with highest HRS score	9.3 (5.2–13.4)
21–40 %	10.1 (5.5–14.7)
41–60%	11.9 (5.0–18.7)
61–80%	15.8 (2.7–29.0)
81–100% with lowest HRS scores	16.7 (8.2–25.2)

Source: Calculated by author from U.S. EPA Superfund site lists.

the higher the proportion of African Americans and Latinos the lower their HRS score. The HRS score is important because remediation funds were allocated partly on the basis of HRS scores. Hence, when I first presented this table during the late 1990s, there was considerable angst in the audience because it implies that EPA was not allocating money to areas with higher proportions of minority populations.

That was also my reaction, until I consulted my notes on many of the sites in New Jersey that I had visited. In fact, by the time I made the first presentation with this table, I had visited the then number 1, 4, 10, 12, 15, 35, 42 and 46-ranked NPL sites, and many other lower ranked sites. The pattern is that all of the most dangerous sites had high HRS scores because the areas depended on groundwater and each of these sites was contaminating or could contaminate groundwater.

For example, about half of New Jersey's drinking water comes from underground supplies and another half from rivers, lakes, and other surface water supplies. In New Jersey, African and Latino Americans disproportionately live in cities and older suburbs that depend upon surface water, not groundwater. Second, for many years, New Jersey was the most aggressive state in nominating sites for NPL status and for remediation, including passing a bond issue to fund a portion of the cleanups. Furthermore, I learned that the most dangerous human health and safety threats had been dealt with, that is, cases where flammable, explosive materials were left had already been remediated. Hence, the proper interpretations of this table is that sites that posed acute human health and safety risks and were known had been controlled, at least in one state, and then the risk managers moved on to chronic contamination of underground water supplies. I cannot assert that the same conclusion is true for other states, but in New Jersey the results are a logical reflection of risk, although they imply environmental inequity.

Implications of being on the Superfund list

The second controversial issue focuses on the implications of being on a federal government list that might lead to nomination as a Superfund site. Logic suggests that being included on the NPL list with a high ranking number is good because it makes it clear that the area needs remediation, and provides resources for cleanup. *However, the Superfund list became a no-build list, that is, companies were reluctant to acquire land for fear of being held responsible for the entire cleanup cost.* I became acutely aware of this when I visited Detroit to study the risk of Halloween fires (Detroit had a history of severe fires on Halloween leading to death, injuries, and property loses). I visited with Mayor Dennis Archer and an assistant who proceeded to lecture me on the negative economic consequences of the EPA list of approximately 35,000 to 50,000 sites that could be NPL sites. This list, they asserted, was making it impossible to redevelop major parts of Detroit. The mayor's position was rewarded when EPA removed about 25,000 from the list, and these sites became "brownfield sites" (Herbert 1995, see also Bryant 2011). In short, the arguments put forward by Mayor Archer, an African American, and other city mayors were that there was more risk to minority and poor people by freezing land redevelopment and not providing jobs than there was by opening up contaminated sites for redevelopment.

Other United States government agencies

While this chapter has focused on the United States Environmental Protection Agency, every U.S. federal and some state and local governments, and businesses have environmental justice programs. The U.S. government programs can be found by searching individual sites. For example, if you search the U.S. Departments of Transportation (DOT), Defense (DOD), Department of Energy (DOE), Treasury, Interior, Agriculture, Commerce, you will find an initial environmental justice plan required by President Clinton's Executive Order 12898, implementation plans and updates to those plans, reference guides, case studies, best, practices and various other efforts that they have made. This is true even for the relatively newly created Department of Homeland Security.

Each department has its own slant on the issue and some collaborate. Some of the most interesting tools are discussed in Chapter 10. For example, *EJscreen*: Environmental Justice Screening and Mapping Tool was released June 11, 2015 by the EPA. It builds high resolution maps and combines them with environmental and demographic data to identify areas that may have high burdens, including particulate matter, traffic density, and distance from NPL sites (see Chapter 10). For those interested in transportation, the DOT site has some very interesting elements, including model surveys and tools to determine if people have reasons to be concerned about being isolated.

Commentators discuss the progress of the 17 federal agencies in achieving environmental justice goals (for example, Mock 2015). However, these assessments need to be taken with a grain of salt because these bloggers are strongly influenced by their particular interests rather than the totality of the EJ effort.

States have their own environmental justice programs. I cannot possibly do justice to the major variations by state. Bonorris (2010) summarized each state's efforts as part of an American Bar Association and the Hastings College of Law program. For example, in New Jersey, former governor James McGreevey signed an executive order on environmental justice on February 18, 2004. As noted earlier, New Jersey was the location for the Camden cement plant case, and McGreevey, a former county prosecutor and strong believer in environmental justice was distressed by the Camden case. The executive order called for meaningful public involvement in state programs; it created a task force to consider issues, and provided for a petition and action plan to address environmental justice claims. The governor, his commissioner of environmental protection and attorney general argued for the executive order. However, a representative of New Jersey Chamber of Commerce argued that it would serve as a disincentive to urban redevelopment and the even environmental leaders wondered if it would stop a facility from being sited (Goldshore, Wolf 2004). I personally worked with former Governor McGreevy and agreed with his commitment. I understand the need for symbols and ceremonies to let people know that their interests have not been totally ignored, but the on-the-ground action about EJ often leaves something to be desired.

Environmental justice has reached down to local government. Many large cities have environmental justice coalitions that you can read about on the web. In 2012, the EPA created an interesting environmental justice program – the "Environmental Justice Showcase Communities," which selected ten local governments, one each in the 10 EPA regions to help local governments address their issues and serve as models for others. The $100,000 per project over two years is not much money, but the local communities (Bridgeport, CN; Staten Island, NY; Washington, D.C.; Jacksonville, FL; Milwaukee, WI; Port Arthur, TX; Kansas City, MO and KS; Salt Lake city, UT; and Port of Los Angeles and Long Beach, CA) all have an environmental justice legacy. It will be interesting to see what they have accomplished at the end of the program.

Quiet side of EJ within the EPA

Rules and regulations

While nearly all elected officials have been aware, sometimes painfully, of the hazardous waste facility-environmental justice issue, other EJ issues have emerged. The U.S. Environmental Protection Agency (EPA) is authorized by the U.S. Congress to create and enforce rules and regulations. Since its creation in 1970, regulatory authority has been EPA's major tool for protecting human health, and the water, air and land environments. Quite a few of these laws were described in Chapters 2 and 3, and EPA's regulatory powers are also included in the case studies in Chapters 4, 7, and 8.

Many of these rules and regulations are controversial. For example, a CNS News (Meyer 2014) story begins by noting that since President Obama took office in 2009, the EPA has issued 2,827 new final regulations, which it points out contains 19 times as many pages as the Gutenberg Bible and 38 times as many words.

Behind this article and other challenges are a tug-of-war between business interests and environmental groups, one calling for more regulatory control and the other for rollback of regulations (McCarthy, Copeland 2014).

While EPA is criticized for creating too much bureaucratic work, environmental justice positions on rules and regulations have been criticized by government officials as inadequate. In 2005, at the request of the U.S. Congress, the U.S. Government Accountability Office (2005) examined EPA's consideration of environmental justice in three rules issued between 2000 and 2004:

- In 2000, a gasoline rule to reduce sulfur content in gasoline and to reduce vehicle emissions;
- In 2001, a diesel rule to reduce sulfur in diesel fuel, and reduce emissions from new heavy-duty vehicles; and
- In 2004, an ozone rule to implement a new ozone air quality standard.

The GAO concluded that the EPA did not devote sufficient attention to environmental justice when it drafted these rules, including even mentioning it when it filled in the required agency forms (see below) used to develop and modify rules, and it was unclear to the GAO how much senior management were briefed about environmental justice issues. Second, The GAO concluded that the groups drafting the rules had limited training or guidelines about environmental justice. Third, the economic analyses, GAO added, contained little information about environmental justice. Finally, EPA has a staff trained in environmental justice considerations, and they were not asked to assist according to the GAO report. The EPA, said GAO, had to be more transparent in its inclusion of environmental justice concerns. The GAO followed up with specific recommendations. These are incorporated into the discussion in the next section.

EPA forms a working group when it decides to develop or modify an existing rule, and the process can take anywhere from a few months to years. Given its historical role in environmental justice in the United States, EPA has chosen to explicitly consider environmental justice in its rulemaking process. This policy decision is clearest in its multi-step Action Development Process (ADP). From the beginning of the thought process through the end of the rulemaking life cycle process, EPA states its objective is to answer three questions:

- How did the public participation process provide transparency and meaningful participation for minority populations, low-income populations, tribes, and indigenous peoples?
- How did the rule-writers identify and address existing and/or new disproportional environmental and public health impacts on minority populations, low-income populations, and/or indigenous peoples?
- How did the actions taken under #1 and #2 two impact the outcome or final decision?

(U.S. EPA 2015a, p. 2)

The U.S. EPA's effort is driven by a decision that specific populations are more vulnerable and that EPA should make a special effort to gain input from national and local representatives of these groups and then determine how to address their concerns.

Toward these ends, the EPA has prepared guidance for staff that writes rules that spells out what should be done (U.S. EPA 2015a). This guidance was also reviewed by a special committee of the EPA Science Advisory Board (U.S. EPA 2015b).

Here, I review EPA's risk management process for rules, the role of the environmental justice considerations and then illustrate the process with some of the more controversial efforts. EPA's Action Development Process (ADP) is an opportunity to review this unusual risk management process. The ADP includes decision makers, workgroups with EPA staff that have background in science, economics, and related subjects, a workgroup chair, and analysts, who usually are workgroup members. The process is built around a plan that will:

- Identify possible environmental justice concerns;
- Obtain meaningful public involvement;
- Evaluate and address key environmental justice issues;
- Discuss environmental justice concerns with environmental justice workgroups;
- Ascertain how proposed alternatives would change environmental justice impacts; and
- Close the cycle by documenting efforts to obtain meaningful input and addressed environmental justice concerns.

The EPA's ADP process classifies the potential impacts of regulations and reforms into categories, and these steps, as well as all of the others in the risk management process, are recorded in ADP TRACKER. (http://intranet.epa.gov/oswer/policy/ejr/index/html).

I have summarized the 16-step process in Box 5.2 and please note that this is my interpretation of the process which might not agree with EPA's staff.

This process is more laborious than I am able to indicate. Each rulemaking is an opportunity to provide more protection to environmental justice communities and yet potentially add cost to operations. Every application is likely to be opposed by individuals and groups asserting that:

- The proposed rule or regulation is not sufficiently protective;
- It will add cost to businesses;
- The change is not justified by the data and analyses provided, which they typically consider to be too soft;
- The proposed change costs the taxpayers too much money in the short run and/or in the long run; and
- The change favors some areas over others, including international ones.

BOX 5.2 Environmental justice procedural steps

- *Steps 1 and 2: indicate a possible environmental justice issue.* Fill-in boxes in EPA computerized form to indicate a possible EJ concern (for example, likely to impact health, environment, provides an opportunity to address a long-standing environmental justice issue). Discuss availability of data, and determine if an EPA environmental justice coordinator should be part of the workgroup. Whatever is entered by the working group at this initial stage and throughout the process becomes available to the public through the agencies Regulatory Development and Retrospective Review Tracker (Reg DaRRT) located on the web (www.epa.gov/regdarrt) These data are subject to revision when EPA has periodic meetings to reconsider its proposed action.
- *Step 3: Preliminary analytic blueprint (PABP).* This is another preliminary step, which I would call scoping. It has five steps: (1) identify environmental justice population that might be interested in the rule-making; (2) develop a preliminary plan to obtain involvement from the environmental justice communities; (3) prepare a preliminary plan to evaluate potential environmental justice impacts on the population; (4) develop a data and expert list to conduct any analysis; and (5) prepare a preliminary list of identified issues that will be addressed.
- *Step 4: Early guidance.* This is a critical early step during which senior managers provide guidance to the working group and discuss feedback about resources needed to conduct the analysis.
- *Step 5: Detailed analytical lab blueprint (DABP):* Step five sets forth what the working committee will do to answer the core questions by describing the rule writers responsible for the preliminary and detailed environmental justice assessment; data requirements and sources; scope of the assessment and methods to be used, including elements not included and reasons for not including them in the full assessments; products of the assessment; and resources required and scheduled to prepare the assessment.
- *Step 6: Management approval of the DABP.* This is a critical stage because it really represents the last major opportunity to substantially alter the analysis. The working group meets with decision-makers and discusses feedback from environmental justice and other groups to determine if the working plan should be implemented.
- *Step 7: Data collection, analysis and consultation, and development of regulatory options.* Step 7 produces the data analyses and suggests options dealing with the potential environmental justice concern.
- *Step 8: Selection of options.* Here the entire team considers the magnitude of environmental justice-related impacts and assesses the extent to which the substantive concerns and participatory ones have been addressed.
- *Step 9: Preparation of the action and supporting documents.* The rule-making group drafts the proposed action, including writing a preamble and

supporting documents. EPA's suggestions to its staff can be found on the internet (http://intranet.epa.gov/adplibrary) and in its recently completed Guidance Report (see U.S. EPA 2015a).

- *Step 10: Final agency review (FAR).* This step represents the final intra-agency opportunity to review what has been produced, and discuss what the responses are to the three primary questions.
- *Steps 11 and 12: Office of management and budget (OMB) review.* Representing the executive branch, the OMB reviews rules and regulations with a focus on their economic implications. (Executive Order 12866 (October 4, 1993) requires that significant regulatory actions to be submitted to OMB for review).
- *Steps 13 and 14: Signature and publication.* The EPA program sends the rule and document to the Office of the Federal Register for official publication.
- *Step 15: Soliciting and accepting public comments.* Once published, the public is presented and given an opportunity to comment. Sometimes, the EPA holds public hearings or meetings near the impacted population in order to hear and respond to concerns.
- *Step 16: Developing the final regulatory action.* This last step is the final opportunity to consider input from external parties, and modify the rule-making. In essence, the rule makers brief upper management, which may lead to a determination that more work needs to be done.

Source: U.S. EPA (2015a) Guidance on Considering Environmental Justice during the Development of Regulatory Actions.

EPA faces communications-related challenges in this process. It needs to make sure that environmental justice advocates understand what is being done, and why and how it might impact them. The goal is to build trust in the EPA, not to undermine EPA's credibility. The internet is difficult for some people, seniors, poor, and several ethnic groups have more limited access to internet than others. They prefer more traditional communication modes (e.g., local radio, newspapers, and community and school systems postings). In the case of tribal nations, the U.S. government must directly reach out for government to government communications.

An EPA Science Advisory Board Committee reviewed the draft EPA guidance (U.S. Environmental Protection Agency 2015b). The Committee supported the EPA's objectives and offered suggestions, including calling for clear definitions of environmental justice populations, susceptibility and vulnerability for its analysts; examples of what includes best practice; diagrams, charrettes, decision trees and other aids for analysts to use; a priority on involving environmental justice communities as early as practical; and guides that would help analysts explain why an action to protect environmental justice communities was not taken. All of these are reflected in the May 2015 EPA Guidance Report (U.S. EPA 2015a). Other suggestions made by the Committee (the author was a member) are not in the guidance document. These involve long-term research and development by EPA about cumulative impacts, differential cost impacts, location of monitoring stations, and other scientific issues that the agency will need to consider.

Case studies

EPA's environmental justice efforts have been controversial. What have these efforts accomplished is a legitimate question. As part of their environmental justice effort, EPA has published case studies that they believe demonstrate the success of the process. Several of these are reviewed below.

Lead renovation repair and painting program (RPP)

Lead paint was discontinued in 1978. Many older homes, disproportionately located in central cities where minorities and the poor live, have high lead levels indoors. Sometimes the lead paint is covered by wallpaper, which can cause a problem when the wallpaper is removed, and other times lead dust falls settling on horizontal surfaces such as windowsills. Young children are at high risk of high lead exposures, which can injure rapidly growing brain tissue. The U.S. Centers for Disease Control and Prevention (CDC) operates a healthy homes program that focuses on indoor exposures to toxins, with lead at the top of the list, and many academic and public service organizations emphasize the importance of eliminating lead exposures. For example, the Environmental Health Coalition (2015), which conducts outreach in low-income neighborhoods to find and remove lead sources, states that lead poisoning is the number one environmental hazard threatening children younger than six in the United States.

In 2008, EPA issued a rule in regard to renovation, repair and painting in older homes with lead paint on the inside and the outside. I have seen cases where the lead had been removed from the inside causing contamination. But why is there a concern about the outside? I was involved in one case where the outside of home was scraped prior to repainting. Unfortunately, windows were left open and paint chips seeped into the homes causing exposure to young children. The EPA RPP is intended to remove lead safely, reduce resuspension of lead into the air, and in other ways protect young children.

The rule is explicit about who is required to participate and what they are expected to do. Anyone who engages in work that could disturb lead paint in pre-1978 housing and children's facilities must participate, which means general contractors, multi-family maintenance staff, and specialty trades such as painters, plumbers, electricians. In other words, if you are demolishing, repairing or adding electrical systems, heating or air conditioning, windows, paining, plumbing, fixing or adding new windows, you should participate. Exclusions are for housing without bedrooms, such as dorms or studios, housing officially designated for elderly or the disabled and housing that is lead free.

The Associated General Contractors of America (2013) wrote a helpful fact sheet, which lays out the requirements for contractors:

- Distribution of EPS's lead education pamphlet "Renovate Right" to clients and obtain a signed receipt before starting work;
- Firm certification to do this type of work in pre-1978 housing and child-occupied facilities;
- At least one certified renovator who has taken a training course and is able to perform the requirements of posting signs before the work begins, containing contaminants within the work area and cleaning the work area when the work is completed;
- The certified renovator must train the other employees;
- Before the job starts, paint must be tested for lead, and this includes places that may be covered by wallpaper and other surfaces, and a report must be prepared indicating what was done;
- Use technology and practices that will protect workers and occupants, such as cover the floors and any furniture that cannot be moved; seal openings; and cover external grounds or use other means to prevent diffusion of lead, and many other steps;
- Clean the site when the job is completed and verify that the site is clean;
- Control and dispose of waste in bags or sheets that will not be disturbed until the material is moved off site for final disposal; and
- Keep records certifying that lead-based paint is not present, and other records associated with the work.

Failure to follow the rules can trigger financial penalties. In 2014, EPA (U.S. EPA 2014) initiated 61 enforcement cases that led to 55 settlements and sent a clear message that the program was important. It remains to be seen how much risk reduction will occur, but minimizing dust, containing the work area, and thoroughly cleaning up have not necessarily been standard practice, and this seemingly small step can substantially close the circle on a mistake made many decades ago.

Definition of solid waste (DSW)

Recycling is preferred to landfilling, incinerating, or tossing recyclable materials into streams or placing it on fields. However, recycling centers are typically disproportionately found in poor neighborhoods. Recycling centers are not automatically managed to reduce the risk of explosions, fires, and other accidental releases. EPA's DSW rulemaking gives the EPA, state and local government's far greater authority to oversee these facilities and try to reduce the likelihood of mismanagement leading to serious human health and environmental consequences (U.S. EPA 2015c).

The 2015 rulemaking has a 35-year history. Beginning in 1980, the EPA issued an interim final rule defining solid waste and exclusions from that definition. In

1985 it issued a final rule, and a major alteration was made in 2008 to emphasize recycling.

The press release for the 2015 rule (Deitz 2014, p. 1) says that the new rule is a "significant step forward in promoting recycling innovation, resulting in both resource conservation and economic benefits, while strengthening protections for environmental justice communities." One key element of the rule is that sites have to have trained personnel and resources to prevent hazard events and then respond should one occur, and the EPA and states have the authority under the Resource Conservation and Recovery Act (RCRA) to intervene during the permitting process or when the facility seeks a variance.

In regard to environmental justice, EPA conducted a special environmental justice analysis and held multiple public hearings (Philadelphia, Chicago) that clearly helped EPA narrow its focus. For example, they compared the location of non-hazardous industrial waste facilities, hazardous waste facilities and EPA's damage reports by community racial and demographic attributes. Based on 250 damage case reports, the affected population of the area is much more likely to be poor and minority than the remainder of the population. There also are more hazardous waste facilities and non-hazardous industrial waste facilities in minority and poor areas, but the proportions are much higher in the damage report set and are statistically significantly different at $p<.05$ (Office of Solid Waste and Emergency Response 2014).

Environmental justice played a significant role in this change of the DSW. Shaw *et al.* (2015) did an excellent job of tracing what they call EPA's "massive [rule is over 500 pages long] final definition of solid waste rule" back to the 1980 definition of waste versus recyclable material. In 2008, the Sierra Club filed an administrative petition arguing that the 2008 rule did not adequately protect against environmental releases. The article quotes Assistant EPA Administrator Mathy Stanilsaus as follows: "it's a major environmental justice milestone that directly addresses mismanagement of hazardous materials at some of these recycling facilities" (Shaw *et al.* 2015, p. 2). Please note that the rule change covers many other provisions that are not as directly related to environmental justice.

Mercury and air toxic standard (MATS)

Metals such as mercury and arsenic are emitted by coal burning fossil fuel plants across the United States. Many of these plants are located in the vicinity of tribal nations that rely on local fish for a large part of their food. Studies show that high levels of metal contamination are in the fish, and these fish are caught and eaten, disproportionately by poor and minority populations. On December 16, 2011, the EPA signed a rule to reduce emissions from power plants (U.S. EPA 2011; 2015d). Notably, the final MATS rule was not markedly different from the original EPA proposal. Existing sources were given four years to comply.

EPA estimated that about 1,400 units are impacted by this rule, mostly coal but some oil facilities. The EPA expects a 74 percent reduction in metal emissions as a result of the rule. EPA's fact sheet states that they reviewed more than 700,000 comments about MATS. EPA estimated that the health benefits are $37 billion to $90 billion in 2016 (which seems high to me) (see Cox 2013; Rabl, Spadaro, Holland 2014), and that the annual cost would be $9.6 billion. Various efforts were made to demonstrate that the changes would drive small facilities out of business, and that EPA's benefits estimates were much too high (EHS Management Forum 2012). Fifteen state chambers of commerce, coal associations and manufacture and energy associations challenged the MATS final rule (Rubrecht, Kelly 2012). The EPA (2011) argued that the lights will stay on and that while some older primarily 40+ year old coal plants might close earlier than anticipated, newer ones could be successfully retrofitted with existing technology over the four years for compliance. It expects that less polluting sources will provide new sources, especially gas. Studies by the Congressional Research Service and others concluded that the system failure arguments were exaggerated.

In regard to environmental justice, the NAACP applauded the MATS. NAACP President and CEO Benjamin Todd Jealous said: "The standards will save millions of dollars in medical expenses by helping to prevent new cases of asthma attacks and other respiratory disease that often strike families that can least afford it, while advancing a healthier quality of life for families across the nation" (Wrobel, p. 1). The article added that the "NAACP is committed to promoting environmental justice and protecting those who are disproportionately affected by air pollution, including low-income communities and communities of color."

Writing for a legal audience, Poloncarz and Carrier (2014) reviewed the U.S. Court of Appeals for the D.C. Circuit's upholding the MATS program. Noting that companies can perhaps delay until 2017, the authors argue that the court upheld EPA's expertise, which is common practice. Indeed, 30 law suits had been filed against MATS, and the court consolidated these into three issues. A key observation is that the court did not agree with the argument that EPA had to take cost of compliance into account.

As of 2015, the EPA rule stands, but companies still have some time to maneuver. The environmental justice community supported the EPA rulemaking with letters to the agency, as well as through the NAACP and other environmental justice-related organizations.

What is next in EPA and for Its environmental justice leadership

I would be naïve to assume that the EPA's efforts to integrate environmental justice processes into its programs will continue. EPA is not the favorite major federal agency among many elected officials. Various commentators have described a looming battlefront around EPA's programs (Leber 2014; Environmental Defense Fund 2014). The big issues are coal-fired power plants, clean water, ozone reduction in the atmosphere, global climate change, and EPA's rulemaking ability. The key point is that the environmental justice movement will be part of this battle. For example, Representative Mike Pompeo (2011) introduced legislation

(HR 2876) that would end the EPA's environmental justice eco-ambassador program, a small program for graduate students pursing a degree in the environmental health sciences, public health, public policy, environmental management, environmental law, and other areas relating to environmental issues. The program provides a 10-week internship of 20 hours per week at an EPA site with a stipend of $6,000 per student started in 2011 (U.S. EPA 2012). This is only a symbolic skirmish, and the major battle is to come, depending upon who controls the Congress and the Executive Branch.

Assuming, however, that EPA will continue to have a significant budget and control of it, we can expect to continue environmental justice efforts. Toward that end, EPA had a 2014 plan and is seeking input into an environmental justice plan for 2020. Noting that environmental justice 2020 is a strategy, not a rule, the agency (U.S. EPA 2015e), presented the following three focal points:

- Deepening environmental justice progress in EPA's programs to improve the health and environment of overburdened communities;
- Collaborating with partners to expand our impact on overburdened communities; and
- Demonstrating progress on outcomes that matter to overburdened communities.

(U.S.EPA 2015e, p. 1)

Following up its ongoing programs, EPA appears to be building a web of environmental justice programs within all of its programs (permit, rules, enforcement, science/tools). It is a prime mover in an Interagency Working Group on Environmental Justice and many other venues. It is continuing to build a network of community partners. Interested parties are directed to Charles Lee, the Deputy Associate Administrator for Environmental Justice, which is not who EPA would have chosen if they were backing away from their EJ commitment.

What did Chapter 5 explain about risk analysis? Summary and learning objectives

Equity among populations, places, and time is long-standing challenge for government. In the United States the first highly publicized case was in a rural poor and largely Afro-American community in North Carolina when the State of North Carolina chose to locate a hazardous waste landfill. That case led the United Church of Christ (UCC) to sponsor a study that demonstrated that minority areas had disproportionately more commercial hazardous waste sites than non-minority ones. The controversy that followed ultimately led to an environmental justice presidential order by President Clinton. In the United States the U.S. EPA has been the major protagonist for environmental justice, and the chapter details issues related to hazardous waste siting, air pollution, lead removal and others. Formal action on environmental justice came later to other nations.

At the end of this chapter readers should be able to answer the following seven questions:

1. What incident triggered the environmental justice movement in the United States?
2. How has the environmental justice movement developed in the European Union?
3. What are the drivers of environmental justice in the Southern Hemisphere?
4. How have U.S. courts been involved in environmental justice?
5. Are there instances of environmental injustice that may be needed to reduce risk?
6. How have rules and regulations become part of the environmental justice movement in the United States?
7. What efforts has EPA been taking to move its agenda forward? What factors and forces will oppose and support these efforts?

References

Anderton D, Anderson A, Rossi P, Oakes J, Fraser M, Webber E, Calabrese E. (1994) Hazardous waste facilities: "environmental equity" issues in metropolitan areas, *Evaluation Review*. 18, 123–140.

Associated General Contractors of America. (2013) Fact sheet: U.S. EPA's lead renovation, repair and painting program. January 31, 2013.

Been V. (1994) Locally undesirable land uses in minority neighborhoods: disproportionate siting or market dynamics? *Yale Law Journal*. 103, 1383–1422.

Bonorris S, ed. (2010) Environmental justice for all: a fifty state survey of legislation, policies and cases, fourth edition, www.abnet.org/environ/resources.html. Accessed August 12, 2015.

Bryant, B, ed. (2011) *Michigan: a state of environmental justice?* New York: Morgan James Publishing.

Bullard R. (1983) *Dumping on Dixie: race, class, and environmental quality*. Boulder, CO: Westview Press.

Bullard R, Mohai P, Saha R, Wright B. (2007) *Toxic wastes and race at twenty years, 1987–2007*. Cleveland, OH: The United Church of Christ.

Carruthers D, ed. (2008) *Environmental justice in Latin America: problems, promise, and practice*. Cambridge, MA: MIT Press.

Chester Residents and Mayfield Z, Morse C, Morse O, McDonald K, McDonald A, Stevenson C, Morse L, Otten R, Morse Rothwell L, Rothwell III A, Santiago M, Santiago R, Murphy, Weiss J, Otten R, Dale R, Rothwell F, and Gilliam, L. (Plaintiffs) vs. Seif J, (Secretary of the Pennsylvania Department of Environmental Protection, the Pennsylvania Department of Environmental Protection, Collier C (director of the Southeastern Region of the Department of Environmental Protection), and the Pennsylvania Department of Environmental Protection – Southeast Region (defendants). (1996) Chester residents concerned for quality living.) Civil action No 96-CV-3960, May 22, 1996.

Colby S, Ortman J. (2014) Projections of the size and composition of the U.S. population: 2014 to 2060. *Current Population Reports. P25-1143*. Washington, D.C.: U.S. Department of Commerce, U.S. Census Bureau.

Commission for Racial Justice. (1987) *Toxic waste and race.* New York: United Church of Christ.

Cox LA. (2013) *Improving risk analysis.* New York: Springer.

Cutter S. (1995) Race, class and environmental justice. *Progress in Human Geography.* 19, 1, 111–122.

Deitz R. (2014) EPA rule promotes responsible hazardous materials recycling, protects communities. http://yosemite.epa.gov/opa/admpress.nsf/596e17d7cac72084525781f 0043629e/d66ab83276a9fd6e8527daa005c3459!Opendocument. Accessed August 4, 2015.

EHS Management Forum. (2012) EPA's mercury and air toxics standards "costly" and time-consuming for coal plants. May 14, 2012. www.environmentalleader.com/2012/05/ 14-epas-mercury-and-air-tocis-standards-c. Accessed August 3, 2015.

Environmental Defense Fund. (2014) EPA's Climate change protections under attack. www.edf.org/climatge/epa-greenhouse-gas-litigation. Accessed August 19, 2015.

Environmental Health Coalition. (2015) Childhood lead-poisoning prevention. www.environmentalhealth.org/index.php/en/what-we-do/healthy-kids/childhood-lead-poisoning-prevention. Accessed August 4, 2015.

Europa. (2015) Migration and migrant population statistics. http://ec.europa.eu/ euroststat/statistics-explained/index.php/Migration_and_migrant_ population_statistics. Accessed August 15, 2015.

Fields L. (2013) Reflecting on the environmental legacy of Nelson Mandela. Compass. Sierra Club. December 18. Compass. Sierraclub/typepad.com/compass.2013/12/ reflecting-on-the-environmental-legacy-of nelson-mandela.part-1.htn. Accessed August 12, 2015.

Georgetown University. (2015) EPA's Gina McCarthy participates in Georgetown encyclical panel. June 17. www.georgetown.edu/news/encyclical-panel-gina-mccarthy-epa. Accessed August 15, 2015.

Goldshore L, Wolf M. (2001) Vitality of environmental justice, put in doubt, then bolstered again. *New Jersey Law Journal.* CLXIV, 8, 1–3.

Goldshore L, Wolf M. (2004) New executive order on environmental justice. *New Jersey Law Journal.* CLXXV, 11, March 15, 1–3.

Greenberg M. (1993) Proving environmental inequity in siting locally unwanted land uses. *Risk: Issues in Health & Safety,* 4, 235–252.

Greenberg M. (1999) *Restoring America's neighborhoods.* New Brunswick, NJ: Rutgers University Press.

Greenberg M. (2014) *Protecting seniors against environmental disasters: from hazards and vulnerability to prevention and resilience.* New York: Earthscan.

Greider W. (1997) *One world, ready or not: the magic logic of global capitalism.* New York: Touchstone.

Herbert J. (1995) EPA administrator takes presents to mayors conference. www.apnnewsarchive.com/1995/EPA-Administrator-Takes-Presents-to-Mayors-Conferences/id-8e354545b8b549dcbcd41093ee6cc49. Accessed August 10, 2015.

Kearney L. (2012) Mining and minerals in South Africa. www.southafrica.info/business/ economy/secors/mining.htm#.VdJAQ_IViko. Accessed August 17, 2014.

Laurent E. (2011) Issues in environmental justice within the European Union. *Ecological Economics.* 70, 1846–1853.

Leber R. (2014) The five battlefronts in Republicans' war on the EPA. *New Republic.* November 10. http://newrepublic.com/aritcles/120228/what-expect-gop-war-epa. Accessed August 19, 2015.

McCarthy J, Copeland C. (2014) EPA regulations: too much, too little, or on track?

Congressional Research Service, 7–5700, July 8, www.crs.gov. Accessed July 7, 2015.

McDonald D, ed. (2002) *Environmental justice in South Africa*. Athens, OH: Ohio University Press.

Meyer A. (2014) New EPA regulations issued under Obama are 38 times as long as Bible. http://cnsnews.com/news/article/ali-meyer/new-epa-regs-issued-under-Obama-are 38 times-as-long. Accessed July 7, 2015.

Mock B. (2015) We graded the feds on their environmental justice programs – here's how they fared. http://grist.org/author/brentin-mock. May 8.

Office of Solid Waste and Emergency Response, U.S. EPA. (2014). Potential adverse impacts under the definition of solid waste exclusions (including potential disproportional adverse impacts to minority and low-income populations). File:///c:/users/mrg/Downloads/Exeutive_Summary_Potential_Averse_Impacts_under_the_definition_of_Solid_Waste. Accessed August 3, 2015.

Poloncarz K, Carrier B. (2014) D.C. Circuit upholds EPA's mercury air toxics standards. stay current, www.paulhastings.com/docs/default-source-/PDFs/stay-current-docs. Accessed August 3, 2014.

Pompeo M. (2011) Stop EPA's student "environmental justice" agenda. Press Release, September 9. http://pompeo.house.gov/news/documentsingle.aspx?(DocumentID=259820. Accessed August 20, 2015.

Pope Francis. (2015) Encyclical on the environment: a dialogue on its moral and policy challenges. http://w2.vatican.va/content/francesco/en/encyclicals/documents/papa-franceso_201150524_enciclica- laudato-si.htn. Accessed August 15, 2015.

Rabl T, Spadaro J, Holland M. (2014) *How much is clean air worth?* Cambridge: Cambridge University Press.

Rubrecht GL, Kelly J. (2012) 15 state associations challenge U.S. EPA's mercury and air toxics standards. http://eem.jacksonkelly.com/2012/04/15-state-associations-challenge-us-epas-mercury-and. Accessed August 3, 2015.

Shaw S, Comella P, Joyce P, Simonsen C. (2015) EPA publishes massive final definition of solid waste rule, Synergy Environmental Inc., Newsletter, January 21, www.synergyenvinc.com/news/epa-publishes-massive-final-definition-solid-waste-rule/. Accessed August 4, 2015.

Singh K. (1999) *The globalization of finance: a citizen's guide*. London: Zed Books.

Steger T., ed. (2007) *Making the case for environmental justice in Central and Eastern Europe*. Budapest: Center for Environmental Policy and Law (CEPL).

United Nations Development Programme. (1999) *Human development report, 1999*. New York: Oxford University Press.

U.S. Environmental Protection Agency. (1992) *Environmental equity: reducing risk in all communities*. Washington, D.C.: EPA.

U.S. Environmental Protection Agency. (1995) Environmental risk study for city of Chester, Pennsylvania. Philadelphia, PA, June. http://epa.gov/region3/environmental_justice/ChesterEnvironmentalRiskStudySummaryReport6-1995.pdf. Accessed August 18, 2015.

U.S. Environmental Protection Agency. (2011) EPA fact sheet: mercury and air toxics standard, clean air and reliable electricity. www.epa.gov/.../pdfs/20111221MATScleanair-reliableelectricity.pdf. Accessed August 3, 2015.

U.S. Environmental Protection Agency. (2012) Environmental justice showcase communities. www.epa.gov/environmentaljustice/grants/eh-showcase.html. Accessed August 10, 2015.

U.S. Environmental Protection Agency. (2014) Enforcement: lead renovation, repair and painting rule – December 2014. www.epa.gov/enforcement/lead-renovation-repair-

and-painting-rule. Accessed August 4, 2015

U.S. Environmental Protection Agency. (2015a) On considering environmental justice during the development of regulatory actions, May. www.epa.gov/ environmental.justice/resources/policy/considering-ej-in-rule-making-guide_final.pdf. Accessed June 16, 2015.

U.S. Environmental Protection Agency, Science Advisory Board. (2015b) SAB review of the EPA's draft technical guidelines for assessing environmental justice in regulatory analysis, Washington, D.C.: U.S. EPA.

U.S. Environmental Protection Agency. (2015c) Definition of solid waste (DSW) rulemaking for RCRA hazardous waste regulations. www.epa.gov/osw/hazard/dsw/ rulemaking.htm. Accessed August 4, 2015.

U.S. Environmental Protection Agency. (2015d) Fact Sheet; Mercury and Air Toxics Standards for Power Plants. www.epa.gov/mats/pdfs/20111122MATSsummary.pdf. Accessed August 3, 2015.

U.S. Environmental Protection Agency. (2015e) Draft EJ action agenda. Washington, D.C. June 18, 2015. http://epa.gov/environmentaljustice/ej2020/index.html. Accessed August 4, 2015.

U.S. Government Accountability Office. (2005) Environmental justice: EPA should devote more attention to environmental justice when developing clean air rules. GAO-05-289. Washington, D.C.: GAO, July.

Varga C, Kiss I, Ember I. (2002) The lack of environmental justice in Central and Eastern Europe. *Environmental Health Perspectives.* 110, 11, A662–A663.

Weisskopf M. (1987) Rights group finds racism in dump siting. *The Washington Post.* April 16. http://pqasb.pqarchiver.com/washingtonpost/access/73811505.html?dids= 73811505:7381 Accessed December 18, 2007.

Williams HP. (2012) Universally acknowledged but yet fundamentally ignored: the (in)justice of environmental policy. *Pinpoint Politics.* http://pinpointpolitics.co.uk/ universally-acknowledged-but-yet-fundamentally-igonored-the-injustice-of- environmental-policy. Accessed August 15, 2015.

Williams L. (1987) Race bias found in location of toxic dumps. *The New York Times.* April 16. http://query.nytimes.com/gst/fullpage.html?res=9B0DEFDA113EF935A25757C 0A96194. Accessed December 4, 2007.

Williams L. (2009) Research confirms St. Lawrence cement plant pollutes nearby Camden waterfront neighborhood. Clean Water Action. www.cleanwateraction.org/press/ research-confirms-st-lawrence-cement-plant-pollutes-nearby-camden-waterfront. Accessed August 15, 2015.

Wrobel B. (2011) NAACP applauds EPA's mercury and air toxics standards. www.naacp.org/.../naacp-applauds-epas-mercury-and-air-toxics-standards. Accessed August 3, 2015.

Zimmerman R. (1993) Social equity and environmental risk. *Risk Analysis.* 1, 649–666.

6

CRITICAL PASSENGER RAIL INFRASTRUCTURE

Introduction

Infrastructure does not get much attention, until it fails, or when someone asks taxpayers to pay to repair and upgrade it. Even without major hazard events, protecting and enhancing infrastructure has become a serious problem and a relatively silent priority. The vulnerability and deterioration of, for example, the United States' collective water, sewer, electric, communication and transportation infrastructures, as well as of buildings is well documented (Committee on Predicting 2012) and risky. The country has fallen behind in rebuilding and upgrading infrastructure. Many local and state government and corporate officials appear to be acting like the mythical little pigs in the fairytale who built their houses out of straw and sticks, and when a wolf attacked fled to the brick house. Relying on the United States federal government to be the third pig and pay for bricks is wishful thinking. Underfunding infrastructure is a smart political idea, until it fails, leaving decision-makers looking for someone to blame when all they need to do is look in the mirror.

For this infrastructure case, I chose the passenger rail service between Washington D.C. and New York City. Arguably, they are the center of government and center of capitalism, respectively, in the United States. The rail corridor linking them is a challenging opportunity to apply risk assessment and risk management ideas and tools. Government and business should have an enormous vested interest in protecting the Northeast Corridor line that links these two centers. If they will not invest in this asset, then I am left wondering what assets that are not symbolic, like Liberty Island and the capitol building in Washington, D.C., are worth investing in.

The importance of rail transportation

Historical and international contexts

You probably know a "train buff," someone who touts the importance of trains, has books, photos, maps and usually model trains, and wants to show all of these to you. For example, in June 2014, my wife and I stopped in Xenia, Ohio, a former rail town, to check out the local Greene County museum. We were greeted by two people; one was a train buff who was overjoyed to learn that this author has ridden the New York City subways, including being stuck in a tunnel twice. He took us to his special upstairs room that had models of the local railroad. For him, the history of railroads in Ohio was the history of good jobs, economic growth, and the creation of a high quality urban–industrial way of life in his Ohio community.

Train buffs may exaggerate the role of railroads, but it is not possible to tell the story of urban-industrial growth in the United States, Europe, as well as parts of Asia, Africa and South America without acknowledging the importance of railroads. In the United Kingdom and the United States, railroads have been contributors to the economy for over 150 years. Before the steam engine, mules, horses and other animals pulled resources from mines along short primitive rails. With the invention and diffusion of steam engines, the importance of railroads markedly increased.

Between 1830 and 1860, the Northeast and Mid-Atlantic regions of the United States were tied to the Great Lakes region, forming the so-called American Manufacturing Belt (Figure 6.1). The rectangular-shaped belt was cornered by St. Louis in the southwest, Baltimore in the southeast, Boston in the northeast, and Milwaukee in the northwest. In 1950, eight of the ten most populous U.S. cities were in this 850 mile (1369 km) by 400 mile (644 km) industrial heartland. A dense rail network intertwined with major river ports and canals to form a powerful economic growth engine. Hauling freight was the initial emphasis, but passenger trains became common, including luxury trains such as Pullmans (after George Pullman). Walter Rostow's (1960) classic book on economic development of the United States asserts that by stimulating the coal, iron, and construction industries, U.S. railroads were a critical economic growth engine.

Impacts associated with railroads epitomize some of the best and worst impacts of United States capitalism, for example:

1. Enormous wealth was created, but disproportionately concentrated in the hands of a few families;
2. Technical achievement of linking the East and West Coast of the United States in 1869, including going through the Rocky Mountains; however, working conditions were severe and in some cases immigrants who built much of the rail line were treated poorly; and
3. Lifetime jobs, high wages, and other benefits to railroad employees; but labor strife, including riots, deaths, and localized economic disruption.

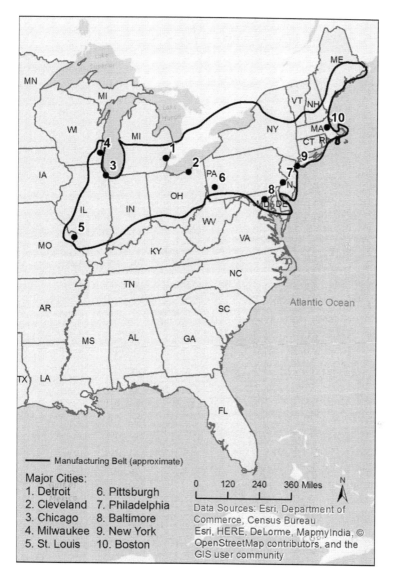

FIGURE 6.1 American manufacturing belt, circa 1950–1970

Canada, the United Kingdom, Germany, France, Belgium, Spain, Russia, Japan, China, Iran, Pakistan, Mexico, and other nations with a need to haul heavy products and move people between cities have similar and fascinating good and bad stories to tell about their railroads.

In the twenty-first century, the *Economist* (2010) characterizes rail transport as the best industry in the world, with enormous increases in productivity of freight hauling, which now has over 40 percent of the United States market, for example. In a globalizing world, the railroad will become an even bigger player in moving goods, and the choice of many daily commuters and interregional travelers in some parts of the world. The future of high-speed passenger rail is less certain because of the need to make and then continue major infrastructure investments.

An uncertain future for high-speed passenger rail

During the 1930s, the United States and Europe built lines and trains that traveled at about 80 mph (129 kmh). In Italy, the train from Milan to Florence topped 120 mph (193 kmh). But World War II intervened, and high-speed trains were less of a priority than moving troops and equipment.

Not until the 1960s, when the Japanese built a train that operated between Tokyo and Osaka at 135 mph (217 kmh), did the race for high-speed rail reengage. Europe launched a major effort that had high-speed trains operating by the mid-1980s in Belgium, Finland, France, Germany, Italy, Portugal, Romania, Russia, Spain, and overall throughout most of the European Union. In Asia, China and Japan have made massive investments, with China's ongoing as it tries to link its many large cities as part of its overall modernization plans. When the author visited China in 2010, he was invited to ride the high-speed rail line between Wuhan and Changsha (about 250 miles, 402 km). The representative of the rail line riding along with the author indicated that China would have the largest rail network of any country in the world. High-speed rail is one way of signaling economic prowess. But despite the enormous investment made by China in high-speed rail, there have been growing pains in the system, and I have to wonder if the government will continue to invest in building the system to reach out to all areas of the country as opposed to focusing on those that are clearly heavily used.

Efforts in the United States to build high-speed rail are much less aggressive and have faced considerable opposition in some locations. Plans exist to upgrade the technology and expand routes. The signature political event was when President Obama (2010) said the following during his State of the Union Address on January 27, 2010:

> We can put Americans to work today building the infrastructure of tomorrow. From the first railroad to the Interstate Highway System, our nation has always been built to compete. There's no reason Europe or China should have the fastest trains, or the new factories that manufacture clean energy products.
>
> Tomorrow, I'll visit Tampa, Florida, where workers will soon break ground on a new high-speed railroad funded by the Recovery Act.
>
> *(Obama 2010)*

The Federal Railroad Administration (2009) and especially the U.S. High-Speed Rail Association (2011) are supporters of rail expansion, focusing their efforts on building new lines in the West and South. The immediate context of this effort to expand rail was a serious recession that increased unemployment, and which led the U.S. government to spend taxpayer dollars in order to increase jobs and add new assets as part of the American Recovery and Reinvestment Act.

In the case of rail, the plan was partly successful. Several parts of the United States, for example, parts of California, embraced the idea and are building new lines. Parts of Texas are planning on high-speed rail, for example, the Dallas area. The major arguments against high-speed rail are that it creates competition with existing highways and airlines, and it is expensive. Some rejected the idea, for example, the governors of New Jersey and Florida. Indeed, President Obama did go to Tampa, and work was proceeding on the line between Tampa and Orlando, Florida (one of the author's daughters was designing rail stations), when the Governor of Florida canceled the project.

Despite the less than universal agreement to increase high-speed rail in the United States, the reality is that Amtrak (2013) annual passenger service has increased from 6.4 million in 1971 when Amtrak began operating to about 32 million in 2014. Furthermore, some states use Amtrak lines and their own network to carry daily commuters. Indeed, with some ingenuity and a lot of time, one can ride on local rail lines from Washington D.C. to Boston.

The Northeast Corridor Line (NEC)

Amtrak's Northeast Corridor between Boston and Washington, D.C. is the most heavily used part of the United States passenger rail system. The *Acela* (higher speed, fewer stops, more expensive) and Northeast Regional (slower, more stops, less expensive) carried over 11 million passengers in fiscal 2013 and was responsible for half of the national revenue (Amtrak 2013). Amtrak has major stops in Washington, D.C., Baltimore, MD, Wilmington, DE, Philadelphia, PA, Trenton, Metro Park and Newark, NJ, New York City, Stamford and New Haven, CN, Providence, RI and Boston, MA. The Washington D.C. to Boston NEC is 450 miles long (725 km) and contains major economic and political centers with the highest population density in the United States. The nine states that the NEC stops in have almost 70 million people (22 percent) of the national population, and these states rank 1–7, 9, and 14 in population density among the 50 states. The strategic importance of the Northeast Corridor Line in the United States for passenger rail service should make it a good example of the use of risk analysis as a process for understanding and managing infrastructure-related risks.

Almost 60 miles of the NEC are in New Jersey, the longest segment of any state in the corridor. In addition to Amtrak's regional service, states have local rail service. Notably, New Jersey has the largest public-operated mass transit system of any state (New Jersey Transit, or NJT), and these same rail lines in part are used by Amtrak and major freight rail systems. Furthermore, New Jersey is the most densely populated and second most affluent state in the United States (second only to Maryland).

Risk analysis to protect the rail corridor

Before providing the details of the risk analyses, I need to be clear about what was done and not done, why some decisions were made, and what was done and yet cannot be described in this chapter. The essence of this chapter is to show what was done to accomplish three risk-related objectives:

1. Objective 1: Replicate the current functioning rail corridor with a mathematical model. Meeting this objective was the most critical step. Without it, the users would not have taken any of the work seriously. Furthermore, they requested that we focus on one key rail station because they asserted that the less complex assets were already well enough characterized for risk management.
2. Objective 2: Build a regional economic consequence model that can be used to assess the damage of hazard events and calculate the benefits of investing to prevent and respond to those events. Users wanted us to focus on two key bridge assets and not on terrorist events.
3. Objective 3: Extend current air pollution models to assess the health impacts of emissions of a chemical agent dispersed along a rail line. This objective was to model a serious rail system event using the rail model built to meet objective 1 and an off-the-shelf air pollution emission model that others can use.

The models that follow could be used by persons with bad intentions. Accordingly, none of the scenarios is related to terrorism, and the risk management discussion below is generic not site-specific.

Objective 1: Simulating rail passenger service

Model elements

The ARENA simulation package, which was developed by Rockwell, (Altiok, Melamed 2007; Rossetti 2010) was chosen to build a model that could replicate reality and test hazard event scenarios. ARENA is a commercially available tool and in the case of a rail lines permits analysts to figuratively build tracks, stations, bridges, and other physical engineered systems into a mathematical model. It allows users to vary trains in service, cars per train, number of boarding-deboarding passengers, and time spent at a station for boarding/deboarding operations during rush hour (a.m. and p.m.) and non-peak hours. Many engineering students have been introduced to ARENA, and therefore we offered it to the rail managers as a tool that they could use as part of their regular operations, as well as to study hazard events. It was not a black box analytical tool that would be a mystery and would require them to depend on the author and his colleagues.

With assistance from New Jersey Transit (NJT) staff, we built a model of the rail corridor between Trenton NJ and New York Pennsylvania Station. Figure 6.2

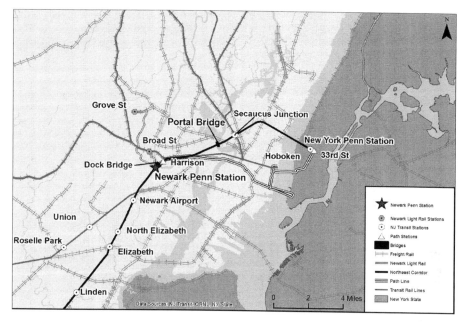

FIGURE 6.2 Area surrounding Newark Penn Station

shows the area around Newark Penn Station where the serious hazard events were to take place.

The main rail line between New York City and Trenton includes two to seven tracks. Newark's Penn Station is the highest use and most complex node in New Jersey, and its track structure illustrated in two dimensions in Figure 6.3. Newark Penn Station began operating in 1935. It has a daily average of 1,800 Amtrak passengers. Weekday boardings for NJ Transit and PATH were over 26,000 and 29,000; and 6180 boarded for Light Rail, respectively (Amtrak 2010; New Jersey Transit 2010). Over 1,000 trains stopped at Newark Penn Station on an average day: 290 NJ Transit, 104 Amtrak, 250 PATH and 386 Light Rail.

The Newark station staff has protocols and spreadsheets for routing and rerouting passengers, in the event of a problem. Comparing their spreadsheets to our simulation model results, their staff remarked that the spreadsheets can only capture a limited number of events, whereas the simulation model has a much greater capacity. The simulation model allows the user to stop the trains, and then operators make adjustments, while the model keeps track of how many people are stranded at different stations and stop locations between stations. When the system is functioning again, trains start running, and the model has recorded how many people were stranded at what location for how long a period of time. I think it is fair to say that these system operators were the strongest supporters of our rail model, and they were able to see how they would use it not only for risk analysis planning but even more than I could for other activities.

If the model can replicate reality, then we can figuratively stop the system at any time and watch what happens. The rail simulation model produces quite a variety of output metrics, only a few of which are used in this chapter. These metrics are as follows:

- The probability that system is down P(D), (i.e. the proportion of the time that the service is stopped in a year);
- The probability that a person is affected by any failure P(E), (i.e. the ratio of people affected on trains or stations to the total number of people using the system);
- Total number of people using the system, NJ Transit, Amtrak, Light Rail and PATH trains;
- Average and maximum number of people waiting at Newark Penn Station and other stations along the NEC;
- Number of disrupted and canceled trains during an incident;
- Average man-hour loss during short service disruptions (the time between the arrival of passenger to the station and the end of the incident);
- Number of passengers held on disrupted trains and its distribution for trains headed toward New York City or toward Trenton (NJ Transit, Amtrak, Light Rail and PATH trains); and
- Number of impacted passengers waiting at stations.

Visualization

Early in the modeling process, we realized that the complexity of the rail system would be a barrier to all but the most knowledgeable transit staff. Massive tables and graphs would not work because going through them was too tedious for senior managers. Hence, we built two animated versions of the model for non-technical audiences. One was the entire area between Trenton, New Jersey, and New York City Pennsylvania Station, which shows trains moving along the tracks and stopping in the stations (the viewer of the animation would see colored dots which represent trains in Figure 6.2). In the simulations that degrade the system, the animated version shows some of the dots stopping and others that are not affected by the event continuing on their destinations. Little boxes on the animation record how many people are stopped and stranded by the failure.

In addition to the regular stations, we added ten stop points as locations where trains can stay on standstill position when there is a system problem. Ten stop points were placed between stations that are more than 4 miles apart. The author, frequent traveler on NJT to New York City to visit his parents, has been held near several of these locations on the tracks.

A 12-minute version of the animation was created, and when that was characterized as being too long by senior decision-makers, then two 2–3-minute versions were created for presentations. The author typically ran the short animated version two or three times for audiences so they could understand what was happening during normal operations, when the system was disrupted, and then after it resumed operations.

A graphic visualization below (Figure 6.3) is of Newark Pennsylvania Station, which shows people deboarding and boarding trains, and the little boxes on each platform keep track of the number of people (they cannot be read in this text but are readable on a screen).

Validation

Initially, potential users, including several of this author's former students who work at the transportation agencies, were skeptical and not interested unless they could be shown that we could represent current reality. Accordingly, we ran the model 25 times for one year and compared the average results to the data provided to us by the rail system managers for number of trains, average travel time, and average number of passengers boarding and deboarding at Newark Penn Station. Data for the Newark Penn Station (Table 6.1), show close agreement between the actual and simulated number of trains at Newark Penn Station.

Average travel times, which include speed of trains and time to board and deboard were also very close (Table 6.2) for both westbound (WB heading toward Trenton) and eastbound (EB toward New York City). Table 6.2 shows four of the most important routes (four of 46).

Finally, average daily passenger boardings and deboardings are summarized in Table 6.3. This comparison of the simulation results against the actual 2010 data show little difference.

TABLE 6.1 Validation results, number of trains at Newark Penn Station, daily average

Train	Simulation	Real data
NJ Transit	289.62 ± 0.0223	290
Amtrak	103.57 ± 0.0052	104
Light Rail	384.56 ± 0.0417	386
PATH	247.63 ± 0.0228	250

TABLE 6.2 Validation results, times between selected stations, minutes

Train and direction	Simulation	Real data
EB Northeast Corridor (trains from NJ to NY Penn Station)	28.28	28
WB Northeast Corridor (trains from NY Penn Station to NJ)	30.55	30
EB Acela (High speed trains from Washington DC to NY and Boston)	35.37	35
WB Acela (High speed trains from Boston and NY to Washington)	27.92	27

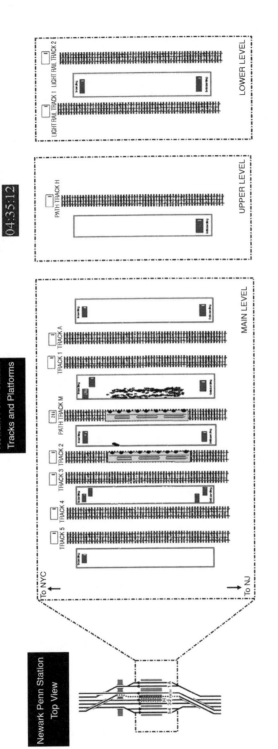

FIGURE 6.3 Two dimensional view of the Newark Penn Station rail station

TABLE 6.3 Validation: boardings and deboardings at Newark Penn Station, average daily values

	Simulation	Real data
NJ Transit boardings	26,525 ± 4.6761	26,449
Amtrak boardings	1,800 ± 0.4107	1,800
Subway boardings	6,103 ± 0.8924	6,152
PATH boardings	29,805 ± 4.8177	29,923
NJ Transit deboardings	26,405 ± 5.9433	26,449
Amtrak deboardings	1,803 ± 0.4881	1,800
Subway deboardings	6,252 ± 1.1593	6,215
PATH deboardings	29,622 ± 4.1459	29,923

The final and most complex validation was to try to capture the flow of passengers during 24 hours. At the time of this work, the NJT staff did not have an actual count; nevertheless they have considerable experience. The AM peak is about half of the PM one because many people deboard at the AM peak and many more board in the evening rush.

While the model results clearly were valid for 2010, they would need to be updated to capture current passenger flows. Assuming the schedules and other data were kept updated, the conclusion is that the model could be used to follow the impact of minor and major events. However, as a further test, we modeled the results of "routine" failure events for the NJT staff as described below.

Classifying hazard events and choosing two major hazard events for analysis

Possible events include chronic, small and annoying delays all the way to massive destruction that kills and injures many people, destroys and degrades parts of the system, and indirectly leads to job and income loss across this and other regions. The logical place to begin is with a search through existing literatures.

Literature review and suggestions from experts

The U.S. Federal Railroad Administration (FRA)'s Office of Safety Analysis maintains a searchable list of every reported accident beginning with January 1975. The web-list has tens of thousands of events with collisions, derailments, and other major event categories. These broad categories are further subdivided into train accidents, high-rail grade crossing, and others. Among the approximately 500 specific causes are worn rail and defective and missing crossties. Human error is apparent in the data, including events attributed to vandalism, employees falling asleep, other worker failures, and other human factors.

There have been attempts to depict the worst train disasters. Kichenside (1997) and Semmens (1994) report the worst train disasters measured by deaths. The BBC

(2007) reported the 17 worst rail disasters from 1981 through 2007. These depictions find that nearly all of the world's worst train disasters were in Africa and Asia and involved brake failures, collisions and derailments, gas explosions, and even cyclones toppling a train into a river.

Given concern about terrorist-initiated events, Jenkins, Butterworth, and Clair (2010) reviewed 181 rail sabotage attempts, including one to derail a high-speed train in 1995 in France. There have also been assessments of the impacts of hazard events such as earthquakes on ports and other transportation systems (Chang 2000; Chang, Nojima 1998; Committee 1999). All the data bases and studies provide insights into what terrorists might do.

For the example in this book, the question is how relevant are these as illustrations in the context of the Northeast Rail Corridor. The question was answered by people who have been working on the rail line. The author and colleagues spoke with Amtrak security staff, staff at New Jersey Transit, as well as colleagues. We asked what kinds of events would be most serious and analysis of what events would provide them with useful planning data.

Amtrak and NJT suggested the focus of the simulations. They did not want terrorist attack scenarios presented to the public. To avoid providing information to those with bad intentions, we did not built a cyberattack scenario, nor events around biological agents, multiple coordinated conventional explosions, dirty bombs and other terrorist-initiated events. Hence, the public demonstration of models, especially this one, may not be the same as their use for internal purposes. If the model works, then the full range of concerns can be addressed out of the public eye by the responsible parties.

One final test: routine delays in service, relatively high probability events with limited consequences

The United States DOT has a goal to reduce the delays of 15 minutes or more for its Amtrak trains (Bureau of Transportation Statistics 2005). Reports for the Northeast Corridor (NEC) and the nation as a whole show large variations by year and location. Compared to the 1970s and 1980s, delays have decreased. Acela Express data for 2012 and 2013 along the NEC show on-time arrival of 94 percent (Amtrak 2012), and Northeast Regional Trains also report a very high level of on-time arrival.

Reporting for the *New York Times*, Grynbaum and Gebeloff (2010) note that 96 percent of daily commuter railroads that serve New York and New Jersey are on time. The *New York Times* staff gathered its own data from three commuter lines and conclude that one in ten trains entering New York Penn Station arrived late, and two-thirds of these by 10 minutes or more. During the rush hour, they report that two in five were late by at least 15 minutes (see also Human Transit 2010). New Jersey Transit, which is a key part of this study, was reported to have the most delays. The reports say that limited tunnels, bridges and platforms account for the delays. These Amtrak and NJ Transit data show that delays of an hour or more are infrequent.

With these data as context, as a final preliminary test of the model, a set of simulations with 15 to 30 minute delays were run, and these were checked by the rail staff against their experience. They observed that the morning rush hour simulations seemed to understate the number of delayed passengers. They provided more refined data. The models were rerun and judged to be reflective of reality.

Objective 2: Economic consequences of a major failure

Regional context

We chose a major mechanical failure that would focus around the Newark Pennsylvania Station facility, which the rail staff indicated was by far the most pivotal one in the State of New Jersey because multiple rail, light rail, and bus lines converge on the site. There are two major bridges north and east of the Newark Penn Station: the Dock Bridge and the Portal Bridge. Figure 6.2 shows the location of the bridges relative to the Newark Station and Figure 6.4 shows the entire New Jersey part of the Northeast Corridor line from Trenton to New York Pennsylvania Station.

The Dock Bridge consists of two vertical lift bridges built during the mid-1930s that crosses the Passaic River immediately north of Newark's Pennsylvania Station. The Portal Bridge is a movable swing-span bridge between Kearny and Secaucus New Jersey that crosses the Hackensack River that dates from 1910.

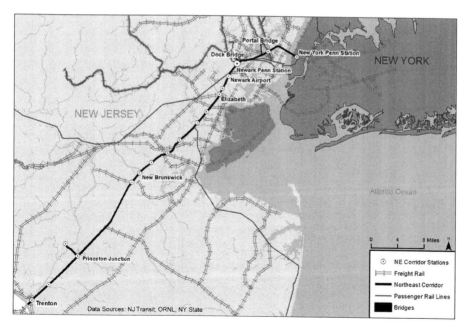

FIGURE 6.4 Location of New Jersey portion of the Northeast Corridor Line

Neither bridge is close to state-of-the-art, and the Portal Bridge sits so low over the river that it has to be open to allow commercial boat traffic. Several officials told the author that it is really a weak link in Northeast Corridor service. The author twice has been on a train that was delayed for more than 15 minutes because of opening of the Portal Bridge. The estimated cost of rebuilding the Portal Bridge is close to $1 billion (Associated Press 2014).

To illustrate a plausible event involving these bridges, we assumed that one would suffer a serious mechanical failure and could not be operated for a year. In fact, this is probably an optimistic assumption because a failure might take more than a year to address. It is further assumed that no one on a train is injured by this event. Hence, the consequences are economic, that is, the delay of rail traffic from Washington D.C. through Boston, and especially would be problematic for commuters between New Jersey and New York City.

Regional economic impact simulation

Context

The objective of regional economic impact tools is to follow the economic ripples of events through the regional economy, that is, beyond the local area where the event originates. People see the immediate impacts of a bridge failures and derailments on television. They may not see other impacts, at least not immediately, unless they are personally involved. A serious prolonged rail-related disruption would lead some people to be late to work and/or lose sleep and time at home. Some would drive to work, increasing traffic congestion, accidents, and even potentially leading to local gasoline price increases. A prolonged event would strain the capacity of other mass transit options. Some people may not be able to get to work, and some freight may not be delivered or be shifted to other modes. If the flow of supplies is disrupted because the same rail network carries freight, then products in commerce will decrease. If the problem lingers, workers will be furloughed and reduce consumption, especially of items that they can defer. Government tax collections would drop because of business losses and consequent reductions in worker earnings. Most important, decision-makers could choose to relocate their business (see below for simulation results).

The simulated bridge failure centers around the Newark Pennsylvania rail station. But the potentially impacted area is much larger. Those that travel on Amtrak could drive or they could take ferries. Commuting patterns between central and northern New Jersey and New York City would be disrupted by the simulated event. Accordingly, a regional economic model was built that joined New Jersey, New York City, and its eastern and northern suburbs that tie in through Metro North and the Long Island Railroad (see below).

Econometric model

Econometric, input-output, computable general equilibrium (CGE), inoperability input-output models, and regional economic model (REMI) can be applied to this economic consequence analysis (Greenberg *et al.* 2007; Haimes *et al.* 2005a,b; REMI 1997; Robinson *et al.* 1999; Rose *et al.* 1997; Santos, Haimes 2004; Treyz 1993). Each of these has advantages and disadvantages. We chose an econometric model to present the overall results because it has the capacity to include impact estimates for a time period of a decade or more. We also built a computable general equilibrium model (CGE) to test for traffic congestion effects from commuters switching from the train to automobiles and buses. (The CGE results are not presented here.)

Econometric simulation models are built from data that link historical relationships among gross national product, consumer spending, labor, and other elements of the economy. For example, if wages and salaries increase and the record over the last 20 years shows that 8 percent of wages and salaries is spent on consumer products, then we assume that the impact of a wage and salary increase on consumer spending is 8 percent.

A region that includes the State of New Jersey and the New York Metropolitan region requires the use of national forecasts to ground the analyses. Also, federal income tax rates, monetary policy and other federal decisions are external to the model. In other words, to the extent that national government forecasts and estimates are substantially inaccurate, then the regional results will be inaccurate.

The model used here includes all of New Jersey's 21 counties, New York City, Nassau and Suffolk, Counties (east of New York City), and Westchester, Rockland, and Putnam counties (north of New York City). The New Jersey part includes 210 equations. The heart of the New Jersey model is a set of equations that model employment, wages, and prices for 40 industries. The New York Metropolitan region equations are similar but less detailed (78 equations).

We assume that the two regions are most directly connected through a shared work force for key industries, as well as shared media, culture, and history. We linked employment through construction, finance, information, manufacturing, wholesale trade, and professional and business services.

Given these connections, major disruptions to New Jersey's economy should also impact on New York, although to a lesser extent. Using this model we should be able to gauge the regional impact of a major rail disruption at the Newark Penn Station. The major limitation of econometric models is the historical relationships in the model may produce misleading results if the economy is rapidly changing in terms of absolute purchases, labor needs and wages. The CGE model helps deal with some of these issues, but has limitations of its own.

Table 6.4 provides results for the simplest low probability event, which is a once a week, one-hour delay that starts at 7:30 a.m. It is assumed the services that pass through the Newark Penn Station are affected from that incident. We ran the model 25 times and averaged the results. The model estimates how many trains are

TABLE 6.4 Simulation results for baseline event of a 1-hour delay once a week (based on assumption that the event occurs at 7:30 a.m. and does not include health impacts)

Performance measures	One hour in a week
Average number of trains disrupted★	25
Average number of train cancelations	100
Average number of passengers held on disrupted trains	9,142
Average number of passengers held on disrupted EB NJ Transit trains	6,339
Average number of passengers held on disrupted WB NJ Transit trains	839
Average number of passengers held on disrupted EB Amtrak trains	849
Average number of passengers held on disrupted WB Amtrak trains	890
Average number of passengers held on disrupted EB Light Rail trains	72
Average number of passengers held on disrupted WB Light Rail trains	153
Average number of impacted passengers at stations★★	44,702
Average number of impacted passengers waiting at Elizabeth	2,226
Average number of impacted passengers waiting at Newark Airport	224
Average number of impacted passengers waiting at Newark Penn	7,513
Average number of impacted passengers waiting at Secaucus★★★	7,513
Average number of impacted passengers waiting at Harrison (PATH station)	4,302
Average number of impacted passengers waiting at NY Penn	639

Notes: ★Disrupted trains represent the trains stopped in actual service.
★★Data for all stations are not presented.
★★★This station serves people coming from northern New Jersey who deboard and travel to New York City or toward Trenton on the NEC.

disrupted, canceled, the average number of people held on disrupted trains, and the average number of passengers waiting at stations. Selected stations are shown.

More specifically, Table 6.4 shows how many passenger trains are disrupted and canceled, and how many people are impacted by a once a week one-hour delay. The impacts of a 7:30 a.m. event are concentrated on the eastbound trains headed toward New York City and primarily in New Jersey Transit trains. When this event was entered into the economic model, the results were measurable but would not be noticeable in the annual economic results.

One reason that this kind of event is not noticeable is the massive economic size of this region. Table 6.5 shows the baseline econometric simulations. I show the actual data for 2010. Then, I provide simulations for 2012 and 2020. For purposes of this research, the key is the impact of the rail events on economic performance. For some applications it is appropriate to review the simulation results of all of these indicators in Table 6.5. However, for the cases that follow, we have concentrated on two of the indicators: nonagricultural employment, and real gross domestic product. In other words all of the comparisons that follow will compare these forecasted results and the post-event results.

TABLE 6.5 Baseline economic simulation results without impact of hazard event

Area and metric	2010	2012	2020	Annual % change, 2010–20
New Jersey				
Non-agricultural employment (000)	3854.1	3923.7	4181.3	0.8
Unemployment rate, %	9.4	7.2	5.0	−6.2
Population (000)	8791.9	8880.5	9192.2	0.4
Personal income ($mill)	450.4	482.0	672.8	4.1
Wage rate ($000)	56.6	59.5	73.5	2.7
Real Gross domestic product (2005=100, $mill)	438.7	459.6	560.3	2.5
Consumer price index NJ (1982 =100)	234.1	242.1	278.8	1.8
*New York region (10 counties)**				
Non-agricultural employment (000)	5169.5	5265.7	5951.7	1.4
Unemployment rate, %	8.8	5.5	5.6	−4.5
Population (000)	12368.5	12429.5	12969.1	0.5
Personal income ($ mill)	668.4	716.7	966.5	3.8
Wage rate ($000)	70.8	68.4	103.7	3.9
Real gross domestic product (2005=100, $mill)	778.9	816.8	942.7	1.9
Consumer price index NY (1982 =100)	240.9	250.8	296.8	2.1

Note: *New York City, Westchester, Rockland, Putnam, Nassau, Suffolk

Major bridge failure scenarios: results

A major event would be loss of one of the main bridges between Newark Penn Station and New York City for a year. Adding the 24 million people who use PATH every year to the over 70 million that ride on NJT, 9 million on Amtrak, and 4.5 million that use Newark totals over 100 million passenger rides that pass through Newark Penn Station would be disrupted by loss of a major asset that could not be replaced for a year. The Dock Bridge, lying just north of Newark Penn Station or the Portal Bridge over the Hackensack River not far from the Secaucus rail station are key vulnerable assets.

The region and U.S. as a whole could not afford to lose these kinds of major assets even if there were no injuries or deaths. To estimate the number of people inconvenienced, we first assume that each person is making a round trip (not always the case), which reduces the estimate to 55 million passengers. Many of these NJT, Light rail and PATH riders make the trip five days a week, but not all do. In order to simulate reality and allow for variations, we calculated average trip usage by different Amtrak and NJT trains, and then ran them in the model, with some variations built in as probabilities of different trains arriving at the Newark Penn Station.

We ran multiple economic simulations to test plausible options. Of these, the last, we think, is most likely. Our first assumption is that there will be efforts to provide resilience to the system. It is simply inconceivable to us that Amtrak and New Jersey Transit would not respond. Hence, the first set of analyses assume that the railroads and the local governments provide a shuttle service from the Newark Penn Station to the PATH rail line in Harrison, New Jersey and to Broad Street station in Newark that goes around a Dock Street bridge failure.

This plausible solution, however, is not without complications. The most obvious is the need to provide carefully supervised boarding and deboarding from Newark Penn Station to buses (assuming their availability) that would travel to Harrison, which is a short distance but separated by a river. There will be substantial crowding, frustrated people, equipment limitations, annoying weather conditions and other circumstances that will slow down the transfer of the riders. It is reasonable to expect that the average trip would be delayed one hour in both directions, that is, a total of two hours a day. A much better result is that the delay would only be one half hour in both directions, or a total one-hour delay. These two were the first simulations of this low probability and high consequence bridge failure.

A more probable option is that only 40 percent are willing to accept a one hour per day delay for a full year, another 40 percent drive in their autos or take buses, and the remaining 20 percent telecommute on any work day (airplanes not considered in these simulations, although it would be an option for those going from Washington D.C. to New York City and Boston). A big issue is the impact on road congestion, which adds to the commute time and/or cuts into leisure time for those who drive. One version shown in Table 6.6 assumes an average loss of two hours a working day getting to work. The more optimistic one assumes that combinations of shift to light rail and other rail at Newark, more buses and autos, plus telecommuting reduces the loss to only one hour a working day.

The third simulation is among the most painful and is a realistic response by business. It assumes a two hour a day loss of time per working day for passengers and one-third of job losses associated with the event are not replaced in the region. That is, businesses in the area permanently relocate their activity outside of the study area. No one knows how many jobs would permanently be lost. However, following the events at the World Trade Center over 100,000 jobs were lost. The Fiscal Policy Institute (2001) reported that most of these had relocated elsewhere in New York City, but that 22,000 relocated outside New York City, principally in New Jersey. Notably, the vast majority of the job losses were by people who held less skilled positions, such as janitors and cleaners, maids and housekeeping workers, and apparel workers.

Before reviewing the simulation results, context is in order. This is a massive economic region of over 21 million people, 10 million jobs, and a real gross domestic product of $1.3 trillion in 2005 dollars. Because this region is so massive and multi-faceted, it has enormous capacity to adjust to negative events, whether they are natural hazards, human-initiated problems, financial miscalculations, or others. This region is the markedly different from some others that the author has studied that have been dependent on a single major employer. For example, the author examined the economic impact of reducing investments in environmental management cleanup programs in some the rural regions where nuclear weapons were developed, tested, built and where nuclear waste is stored. In these small economic regions, a relatively small reduction in a single government program causes a local recession (Greenberg, Miller, Frisch, Lewis 2003). A region like NJ-NYMR has the ability to absorb major events, especially over time. One of the strengths of econometric models is that they play out the event while at the same time continuing regional economic growth. Internally, as in this case, an initial economic blow is delivered but unless it is accompanied by decisions that permanently remove economic activity from the region, the region rebounds. In this set of simulations, we caused the event in the year 2012 and the big economic hit occurs in 2013. Gradually, the national and regional economies grow, the impact is absorbed unless there is a major permanent loss of jobs caused by decisions that the region is no longer viable (scenario #3 below).

The 2-hour delay with resilience shows job losses and by the year 2020, the economy has come back. But about 10,000 jobs are lost by 2020 (#1 in Table 6.6). New Jersey, where the event occurs is disproportionately impacted. Assuming decision-makers feel that the problem would be fixed and commuters could tolerate the loss of time for a year, the impact in a region of this size is relatively modest. It becomes even more modest if the time loss were cut from two hours to one hour (#2 in Table 6.6). The job loss in the region drops to 5,100 and the GDP loss is reduced.

The last scenario (#3 in Table 6.6) is the one we believe is the most likely for an event that lasted for a year without a clear ending date. Some decision-makers would figure out ways to provide temporary housing for their employees and shuttles around the problem. But others would not have the patience or the budget. We assume for purposes of this simulation that among those who are losing productivity, one-third would choose to leave the area. The job loss estimate compared to the baseline is 41,000 of which three-fourths are in New Jersey.

A total of 41,000 jobs in a region with about 10 million does not seem like much, only 0.4 percent, but in an era when the unemployment rates is over 6 percent and we expect it to be 5 percent by 2020, which may be an optimistic baseline forecast, these jobs would be noticed. But is this a major loss? For context, New Jersey lost 114,000 jobs from December 2007 through December 2008, which makes this loss seem small measured over almost a decade. A major difference was that the losses during 2007–2008 were part of a series of international events that have not been fully addressed and required major actions on the part of the U.S. government, the financial and housing industries and other nations. Arguably, the great recession that began in 2008 could have been prevented or mitigated, but only with a complex policy consensus by various parties.

In contrast, our event, a single bridge failure is virtually preventable by the owners and operators of the bridge in question. Furthermore, we deliberately picked one of the simplest problems to overcome by shuttling people a short distance. There are

TABLE 6.6 Comparison of baseline economic results and impacted results: full year loss of major bridge asset and different levels of resilience

Region and metric	2010	2012	2020	Difference between baseline and impacted, 2010–2020
0. Baseline				
New Jersey				
Non-agricultural employment (000)	3854.1	3923.7	4181.3	–
Real gross domestic product (2005=100, $mill)	438.7	459.6	560.3	–
New York region				
Non-agricultural employment (000)	5169.5	5265.7	5951.7	–
Real gross domestic product (2005=100, $mill)	778.9	816.8	942.7	–
1. Impacted, limited resilience, 2 hour delay per day				
New Jersey				
Non-agricultural employment (000)	3854.1	3899.0	4175.6	−5.7
Real gross domestic product (2005=100, $mill)	438.7	459.2	558.9	−1.4
New York				
Non-agricultural employment (000)	5169.5	5257.0	5947.7	−4.0
Real gross domestic product (2005=100, $mill)	778.9	815.8	941.7	−1.0
2. Impacted, resilience, 1 hour delay per day				
New Jersey				
Non-agricultural employment (000)	3854.1	3910.7	4179.4	−1.9
Real gross domestic product (2005=100, $mill)	438.7	459.2	559.1	−1.2
New York				
Non-agricultural employment (000)	5169.5	5261.3	5948.5	−3.2
Real gross domestic product (2005=100, $mill)	778.9	816.2	941.9	−0.8
New Jersey				
Non-agricultural employment (000)	3854.1	3903.7	4177.1	−4.2
Real gross domestic product (2005=100, $mill)	438.7	459.2	559.0	−1.3
New York				
Non-agricultural employment (000)	5169.5	5258.7	5948.0	−3.7
Real gross domestic product (2005=100, $mill)	778.9	816.0	941.8	−0.9
3. Impacted, 2 hour delay and no replacement of one-third of job losses				
New Jersey				
Non-agricultural employment (000)	3854.1	3899.0	4151.7	−29.6
Real gross domestic product (2005=100, $mill)	438.7	459.2	558.6	−1.7
New York				
Non-agricultural employment (000)	5169.5	5257.0	5940.6	−11.1
Real gross domestic product (2005=100, $mill)	778.9	815.8	940.8	−1.9

other bridge and road failures in this region that would be hard to work around. If this was a terrorist attack, we could anticipate attempts to damage multiple links in the rail system and highways system, which would be extraordinarily difficult to overcome without a substantial investment. In short, in contrast to other rail structure events we could have tested, this one is relatively modest, albeit painful.

Overall, combining the rail simulation model results with economic simulation capacity allows decision-makers to assess the economic consequences of natural and human hazard events, and think about which of these is more and less tolerable before committing limited resources to prevention and resilience.

Objective 3: Chlorine tank leak: low probability, high consequence with health impacts

A long list of natural and human-initiated events could kill and injure people, as well as damage the environment and assets. Earlier I indicated that this book would not include a publicly available terrorist-initiated event. Also, NJT and Amtrak indicated that the Newark Penn Station was a key location for them. Hence, an industrial emission scenario was created around the Northeast Rail Corridor near the Newark rail complex.

An industrial train containing liquid chlorine leaves its factory and heads south along the rail line. Improbably, one car has a small hole and emits liquid chlorine as it follows the rail line, and improbably the leak is not stopped for 90 minutes. The event is described in detail below.

Air pollution simulation model

Air pollution plume models estimate how particles and gases disperse. Emissions can be episodic, such as from periodic manufacturing operations, a fire, or leak from a factory or rail car, or they can be continuous such as from a scrubber controlling sulfur emissions at a petroleum refinery, and home heating during the winter. The impacts of emissions depend on the following set of attributes at the site.

1. Biological, chemical, and physical characteristics of the emitted substance;
2. Velocity, temperature, rate of release and height of the emission source;
3. Characteristics of the surrounding environment, such as buildings and hills that could redirect and absorb some of the emitted material;
4. Immediate environmental conditions, notably wind direction, speed and turbulence;
5. Human and ecological receptors directly exposed because they are outside or in nearby schools, hospitals, houses, enclosed arenas and others; and
6. Capacity of local responders to evacuate and/or direct shelter in place.

Chlorine tank leak scenario with the SCIPUFF model

Chlorine, a ubiquitous substance, is widely used for purifying potable water and wastewater, and as an intermediate chemical and many other products. Manufactured in northern New Jersey and of considerable concern to risk analysts, the State of New Jersey, and the American Chemistry Council (see below under risk management), chlorine and ammonia account for much of chemical shipments by rail in the United States. There have been chlorine incidents. In 2005, a train derailment near Graniteville, South Carolina, ruptured a tank car with chlorine and nine people were killed, 75 injured, and over 5,000 people living within a 1 mile radius were evacuated for several days. The estimated cost of this event was $126 million (Federal Railroad Administration 2005). A simulation study that assumes a chlorine railcar rupture near the Washington, D.C. mall during a major public event was estimated to kill 17,500 people. In general, chlorine is among the chemicals of greatest concern to the American Chemistry Council (2012). Please also note that chlorine's properties to suffocate were well known about a century ago, when it was used as a chemical weapon during World War I (see Chapter 4).

Several dozen mathematical models are available to simulate air pollutant dispersion. SCIPUFF (Second-Order Closure Integrated Puff) was used. Validated in the field and laboratory (Sykes, *et al.* 1999, Sykes, Gabruk 1997), it uses a collection of Gaussian puffs to create time-varying three-dimensional concentration profiles, and predicts both the average concentration and the concentration variance out from the sources. SCIPUFF can use time-varying meteorological inputs. Concentrations of contaminants are estimated at locations, over a regular grid, or for contours of concentration profiles. The model permits adjustment for terrain, particle and gas movement, degradation, short and long range transport, and direct input of meteorological information.

The SCIPUFF implementation used in this chapter was from the Hazard Prediction and Assessment Capability (HPAC) system (DTRA 2003), which provides dispersion modeling in addition to chemical, biological, and nuclear databases for source definitions. HPAC has been tested in the URBAN 2000 field experiment (Allwine, Shinn *et al.* 2002) and in various other comparative evaluation studies (Chang, Hanna *et al.* 2005; Warner, Platt *et al.* 2004; Urban *et al.* 2011).

High risk scenario

There is a major chlorine manufacturing facility in northern New Jersey, and trains leaving the site can take four paths. One of these follows the Northeast Corridor passenger rail line before turning west. A leak occurs from one of chlorine-containing rail cars, and SCIPUFF predicts concentrations along the corridor. The public health impacts are interpreted using the guidelines developed by the National Advisory Committee for the Acute Exposure Guideline Levels (AEGL) for short-term exposure. AEGLs help companies and government think about facility location and air pollution controls, and they are used for alerts and emergency responses (NRC 2001, 2004).

AEGL values are presented for three exposure levels: AEGL3 is the threshold for lethal effects; AEGL2 is threshold for serious, long-lasting effects or an impaired ability to escape; and AEGL1 is the threshold for notable discomfort. In addition, AEGL values are estimated for specified exposure periods, typically 10 minutes, 30 minutes, 1 hour, 8 hours, and so on. Human health risks greatly depend on whether the high levels of concentrations persist, and whether the individual was present at that location during the period of high concentrations (see Figure 6.5).

The dark shades on the maps that follow show a potentially lethal dose of chlorine without medical treatment. The gray implies a high level of exposure that might require medical treatment, and less intense gray may be associated with watery eyes and odors.

Chlorine leak event scenario and results

The illustration shown in the book starts near Kearny, New Jersey. A freight train leaves the chlorine manufacturing site and merges into the main Northeast Corridor line. Traveling at 5 miles/hour with low wind speed, a rail car begins to leak chlorine at 10 kg per second. Figure 6.6 shows five stages as the train travels south and west. Stage 1 is a small plume at 10 minutes, with a high dose near the

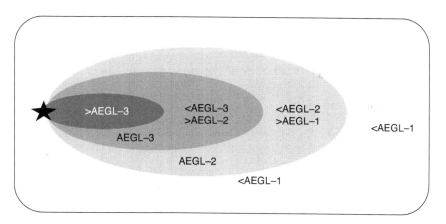

FIGURE 6.5 Schematic of impact from a hazardous release

TABLE 6.7 AEGLs for chlorine

AEGLs, ppm	10 minutes	30 minutes	1 hour	4 hours	8 hours
AEGL1	0.5	0.4	0.5	0.5	0.5
AEGL2	2.8	2.8	2	1	0.5
AEGL3	50	28	20	10	7.1

Note: AEGLs are in parts per million or milligrams per cubic meter, NRC, 2004.

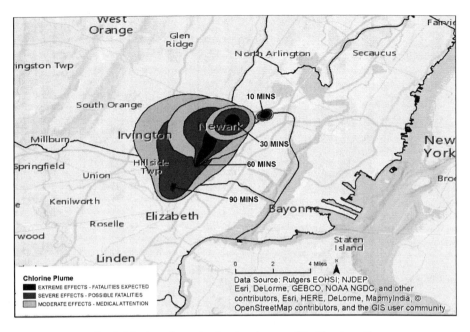

FIGURE 6.6 Path of chlorine plume in simulated event (10–90 minutes)

train. At 30 minutes (the darkest black area within the 30 minute ellipse) the plume has reached Newark Penn Station and the surrounding area. At 40 minutes the slow traveling train and its plume are heading southwest toward Newark International Airport. The dose in the lethal zone is diminishing because of diffusion and chemical reactions, but is still potentially lethal. At one hour, the plume has drifted over the New Jersey Turnpike, Route 1 and is on the edge of Newark International Airport. And the most southern part of the slide shows that the cloud is starting to dissipate at 90 minutes as it heads toward Elizabeth. This simple figure summarizes 194 snapshots of the simulated plume as it heads southwest along the NEC.

Before presenting the results of the chlorine tank car release scenario, it is imperative that the reader understand that this is one illustration of risk scenarios that can be tested by combining rail network and air pollution models. The models have the capacity to analyze hundreds of scenarios. These assessment tools were built to be planning tools that would allow experts to vary conditions.

For purposes of the analysis, I focus on people in the high exposure zone. Using United States census and local data, we counted the number of people who live in this zone – 36,000. Using the simulation model during morning rush hour, we counted those estimated to be at Newark Penn Station, the Harrison PATH station, Grove Street, Broad Street. This number is 13,000 at the train stations. In other words, about 50,000 are exposed by the event. Notably, 75 percent of the residents are African American and Latino compared to 31 percent in the State of New Jersey as a whole. In other words, this event would have environmental justice consequences.

In order to understand the health impacts of the event, the author spoke with colleagues who are familiar with respiratory exposures from chemicals, and researchers from the U.S. Army Corps of Engineers and U.S. Department of Homeland Security who have experience with chlorine and have worked on chlorine risk assessments.

Based on these discussions and our own research, we constructed two outcome scenarios. The first, called less impact, assumes that 1 percent, or 500 people would die as a result of the exposure and another 10 percent would be injured (5,000). Of those injured, half would return to work in three days (2,500), 25 percent in two weeks (1,250), and 25 percent would suffer permanent injury and not be able to return to work (1,250). The relatively low number of people who die and are injured are based on the assumption that the vast majority of people are inside buildings and cars. The second scenario, more impact version, assumes that 5 percent would die (2,500), and that 20 percent would be injured (10,000). Of those injured 25 percent would return to work in three days (2,500), another 50 percent would return to work in two weeks (5,000), and 25 percent would be permanently disabled (2,500). In reality, both exposure scenarios probably underestimate what would happen. A major issue in this scenario is that a large number of people would be outdoors on platforms and while people often evacuate in an orderly fashion, the nature of this event is such that orderly evacuation will be a challenge because of the limited number of exits from the platforms and the likelihood that some individuals will panic causing the entrances to be blocked and further injuries.

Furthermore, access to individuals who have been injured in the street will be difficult, but will be much more difficult for those at the crowded train station. This event assumes that we begin during rush hour, and it is difficult to believe that rescue personnel will be able to gain access to all of the people that would be exposed and will have a sufficient amount of equipment to prevent the injuries, even if they do have access. Also, while we would expect people to stay inside, many might not. In short, the two scenarios may understate the consequences.

There are 15 schools and one hospital in the red zone. In order to avoid double-counting children and school employees, we have not counted any of them in the red zone calculations. Nor have we included the people who do not live in the area who would be in buses or automobiles passing through. We have not included employees, and assumed that there are no recreational events at the Prudential Arena in Newark, the soccer stadium in Harrison, and the PAC Theater that lies a short distance from the Newark Penn Station. By starting the event at 7:30 a.m. and trying to avoid any double-counting, the 50,000 estimated to be in the red zone is likely an underestimate. Based on the literature and those we spoke with, this is the first attempt at a risk analysis where the chemical event for chlorine is moving rather than emanating from a single fixed source.

Being in the not fatal exposure zone implies less exposure, but it does not mean that some exposed individuals would not experience health effects, ranging from overstimulation of their cardiovascular system to mild irritation. Furthermore, there might be indirect health impacts caused by auto accidents, exhaustion on the part of medical teams and other health-related consequences. Consequently, while we estimated the number of people in each of the three zones, this must not be interpreted as a direct measure of mortality or morbidity. There are too many confounding factors, and we tried to be conservative and not grossly overestimate the risk.

I assume that even under the worst conditions that require evacuation, people will be able to return to their homes in two days. The question is will there be economic stigma? And more important, how much and for how long? While my focus has been on the potentially fatal exposure zone, I present some aggregate data for the surrounding areas.

Even assuming that no one from the potentially non-lethal zones needed hospitalization, the challenge to risk managers is formidable. At a minimum some people would evacuate, which would lead to injuries and fatalities. Table 6.8 shows the large number of people, dwelling units, daytime population in the larger zones that include the lower exposure zones. This does not include people in industrial facilities, infrastructure, and other non-residential facilities.

I do not have sufficiently detailed data to estimate the economic consequences of this event on this large region. It would be imperative that the daytime population who work in the area be separated from the resident population to avoid double-counting or even triple counting in the case of those who took the light rail, deboarded at the train station, and worked in a local building. I would want to know how many people were employed in the local hospitals, the colleges and universities, and schools in the area. It is imperative that we learn about triaging capacity from officials. And we need feedback from officials to estimate the costs of preventing the event and adding resilience to the system.

TABLE 6.8 Data to estimate direct, indirect and induced economic consequences of chlorine event

Group and attributes	High exposure zone	Other zones and rest of municipality
Total resident population, 2010	36,079*	1,014,171
African-American resident population, 2010	13,991 (38.8%)	374,546 (36.9%)
Hispanic resident population, 2010	13,602 (37.7%)	269,819 (26.6%)
Number of owner occupied housing units, 2010	2,300	169,056
Number of rental units, 2010	10,973	171,991
Number of schools	15	534
Number of hospitals	1	10
Daytime population, 2010	NA	1,153,956

Notes: *Does not include an estimated 13,000 exposed at railroad stations.

Modeling the consequences outside of the potential fatal exposure zone necessitates considerably more data and interaction with officials. The analyst would also need to add equations in the economic model that allow measurement of feedbacks between these events and property values, sales, loss of taxes and other economic consequences. All of this is feasible, and would allow a more robust estimate of the non-directly human health-related consequences. More than one person, however, told the author and his colleagues, that they did not want to know the full extent of the human health and safety consequences.

Limitations of the tools used for the passenger rail risk assessments

The rail simulation model validations were able to reproduce rail operations, frankly more accurately than the author had anticipated. Furthermore, the animated versions have proven to be very popular with audiences ranging from senior managers to undergraduate students. The animations have been a good teaching tool. The author can figuratively stop normal rail traffic, explain a change to the conditions of the rail system, and then resume the analysis or rerun it. One major limitation of the rail model is the need to make sure that the data are current. A second major limitation is that while ARENA is a standard industrial systems model, these simulations cannot be done by a novice. Anyone who would want to plan with this kind of a model will need to devote a portion of a position to keeping the data up to date and then operating the package.

The air pollution model worked as well as we had anticipated, perhaps it was a bit too vivid because the snapshots showing the spread of the event sent shivers through some audiences. The author has had to remind audiences that these are simulated results. A limitation is that considerable expertise is required to use the software properly and data are required about local terrain and other attributes that need to be taken into account. Those who would plan with SCIPUFF will need to spend time determining what agents to model and under what conditions. In order to be an effective tool for risk analysis, the final user of the results has to play an important role in picking the events. For this public exercise, we deliberately picked a relatively common substance and an equally common way of shipping it. The users and analysts have to reach a consensus on the best and most effective use of these air pollution simulation tools.

The economic model is a standard one, and depending upon the needs of the user community another model(s) might be more appropriate. All of the economic simulation models demand a great deal of expertise, development and adjustment time, and a person or persons who can work with multidisciplinary colleagues.

I have lived in the world of policy analysis for more than four decades. Hence, I urge agencies and companies considering these kinds of models to select the tools on the basis of serving risk analysis and other organizational planning objectives, if at all possible. This may mean picking tools that are less predictive for risk analysis, but if these tools are used for other purposes, then there will be an ongoing investment in them, which I know from painful experience is better than developing a good model and watch it abandoned in two years when the next executive assumes power and changes the agenda. In other words, try to have the tools used for multiple purposes institutionalized so that they can be updated and used when needed.

Risk management

Rail network, economic impact, and air pollution simulation models can help assess some low probability and high consequence events in densely developed locations. The results are not to be taken at face value, yet they clearly illustrate major vulnerabilities in this region. There is a need to consider a range of preventive steps as well as resilience options, many of which could be difficult and expensive to implement, and therefore the sooner the analyses are conducted and the results are studied the better.

Given concern about homeland security, I am constrained in regard to what I can say in this section. What I use comes from published reports and publicly announced activities, and is primarily based on standard practices.

Prevention

Prevention starts with surveillance. In the case of rail, as a boy living in New York City, I remember subway trains sounding warnings to men who walked the tracks looking for problems and then repairing them. We know that bridges are particularly vulnerable, not only because they represent a target that is hard to repair, but also because they are relatively fragile compared to on-land rail elements. As a teenager, our neighbors had a son named John who worked underground looking for problems in the rail tunnels. John told me that it was tough work, and that he hoped that someone like me would invent a robot that would take his job because he did not think that it would be easy to attract workers like him in the future. My neighbor John's wish is being realized. Engineers have been developing and testing sensors that show the wear and tear on infrastructure, especially bridges, and can spot objects that are not supposed to be on the tracks. Small robots and sensors will replace workers like John. For rail managers that want to send workers along the tracks, training videos are available for workers on what to do and not do when they see something and someone that poses a risk. Our group developed one for the U.S. Department of Homeland Security.

Sometimes, prevention means not ignoring the obvious. More than one rail line has been shut down by snow laden trees falling on tracks, electrical, and other engineered systems. Preventive pruning during the warm months means a lower probability of a storm knocking out infrastructure.

Intruders are a danger to all of us and to themselves. Yet, they need access to cause damage. Managers can install barriers outside a station along the tracks and various other key locations. A police presence can deter an individual with bad intentions, and some security forces use dogs as an added deterrence. Sometimes, however, a non-uniformed security officer can see or hear something that uniformed officers cannot. Cameras can help, but may not provide sufficient time to stop a determined intruder.

The above kinds of prevention tools are widely accepted, but others are not. By far the most controversial issue is in regard to passengers as sources of information. In 2010, an "If You See Something, Say Something™" policy was instituted in New York City and has diffused to many jurisdictions and businesses. Using data collected by the Maryland Transit Administration (MTA), the author and associates (Maryland 2011; Greenberg *et al.* 2012) found that 54 percent of surveyed riders responded that they "very likely" would report something suspicious, and yet focus groups showed equivocation by many. Racial and ethnic profiling is a major concern of many people.

This "no-brainer" policy has been strongly opposed by some because they argue that see something say something tramples on the Bill of Rights, and more pointedly it is a modern day program that asks people to spy and report on each other (Gunn 2012). Molotch's (2012) argues that see something say something undermines public safety because it has not helped capture terrorists, wastes the time of staff and the public, and makes it more difficult for trained professionals to do their jobs. Continued monitoring is essential to gauge how to enhance the effectiveness of this policy as a public health preparedness tool for rail systems.

Yet another debatable source of prevention is searching rail passengers and their baggage. Airline passengers have become accustomed to arriving early, having their baggage and their bodies scanned. Arguably, one reason why rail has passed airplane on short flights along the east coast and elsewhere are searches at airports. Pilot tests have been made of rail passenger searches (Wiessner 2006). But the rail industry is reluctant to agree to searches and probably give away a competitive economic advantage that it appears to enjoy.

In regard to the chlorine event that was analyzed in this chapter, it can be prevented by policy decisions. Chlorine can be shipped in solid form, rather than in liquid form, but a different manufacturing process is needed. The train should stop, if the rupture is noticed, and the train should stop if the operator is not poisoned and able to operate the train. The rupture in the rail car could be closed earlier than was allowed for in the model. The rail path we chose could be closed off. Health effects can be lessened by rapid evacuation and/or shelter in place, which depends upon the location of the plume relative to the receptors. There have been two incidents with rail cars carrying chlorine in this area during the two years before this study. Neither resulted in a serious problem because there was no breach of the rail cars.

While the chlorine rail car event is low probability, it is plausible. Indeed, a much more severe version could have been developed. State and the U.S. federal government, as well as the Chlorine Institute have developed a Rail Transportation Security Plan. Frankly, I do think that this event will occur, and yet by demonstrating that it is plausible for a lethal dose of a common chemical to appear over a major train station, threaten a major airport, be carried by the train, demonstrates the value of using not only the rail model but combining it with the plume model in a densely developed urban area. This package of three tools is directly applicable to a variety of scenarios not only in this region but in many other locations in the United States and the rest of the world.

Resilience

Historically, rail systems could not be disabled by a cyberattack because they did not depend upon vulnerable computer systems. As the computer world expands, the vulnerability of rail increases, which implies a need for backup systems. Other infrastructure systems have installed backups and rail can emulate these approaches, albeit at some cost. Resilience in the case of passenger rail means using light rail, alternative heavy rail, buses, including school buses, car pools, ferries, and other mobile assets to move people around damaged areas, and instituting telecommuting, if that is possible.

The chlorine scenario and others like it require specially trained medical, fire department and police personnel to facilitate triaging and evacuation to facilities where injured individuals can be cared for. In this context, World War I and World War II employed special trains equipped to evacuate severely injured personnel. In the context of the study area for this project, the author and colleagues have proposed a special train that would pick up casualties and transport them to a hospital located adjacent to the NEC in central New Jersey. The challenge for those proposing the special train and short rail link to the hospital is cost. This project would ask the public to layout millions of dollars for a facility and rail link that no one ever wants to use.

Organization

Risk management is about figuring out what to do to prevent hazard events and how to respond to restore some normalcy when they do occur. Risk management requires outstanding organizational capability. For example, business, under attack by cyber thieves, has become reluctant to share the data (see Chapter 11). However rail security requires sharing. In 2007, United States first partnership between government and the private freight industry was signed between New Jersey's Homeland Security Department and CSX, which is the largest private rail operator in the United States with almost 2000 miles of track, 1,300 grade crossings and more than a half dozen rail terminals and yards in the northeast. CSX accounts for more than half the freight rail shipped in New Jersey. The agreement between CSX and the State of New Jersey gives the state access to the CSX database so that they can determine what hazardous materials are in transit at any time (National Terrorism Preparedness Institute 2007). It is no accident that the release by government and CSX used chlorine as an example of why this agreement was necessary.

More broadly, in 2008, New Jersey announced a plan on how it would respond to mass casualty events. Indeed, this plan was activated on January 15, 2009 when

U.S. Airways flight 1549 crash-landed in the Hudson River and all the passengers were rescued.

Intergovernmental cooperation is assumed but needs reinforcement with agreements. In 2013, New Jersey announced a passenger rail plan to respond to major events (Cortacans 2013). The plan divides the state's rail stations (there are over 300 in New Jersey) into categories based on riders and nearby assets as well as by the location of key bridges and tunnels. Thirty-eight stations fall into the most important group. The next phases address coordination among agencies/departments, and securing resources in the case of an event or multiple events. The plan includes a step-by-step articulation of who should respond in different locations and the role of local hospitals, police, fire and EMS personnel. This plan would be used if the chlorine event in this chapter ever occurred.

What did Chapter 6 explain about risk analysis? Summary and learning objectives

Shipping freight by rail has become more important as international shipments grow as part of globalization, and passenger rail is increasing in locations as an alternative to mid-range airplane traffic and automobile use. The 450 mile (724 km) Northeast Rail Corridor between Washington, D.C. and Boston is a critical asset for both passengers and freight. This chapter zeroed in on a 60 mile (96.5 km) section between Trenton, New Jersey and New York City's Pennsylvania Station. The chapter demonstrated that a data-rich mathematical model supported by cooperating rail managers could replicate the performance of the rail system during the rush hours and off-peak hours. Having demonstrated this capacity, the author degraded the system with small and then major events.

The regional economic model built and then adapted for this application measured the economic impact in terms of lost jobs and regional income, as well as other outcomes not shown in the chapter. The combination of a loss of a major bridge asset for a year and relocation of some jobs out of the region as a result of the event underscores the need for carefully considered prevention and resilience in regard to critical infrastructure systems.

An air pollution model was combined with the rail model to illustrate the serious potential human health impact of a major chemical leak caused by a leaking rail car along the Northeast Corridor line. This event illustrates the need for sharing information, training first responders, and otherwise being prepared for the worst. Indeed, government and business are working on plans and agreements that would markedly improve resilience.

At the end of this chapter readers should be able to answer the following seven questions:

1. How important has rail been in national economic development, especially shipment of goods?

2. How can a rail system's flow of passengers be replicated by a mathematical model, and then how can the model be used to study hazard events?
3. How can direct, indirect and induced regional economic impacts be estimated by economic impact models?
4. How can an air pollution model approximate the diffusion of contaminants over a region?
5. How can analysts combine rail network, air pollution and economic models be used to assess the consequences of hazardous rail events?
6. How can analysts use these models to assess the best options for preventing the most consequential events from occurring?
7. How can these models be used to develop post-event resilience strategies?

References

Altiok T, Melamed B. (2007) *Simulation modeling and analysis with ARENA.* New York: Elsevier, Inc.

Allwine K, J Shinn J, Streit G, Brown M. (2002) Overview of urban 2000. *Bulletin of the American Meteorological Society.* 83, 4, 521–536.

American Chemistry Council, CHEMTREC, the Chlorine Institute, Compressed Gas Association, National Association of Chemical Distributors. (2012) Transportation Security Guidelines for the U.S. Chemical Industry. http://cl2.files.cms-plus.com/PDFs/trnsecurguidnce06-02.pdf. Accessed June 24, 2012.

Amtrak. (2010) Amtrak fact sheet, fiscal year 2010, State of New Jersey, www.amtrak.com/pdf/factsheets/NEWJERSEY10.pdf. Accessed April 11, 2012.

Amtrak. (2012) Acela express on-time performance. www.amtrak.com/serlet/ContentServer?overrrideDefaultTemplate=OTTPage. Accessed April 11, 2012.

Amtrak. (2013) Amtrak sets ridership record and moves the nation's economy forward – America's Railroad helps communities grow and prosper. www.amtrak.com/ccurl/730/658/FY13-Record-Ridership-ATK-13-122.pdf. Accessed December 9, 2014.

Associated Press. (2014) New Jersey's Portal Bridge, bane of the Northeast Corridor, is due for upgrade. www.washingtonpost.com/politics/new-jerseys-portal-bridge-bane-of-the-northeast-corridor-is-due-for-upgrade/2014/11/15/36c34662-6d1e-11e4-a31c-77759fc1eacc_story.html. Accessed December 18, 2014.

BBC. (2007) World's worst rail disasters. December 19, 2007. http://news.bbc.co.uk/2/hi/south_asia/3650835.stm. Accessed May 3, 2012.

Bureau of Transportation Statistics. (2005) Amtrak on-time performance. www.bts.gov/publications/transportation_statistics_annual_report/2005.html. Accessed April 11, 2102.

Chang S. (2000) Disasters and transport systems: loss, recovery and competition at the Port of Kobe after the 1995 earthquake. *Journal of Transport Geography.* 8, 53–65.

Chang J, Hanna S, Boybeyi Z, Franzese P. (2005) Use of Salt Lake City URBAN 2000 field data to evaluate the urban hazard prediction assessment capability (HPAC) dispersion model. *Journal of Applied Meteorology.* 44, 4, 485–501.

Chang S, Nojima N. (1998) Measuring lifeline system performance: highway transportation systems in recent earthquakes. Proceedings of the 6th U.S. National Conference on Earthquake Engineering, Seattle, USA, Paper No. 70.

Committee on Assessing the Costs of Natural Disasters, National Research Council. (1999) *The impacts of natural disasters: a framework for loss estimation.* Washington, D.C.: National Academy Press.

Committee on Predicting Outcomes of Investments in Maintenance and Repair for Federal Facilities. (2012) *Predicting outcomes of investments in maintenance and repair of federal facilities.* Washington, D.C.: The National Academies Press.

Cortacans H. (2013) Readying? the rails: the New Jersey EMS railway plan. www.emsworld.com/article/10949279?new-jersey-ems-railroad-security-plan. Accessed December 16, 2014.

DTRA. (2003). Hazard prediction and assessment capability (HPAC) user guide version 4.0.3. San Diego, CA, Prepared for Defense Threat Reduction Agency (DTRA) by Science Applications International Corporation.

Economist. (2010) High-speed railroading. www.economist.com/node/16636101. Accessed December 9, 2014.

Federal Railroad Administration, U.S. Department of Transportation. (2009) Vision for High-speed Rail in America: High-speed Rail Strategic Plan. Washington, D.C: FRA.

Federal Railroad Administration, Office of Safety. (2005) Norfolk Southern (NS), Graniteville, South Carolina, January 6, 2005. Available at: www.ntsb.gov/investigations/summary/RAR0504.html. Accessed June 20, 2012.

Fiscal Policy Institute. (2001) World Trade Center jobs in fact take a heavy toll on low-wage workers. www.fiscalpolicy.org November 5, 2001. Accessed May 21, 2012.

Greenberg M, Mayer H, Herb J. (2012) Engagement of minority communities and public awareness programs: review of the Maryland Transit Administration (MTA) 2011 and 2010 customer satisfaction survey data. Washington, D.C.: Science and Technology Directorate, Office of University Programs, National Transportation Security Center of Excellence, April.

Greenberg M, Lahr M, Mantell N, Felder F. (2007) Understanding the economic costs and benefits of catastrophes and their aftermath: a review and suggestions for the as-federal government. *Risk Analysis.* 27, 1, 83–96.

Greenberg M, Miller KT, Frisch M, Lewis D. (2003) Facing an uncertain economic future: environmental management spending and rural regions surrounding the U.S. DOE's nuclear weapons facilities, *Defence and Peace Economics.* 14, 1, 85–97.

Grynbaum M, Gebeloff R. (2010) 95% of trains are on time? Riders beg to differ. *New York Times.* www.nytimes.com/2010/07/27/nyregion/27ontime.html. Accessed April 11, 2012.

Gunn, D. (2012) Does "See something, say something" do nothing? *New York Magazine.* September 21, 2012. http://nymag.com/news/intelligencer/mta-anti-terrorism-2012-10. Accessed November 2, 2012.

Haimes Y, Horowitz B, Lambert J, Santos J, Lian C, Crowther K. (2005a) Inoperability input-output model for interdependent infrastructure sectors. 1: Theory and methodology. *Journal of Infrastructure Systems.* 11, 67–79.

Haimes Y, Horowitz B, Lambert J, Santos J, Crowther K, Lian C. (2005b) Inoperability input-output model for interdependent infrastructure sectors. 1: Case study. *Journal of Infrastructure Systems,* 11, 80–92.

Human Transit. (2010) If on-time performance is 96%, why am I always late? www.humantransit.org/2010/07/if-ontime-performance-is-96-why-am-i-always-late. Accessed April 11, 2012.

Jenkins B, Butterworth B, Clair J-F. (2010) Off the rails: the 1995 attempted derailing of the French TGV (high-speed train) and a quantitative analysis of 181 rail sabotage attempts. San Jose, CA, Mineta Transportation Institute.

Jenkins, B., Butterworth, B., and Shrum, K. (2010) Terrorist attacks on public transportation: a preliminary empirical analysis. San Jose, CA, Mineta Transportation Institute at San Jose State University; 2010. MTI Report WP09-0J.

Kichenside G. (1997) *Great train disasters — the world's worst railway accidents*. Shreveport, LA: Parragon Publishing.

Maryland Marketing Source, Inc. Maryland Transit Administration. (2011) Customer ridership study. Randallstown, MD, Maryland Marketing Source, Inc.

Molotch H. (2012) *Against security: how we go wrong at airports, subways, and other sites of ambiguous danger*. Princeton, NJ: Princeton University Press.

National Association of Railroad Passengers. (2010) Ridership Statistics. www.narprail.org/site/assets/files/1038/nec-2015.pdf. Accessed June 5, 2016.

National Research Council. (2001) Standing operating procedures for developing acute exposure guideline levels for hazardous chemicals. Washington, D.C., Subcommittee on Acute Exposure Guideline Levels, Committee on Toxicology, Board on Environmental Studies and Toxicology, Commission on Life Sciences, National Research Council.

National Research Council. (2004). Acute exposure guideline levels for selected airborne chemicals, Volume 4. Washington, D.C.: National Academy Press.

National Terrorism Preparedness Institute (2007) N.Y. and N.J. announced rail security plan. http://contingencyplaning.com/articles/2007/08/01/ny-nj-announce-rail-security-plan. Accessed December 16, 2014.

New Jersey Transit. (2010) NJ Transit facts at a glance, fiscal year 2010. www.njtransit.com/pdf/FactsAtaGlance.pdf. Accessed December 26, 2011.

Obama B. (2010) Remarks by the President in the state of the union address, January 27, 2010. www.whitehouse.gov/the-press-office/remarks-president-state-union-address.html. Accessed April 11, 2011.

REMI, Inc. (1997) *The REMI EDFS-53 forecasting and simulation model*, volume 1, model documentation, Chapter 4. Amherst, MA, Regional Economic Modeling.

Robinson S, Yúnez-Naude A, Hinohosa-Ojeda R, Lewis, J, Devarajan S. (1999) From stylized to applied models: building multisector CGE models for policy analysis. *The North American Journal of Economics and Finance*. 10, 5–38.

Rose A, Benavides J, Chang S, Szczesniak P, Lim D. (1997) The regional economic impact on an earthquake: direct and indirect effects of electricity lifeline disruptions. *Journal of Regional Science*. 37, 3, 437–458.

Rossetti M. (2010) *Simulation modeling with ARENA*. New York: John Wiley & Sons. Inc.

Rostow W. (1960) *The stages of economic growth: a non-communist manifesto*. Cambridge: Cambridge University Press.

Santos J, Haimes Y. (2004) Modeling the demand reduction input-output (I-0) inoperability due to terrorism. *Risk Analysis*. 24, 6, 1437–1451.

Semmens P. (1994) *Railway Disasters of the world: principal passenger train accidents of the 20th century*. Somerset, UK: Patrick Stephens Ltd.

Sykes R, Cerasoli C, Henn D. (1999) The representation of dynamic flow effects in a Lagrangian puff dispersion model. *Journal of Hazardous Material*. 64, 223–247.

Sykes R, Gabruk R. (1997) A second-order closure model for the effect of averaging time on turbulent plume dispersion. *Journal of Applied Meteorology*. 36, 165–184.

Treyz G. (1993) *Regional economic modeling; a systematic approach to economic forecasting and policy analysis*. Boston, MA: Kluwer Academic Publishers.

Urban, JT., Warner S, Platt N. (2011) Assessment of HPAC urban modelling capabilities using data from the joint urban 2003 field experiment. *International Journal of Environment and Pollution*. 44, 1–4, 24–31.

U.S. High Speed Rail Association. (2011) 21st century transportation for America, www.ushsr.com/hsrnetwork.html. Accessed April 8, 2011.

Warner S., Platt N, Heagy J. (2004). Comparisons of transport and dispersion model predictions of the joint urban 2003 field experiment. *Journal of Applied Meteorology and Climatology*. 43, 6, 829–846.

Wiessner C (2006) US tests rail security plan in New Jersey. www.redorbit.com/news/genreal/384380/US-test-rail-security-plan-in-ne-jersey. Accessed December 16, 2014.

7

FRESH WATER, LAND USE, AND GLOBAL CLIMATE CHANGE

Introduction

Every decade, several environmental subjects become publicly prominent, causing otherwise disinterested people to become curious and concerned. As I watch the media cultivate the public's emotional reactions, I think of these events as "media tsunamis" climaxed by a large wave of interest that eventually attenuates, unless a similar event reoccurs. During my lifetime these media tsunamis have included atomic warfare, Earth Day, stratospheric ozone depletion, the TMI/Chernobyl/Fukushima nuclear power plant failures, and more recently fracking and global climate change (GCC).

The GCC message is that human fossil fuel use has caused upper atmospheric changes leading to alterations in the frequency, duration, timing and type of precipitation; rising sea-level; acceleration of the world's water cycle; more frequent and massive storms that kill and injure people and destroy their possessions, while in other places and times lead to longer and more severe droughts (International Panel 2001, 2007; Karl et al. 2009; Lins et al. 2010; Vorosmarty, Sahagian 2000; Vorosmarty et al. 2000, 2010). The media message is predominantly negative information, which is more salient to the public than positive news.

Disputes about imperfect data and models and denials of GCC have tended to elevate global climate change to a topic of public conversation. For example, a few years ago, the author attended a reunion. After falsely assuring each other that our appearances had not changed much during the last 50 years, several of my fellow graduates raised global climate change and its potential impact upon their children and grandchildren. We discussed the subject with an intensity that would have made our professors proud had we been so inclined to engage in such serious discussions a half century earlier. My classmates recognized that they were contributing to the problem through their consumption, yet other than making personal adjustments in their purchasing, they felt powerless about making a contribution to reversing global climate change.

My contributions to that conversation are reflected in this chapter, centering around the larger issue of resource use, economic development and land use. I told my classmates that they might make a difference not only by focusing on their individual behaviors and purchases but they could play a role in local land-use decisions. With some exceptions, humans have been permitted and encouraged to use ever increasing amounts of the Earth's resources, thereby reducing the capability of ecosystems in the long run to provide nutrients, food, wood, and clean water and air, and relying on scientific ingenuity to invent ways to sustain high rates of economic growth. I suggested to my colleagues that they consider engaging in land-use planning meetings in their local jurisdictions where they would come face-to-face with balancing short-term preferences expressed in the local town plans against the need to manage land use and the environment for the longer term and provide space for disadvantaged people rather than opposing it.

My former classmates and I are senior citizen middle-income people living in places with economic resources and political capacity that can adapt to GCC, but a measure of our society is how would we assist poor people living in places with limited resources and political power adapt, as described in the last part of the chapter.

Toward that end, this chapter uses freshwater resources as an illustration to discuss risk issues related to natural resource use. After looking at the water resources issue from the global perspective, and providing a brief case study of China's efforts to solve one of its water resource issues, the chapter focuses on South America, Australia, and especially Africa, in other words, the Global South, where the challenge of land-use conversion, water resource shortages or deluges, population growth and migration, and conflict are already serious stressors.

Because I chose to report on every continent to some extent, readers may find some of this presentation tedious and you are not discouraged from skimming through all the details and concentrating on the major observations, with the exceptions of the final discussion of alternative futures.

A global perspective on freshwater resources

The literature on resource use is voluminous, including ethical, legal, political, scientific, engineering and other challenges that arise from unfettered economic development and land-use changes (Bailey 2010; Foley *et al.* 2005; Beck 1992; Black 1998; Black, King 2009; Gleditsch *et al.* 2007; Meadows *et al.* 1972; Sabin 2013). Water resources are a longstanding challenge, arguably the most serious, and global climate exacerbates the challenge. I begin with pre-twenty-first-century papers and reports, and then move the focus to more recent reports.

I consider Peter Gleick of the Pacific Institute the guru of freshwater-related-world-wide risks. Gleick's (1993, 1998, 2008) books identify key issues and places at high risk for a variety of water-resource-related issues. Homer-Dixon (1994) links water resource scarcity to violent conflict. Wolf *et al.* (1999) illustrate the complexity of managing international river basins and in some cases water within the same country (see Chapters 2 and 3 for an intrastate example). Liverman and O'Brien (1991) reported on water resource issues in Mexico 25 years before this chapter was written. They state that climate models imply warmer and drier conditions, which means more evapotranspiration in Mexico, and any increases in precipitation would not compensate for these losses. The authors indicated that these changes would impact much of Mexico, in some cases severely, especially agricultural production, urban areas, and industrial freshwater supplies. As a harbinger of much of the literature, Liverman and O'Brien note that the results vary by analytical model and that the current set of models do not replicate Mexico's current climate, which is a candid observation and a signal about the important role of uncertainty in the water and many other resource-related risk issues.

Freshwater supply, global climate change, and land use

It is fascinating that so many scientific reports start with a focus on global atmospheric physics, the hydrological cycle, soil science, and yet in the end they observe that social, economic and political factors are of equal or even greater importance than global climate change in exposing people and places to acute and chronic water-related risks. For example, Vorosmarty *et al.* (2000) studied selected major river basins for the period 1985–2025. The year 1985 represented the baseline, and variations in water demand were introduced into their analysis assuming various levels of population growth, migration, changes in other water uses, as well as variations in climate change predicted by simulation models. Acknowledging uncertainty in the input data, the authors report that one-third of the world population faces "relative" water scarcity and 450 million severe water scarcity. Vorosmarty *et al.* (2000) conclude that growing water demand not climate change is the major challenge.

Vorosmarty *et al.* scaled their data from larger regions to smaller ones and then to even smaller areas. As the scale went from macro (global), to meso (regional), to micro (local), they reported intensification of serious water-supply shortages requiring major adaptations. Vorosmarty *et al.* (2000) illustrate their observations with the Chang Jiang River (Yangtze) and the Yellow Rivers in eastern China (see below).

Many studies that begin with global climate change quickly identify other factors that contribute to freshwater supply problems. Vorosmarty and Sahagian (2000) identify the impact of large engineered projects for irrigation, hydroelectric power, and other human needs on the global water cycle. The authors estimated global water withdrawals in the year 2000 as 4,000–5,000 km^3/yr. They observed nearly exponential growth in water demand during the late twentieth and early twenty-first centuries. The current level of global demand, the authors suggest, is not an immediate threat because estimated runoff from the continents is about 40,000 km³/yr, in other words, 10 percent–15 percent of the total is withdrawn. The authors caution, however, that the balance of withdrawal to availability varies markedly by region, with arid places in Africa and Asia already facing shortages.

Most withdrawals are for irrigation (60 percent–70 percent). Vorosmarty and Sahagian identify major engineered sources. United States residents will not be surprised to learn that California and the high plains and southwest rank 3–5 on Vorosmarty and Sahagian's list of underground water mining areas. Yet these U.S. withdrawals are dwarfed by water mining in the Sahara and Arabia. The latter two account for over 75 percent of all aquifer mining in the world, or 65 times as much as the United States' regions. Given the high evapotranspiration rates in the Sahara and Arabian areas, most of this water quickly transfers back to the atmosphere.

Large freshwater lakes and associated groundwater are another source tapped for irrigation, population and other uses. Vorosmarty and Sahagian identify the Caspian and Aral seas as major sources of diversion, with the Caspian Sea and associated groundwater responsible for almost 20 percent of the world-wide diversion. The Caspian is the largest inland body of water, and Azerbaijan, Iran, Kazakhstan, Russia and Turkmenistan all border on it. The Aral Sea, located in Kazakhstan and Uzbekistan, has been severely depleted for irrigation projects, and it is only about 10 percent of its original size. The Aral Sea is the poster child for water mining of a surface water system. Viewing it today compared to pre-Soviet diversion is shocking (Figure 7.1) (see also Oelkers, Hering, Zhu 2011).

The authors also describe desertification, wetland drainage, soil erosion in agricultural areas, deforestation, and dam building as other sources of diversion from the water cycle. At the global scale, these are responsible for less than 5 percent of the total listed by Vorosmarty and Sahagian. However, at local scales these diversions can lead to serious water shortages.

Vorosmarty and Sahagian indicate that sea-level rise increases will threaten some freshwater supplies and engineered systems, and they conclude that dams and other impoundments will not increase a great deal because of technical, socioeconomic and environmental barriers faced in building them (see also Gleick 1998). The authors also point to increased deposition, and changes in chemical and biological characteristics of the water as threats that are not yet understood.

Vorosmarty and Sahagian conclude their paper with sharp criticism of the lack of efforts to gather data on risk to global water supplies. They note that we should be learning more about freshwater supplies by expanding the network of monitoring stations. Instead they point to degradation of the monitoring network due to commercialization, failure to maintain the systems, and claims of intellectual property rights regarding data. The authors note that registries of water engineering works area are incomplete and dated, and some locations are inaccurate. Vorosmarty and Sahagian identify a lack of biophysical data, and operational data on water engineering systems as another constraint on learning about current and future shortages.

Land-use changes from rural to urban markedly reduce water recharge.

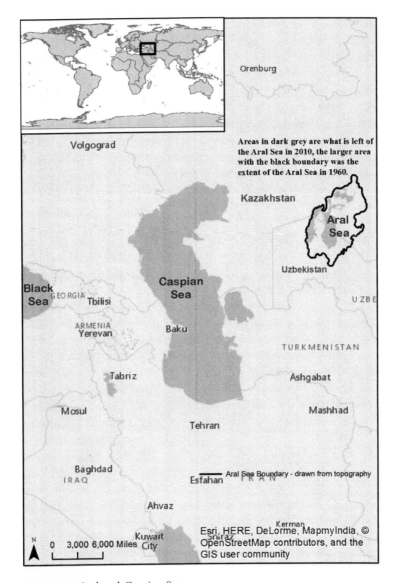

FIGURE 7.1 Aral and Caspian Seas

However, other land use changes cannot be overlooked. Kim and Jackson (2011) compared the impacts of land-use changes on groundwater recharge, finding that conversion of grasslands to woodlands would bring about greater recharge, whereas woody plant invasion or a forestation into grasslands and croplands reduce recharge. Cultivation should increase recharge but cultivation introduces the risk of contamination and salinization of groundwater.

Conflict over water is a historic problem and recent reports document the potential for conflict as potable sources shrink and demand increases (Wolf *et al.* 1999; Greenberg 2009; Grover 2007; Fisher, Huber-Lee, Amir 2005; Gleick 2008; Dinar *et al.* 2007; Trondalen 2008; Zeitoun 2008). *Overall, the tone of the global literature about freshwater is decidedly pessimistic, with continuing losses of water from the hydrologic cycle and competition for a diminishing available supply.*

An optimist might trust or at least hope that some of the most productive agricultural regions could provide food to those regions stressed by economic development, population growth and threatened by changing climate. Rosenzweig *et al.* (2004) examined historically productive food growing areas in Argentina, Brazil, China, Hungary-Romania, and the United States to assess that possibility because these countries produce about 70 percent of the world corn and over 90 percent of soybeans on about one-third of global arable and irrigated land. Using state-of-the-art models, and estimates of population and economic development, their findings are not encouraging. They conclude that these relatively water-rich areas appear to have sufficient water to maintain their current production. However, only Brazil, they find, can relatively easily accommodate expansion of irrigated land. The others are unlikely to be able to reliably produce additional food either in the near term (the 2020s) or medium-term (2050s). Rosenzweig *et al.* emphasize the need for adaptation, including changes in planting schedules, and changes in crop genetic characteristics that would make them more tolerant to heat pasts and pesticides.

When people think of water loss and drought, the usual image is of already dry areas in Africa and Arabia. However, places that rely on melting snow or ice, which is the main source of freshwater for one-sixth of the world population, appear to be at high risk. Barnett, Adam, and Letenmaier (2005) observed that global climate change means less winter precipitation in the form of snow and the melting of the winter snow occurs earlier. These changes shift peak river runoff to late winter and early spring rather than summer and autumn. Assuming no major interbasin water transfers, the authors expect serious water-related risk management challenges. For example, the Columbia River basin in the U.S. drains into the Pacific Ocean. Less winter snowfall and earlier melting suggest that water releases will force a choice between water for hydroelectric energy production and earlier releases for salmon runs. The salmon are protected, and tribal nations in the area will have strong legal rights to assert. Will this region accept a 10 to 20 percent reduction in hydropower generation in this region? I doubt it without considerable angst.

Barnett, Adam, and Letenmaier project that the Himalaya-Kush region of India and China will be the most impacted area. Melting snow supplies 50 to 70 percent of the water flow during the summer in one of the most densely populated parts of the globe. This may be the most consequential case in the world based on the number of people at risk, but there are others. For example, the authors report substantial glacial melt in the Peruvian Andes Mountains, that will eventually force the population to adapt the way they live.

Water for food production is the most difficult problem across the globe.

Rockstrom, Lannerstad, and Falkenmark (2007) examined water sources and needs for agriculture in 92 countries with the goal of estimating how much water would be required to meet the world's growing population out to the year 2050. Even with conservative estimates about food needs and assuming technological changes to improve efficiency, they do not know how irrigation (so-called "blue water") can be sufficiently expanded to meet the needs, and they concluded that more "green water" from rainfall will be required, which they judge to be problematic.

Key areas are sub-Saharan Africa and South Asia. They both are tropical savannah agro-ecosystems characterized by seasonal rainfall, intermittent dry spells, drought years, and higher evaporation, and sometimes poor soils. The first never had a green revolution but the second did and will need a second one. Seventy percent of the world's 1.1 billion poor and a majority of the 850 million malnourished live in these areas (Rockstrom, Lannerstad, Falkenmark 2007; Sanchez, Swaminathan 2005; Conway 1997).

Until recently, freshwater supply was almost exclusively a risk management issue for local, river basin and national governments. It has become obvious that actions taken in one country impact other countries. Hoekstra and Mekonnen (2012) estimated annual average water footprints for the period 1996–2005. China, India, and the United States other countries with large water footprint within their own territory had averages of 1207, 1182, and 1053 gm^3 per year, respectively. This is not surprising because of their large population and industrial base. About 38 percent of the water footprint of global production lie within these three countries. The agricultural water footprint is the largest share.

These and other countries are major parts of a growing direct and indirect international trade in freshwater. Major water exporters are the United States, China, India, Brazil, Argentina, Canada, Australia, Indonesia, France and Germany. The largest importers are the United States, Japan, Germany, China, Italy, Mexico, France, the United Kingdom and the Netherlands (Figure 7.2). The biggest net virtual water importers are North Africa and the Middle East, Mexico, Europe, Japan, and South Korea. These hidden water trades are part of cotton, soybean, oil palm, sunflower, and other derived products (43 percent of the total sum of international water flows). Cereals, industrial products coffee, tea, and cocoa, and even beef cattle are other parts of other indirect water trade.

Hoekstra and Mekonnen (2012) estimated national external water dependency. Some European countries such as Italy, Germany, the United Kingdom, and the Netherlands have external water footprints that constitute 60 percent to 90 percent to their total water footprint. It is not a surprise that the most dependent nations with a large external water footprints are in places with limited freshwater supplies: Malta, Kuwait, Jordan, Israel, the United Arab Emirates, Yemen, Mauritius, Lebanon, and Cyprus – all with a dependency of over 70 percent (see Figure 7.3). By comparison the external water dependency of the United States is 20 percent.

Dalin *et al.* (2012) examined global trade in water-consuming products for the period 1986–2007. They found substantial increases, with two standing out. The U.S. has substantially increased trade with Mexico, and China has massively

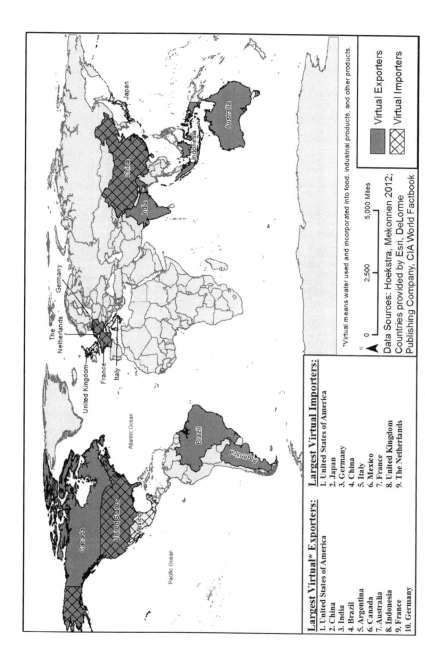

Largest Virtual* Exporters:
1. United States of America
2. China
3. India
4. Brazil
5. Argentina
6. Canada
7. Australia
8. Indonesia
9. France
10. Germany

Largest Virtual Importers:
1. United States of America
2. Japan
3. Germany
4. China
5. Italy
6. Mexico
7. France
8. United Kingdom
9. The Netherlands

Virtual Exporters

Virtual Importers

*Virtual means water used and incorporated into food, industrial products, and other products.

N

0   2,500   5,000 Miles

Data Sources: Hoekstra, Mekonnen 2012;
Countries provided by Esri, DeLorme
Publishing Company, CIA World Factbook

FIGURE 7.2 Major water importer and exporter nations

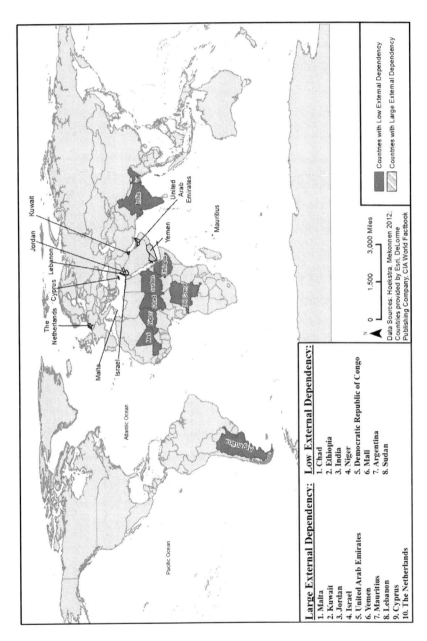

Large External Dependency:

1. Malta
2. Kuwait
3. Jordan
4. Israel
5. United Arab Emirates
6. Yemen
7. Mauritius
8. Lebanon
9. Cyprus
10. The Netherlands

Low External Dependency:

1. Chad
2. Ethiopia
3. India
4. Niger
5. Democratic Republic of Congo
6. Mali
7. Argentina
8. Sudan

Data Sources: Hoekstra, Mekonnen 2012;
Countries provided by Esri, DeLorme
Publishing Company, CIA World Factbook

N

0   1,500   3,000 Miles

Countries with Low External Dependency

Countries with Large External Dependency

FIGURE 7.3 Water dependent nations

increased its imports of soybeans, especially from Brazil, and secondarily from Africa and Argentina. The authors note that changes disproportionately appear to be from more water efficient sources, which is a good sign, globally, but not necessarily for the area losing the water.

Buying products that consume water is an indirect from of increasing a national water footprint. Land grabbing is a direct form. Rulli, Saviori, and D'Odorico (2013) focus on the transfer of the right to own or use land and water purchased by foreign investors. The following five countries in rank order are the largest land grabbers: the United Kingdom, the United States, China, United Arab Emirates and Israel. These five are responsible for approximately one-third of the land grabbed. At the top of the list of countries where land has been grabbed are the Democratic Republic of Congo, Indonesia, the Philippines, Sudan, and Australia. In other words, much of the land grabbing is in Africa and South Asia (Figure 7.4). The authors point out that land grabbing has rapidly increased, and they characterize it as a new form of colonialism that began after 2008. At the time of this writing, this was less than 2 percent of the world's agricultural land, but I would expect it to substantially increase.

Not everyone, including this author, believes that we have an intractable water-risk problem that cannot be managed. Some authors believe that nations have an opportunity to be resilient to the loss of freshwater supplies. Pahl-Wostil (2007) assert that the challenge is to be able to supply water within a range of environmental conditions, which requires information be provided to managers and for managers to adjust. Part of the adjustment is building low-cost community scale systems that can be activated as needed (see also Gleick 2008). Oelkers, Hering, and Zhu (2011) point to the greater use of inexpensive desalinization around the world (see also Gleick 2008). However, desalinization provides less than 1 percent of global freshwater needs and energy has to be used to desalinate, which typically has meant fossil fuels. They also call for improved management of this freshwater, which is a universal desire but a lot easier to say than to accomplish. A key point that I return to later in the chapter is that freshwater resource management decisions are made by thousands of people, and there will be a continuum of such decisions, some of which will permit adaptation, but only some of many.

Part of the resistance by some parties is that they do not trust the science, especially at regional and local scales. The science of water resources modeling has a long history and efforts to produce less uncertainty in global climate change forecasting has led to many interesting modeling studies. Most of the initial set of models used one or two sets of assumptions to simulate outcomes. More recent efforts have used multiple models. Prudhomme *et al.* (2014) produced a set of 35 simulations based on global hydrological climate models, showing the likely increase in global severity of drought by the end of the twenty-first century, with regional hotspots including South America and central and western Europe in which the frequency of drought increases by more than 20 percent, and they also identify southern Europe, the Middle East and the southeast United States, Chile and Southwest Australia as possible hotspots for future water security issues. But

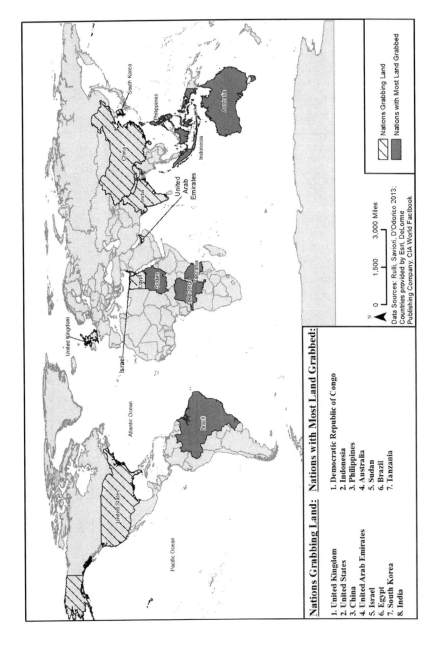

Nations Grabbing Land:

1. United Kingdom
2. United States
3. China
4. United Arab Emirates
5. Israel
6. Egypt
7. South Korea
8. India

Nations with Most Land Grabbed:

1. Democratic Republic of Congo
2. Indonesia
3. Philippines
4. Australia
5. Sudan
6. Brazil
7. Tanzania

Data Sources: Rulli, Saviori, D'Odorico 2013;
Countries provided by Esri, DeLorme
Publishing Company, CIA World Factbook

0   1,500   3,000 Miles

Nations Grabbing Land

Nations with Most Land Grabbed

FIGURE 7.4 Land grabbing nations

they note a great deal of uncertainty in multiple components of the exercise, especially as the scales go from global to regional and local scales.

Haddenland *et al.* (2014) used seven global hydrological models to compare global water resources impacts of man-made structures (dams, reservoirs) and global climate change. They found that these kinds of human structures are usually not that important except in some places where they are markedly important. In these vulnerable places mean runoff decreased 15 percent by impoundments and consumptive use. The Indus (Tibet, India, and Pakistan), and Huang He (China) river basins are presented as examples. Other places identified by the authors as impacted are the Colorado, Nile, Orange, Murray-Darling, and Mississippi river basins. However, even this multi-model effort produces highly uncertain results.

Schewe *et al.* (2014) using multiple models concluded that some places will suffer more than others from climate change and land-use changes. They identify global hydrological models as highly uncertain, which they indicate means that they cannot give precise and certain estimates of runoff and evapotranspiration.

Dalin *et al.* (2015) build an interesting set of models that include the capacity to estimate hydrologic outputs and economic consequences, and include interesting components such as trade out to the year 2030. They find that factors such as increasing demand for rich foods will increase the challenge of feeding people and balancing water between agriculture, environment, and urbanization. Oki and Kanae (2006) summarize the challenges of understanding the physical components of freshwater. They note that the scientists need better hydrologic system data, and yet they observe that the social factors that drive water use, pollution, and other elements of availability are a bigger challenge than science and engineering.

New York City's and China's massive engineered fresh water projects

When I was a sophomore in high school, I was fortunate to receive a scholarship to study with a professor at nearby Hunter College in New York City. My internship turned out to be an opportunity to work with Anastasia Van Burkalow who was working on a study of New York City's water supply system. Van Burkalow (1959) described New York City's system as delivering 1.2 billion gallons of water a day to 8 million New York City residents and over a million more that host one of the three aqueducts that move water from the northern suburbs to the Hillview Reservoir in Yonkers (see Chapter 2 to see discussion of security of the reservoir).

The three aqueducts, include the Delaware aqueduct, which at over 100 miles is the longest tunnel in the world. New York has also built a massive (estimated at $2.1 billion) filtration plant and is in the process of finishing a new tunnel that it began in 1970. This new tunnel is 24 feet wide (7.3 m) and slowly shrinks to less than 20 feet when it reaches Queens, New York. It will allow New York City to close the first two aqueducts to repair leaks. New York City had well over 100 years to build this system, and it has purchased a massive area to store billions of gallons of water, move it over 100 miles, and filter it. The cost of building this system in 2015 dollars is difficult to estimate. But using inflators I estimate it to be $20 billion +/- $5 billion. Frankly, given twenty-first century local politics, I would say that the chances of building these massive engineering projects today in New York City would range from slim to none.

On the other side of the world, 6,800 miles (10,944 km) away from New York City is Beijing the capital of China which has had severe water scarcity issues during the dry season and heavy flooding during the short wet season. The Chang Jiang is among the largest rivers in the world and the Yellow River is the second longest in China. They flow through some of China's largest cities, including Chongqing, Wuhan, Nanjing, and Shanghai (Figure 7.5). China is building a major set of tunnels and canals from southern China to divert water north, including to Beijing. The eastern and western routes will deliver water toward Tianjin and northwest China, respectively. The central route will direct water to the Beijing area. The central project has required farmers to cut their water use, the relocation of over 300,000 people to make way for a reservoir, and raised concerns about water quality. In 2008, the costs for the eastern and central routes were estimated at $37.4 billion, and these costs will increase. Ma *et al.* (2006) argue that while water will be diverted from the south to the north, northern China currently supplies a great deal of food to southern China and the flow of water will allow northern China to provide water back to southern China through the food. Bermittella, Rehdanz, and Tol (2006) suggest that the transfer could benefit China

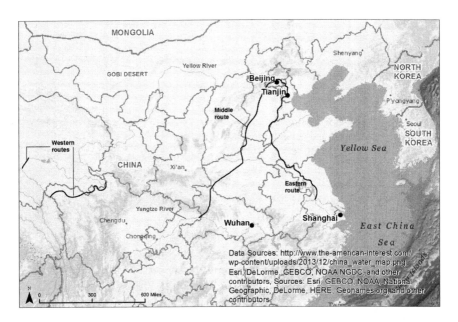

FIGURE 7.5 Beijing and other south-north projects, China

as a whole through more products, including food, flowing south and less freshwater related risk in northern China. The results are uncertain and a topic of considerable debate.

The controversial Three Gorges Dam project is typically used to illustrate China's massive, in many cases, unprecedented mega-scale engineering projects. The north–south water transfer projects are considerably larger and more costly than the Three Gorges project. The north–south projects are a mega-scale gamble that the Chinese government is taking, one that New York City took a century ago and continues to work on. Few countries would even have the resources to contemplate such massive engineered projects, none in the global Southern Hemisphere.

The southern hemisphere: Australia, South America and Africa

The Southern Hemisphere has been neglected in the literature. However, the literature is growing (Adger *et al.* 2003; Bicknell, Dodman, Satterthwaite 2009; Carmin, Anguelovski, Roberts 2012; Davoudi, Crawford, Mehmood 2009; Dessai *et al.* 2009). Here, I focus on three important areas that face a variety of freshwater-related challenges.

Australia is a relatively affluent country, indeed, on a per capita basis it is the most affluent in the Southern Hemisphere. But Australia has freshwater related vulnerabilities: the lowest percentage of rainfall captured as runoff and also the lowest volume of runoff of any inhabited continent. Its rivers are small and often contain brackish waters with highly variable flow patterns. Hence, Australia faces water volume and quality threats. Goater *et al.* (2011) call for adaptive governance strategies that center on proactive risk planning, being receptive to new technologies, and especially collaborations that cross Australia's jurisdictional boundaries.

The authors emphasize human health effects, mentioning not only the common impacts of water scarcity but also waterborne infections, risks arising from chemical contaminants, and human acceptance problems associated with color, taste and odor, such as from iron and manganese,

Goater *et al.* suggest identifying those Australian regions most at risk of water scarcity and water quality issues. They call for a list of existing community adaptive strategies and good existing practices as examples that other communities can emulate. They note that risk assessments for water-related diseases are hindered by the uncertainty surrounding the effects of climate change. Goater *et al.* (2011) assert that it is difficult to isolate relationships between water supply, adaptive capacity of communities and human health outcomes, and that work on these subjects is essential.

South America has some of the wettest and driest places on Earth. Vorosmarty *et al.* (2013) used a risk analysis framework to study South America's water-related risks, noting that along with Asia, South America is not only characterized by growing economies but also the most serious cases of sudden dangerous weather changes (see also Freeman, Warner 2001). They add that flooding risks are continuing to rise (see also United Nations International 2011). In that context, the authors derived vulnerability (damage) functions for urban and rural populations in South America, maps of precipitation, urban and rural populations, a geography of major precipitation events, and populations exposed to these during the period 1960–2000, and likely to be exposed in the near term future. Their objectives were to rank the risk sources and variability in climate variability, and estimate how these impact population growth and redistribution (see Kates *et al.* 2001 and Downing, Olsthrom, Tol 1999 for other illustrations of efforts to do place-based assessments).

The authors used a variety of data sources, such as remote sensing, ground-based hydrometeorological networks, data assimilation and simulation to monitor and map extreme weather at the regional scale, including likelihood of amount of precipitation, flood stage, erosion, landslides, and mudslides. They superimposed these data on population distribution maps. Vorosmarty *et al.* (2013) acknowledge that they had to reconcile data collected from all over South America. With that caveat noted, using data from 1960–2000, they varied assumptions about population growth and distribution as well as about changes in climate. Rainfall and population time series were used with vulnerability functions to create a geography of exposure and risk in response to extreme precipitation. Their continental geography study compares average rainfall and multipliers of average rainfall in order to find places that have and are likely to experience serious events. Western Argentina/Chile, the region surrounding Santiago and the Andes, northeastern Brazil, as well as portions of Venezuela are estimated to have many acute water-related hazard events.

In regard to rural areas, pre-existing conditions continue to place many people at risk, followed by demographic shifts into high water-risk areas. Notably, estimated climate change was the least significant predictor of damage in rural areas of South America. Urban populations grew substantially in South American during the 40 year study period (almost twice as much as rural), and the authors estimate that urban areas constituted over three-quarters of the added risk, and that the number of urban people at risk nearly tripled during the four decades. Vorosmarty *et al.* observe that that only 10 percent of the incremental change could be attributable to climate change.

The South American water-risk maps produced by this group are quite revealing, and I recommend that those with an interest examine them along with those by Balk, Montgomery, and Liu 2012; Pielke and Downton 2000; United Nations International 2011; and Dilley *et al.* 2005.

Vorosmarty *et al.* present the following risk management options:

- Invest in early warning systems;
- Build up response capacity and preparedness;
- Increase investment in storage reservoirs, flood control and other engineered systems when resources are available and the investments would not be substantially destructive of environmental and settlements;

FIGURE 7.6 South America water risk areas

- Emphasize wherever possible upstream land management (natural wetlands, floodplains, riparian areas); and green areas; and
- In general, upgrade water, sewer, and other infrastructures to try to keep pace with growing urbanization.

This research illustrates the value of mapping the best available data and displaying it as a way of showing the geographical dimensions of risk, and this paper and some others do an excellent job of emphasizing the impacts of natural events and of pointing to human factors shaping risk profiles.

Africa is assumed to be the continent most impacted by global climate change (World Bank 2003). De Wit and Stankiewicz (2006) studied the impact of reduced precipitation on geometry of drainage in Africa, and hence availability of surface water. The authors posit a nonlinear response of drainage to rainfall. Regions with 1,000 mm of precipitation per year or more would lose 17 percent of their draining capacity under a serious global climate change scenario. Those regions with less than 500 mm a year of rainfall have no clear drainage system. Regions receiving 500 mm per year are predicted to lose about half of their surface drainage. These latter regions account for 25 percent of Africa, including major sections of South Africa, Botswana, Zimbabwe, Angola, Sudan, Chad, Niger, Senegal, Morocco, and Algeria. The authors' models suggest that southern Africa will suffer the most. The authors are concerned about conflicts among and within nations because so many of the rivers also serve as important political and ethnic boundaries. The authors call for cooperative planning and negotiation to avoid conflict. The underlying problem is that the little drainage in some areas will be further reduced by global climate change.

Collier, Conway, and Venables (2008) agree with the consensus that Africa will be the continent most severely impacted by global climate change. This is because of its limited capacity to adapt, and high dependence on agriculture. While some parts of Africa, such as East Africa, could receive additional water, much of southern Africa will be hotter and drier. Crop yields will be reduced by an overall reduction in water and exacerbated by extreme weather events. The authors identify migration, changes in production and changes in crop patterns as close to intractable challenges. The authors believe that the responsibility to manage the risk will fall to private enterprise, and that the role of government will be to provide information, incentives, and economic environments conducive to facilitate such changes. Collier, Conway, and Venables assert that adaptation will be impeded by Africa's large number of small countries and ethnic groups, which will hinder migration. Africa, they argue, does not have a long history of successful adaptability to changing conditions, and it will have a difficult time adjusting to new agricultural products when the need arises.

The Intergovernmental Panel on Climate Change (2007) concludes that current conditions of chronic hunger will worsen because the proportion of depleted water resources is increasing. The literature expresses concern about the spread of malaria-carrying mosquitoes into higher elevations, especially above 1,000 m, in other words, the highlands of East Africa. This problem is expected to be exacerbated by inadequate drug treatment programs, drug resistance, land-use change, and various socio-demographic factors, especially poverty. Sea-level rise by a meter or more could occur and would affect some 6 million people in the Nile Delta. There could be considerable impact on the infrastructure system related to flooding.

Migration should increase, or at least the need for it should increase. Collier, Conway, and Venables point out that drought in the Sahul (Australia, New Guinea,

Tasmania, and neighboring islands) should lead to a serious migration issue. Another example is the movement of population from arid and landlocked Burkina Faso (formerly Upper Volta) to coastal Côte d'Ivoire (Ivory Coast). The Burkina Faso government had collapsed and power was not settled at the time this chapter was written.

Africa will become more prone to water-related shocks and needs to be able to shift to drought resistant crops (such as cassava) and it will hard pressed not to use genetically modified crops. But this is a problem heightened by the reality of EU countries resisting genetically modified crops. Africa has experienced considerable deforestation, which only exacerbates the vulnerability as noted earlier in the chapter. Water has been a source of conflict as pastoralists seeking water resources clash with sedentary arable farmers. Africa epitomizes severe water-related stresses.

Durban, South Africa

Large cities with resources have been responding to threats posed by floods, droughts, and long-term changes in their water supply. For example, New York City has had one of the most dependable freshwater supplies because of investments it began over a century ago in three reservoir systems outside the city itself, which were supported by water tunnels and a filtration system, and China has a program to address its most striking water problems with engineered systems (see above). We should expect cities like New York, London, Paris, Tokyo, Beijing, and many others world cities to have the resources to devise and begin to implement plans in regard to freshwater supply and water hazard events.

Cities in poorer countries face a different reality. Durban, South Africa is a Southern Hemisphere city located on the poorest continent. Durban (or *eThekwini*, meaning "bay/lagoon") is a port and manufacturing city on the Indian Ocean, also famous for beaches that attract tourists (Figure 7.7). In the African context, Durban with about 3.6 million people is a critical asset.

Durban faces major water-related challenges. These start with poverty. The Health Sciences Research Council (2004) estimated that 57 percent of individuals living in the nation of South Africa lived below the poverty level as we entered the twenty-first century. Cape Town was estimated to have the lowest poverty rate among South African cities: 30 percent. Pretoria and Johannesburg's were estimated to be 35 percent and 38 percent, respectively. Durban's portion in poverty was 44 percent. The Human Health Sciences Research Council constructed a poverty gap measure, and calculated that the poverty gap has grown, and that Durban's had grown more than other South African cities. Nicolson (2015) observed that South Africa faces a triple threat of poverty, unemployment, and inequality. Budlender, Woolard, and Leibbrandt (2015) contend that current measures of poverty underestimate poverty in South Africa, and that the actual rate exceeds 60 percent.

Supplying freshwater, keeping the water from being polluted, managing storms and floods in cities like Durban, especially in poor neighborhoods, is a daunting challenge because many of the poor live on the outskirts of the developed areas in

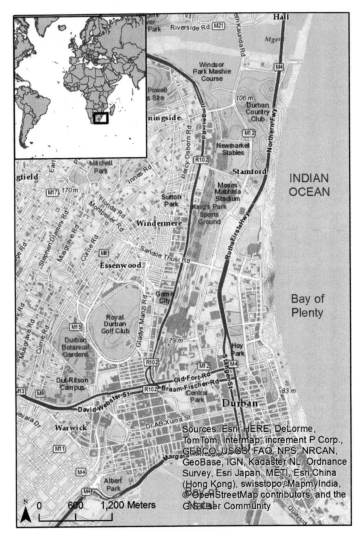

FIGURE 7.7 Durban area

poorly constructed housing, without water or sewer connections and no capacity to manage flood waters. Protecting these people is difficult because water, sewers, and flood protection are only one set of needs, which include food, education, and health. The pressure to make investments that will do the most good for the most people is exacerbated in places like Durban where there is no cushion to fix bad investments. Furthermore, because Durban has important economic assets that are vulnerable, emphasizing the needs of capital and ignoring the needs of the poor living in the most vulnerable circumstances as hopeless is easy enough to do, at least intellectually.

The focus of this case study is the fascinating effort by Durban officials to develop a plan that would address many public needs. Figure 7.8 is a logic diagram of their process. The "managers" were managers/technical experts.

The managers targeted three time horizons: 0–4, 0–50, and 0–100 years. They listed economic, engineering, social and political adaptations. A total of 47 were compiled, and because many of these overlapped, these 47 were grouped into 16 categories. A list of water adaptation categories was as follows:

- Water-related spatial planning;
- Water-related asset protection;
- Sea-level rise preparedness;
- Community water management;
- Water-related municipal climate change capacity; and
- Construction of Spring Grove dam.

With the exception of the Spring Grove dam, each option contained multiple related options. For example, sea-level preparedness included revising coastal set-back lines, and preparing coastal management plans.

The 16 categories were studied following two paths. One path estimated the capital and operating costs of the options, and then estimated the financial costs of implementing each (see right side of Figure 7.8). The managers focused on actions to protect many people against major hazard events (see left side of Figure 7.8). Standard cost-benefit analysis was not used because the managers made an explicit decision to protect people rather than focus on capital assets. They said that they wanted local values and priorities to heavily weight priorities.

Emphasizing people in the Durban context means that gross domestic product would not be used as a key metric because of inequalities in the distribution of assets among people and sub-areas of the city (Stiglitz, Sen, Fitouss 2010; Tol 2002; World Bank 2010). The authors also reported that changing water-run off, ranges of temperature, soil moisture, and other influences on the water cycle have been studied, and that uncertainty is too high to be used in modeling studies that demand high quality data. The researchers also were wary of using standard discount rates because they argue that these metrics overvalue the present compared to the future. Given budgetary constraints, the group believed that projects like watershed management, community preparedness, zoning and other institutional responses would be undervalued, and that this city needed solutions that were flexible and adjustable to diverse needs (see Hounsome, Iyer 2006; International Institute for Environment and Development (IIED) 2009; Mather, Roberts, Tooley 2011; Momba *et al.* 2006; Roberts 2008, 2010; Roberts *et al.* 2012).

As noted above, the analysts clustered 47 policy options into 16 "municipal adaptation clusters" and evaluated these under four future conditions or scenarios (Cartwright *et al.* 2013):

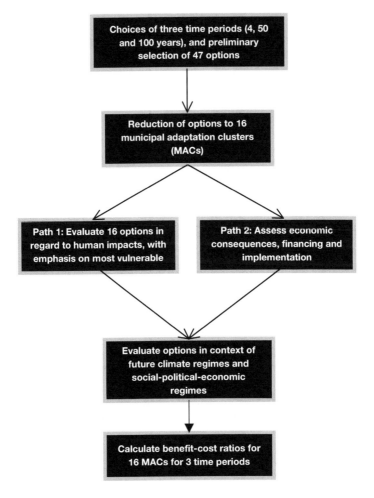

FIGURE 7.8 Design to assess costs and benefits of Durban's options

Source: Adapted and simplified from Cartwright *et al.* (2013), Figure 2, p. 148.

- *"Ready for the storm"*: Climate change is happening, and the city needs to apply its resources to prevent some consequences and be resilient to a wide range of others, especially risks to the most vulnerable populations.
- *"Plain sailing"*: Climate change has minor impacts, and resources therefore can be applied to development and to reduce human inequality.
- *"Even keel but going south"*: This scenario assumes only minor changes in climate but massive development that can multiply the negative impacts of minor climate changes. The local government focuses on coping with poor land use and growth decisions.

- *"Leaky boat, stormy sea"*: This is the worst case future with substantial climate changes and poor land use and development choices leading to disease outbreaks, droughts, floods, sea-level rise and crop failures.

As part of this exercise in risk analysis, the 16 adaptation clusters were evaluated for political support, job creation, historical evidence of use in the area, technical complexity, and likelihood of failure, as well as the benefits and costs analyses.

The managers calculated and mapped the results so that audiences could see the number of people potentially benefiting and the frequency of them benefiting. As part of this effort to be transparent, the managers weighted consequences. For example, if lives were assumed to be saved, then a weight of 0.7 was applied to the adaptation cluster. "Significant," "moderate," and "small" estimated benefits were weighted by values of 0.2, 0.07, and 0.03, respectively. Clearly, their weighting scheme emphasizes adaptation policies that will save people's lives. These weights were multiplied by number of people impacted and frequency of their impact to produce a "population impact equivalent" for each of the 16 adaptation clusters that were examined across space and time.

This approach contains a great deal of subjectivity (see Chapters 2 and 3 for similar risk management approaches). The transparency of the approach makes it easy to understand. The four most highly scored adaptation clusters in the 0–50 year span are reproduced in Table 7.1.

The managers do not claim that they represent residents' views and values, nor the owners of large capital investments. In essence, any option that required large capital investment (such as the dam project) had low ratings. The managers are part of the decision-making group in the region and this low rating of costly projects likely reflects the fact that they live in a world where money for large capital projects is not available. They could not do what China, the United States and some other nations have done. At the top of the preferred list are solutions that can be controlled by risk managers at the local scale, such as revising set-back lines, developing coastal plans, and organizing a cross-department advisory team. I was surprised that the set of natural capital regulation and acquisition options was only ranked thirteenth of 16. I assume that the project team must feel that it is not feasible to obtain and manage land in this highly stressed environment.

I suspect that residents would have increased the rating of providing an early warning system, and a health awareness system, which ranked seventh and eighth, respectively, out of the 16 adaptation clusters. Overall, these results suggest that the team that rated the options is not looking to make massive transformative changes for the future. Instead, it is trying to build organizational capacity and flexibility to respond.

An interesting set of comparisons is between the four scenarios in columns 2–5. The ratios in Table 7.1 are 50 percent to 300 percent higher when development can be locally controlled and when global climate change turns out to be less destructive of the Durban environment.

Summarizing, this clever study shows that it is possible to study adaptation

TABLE 7.1 Benefit-cost ratios for 0–50 year time span: most highly ranked and lowest ranked adaptation options, Durban

Options (1=highest preference, 16=lowest ranked preference)	Ready for the storm	Plain sailing	Even keel but going south	Leaky boat, stormy seas
Sea level rise preparedness (revise coastal set-back lines, develop coastal plans)	66.4 (1)	50.6 (2)	38.1 (2)	18.6 (2)
Cross departmental advisory forum among departments and technical experts teams	62.2 (2)	63.0 (1)	59.4 (1)	45.9 (1)
Municipal wide adaptation capacity (develop socioeconomic capacity)	26.5 (3)	25.7 (3)	23.2 (2)	16.4 (3)
Water-related municipal climate change capacity (analysis of future run-off scenarios and social and institutional capacity to respond)	25.0 (4)	23.6 (4)	20.8 (4)	13.9 (4)
Options 5–12 not shown in table★	NA	NA	NA	NA
Natural capital regulation and acquisition (land use management, systems plans, land acquisition, enforcement, integrating municipal plans)	2.3 (13)	2.3 (13)	2.1 (13)	1.5 (13)
Water-related asset protection (revise plans for coastal assets and sea-level rise scenarios; monitor/ maintain stormwater system, devise drainage plans)	0.4 (15)	0.3 (15)	0.2 (15)	0.1 (15)
Construction of the Spring Grove dam	0.3 (16)	0.2 (16)	0.1 (16)	0.1 (16)

Note: ★The full set of ratings is available in the Cartwright *et al.* (2013) paper.

Source: Adapted from Cartwright *et al.* (2013), Table 1, p. 149.

options in environments with the focus on vulnerable people, which means shifting the priority away from economic assets. This hybrid of traditional economic and socioeconomic analyses can be extended by other groups that develop their weights, as well as change the adaptation strategies. This group of managers recognized the temporal uncertainty issue by building scenarios for three different time periods and for four climate and development scenarios.

Which alternative future for which population

Arguably freshwater is our most endangered precious resource (Black, King 2009; Fagan 2011; Solomon 2011; Satterthwaite *et al.* 2009; Greenberg, Ferrer 2012).

Using freshwater as a sentinel ecological resource, this chapter has shown that uneven development, population growth and local land-use decisions have been increasing pressure on freshwater sources. Concerns about global climate change increase the pressure and the risk.

We know that adaptation will follow, but what kind of adaptation and who will benefit or at least be no worse and who will suffer major disruption (Hallegatte 2008; Kates 2000; Laugesen, Fryd 2009; Lee 1999; Pahl-Wostil 2007; Pelling 2011)? I doubt that readers will be surprised when I conclude that affluent largely western nations in the northern hemisphere have a better chance to adapt without entirely changing their lives because of their economic, political, and military power (see chapter 9 where that does not happen in fiction). I have visited Las Vegas, Nevada many times and am always amazed that a place with an average annual rainfall of 4.2 inches has over 2 million residents in the metropolitan area. On my family visits, family and friends were sure that the city and casino industries would use their resources to purchase whatever water they need. The same is true of some other areas in the United States, the Middle East, Europe and Asia and any other places that have sufficient capital and power to get what they need.

Other people living in or near these dry but wealthy places will need to adapt, especially the farmers, ranchers, mineral site operators, and others who will not be able to deny water to growing metropolitan areas. Government and business will develop and implement technology that will promote more efficient water use, but eventually without political support water will go to large urban areas with sunken investments in infrastructure and people.

The picture is far more challenging in rural and smaller cities, especially in developing nations. Durban appears to me to be more the exception than the norm. How many other cities will use the kind of process used in Durban? I assume that the major world powers will not completely abandon much of the world's people, although the science fiction world of Chapter 9 suggests that they might. Yet, it is equally hard to believe that smaller and even medium-sized cities without major economic and political assets will continue to receive their share of freshwater in dry environments. I expect the world to have twenty-first century equivalents of nineteenth- and twentieth-century abandoned mining and industrial towns. Rural areas will have their water redirected to large wealth creation and retention centers.

Figure 7.9 diagrams my thoughts about the process beginning with increasing development and population growth, then increasing water demand, while at the same time there are periodic droughts and long-term loss of freshwater from pollution and mining and grabbing of water and land. Some areas are able to adapt by using technology and education, but others face increased competition for water that leaves them vulnerable to other natural hazard events, eventually leading to migration and redefinition of human life in those environments.

This vision of inequity and disruption calls for wealthy nations to invest in these marginalized areas. Assistance may allow the populations a chance to use local

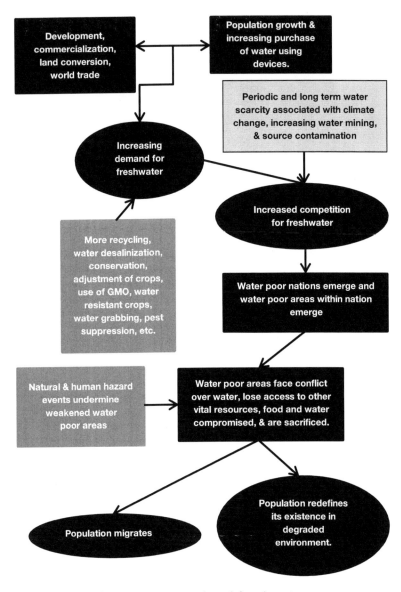

FIGURE 7.9 Creation of water scare areas and need for adaptation

knowledge to redefine human life in these stressed environments. When life in some of these clusters becomes too expensive to manage and the cost to the stranded population is too high, some nations and areas within the host nations will need to open up their borders to migrants. For me, the questions are how many of these degraded clusters will be created and how long will it take for them to be to the point of no return, and then how many will be aided in adapting? Global climate change will not be the major cause, but it will accelerate the process in favor of concentration in areas with large fluid, sunken and political capital.

What did Chapter 7 explain about risk analysis? Summary and learning objectives

Most of the Earth is covered by water, but only about 2 percent is freshwater. This chapter shows that increasing development, population growth, land-use changes, water mining and pollution and now the threat, if not reality, of climate change are leading to difficult choices. The global picture shows problems on every continent and serious problems in some locations. Typically, these stressed areas are already semi-arid areas or places that rely on snowmelt. Clusters of vulnerability become clearer as the scale shifts from continent to region and finally to locality. Science does not yet allow certain forecasts of the most vulnerable places but as it improves the band of uncertainty decreases. While science has focused at the global and regional scales, the key scale is national and local. Land-use decisions, economic development choices and many other critical risk-related decisions have historically been in the purview of local and state governments. It follows that there are many opportunities to make good and bad choices.

The chapter uses Durban, South Africa, as a moderately sized city in a poor part of the world as a model for trying to cope with the freshwater-related supply and storms in a social environment stressed by poverty. Using a combination of hybrid traditional cost and benefit tools managers have tried to make explicit and transparent choices about their future.

At the end of this chapter readers should be able to answer the following seven questions:

1. What is the current level of understanding of the impact of global climate change on freshwater supplies?
2. What areas are most likely to be severely impacted by global climate change?
3. How do land-use decisions as the expression of economic development and population choices impact the freshwater supply?
4. What major project has China undertaken to manage water-supply risks in Beijing and elsewhere in northeastern China, and how is it similar and different from what has been done in New York City?
5. Why does the Southern Hemisphere appear to be disproportionately vulnerable to freshwater supply risks?
6. How does Durban, South Africa illustrate a way of managing water-related risks that is sensitive to a large poor population?
7. How will global climate change likely contribute to clusters of water-poor areas that will require government and private intervention to maintain or assistance to support migration?

References

Adger W, Huq N, Brown K, Conway D, Hulme M. (2003) Adaptation to climate change in the developing world, *Progress in Development Studies*. 3, 3, 179–195.

Bailey A. (2010) Population geographies and climate change. *Progress in Human Geography*. 35, 5, 686–695.

Balk D, Montgomery MR, Liu Z. (2012) *Urbanization and climate change hazards in Asia*. Bangkok: Asian Development Bank.

Barnett T, Adam J, Letenmaier D. (2005) Potential impacts of a warming climate on water availability in snow-dominated regions. *Nature*. 438, 303–309.

Beck U. (1992) *Risk society*. London: Sage.

Bermittella M, Rehdanz K, Tol R. (2006) The economic impact of the south-north water transfer project in China: a computable general equilibrium analysis, climate change modeling and policy. http://papers.ssrn.com/sol/3/papers.cfm?abstract_id=952938. Accessed December 26, 2015.

Bicknell, J, Dodman D, Satterthwaite D., eds. (2009) *Adapting cities to climate change: understanding and addressing the development challenge,* London; Earthscan.

Black R. (1998) *Refugees, environment and development*. Harlow: Addison Wesley Longman

Black M, King J. (2009) *The atlas of water: mapping the world's most critical resources*. Oakland, CA: University of California Press.

Budlender J, Woolard I, Leibbrandt M. (2015) How current measures underestimate the level of poverty in South Africa. The conversation. http://theconversation.com/how-current-measures-underestimate-the-level-of-poverty-in-south. Accessed September 3, 2014.

Carmin J, Anguelovski I, Roberts D. (2012) Urban climate adaptation in the global South: planning in an emerging policy domain, *Journal of Planning Education and Research*. 32, 1, 18–32.

Cartwright A, Blignaut J, De Wit M, Goldberg K, Mander M, O'Donoghue S, Roberts D. (2013) Economics of climate change adaptation at the local scale under conditions of uncertainty and resource constraints: the case of Durban, South Africa. *Environment & Urbanization*. 25, 1, 139–156.

Collier P, Conway G, Venables T. (2008) Climate change and Africa. *Oxford Review of Economic Policy*. 24, 2, 337–353.

Conway G. (1997) *The doubly green revolution: food for all in the twenty-first century*. New York: Penguin Books.

Dalin C, Konar M, Hanasaki N, Rindaldo A, Rodriguez-Iturbe I. (2012) Evolution of the global virtual water trade network. *Proceedings of the National Academy of Sciences*. 109, 16, 5989–5994.

Dalin C, Qiu H, Hanasaki N, Mauzerall D, Rodriguez-Iturbe I. (2015). Balancing water resource conservation and food security in China. *Proceedings of the National Academy of Sciences*. 112, 15, 4588–4593.

Davoudi, S, Crawford J, Mehmood A, eds. (2009) *Planning for climate change: strategies for mitigation and adaptation for spatial planners* London: Earthscan.

Dessai, S, Hulme M, Lempert R, Pielke R, Jr. (2009) Do we need more precise and accurate predictions in order to adapt to a changing climate? *Eos* 90, 13, 111–112.

De Wit M, Stankiewicz J. (2006) Changes in surface water supply across Africa with predicted climate change. *Science*. 311, 5769, 1917–1921.

Dilley M, Chen R, Deichmann U, Lerner-Lam A, Arnold M. (2005) *Natural disaster hotspots: a global risk analysis*. Washington, D.C: The World Bank.

Dinar A, Dinar S, McCaffrey S, Mckinney D. (2007) *Bridges over water: understanding trans boundary water conflict, negotiation and cooperation*. Hackensack, NJ: World Scientific.

Downing T, Olsthrom A, Tol R. (1999) *Climate change and risk*. London: Routledge.

Fagan B. (2011) *Elixir: a history of water and humankind*. New York: Bloomsbury Press.

Fisher F, Huber-Lee A, Amir I. (2005) *Liquid assets: an economic approach for water management and conflict resolution in the Middle East and beyond*. Washington, D.C.: RFF.

Foley J, DeFries R, Asner G, Barford C, Bonan G, Carpenter S, Chapin F, Coe M, Daily G, Gibbs H, Helkowski J, Holloway T, Howard E, Kucharik C, Monfreda C, Patz J, Prentice C, Ramankutty N, Snyder P. (2005) Global consequences of land use. *Science*. 309, 5734, 570–574.

Freeman P, Warner K. (2001) *Vulnerability of infrastructure to climate variability: how does this affect infrastructure lending policies?* Report Commissioned by the Disaster Management Facility of the World Bank and the ProVention Consortium. Washington, D.C.: The World Bank.

Gleditsch N, Nordas R, Salehyan I. (2007) *Climate change, migration, and conflict*. New York: International Peace Academy.

Gleick P. (1993) *Water in crisis*. Oxford: Oxford University Press.

Gleick P. (1998) *The world's water: The biennial report on freshwater resources*. Washington D.C.: Island Press.

Gleick, P., ed. (2008) *The world's water 2008–2009*. Washington D.C.: Island Press.

Goater S, Cook A, Hogan A, Mengersen K, Hieatt A, Weinstein P. (2011) Strategies to strengthen public health inputs to water policy in response to climate change: an Australian perspective. *Asia-Pacific Journal of Public Health*. Supplement to 23, 2, 80S–90S.

Greenberg M. (2009) Water, conflict, and hope. *American Journal of Public Health*. 99, 11,1928–1930.

Greenberg M, Ferrer J. (2012) Global availability of water. In R. Friis, ed., *The Praeger handbook of environmental health*. Vol. 3, Water, Air and Solid Waste. 1–20. New York: Prager.

Grover V, ed. (2007) *Water: a source of conflict or cooperation?* Enfield, NH: Science Publishers.

Haddenland I, Heinke J, Biemans H, Eisner S, Florke M, Hanasaki N, Konzmann M, Ludwig F, Masaki Y, Schewe, J, Stacke T, Tessler Z, Wada Y, Wisser D. (2014) Global water resources affected by human interventions and climate change. *Proceedings of the National Academy of Sciences*. 111, 9, 3251–3256.

Hallegatte S. (2008) Strategies to adapt to an uncertain climate change. *Global Environmental Change*. 19, 2, 240–247.

Health Sciences Research Council. (2004) Fact sheet on poverty in South Africa. Pretoria, South Africa.

Hoekstra A, Mekonnen M. (2012) The water footprint of humanity. *Proceedings of the National Academy of Sciences*. 109, 9, 3232–3237.

Homer-Dixon T. (1994) Environmental scarcities and violent conflict: evidence from cases. *International Security*. 19, 5–40.

Hounsome R, Iyer K. (2006) Headline climate change adaptation strategy for Durban council for scientific and industrial research, Report prepared for Thekwini Municipality, Durban, South Africa, available at http://durbanportalnet/ClimateChange/Policy%20and%20Legislation/eThekwini%20Policy%20and%20Guidelines/Durban%20Climate%20Change%20Headline%20Adaptation%20Strategy%202006pdf. Accessed December 27, 2015.

International Institute for Environment and Development (IIED) (2009) Bringing the economics of climate adaptation to life, available at http://pubsiiedorg/pdfs/G02737pdf. Accessed August 12, 2015.

Intergovernmental Panel on Climate Change (IPPC) (2007) *Climate change 2007: synthesis report. Contribution of working groups one, the scientific basis. Contribution of working group I, II, and III to the fourth assessment report of the Intergovernmental panel on climate change.* Geneva: IPCC.

Karl T, Melillo J, Peterson T. eds. (2009) *Global climate change impacts in the United States.* Cambridge, UK: Cambridge University Press.

Kates R. (2000) Cautionary tales: adaptation and the global poor. *Climatic Change.* 45, 5–17.

Kates R, and 22 others (2001) Sustainability science. *Science.* 292, 5517, 641–642. (doi:10.1126/science.1059386)

Kim J, Jackson R. (2011) A global analysis of groundwater recharge for vegetation, climate, and soils. *Vadose Zone Journal.* 11, 1, 1–35. Vzj.geosceinceworld.org/content/11/1/vzj2001.0021RA.full. Accessed August 24, 2015.

Laugesen C, Fryd O. (2009) *Sustainable wastewater management in developing countries: new paradigms and case studies from the field.* Reston, VA: ASCE Press.

Lee K. (1999) Appraising adaptive management. *Conservation Ecology.* 3, 3–16.

Lins H, Hirsch R, Kiang J. (2010) Water – the nation's fundamental climate issue: A white paper on the U.S. Geological Survey role and capabilities. Circular 13, Washington, D.C.

Liverman D, O'Brien K. (1991) Global warming and climate change in Mexico. *Global Environmental Change.* 1, 5, 351–364.

Ma J, Hoekstra A, Wang H, Chapagoon A, Wang D. (2006) Virtual versus real water transfers within China. *Philosophical Transactions B.* 361, 835–842.

Mather, A, Roberts D, Tooley G. (2011) Adaptation in practice: Durban, South Africa in Otto Zimmermann, K ed., Resilient cities and adaptation to climate change, *Proceedings of the Global Forum* 2010, 543–563.

Meadows D, Meadows D, Randers J, Behrens W III. (1972) *The limits to growth.* New York: Universe.

Momba MNB, Tyafa Z, Makala N, Brouckaet B, Obi C. (2006) Safe drinking water still a dream in rural areas of South Africa, case study: Eastern Cape province. www.wrc.org.za. Water SA, 32, 5, 715–720.

Nicolson G. (2015) South Africa: Where 12 million live in extreme poverty. *Daily Maverick.* www.dailymaverick.co.za/article/2015-02-03-south-africa-where-12-million-ive-in. Accessed September 3, 2015.

Oelkers E, Hering J, Zhu C. (2011) Water: is there a global crisis? *Elements.* 7, 3, 157–162.

Oki T, Kanae S. (2006) Global hydrological cycles and world water resources. *Science.* 313, 5790, 1068–1072.

Pahl-Wostil C. (2007) Transition towards adapted management of water facing climate and global change. *Water Resources Management.* 21, 49–62.

Pelling M. (2011) *Adaptation to climate change: from resilience to transformation.* London, Routledge.

Pielke R, Downton M. (2000) Precipitation and damaging floods: trends in the United States, 1932–97. *Journal of Climate.* 13, 3625–3637.

Prudhomme C, Giuntoli I, Robinson E, Clark D, Arnell N, Dankers R, Fekete B, Franssen W, Gerter D, Gosling S, Hagemann S, Hannah D, Kim H, Masaki Y, Satoh Y, Stacke T, Wada Y, Wisser D. (2014) Hydrological droughts in the 21st century, hotspots and uncertainties from a global multi-model ensemble experiment. *Proceedings of the National Academy of Sciences*, 111, 9, 3262–3267.

Roberts D. (2008) Thinking globally, acting locally: institutionalizing climate change at the local government level in Durban, South Africa. *Environment and Urbanization.* 20, 2, 521–538.

Roberts D. (2010) Prioritizing climate change adaptation and local level resiliency in Durban, South Africa. *Environment and Urbanization.* 22, 2, 397–413.

Roberts, D, Boon R, Diederichs N, Douwes E, Govender N, Mcinnes A, Mclean C,

O'Donoghue S, Spires M. (2012) Exploring ecosystem-based adaptation in Durban, South Africa: "learning- by-doing" at the local government coal face. *Environment and Urbanization.* 24, 1, 1–29.

Rockstrom J, Lannerstad M, Falkenmark M. (2007) Assessing the water challenge of a new green revolution in developing countries. *Proceedings of the National Academies of Sciences.* 104, 15, 6253–6260.

Rosenzweig C, Strzepek K, Major D, Iglesias A, Yates D, McCluskey A, Hillel D. (2004) Water resources for agriculture in a changing climate. *International Case Studies.* 14, 345–360.

Rulli M, Saviori A, D'Odorico P. (2013) Global land and water grabbing. *Proceedings of the National Academy of Sciences.* 110, 3, 892–897.

Sabin P. (2013) *The bet.* New Haven, CT: Yale University Press.

Sanchez P, Swaminathan M. (2005) Cutting world hunger in half. *Science.* 307(5708), 357–359.

Satterthwaite, D, Huq S, Reid H, Pelling M, Romero-Lankao M, Romero-Lankao P. (2009) Adapting to climate change in urban areas: the possibilities and constraints in low- and middle-income nations. In Bicknell J, Dodman D, Satterthwaite D, eds., *Adapting cities to climate change: understanding and addressing the development challenge*: 3–50. London: Earthscan.

Schewe J, Heinke J, Gerten D, Haddeland I, Arnell N, Clark D, Dankers R, Eisner S, Fekete B, Colon-Gonzalez F, Gosling S, Kim H, Liu X, Masaki Y, Portmann F, Satoh Y, Stacke T, Tang Q, Wada Y, Wisser D, Albrecht T, Frieler K, Piontek F, Warszawski L, Kabat P. (2014) Multi-model assessment of water scarcity under climate change. *Proceedings of the National Academy of Sciences.* 111, 9, 3245–3250.

Solomon S. (2011) Water: the epic struggle for wealth, power and civilization. New York: Harper Perennial.

Stiglitz J, Sen A, Fitouss J-P. (2010) *Mismeasuring our lives. Why GDP doesn't add up.* Commission on the Measurement of Economic Performance and Social Progress. New York, New York: The New Press.

Tol R. (2002) Estimate of the damage costs of climate change. *Environmental and Resource Economics.* 21, 47–73.

Trondalen J. (2008) *Water and peace for the people: possible solutions to water disputes in the Middle East.* Paris: UNESCO.

United Nations International Strategy for Disaster Reduction. (2011) *Revealing risk, redefining development.* Global Assessment Report on Disaster Risk Reduction. Geneva: UNISDR.

Van Burkalow A. (1959) Geography of New York City's water supply. *Geographical Review.* 49, 3, 369–386.

Vososmarty C, Bravo de Gueni L, Wollheim W, Pellerin B, Bjerklie D, Cardoso M, D'Almedia C, Green P, Colon L. (2013) Extreme rainfall, vulnerability and risk: a continental-scale assessment for South America. *Philosophical Transactions of the Royal Society.* rsta.royalsocietypublishing.org. Accessed August 21, 2015.

Vorosmarty C, Green P, Salisbury J, Lammers R. (2000) Global water resources: vulnerability from climate change and population growth. *Science.* 289, 5477, 284–288.

Vorosmarty C, McIntyre P, Gessner M, Dudgeon D, Prusevich A, Green P, Glidden S, Bunn S, Sullivan C, Reidy Liermann C, Davies P. (2010) Global threats to human water security and river biodiversity. *Nature.* 467, 555–561.

Vorosmarty C, Sahagian D. (2000) Anthropogenic disturbance of the terrestrial water cycle. *BioScience.* 50, 9, 753–765.

Wolf A, Natharius J, Danielson J, Ward B, Pender B. (1999) International river basins of the world. *International Journal of Water Resources Development.* 15, 387–428.

World Bank (2003) *Poverty and climate change: reducing the vulnerability of the poor through adaptation.* Washington, D.C.: World Bank.

World Bank. (2010) *The cost to developing countries of adapting to climate change: new methods and estimates,* Global Report on the Economics of Adaptation to Climate Change Study Consultation Draft. Washington, D.C.: World Bank.

Zeitoun, M. (2008) *Power and water in the Middle East: the hidden politics of the Palestinian-Israeli water conflict.* New York: I.B. Tauris.

8

BIOLOGICAL TERRORISM

Introduction

The book of *Exodus* in the Old Testament tells of ten plagues visited on Egypt and of the escape of the Israelites when the Red Sea parted. Some doubt that these events ever occurred. Researchers have offered alternative explanations. In regard to the parting of the Red Sea, strong winds, not unusual for the area, could have parted the Red Sea long enough for the exodus. Another idea is that a comet collision blackened the sky and cast ash on the land with devastating consequences that could help explain at least some of the ten plagues.

A third explanation of events is a volcanic eruption on the Greek Island of Santorini (Thira), about 1,000 km (621 miles) away. The volcanic eruption could have led to massive waves that parted the Red Sea long enough for the people to escape, and then swamped the pursuing chariots. The eruption is asserted to have cast an enormous amount of acidic ash into the air, which headed southeast toward Egypt. The ash fell, killed fish, animal and plant life. Red tide formed, which set off a chain that turned the water blood red, reduced oxygen in the sea, provided an overabundance of nutrients to frogs, gnats, lice, and flies that died. These were incorporated into the food chain, leading to anthrax among cattle. This devastating chain continued and with good imagination could be the cause of the ten plagues (Marr, Malloy 1996; Sparks 2007).

Whether you believe the biblical account or the speculative scientific ones, anthrax mentioned in one of the alternative explanations and other biological organisms are a concern in the twenty-first century. Governments facing external and internal enemies with moral, political, strategic and personal objectives are well aware of the threat. Along with an all-out nuclear war involving explosions of high-yield weapons across the globe, spread of radiation, darkening of the skies, and other possible effects such as uncontrollable fires, starvation, and other outcomes of a nuclear war, biological agents should be high on the list of acute hazard events to worry about.

Some of this concern is amplified by media. For example, writing in the *Toledo Blade*, in 2000, the year prior to the anthrax attacks, Michael Woods (2000) called anthrax an "agent of doom," labelling it as the "100-megaton bomb in the arsenal of bioterrorism and biological warfare." He cites a study that indicates that a small amount of powdered anthrax material, seeded into the air of a city, could kill more than 1 million people. In contrast, he adds that 80,000 would die in the explosion of a 12.5 kiloton atomic bomb. Of course, not every media story compares degrees of gloom and doom, and some do acknowledge uncertainty. Yet, as pointed out in Chapter 3, the media understand the power of negative information and use it to cultivate and maintain audiences. Even without media enhancement, bioterrorism is a major concern of nation-states and non-governmental organizations because some extremely dangerous organisms are relatively easy to obtain, turn into weapons and dispersed, especially anthrax (Block 2001).

This chapter uses anthrax to examine efforts to prevent bioterrorism, which includes the use of risk assessment and risk management. Risk assessments are based primarily on animal data (see Chapter 2), which leads to high uncertainty in defining actionable levels for risk managers who are pushed to remove all exposures after an event and prevent exposures with prophylactic drugs and antibiotics, which are expensive and not risk-free.

Biological warfare and terrorism agents

Historical and international contexts

Hostile parties and individuals have used cadavers, including disease-infected ones, to pollute water and food supplies (Eitzen, Takafuji 1997). Shortly after the 2001 use of anthrax that affected postal workers (see below), National Public Radio (2001) broadcast a story about the historical use of biological agents. Beginning with the ten plagues on Egypt, the story mentions the use of a fungus by the Assyrians to poison their enemies' water supplies; the use of plague infested cadavers to start a plague in the Tartar army in 1346; and the use of smallpox-laden blankets to kill Indians during the French and Indian Wars in 1754. Moving forward, the first major weaponized use of biological agents was during World War I when German agents used *Burkholderia mallei* to cause glanders in livestock. Glanders is caused by a bacterial infection, which is found in contaminated food or water. In order eliminate it, large numbers of animals were slaughtered, a practice that has continued to the present (see below).

Jonathan Tucker, an expert in chemical and biological weapons for the United States government, including for the Congressional Office of Technology Assessment and a weapons inspector in Iraq, not only kept track of the use of chemical weapons (see Chapter 4), but also biological ones. He analyzed international data about chemical, biological, nuclear and other reported incidents from

1960 through January 1, 1999, finding that 121 of the reported 415 incidents were biological (second to chemical incidents) and the vast majority were hoaxes. But not all of them were. In 1972, Chicago police arrested two college students who founded a terrorist group (R.I.S.E.) for plotting to put typhoid and other bacteria in the city's water supply. In 1984, in order to influence an election, the Bhagwan Shree Rajneesh group infected salad bars, and other public buildings with *Salmonella typhimurium* bacteria in the city of Dalles, Oregon. Over 700 people suffered food poisoning. In June 1993, the religious group Aum Shinrikyo released anthrax spores in Tokyo. However, the terrorists used a strain of the bacteria used for vaccines. No one died. Tucker's (1999) paper predicts that there will be many more hoaxes and small-scale attacks on food supplies. This report was prior to the 2001 anthrax attack in New Jersey, which dispersed anthrax spores through the U.S. postal service.

Government agencies monitor the most serious agents, and these are added to the list of banned products by the Biological Weapons Convention. The Biological Weapons Convention of 1975, agreed to by more than 160 states, banned developing, producing, acquiring, retaining, and producing biological agents intended for warfare purposes and delivery systems (Carus 2002; Grundmann 2014).

CDC biological weapons classification

An easy to understand list of the biological warfare agents has been published by the U.S. Centers for Disease Control and Prevention (Table 8.1). A caveat is that the CDC list focuses on the United States. The priority list could shift for applications in South America, Africa, parts of Asia and some other places based on agent availability, ability to turn it into a weapon and deliver it. For example, anthrax spores are easier to find in Africa and other less urban industrial nations than North America, Europe, and other urbanized places. Readers in more rural areas are advised to consult the World Health Organization's (WHO) website for more information.

The CDC classifies potential biological agents into three categories. Table 8.1 shows the classification and presents a brief explanation for the classification. The agents in group "A" are the most serious concerns because of their inherent toxicity, as well as availability and ability to use as a weapon. Anthrax, at the top of the list alphabetically, will be the case in this chapter. However, before focusing on anthrax it is important to note that anthrax is only one of the agents in the most dangerous "A" list. All of these biological organisms could be used as weapons, leading to high mortality, panic, and requiring large investments to reduce the impacts in the event of a bioterrorist attack.

I briefly describe the "A" list of biological agents. The historical significance of botulism, bubonic plague, and smallpox are undeniable. Rotz *et al.* (2002) reviewed CDC's assessment of biological agents. The group took into account potential public health impact, dissemination potential, and preparations for risk

TABLE 8.1 CDC/NIAIFD classification of potential biological agents used for bioterrorism attacks

Category	Agent	Concerns
A	Anthrax (*Bacillus anthracis*) Botulism (*Clostridium botulinum* toxin) Plague (*Yersinia pestis*) Smallpox (*Variola major*) Tularemia (*Francisella tularensis*) "rabbit fever" Viral hemorrhagic fever (e.g., Ebola, Marburg, Lassa, Machupo)	Easily spread from person to person Could cause high mortality rates Could cause panic and social disruption Requires a great deal of planning and implementation to protect human health
B	Brucellosis (*Brucella* species) Epsilon toxin (*Clostridium perfringens*) Food-safety threats (e.g., Salmonella species, *Escherichia coli* O157:H7, *Shigella*) Glanders (*Burkholderia mallei*) Melioidosis (*Burkholderia pseudomallei*) Psittacosis (*Chlamydia psittaci*) Q fever (*Coxiella burnetii*) Ricin toxin (*Ricinus communis*) and Abrin toxin (*Abrus precatorius*) Rosary peas Staphylococcal enterotoxin B Typhus fever (*Rickettsia prowazekii*) Viral encephalitis (e.g., Venezuelan equine encephalitis, Eastern and Western equine encephalitis) Water-related hazards (e.g., *Vibrio cholerae, Cryptosporidium parvum*)	Moderately easy to disseminate Result in moderate morbidity rates and low mortality rates Require specific enhancements of the CDC's diagnostic capacity and enhanced disease surveillance
C	Emerging infectious diseases Nipah virus Hantavirus	Are available Can be easily produced and disseminated Show potential for high morbidity and mortality rates and major health impact

Source: Adapted from Office of Laboratory Services, CDC 2015; Rotz *et al.* 2002.

management, and they also included public perception. Anthrax, smallpox, viral hemorrhagic fever, and cholera were the four on the highest public perception list.

In the United States, the Centers for Disease Control and Prevention (2015a) estimate about 145 cases of botulism a year. Botulism can come from eating food contaminated with the toxin (about 15 percent of all cases and typically from home-canned food). Sometimes the toxin penetrates through a wound (20 percent), often from contaminated needles (Centers for Disease Control and

Prevention 2015a). The majority of cases (65 percent) are infant botulism where the toxin has been digested in food, such as honey, and sometimes the agent is in dirt and dust.

Plague is caused by a bacterium that is injected into the host by rodent fleas found in an animal that has the plague. Millions of people were killed by the plague in Medieval Europe. Cases are reported in Asia, Africa, and the United States (Centers for Disease Control and Prevention 2015b).

Smallpox is contagious disease caused by a variola virus that is spread by prolonged face-to-face personal contact and by contact with fluids and objects that are contaminated (Centers for Disease Control and Prevention 2015c). Smallpox was thought to be eradicated in the United States in 1949, with only laboratory stockpiles kept to create vaccines. But there is a concern that it could be turned into a weapon.

Using my students as evidence of familiarity, few people have heard about tularemia. Tularemia is a disease that can devastate hares, rabbit, and rodent populations (Centers for Disease Control and Prevention 2015d). Humans can be infected by tick and deer fly bites, by skin contact with infected animals, inhalation of contaminated dusts, and laboratory contact. About 150 cases a year occur in the United States, mostly in Arkansas Massachusetts, Missouri, and Oklahoma, and a few in almost every state, except Hawaii.

Last on the "A" list are viruses capable of causing multiple organ system failure. The hosts are mice, rats, other rodents, and mosquitoes and ticks. But not every host is known. The major public health concern is weaponizing one or more of a diverse set of viruses, such as Ebola.

Category "B" contains some extremely dangerous agents that might be on the "A" list in some countries. The "C" group primarily is to keep track of emerging agents.

With so many agents to be controlled, I chose anthrax because of its inherent toxicity, risk assessment issues, and especially because there have been three recent events in the United States, one of which I am very familiar with.

Anthrax

Exposures and consequences

Anthrax is an acute disease caused by *Bacillus anthracis*, a one cell rod-shaped bacterium (Figure 8.1). Several attributes make anthrax a dangerous biological weapon. Anthrax bacterium can lie dormant for decades. When anthrax spores come into contact with lesions on a host, they can reactivate and multiply. Sheep, goats, and cattle are infected when grazing and eating, and their mortality is extraordinarily high.

Humans are exposed through skin contact (cutaneous), inhalation (lungs), and digestion (gastrointestinal). A human working with sheep can be exposed by handling or breathing wool from infected sheep. Exposure to inadequately cooked

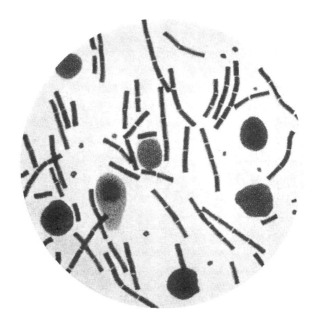

FIGURE 8.1 Anthrax spores and rods

meat from an infected animal is a clear hazard. These threats have existed for centuries. Cherkasskiy (1999) estimates that every year hundreds of thousands of animals are killed by anthrax.

Louis Pasteur developed the first vaccine in 1881. Western nations have developed vaccinations for domesticated animals. Anthrax has dramatically declined in relatively affluent nations, but remains a major threat in less well-endowed nations with limited human and animal health programs. Nevertheless, because anthrax spores can exist for many decades in dormant states, they must not be ignored by risk managers in any location, especially among workers who come into contact with animal cadavers and hides, such as rag pickers and wool sorters.

Bioterrorist threat

In the United Sates and most urbanized nations, airborne emissions of weaponized anthrax are the most threatening mass casualty threat. Large and the smallest particles can be intercepted by the body, but 1–5 um (microns) particles can deposit in the air sacs (alveoli). From there they damage the lungs and move into the blood stream, being protected by a capsule around the bacterium. This is not to say that digestive or skin exposures are of no concern. However, more agent is needed to cause impact through these exposures than through the respiratory system, a point relevant to bioterrorism.

Another concern about anthrax is that it produces symptoms that are not unique to it, and by the time anthrax is diagnosed it may be too late to intervene. Symptoms can appear within a week, but cases of inhalation anthrax may appear six weeks after exposure. Cutaneous anthrax produces a sore and then a blister. These symptoms can be missed until the blister produces an ulcer with a black area in the center, which is a clear signal of anthrax. Indeed, anthrax is the Greek word for coal, for which the disease is named because of the black sore that appears. Gastrointestinal anthrax symptoms are loss of appetite, nausea, diarrhea, and fever. Unfortunately, these symptoms are also not unique to anthrax. Inhalation anthrax is also not so obvious to diagnose. The initial symptoms are cold and/or flu-like symptoms, including a sore throat, muscle aches, and a low grade fever. These symptoms increase over time. Antibiotics (ciprofloxacin, doxyclcycline, and penicillin) can kill the anthrax spores, but timing is critical.

Studies of the impact of airborne anthrax place it at the top of the most serious bioterrorism threats. Grundmann (2014) reported on a World Health Organization (WHO) hypothetical analysis in a city of 1 million residents. About 180,000 would be exposed to a release of anthrax spores. Of those, 95,000 deaths might occur and 30,000 would be injured and required medical assistance. The next most serious consequences would be from plague, with 44,000 deaths and 36,000 injuries. These frightening numbers should not be taken at face value because the study was published over 45 years ago. Simulation modeling has improved, and our knowledge of how to react has markedly improved. But in the following section, we will review several other hypothetical and actual studies of anthrax that show marked vulnerability to anthrax that can only be controlled with the most careful planning and execution of risk management plans.

Vaccination can prevent a serious case of anthrax. The vaccine can be administered prophylactically to health-care workers, soldiers, laboratory employees, and those who handle animals (veterinarians) and animal products (livestock producers) who can be exposed as part of their jobs. The high risk group now includes mail handlers and first responders to an anthrax event. The Centers for Disease Control and Prevention have recommendations for the vaccine as well as for the use of protective clothing and respirators (Centers for Disease Control and Prevention 2015 f, g, h). These recommendations are not rigid and are period-ically updated by an expert panel. For example, in 2010, a CDC Advisory Committee (Advisory Committee 2010) offered the following recommendations:

- reduce the number of pre-event doses doses from 6 to 5;
- administer the dose directly into the muscle rather than subcutaneous (between the skin and muscle into the fat layer);
- provide post-exposure dose to pregnant women;
- provide guidance to workers as part of an occupational health program about pre-exposure vaccination; and
- administer 60 days of antibiotic prophylaxis in conjunction with three doses of vaccine for previously unvaccinated persons after exposure to anthrax bacteria.

Recent events in the United States

The United States has seen a marked increase in threatened biological agent attacks. Carus (2002) reported that a total of 153 cases of actual or threatened use of biological agents were reported in the United States between 1990 and 1999, which is more than five times the reported cases for 1900 through 1989. Carus uses "threatened use" to mean federal government investigations that resulted in the seizure of biological agents that were intended to be used against the U.S. population. The users were both individuals and groups that had secular, religious, criminal and other reasons for their plots. With this context, the anthrax attack in 2001 was not a threatened use or aborted one. It occurred.

The 2001 anthrax attack

The Centers for Disease Control and Prevention (2013a) points out that over 90 percent of the anthrax cases in the United States during the period 1955–1999 were related to handling animal hides and other animal products. Only 6 percent were inhalation. The lowest rate of lethality, <1 percent, has been for cutaneous anthrax treated with antibacterial agents.

The highest human morality rate was almost 90 percent for the airborne emission in Sverdlovsk (Meselson *et al.* 1994). Concern about exposure in the United States was piqued by the Sverdlovsk anthrax spore release. Briefly, in 1979, a military facility in the former Soviet Union leaked anthrax in a very narrow band to the south of the city. At least 64 people died. The United States accused the USSR of violating an agreement about biological weapons. The Meleson *et al.* paper was a product of a team of U.S. and USSR researchers who jointly investigated this hazard event.

When anthrax was sent through the U.S. mail in 2001, the public and government agencies were alarmed. I briefly summarize some of the facts as we understand them and focus on the impact of this event on subsequent U.S. government risk management efforts. The 2001 anthrax attacks began on September 18, 2001, one week after the September 11 attacks on the World Trade Center in New York City, the Pentagon crash, and the airplane crash in Shanksville, Pennsylvania. Letters containing anthrax spores were mailed to two Democratic Party Senators and several news media offices. Five died and 17 others were infected (Federal Bureau of Investigation 2001; Jernigan *et al.* 2002). After many investigations, in 2005, Bruce Ivins, a scientist at the U.S. government's biodefense labs at Fort Detrick in Frederick, Maryland, was identified as a major suspect. On July 29, 2008, Ivins died from an overdose of acetaminophen (Federal Bureau of Investigation 2001).

I point to four elements of this homegrown terrorist case that are directly relevant to risk assessment and management:

- *Location*: The anthrax-laden letters were mailed from Princeton, New Jersey to ABC, CBS, and NBC News, to the *New York Post*, and several other media outlets. But claims were made that there were other mailings from the United States and outside the country. In other words, mail proved to be a good delivery mechanism.

- *Type of anthrax bacteria*: The anthrax spores in the letters were from the same source (Ames strain) but in several forms. There was also concern about variations and even mutations in the strains, and in their protective coatings. For example, one concern was that smallpox virus had been added to the anthrax spores, and other assertions were made that the anthrax was being manufactured to be more deadly. Assertions were made that bentonite (a clay) was part of anthrax package (assumed from Iraq) and another had silicon as part of the anthrax weapon. In short, rumors about the anthrax strain were rampant and these heightened concern that this event was part of a larger biological attack. These speculations amplified risk perceptions.
- *Victims*: The 22 victims lived in different places and while some had attributes in common, others did not share these locations, jobs, and ages. A 2004 study proposed that the total number of people harmed by the anthrax attacks of 2001 should be raised to 68 (Cymet, Kerkvliet (2004). The epidemiological investigations took a lot more time than elected officials were expecting, albeit not from the perspective of those who realize that thorough investigations require time and patience.
- *Attackers*: Who did it? The FBI concluded that Bruce Ivins was the sole perpetrator. Others were vetted including government employees, U.S. right-wing extremists who were trying to kill Democrat U.S. senators in order to obtain a majority in the U.S. Senate, and given the circumstances of 2001, Iraq, Syria, and al-Qaeda and even high ranking U.S. Government officials were suggested. All of the uncertainty kept the issue in the media and before the public; it was a great media newsworthy story.

The so-called Amerithrax investigation (FBI name for it) required following up many leads, which took considerable time and resources. FBI famous cases and criminal series provide factual data on the FBI's efforts. For example, the FBI reports covering the period 2001–2011 indicate that 25 to 30 full-time investigators from the FBI, U.S postal service, and other law enforcement agencies, as well as from the District of Columbia, and Justice Department expended hundreds of thousands of investigator hours on the cases, interviewing more than 10,000 witnesses on six continents, and conducting 80 searches and other data gathering from over 60 sites. Readers who want detailed accounts of are recommended to read (Coen, Nadler 2009; Cole 2009; Graysmith 2003; Sarasin 2006; Willman 2011). A broader picture of the event is found in two books by Richard Preston (1995, 2003), which are eminently readable. Summarizing, the effort to piece the parts of attack through the mail was given the kind of media attention normally reserved for major wars, attacks on elected officials, and major criminal events.

Away from the media, the 2001 attack required a massive decontamination effort. More than two dozen buildings were contaminated with anthrax.

Decontamination required a specialized labor pool, air scrubbers, chlorine dioxide gas, and other materials. Piecing together newspaper reports suggests that the decontamination of the Brentwood postal facility in Washington, D.C., the Hamilton, New Jersey postal facility, and government buildings in Washington D.C. cost almost $250 million. Johnston (2007) estimated that the cost exceeded $1 billion. The postal service placed biohazard detection technology in its distribution centers, and these devices have been placed in selected other locations. They also devised different methods to sanitize the mail, including the use of radiation and various biological agents. After the postal mailing events, substantial investments were made in bio warfare research and preparedness programs. The National Institute of Allergy and Infectious Diseases (NIAID) budget increased by $1.5 billion in 2003. In 2004, Congress passed the Project Bioshield Act, which provides $5.6 billion over ten years for the purchase of new vaccines and drugs (White House 2004).

One theory, proven to be false, was that Iraq was the source of the attack (Harnden 2001). Another idea was that someone with a little training in biology and chemistry could manufacture a weapon from anthrax spores. That is possibly true, but only on a limited scale and with considerable risk to the individual. The passage of the Patriot Act was largely attributable to the 9/11 attacks, but the anthrax events also were part of the argument made for the Patriot Act.

Quite a few expensive lessons were learned from the post-events. On March 14, 2005, more than three-and-a-half years after the anthrax-laden letters passed through the facility, the Hamilton, NJ post office reopened. The Associated Press (2005) reported that

> the opening had more the air of a gala than a normal day at the post office. Officials were on hand with cake and the low-slung building was decorated with balloons.

The estimated cost of reopening the post office was $80–$100 million, which included fumigating the building with chlorine dioxide, stripping all the walls bare and replacing all the mail sorting equipment and the furniture, as well as adding sensors to detect biological agents. Only ten of the 500 employees were reported to have refused to return to work at the post office. On the tenth anniversary of the event, Duffy (2011), a journalist for the *Times of Trenton* (nearest city to the post office) summarized the event and asked residents and the mayor of Hamilton about it. The story is remarkably devoid of passion about the event, and perhaps the only interesting part of the story is near the end where the reporter observes that before 2001, the National Institute of Health spent close to $200 million per year on biodefense related projects, and a decade later the total was $1.3 to $1.6 billion.

A U.S. GAO report (2004a) asserted that the public health agencies underestimated postal worker risk and had delayed the releasing information about spore counts because they did not know what these counts meant (see below under risk assessment for a discussion). The GAO emphasized the need for better guidance to the postal service. A second GAO report (2004b) to Bill Frist, Majority Leader of the U.S. Senate observed that three major lessons learned were planning and experience, effective communications, and a strong public health infrastructure were all essential (an illustration of the sixth risk analysis question).

The 2014 CDC laboratory event and the 2015 shipping anthrax events

On June 5, 2014 employees in CDC's Bioterrorism Rapid Response and Advanced Technology (BRRAT) laboratory were working on a method that might allow more rapid detection of anthrax (Frieden 2014; Centers for Disease Control and Prevention 2014). CDC has four types of laboratory facilities that build on the safety of the previous levels. BSL-1 labs deal with nonpathogenic microbes; BSL-2 facilities have moderately hazardous ones; BSL-3 and BSL-4 laboratories work on dangerous microbes, such as those that cause tuberculosis, and Ebola and Marbury viruses.

CDC staff had a sample of live and infectious anthrax bacteria and sought to sterilize them so that they could be moved to another laboratory where equipment was to be used to conduct experiments. Believing that the sample was not active, they moved it from BSL-3 to BSL-2 laboratories. Eight days later a laboratory scientist noted growth on the plate with the supposedly sterile anthrax sample. The plate apparently had only been treated for 10 minutes rather than the required 24 hours.

CDC initially located 81 employees who might have been exposed. Each was evaluated, and those found to be potentially exposed were treated with antibiotics. The anthrax samples were returned to the BSL-3 laboratory, and work in the laboratories was temporarily halted. None of the employees reported symptoms. Nevertheless, this incident is important because it was embarrassing to the United States' bioterrorism research efforts and underscored inherent vulnerability when dealing with extreme biological hazards.

Reporting to the House Energy and Commerce Subcommittee on Oversight and Investigations on July 16, 2014, Dr. Tom Frieden, CDC director, attributed the incident to the following:

* Lack of approved plan to guarantee that the research design was appropriate and met safety requirements;
* Sterilization techniques not approved;
* Transfer of anthrax sample without certainty that they were dead;
* Use of a more dangerous anthrax strain than was necessary;
* Staff were not sufficiently knowledgeable about inactivation of anthrax;
* Lack of standard operating procedure for inactivation and transfer of the agent to other laboratories;
* Difficulty in rapidly identifying the full universe of individuals;
* Inability to immediately identify who could have been exposed; and
* Inadequate communications of events in the laboratory setting.

Frieden noted that several other incidents had been identified in the BRRAT labs in 2006, 2009 and 2014, and that CDC was reconstructing laboratory procedures and policies to prevent this type of event. Frieden discontinued experiments involving toxins and selected other agents until staff were able to implement safer approaches. A moratorium was placed on biological material leaving any CDC BSL-3 or BSL-4 laboratory, and personnel actions were taken with staff responsible for the event. These and other steps were necessary to assure Congress that the work of CDC's laboratories was protecting human health and safety rather than potentially harming it. The focuses of the director's remarks were improving the safety culture of the CDC laboratory scientists.

Public trust was shaken again in 2015 when the media reported that the U.S. Department of Defense (DOD) inadvertently shipped live anthrax spores from the Dugway Proving Ground in southwest Utah (located about 40 miles from the Tooele chemical weapons site reviewed as part of Chapter 4) in the mail to a military facility in South Korea and to government facilities in nine states. As the story evolved, the news has both gotten better, that is, no one was reported as having contracted anthrax, but worse because the Defense Department revealed that FedEx was used to ship the spores (Lamothe 2015; Starr 2015; Toor 2015; Hennigan 2015, Reuters 2015). A week later, the news showed no cases, but that as many as 66 laboratories in 19 U.S. states and three countries had received these mailings. The media reported, 31 military and civilians were receiving antibiotics prophylactically. Major print and television media continue to report on this story and more laboratories in more states and more countries have been reported to have received anthrax in the mail.

The bottom line is that government officials and the public must be able to trust CDC and other government and non-government researchers will properly manage anthrax and other biological agents. This means unassailable safety equipment and construction, as well as practices and legal requirements, which do not all exist at this time.

Risk assessment: uncertain steps forward

The biological agent risk assessment literature is among the most challenging because of the lack of both low exposure data and human data. In the wake of the 2001 postal attack, Coleman et al. (2008) criticized the lack of effort to distinguish between fact and speculation about the risk of inhalation anthrax, asserting that the widespread idea that a single spore can cause death is not substantiated by data. They point out that hundreds of millions of dollars were spent to remove every spore from several post office buildings after the 2001 anthrax spore event. Coleman et al. (2008) reviewed a variety of studies to make their case that there is threshold for how clean is clean enough. For example, Cohen and Whalen (2007) found that that exposure to 600 spores per day resulted in low risk. Brachman et al. (1960) calculated that 500 spores were not necessarily dangerous. Citing animal data from chimpanzees, monkeys, dogs, rabbits, guinea pigs, and sheep studies, they presented a strong argument that a threshold exists and that a lethal dose is most likely to occur from an exposure of 10,000+ spores. In regard to public policy, the authors question the zero tolerance policy toward anthrax spores (see also Raber, Hibband, Greenwalt *et al.* 2011).

Hong, Gurian, and Ward (2010) studied anthrax exposure as a time-space cluster problem, that is, they build models to consider the case of aerosol releases and tested their models with a hypothetical office containing an HVAC system. The models were used to track the concentration of anthrax spores after release, and when spores are disturbed and resuspended in the air. Assuming that the models mirror reality, which the authors do not assert, they suggest that these risk assessment models could be used to estimate the need for environmental cleanup, timing of the human reoccupation of decontaminated structures, and administration of prophylactic antibiotics. The authors are clear about some of the major uncertainties in their study, including the need to rely on high-dose animal models to estimate low-dose human response, a wide range of deposition velocities related to room circulation characteristics and materials. The study is a fascinating effort to dig into and explicitly treat some of the more complex parts of biological agent exposure. The number of uncertainties in the model is striking, even for a hypothetical case.

A third anthrax infectivity study examined quantitative dose-response models and how outcomes change over time. Toth *et al.* (2013) found insufficient human data to allow dose-response modeling based on the U.S. Postal Service incident in 2001, the Sverdlovsk release in 1979, and among workers handling contaminated animal products. Using a data set culled from industrial exposures, they built an exponential model producing the results in Table 8.2. It has the classic s-shaped curve described in Chapter 2 (Text Box 2.1), that is, a threshold before infection, a steep increase as the dose increases and a leveling off. They fit their exponential model to the Sverdlovsk data, and showed that the exposure-infection-symptomatic illness-death model is a good fit to the data. Based on their model, they indicate a dose of 600 spores would produce infection in 2 percent to 6 percent of untreated people, which depending upon country and during peacetime conditions should not be deemed tolerable.

TABLE 8.2 Infection doses for anthrax extrapolated from thirteen mathematical models

Dose to infect 50,10, 1 and 0.1%	Exponential time dependent model, # of spores	Median and range of other models, # of spores
ID_{50}	11,000	11,000 (4,130-96,800)
ID_{10}	1,700	1,700 (50-21,000)
ID_1	160	250 (1-9,900)
$ID_{0.1}$	16	38 (0.1-5,700)

Source: Toth *et al.*, 2013, Table 1.

The authors used their model to calculate the doses measured by spore counts that would infect 50 percent, 10 percent, 1 percent, and 0.1 percent of the exposed population, and they compared these results to 12 other mathematical models (Table 8.2). These were 11,000, 1,700, 160, and 16 spores, respectively. These results underscore the difficulty of extrapolating high-dose primate and human data down to low-dose exposures as described in Chapter 2. This is at the heart of the how clean is clean enough policy issue. More specifically, how clean does a site have to be for it to be politically clean? Is it cleaned to 1,700 or 600, or must no spores be found?

Risk management

Risk managers have a variety of options for managing biological threats, such as anthrax spores; none of these options is without risk (Milanovich 1998). The first is surveillance of persons with bad intentions (Wagner, Moore, Aryel 2006). In Chapter 2, I presented an influence diagram that suggested the creation of an anti-terrorist unit that would try to prevent a terrorist event. In the case of anthrax or other biological agent attack, the security unit would look for four assets required for a successful attack:

- Availability of the agent or ability to produce it;
- Storage of the agent;
- Ability to turn the agent into a weapon; and
- Ability to deliver the agent.

Intervening to block any of these four stages from occurring belongs to security forces. Governments have made progress developing so-called "fingerprinting" of biological agents, and a great deal of effort is being invested in these largely clandestine efforts.

Environmental monitoring and public health surveillance are critical. Surveillance of biological threats is more challenging than for radiation and chemical agents. In the case of radiation, Geiger counters can detect exposures and acute symptoms will rapidly appear. In the case of chemical agents, significant exposures appear within a few days, typically sooner (Chapter 4). But biological agents may not produce symptoms for days, even weeks, by which time the exposed individual may be in a different location. Furthermore, many of the symptoms are attributable to a severe cold, the flu, digestive and other ailments.

The Department of Homeland Security has built a BioWatch program to detect agents in over 30 populous cities (White House 2004). Rapid and accurate detection is extremely important. The major criticisms for this type of risk management response are as follows:

- high cost;
- failure to detect all releases;

- an invitation to bad intentioned individuals to attack places without BioWatch;
- lack of optimum siting of detection equipment; and
- false positives that eventually would lead to the public ignoring warnings.

On the other hand, one successful detection of an actual release that prevents airborne dispersion would make the expense more than worthwhile. In the rail simulation case (Chapter 6), the researchers considered the option of an anthrax spore release scenario without detection apparatus, another with equipment that did not provide quick feedback, and then one that provided immediate detection and reporting. That thinking was not published, but showed the benefit of having such capability in key locations.

Part of the issue in bioterrorism cases is protecting first responders. A great deal of thought and resources have been focused on providing more protective clothing, including self-contained breathing apparatus.

Appropriate communication is part of any risk management package. If there is a suspected exposure, and the cause is uncertain, informing the general public that there is or could be an exposure may cause public panic. Early disclosure of a suspected problem could save lives, but if proven false could be costly to people and risk managers who will be accused of crying wolf when there is no wolf present. This is the toughest choice for decision-makers. Spending money on a false alarm may be tolerable once or twice, scaring the public may be tolerable once and maybe twice, but not informing the public when they may have been exposed or is likely to be considered inexcusable negligence (see Chapter 3).

The chance of false positive is particularly high in dense urban centers and during times when other diseases are prevalent, for example, during the flu and allergy season when bad colds are common. The lack of clarity about causes of respiratory symptoms means a delay in detecting, confirming and acting to reduce exposures and treat sick people. That delay may be longer where the local government is not well prepared. Before action can be taken, it is likely that health officials will need to be sure that there is a cluster (time and space) of cases significantly higher than would be anticipated and cannot be attributed to competing diseases. The Centers for Disease Control and Prevention (2015g) has provided guidelines for surveillance of symptoms, but frankly not all states are equally adept at following through to find clusters of acute diseases or chronic diseases. Overall, the worst case scenarios would be exposures during periods when there are competing diseases producing similar symptoms in places where health programs have limited resources and the surrounding population does not trust authorities.

Investing in preparedness is not only expensive but also requires unprecedented cooperation among organizations. In order to increase the survival rate of exposed people and reduce exposure, stockpiles of medication to combat the infection and vaccinate people are essential within 24 to 48 hours. Hence, state governments must have identified the location of the outbreak, the number already impacted and likely to be impacted, and states must reach out to marshal antibiotics and vaccines (Federal Emergency Management Agency 2007). The Cities Readiness Initiative with 72 participating cities (Centers for Disease Control and Prevention 2013c) is charged with gathering and distributing supplies within 48 hours, including reaching out to drug manufactures that may have an inventory.

Informatics can tie together surveillance data and communicate it to epidemiologists for interpretation. Risk managers may then craft and broadcast information and advice to the public and public organizations. The bottom line is that decision-makers cannot afford to miss a real incident, nor however, must they repeatedly communicate false alarms, as noted earlier. Frankly, I would not want to make a career out of being the one who has to make the final call in regard to these highly uncertain scenarios.

Paths of agent transmission need to be considered by risk assessors and managers. Anthrax, botulism, tularemia, and ricin can be transmitted from person to person, but are not contagious. In contrast, cholera, plague, smallpox, and typhus are contagious, with the latter group likely requiring quarantine of the exposed population, clearly among the more unpopular steps that managers can require.

Since we cannot be sure where an attack will occur, government must balance the needs of reducing morbidity and mortality against the impact of surveillance on civil liberties and the cost of having expensive unused drugs sitting on shelves until their utility expires. In regard to stockpiling biological countermeasures, government is looking for shelf-life extension programs that aim to cycle necessary drugs through the emergency stockpile and then cycle them for nonemergency situations.

There are medical countermeasures to treat some biological agents (anthrax, botulism plague, smallpox, tularemia, and typhus). Some of the A and B agents, such as Ebola, viral hemorrhagic fevers, West Nile Virus and some others have no countermeasures. Even the best government security agents cannot always stop someone or a group from using biological weapons. Given this reality, government needs to be continually scanning for individuals who might be inclined to use a biological weapon. It has the responsibility to consider the likely targets, the groups most likely to launch an attack, and the places where those attacks might occur. It then must make a determination of the magnitude of the risk to the population, civil liberties, and the economy compared to the resources needed to prevent the risk or be resilient to an attack.

Risk assessment and risk management meet at cost-effectiveness

Every risk management decision is an opportunity to quietly succeed and publicly fail. The risk assessment section showed that the studies indicate that every anthrax spore does not have to be eliminated. How clean is clean enough is a risk-informed decision that ultimately is political. Did the government have to literally reconstruct the entire Hamilton, New Jersey postal building at enormous expense? I suspect that the answer is no. Given that spores are survivors and could reactivate, would the postal workers have returned without sanitizing the site? In all good consciousness could the post office have told them that no threat remained if the site was cleaned to 500 spores? I suspect that the answer was no, and that government had to remove every spore that they could find and replace all the equipment in order to restore trust, which was extraordinarily expensive.

Risk assessment and management options

How to treat people when there is a serious threat or when there has been an event is a another challenging decision. Wein, Craft, and Kaplan (2003) built a risk model to assess the impact of an aerosolized anthrax attack. The authors used a Gaussian plume model to disperse spores at a height of 325 feet over a city-centered region with a population of 10.8 million people. The model assumes that 2.2 pounds of anthrax is released. Using data from the 2001 anthrax attack and Sverdlovsk release in the Soviet Union, their models include wind speed and inhalation rates, among other variables. The model predicts 1.5 million infections in an area 120 miles long and 11 miles wide (see also Ishibashi, Jolivet, Kelly 2001 for an excellent presentation).

If this hypothetical event were really to occur, antibiotics would need to be immediately delivered and administered. The authors critique CDC's schedule for delivering drugs as too slow to reduce the death toll. They urge the CDC to consider local stockpiling and urge the public to follow through with the treatment. Wein, Craft, and Kaplan estimate that if everyone had a stockpile at home the number of deaths would drop to about 60,000, which is a marked improvement compared to the 600,000 deaths estimated under one scenario and 250,000 under another. The authors note that if compliance with the drug regime drops 10 percent (people do not take the pills for 60 days) the death rate would increase 50 percent.

This is not the place to try to debate the recommendations from this important study. A downside is that wide distribution of these antibiotics would hasten the development of drug-resistant bacteria and vaccines are not well received by some people. In regard to risk assessment, the paper demonstrates the enormous number of variables influencing the outcomes.

Wein, Craft, and Kaplan (2003) deserve praise for this research. It not only includes an air dispersion model, but it also has a dose-response model, a disease progression one, and uses a queuing model for distributing the drugs in each service area. Because of the critical importance of time in reducing consequences, the queuing model allows the authors to estimate how many health professionals would need to fly into these areas and distribute drugs, thereby saving lives. With a provider for every 700 people (over 14,000 providers for a region of 10 million), the authors estimate that the number of deaths could fall to 1,000. This hypothetical anthrax event illustrates the challenge of balancing prevention and resilience of low probability, high consequence events against predictable high costs. If the event never occurs or is minor, then decision-makers will be charged with wasting scarce resources on science-fiction like catastrophes.

Fowler *et al.* (2005) examined the cost-effectiveness of four options for reducing the health effects of an aerosolized anthrax bacteria attack:

- No prophylaxis
- Vaccination alone
- Antibiotic alone
- Post-exposure vaccination and antibiotics.

The authors developed a simple decision model that follows the treatment options at every stage. The first option is vaccination prior to the attack. Follow-up options are post-attack antibiotics and vaccination. The last is no prophylaxis. Fowler *et al.* estimated the costs of the treatments, the costs of death, estimated the likelihood of an attack, successful treatment, and negative effects of treatment, and made assumptions, assisted by experts, on a variety of other model inputs as follows:

- Probability of an attack;
- Number of spores released;
- Age and sex of population;
- Migration into the region;
- Birth rates of the population;
- Percent of population exposed during an attack;
- Percent of population exposed developing symptoms of respiratory anthrax without treatment (95 percent);
- Percent of population who become ill after receiving the treatment(s);
- Viable vaccine supply is available;
- Vaccine cost is known;
- Costs of medical treatment of population compared to self-treatment;
- Discount rate (used 3 percent); and
- Treatment costs of those who contract anthrax.

The authors would also need to simulate various wind directions and local terrain for a real case (see Chapter 6 for a chlorine example). Recognizing and acknowledging the large number of variables that required estimates, the authors ran 10,000 simulations using a Monte Carlo approach to try to distinguish between the four options.

As population at risk increased and the probability of an attack decreased, the option of pre-attack vaccination became less cost-effective. The authors estimated that $500 million to $1 billion could be spent with little benefit. The combination of vaccination and antibiotics is the most beneficial in regard to lengthening quality of life years and least expense. Yet, the differences between the cost-effectiveness of the choices are relatively small on a per-person basis and the uncertainty is high in many important variables. Even if decision-makers do not accept the generic recommendation, the study demonstrates the value of a systematic approach that can pin down of role of different decision-informing factors.

Risk communication

Communications in response to imminent threats literally can make a difference between life and death. As an observer of field exercises, I know that participants are trying to improve their individual performance. Yet, much depends upon coordination among them and their organization. Police, emergency-responders, local and state public health officials, physicians, physicians' assistants, nurses, hospital and clinic staff all need to understand their jobs, and it would help if they understand the jobs of their colleagues. Each region needs to have trained scientists and health-care professionals to detect and respond to a potential biological agent exposure, and if necessary a process for dealing with exposed members of the public. I cannot possibly understate how important communications are as part of these processes. Large cities like New York, Los Angeles and others have recognized this reality and have established protocols that spell out who are responsible for essential actions. Under the pressure of an actual event, mistakes are to be expected. Consequently, exercises that mimic what would happen are critical, even if expensive.

A distressing possibility is that we cannot be certain that public health professionals will fulfill their responsibilities if there were an anthrax spore release, or other serious event. Their focus might be on taking care of their family members (Barnett et al. 2012).

Communication with the at risk public is another high priority (Chapter 3). Pollard (2003) examined six surveys that asked the public about what information they wanted and who they wanted it from during an anthrax spore event. These surveys were in 2001 and 2002, and they included mail, phones and web tools for gathering the data. Survey sizes ranged from 1,015 to 4,397. Looking across the surveys, in regard to what the public wanted to know, over 90 percent want to know what "germ" has been released and how it could be transmitted. Almost 90 percent want to know what they should do to reduce the risk to them and their families, and recommendations for treating the illness if it occurs. About 70 percent wanted to know the number of people who were ill, hospitalized or dead and the location of the cases, and the any travel advisories or restrictions. Lastly, 40 percent wanted to know who was responsible. Clearly, these kinds of results are consistent with the public focusing on their own health, their activities, and then the causes of the problem (see Chapter 3).

The expected was also found for which information sources they preferred. Almost 70 percent would turn to local television and radio for the news, and the second source they would turn to for information was their physician and other medical personnel (about 45 percent). By comparison, only 20 percent to 33 percent would turn to the internet and toll-free government sources. However, the source they turn to is not necessarily the source they trust. For a national event, 70 percent to 80 percent trust a CDC scientist and the U.S. Surgeon General. By comparison, less than half trusted the Secretary of HHS or Homeland Security "quite a lot" or "a great deal." If the event were local, over 70 percent of the public wants to hear from their local doctor, the local health department, doctors from a local hospital, followed by the local police and fire department. At the bottom of the list were the local governor and religious leaders. In other words, the public wants to hear from experts in science and these individuals need to be trained and available to the mass media, both national and local for these events. A caveat is that these communication preferences might vary by region, but I doubt it.

Back to risk management with a focus on resilience

I believe bioterrorism is the most difficult terrorism risk management challenge the U.S. and other urban industrial nations face. It is true that national governments like the United States provide funds and guidelines for education; they regulate agents; oversee institutions that deliver medication and medicate people. National governments support science of all kinds that will help detect and respond to events. In the United States, the Centers for Disease Control and Prevention (2015g) have a clear plan for what they are doing and plan to do for anthrax and other agents. CDC does the following:

- Funds and provides guidance, training in emergency response;
- Coordinates with health departments;
- Regulates the possession, use and transfer of biological hazards;
- Promotes science and practices to strengthen preparedness and responses;
- Works with hospitals, laboratories, emergency-responders to make sure that they have medicine and supplies; and
- Develops guidance to protect the health and safety of workers.

The list of reports and actions, as well as efforts to prevent and manage bioterrorism risk from anthrax spores and other agents is impressive (Centers for Disease Control and Prevention 2013a,b; Cheng *et al.* 2013; Federal Emergency Management Agency 2007; Franco, Bouri 2010; Institute of Medicine 2003; Lesperance *et al.* 2011; Raber *et al.* 2011; Tyshenko 2007; Wood, Blair 2009). Furthermore, we know that surveillance devices are becoming smaller and more plentiful, which will help with detection. The federal level, in short, is increasing the chances of timely and effective responses.

If there is a weak link, it is some state and local governments. With serious budget issues in an era where budgets are under increasing pressure, it will be difficult for state and local government to quickly detect an event, to respond to it in a timely way, and deliver service in time and prevent panic (Ziskin, Harris 2007; see Chapter 11). In regard to risk management, I believe that planning for bioterrorism is the most complex risk management challenge because of extraordinary pressure to prevent events; budget restrictions; legal and ethical considerations; and leadership challenges at state and local levels. If at all possible, investments should be part of investments in the public health and security infrastructures.

What did Chapter 8 explain about risk analysis? Summary and learning objectives

Biological organisms have caused the death of countless people and animals. Nearly all of the agents have come into contact with people through normal activities. Bioterrorism is different, involving the conversion of biological organisms to weapons for political, social, economic and personal reasons. After anthrax was mailed to elected officials through the postal service in 2001, the United States markedly increased its programs to monitor and respond to potential bioterrorist attacks, especially in large cities. The Centers for Disease Control and Prevention, Department of Homeland Security, Department of Health and Human Services, Department of Defense and other federal agencies are involved in prevention and risk management programs and partner with large cities and states. Other nations are equally committed to preventing and responding to acts of bioterrorism.

The CDC has created a short list of very dangerous agents, and this chapter used anthrax to illustrate the challenges of assessing and managing these most serious agents. The risk assessment challenge is that there is little human data for inhalation anthrax and the data that are available have limitations. Using animal data and limited human data, authors have found a highly uncertain estimate of how many spores can cause deaths. The numbers depend upon the assumptions built into the model. Hence, when the post office event occurred in 2001, the federal government spent hundreds of millions of dollars to try to kill every spore. When breaches of protocols occurred in 2014 at CDC labs and in 2015 in regard to Army shipments of anthrax through postal service, there were extremely strong reactions by government, arguably overreactions. However, without these strong reactions the already damaged reputations of the organizations would have suffered even more.

Some important risk management decisions were made after the 9/11 events in the United States and the anthrax events that occurred shortly thereafter. Stockpiling of vaccines and drugs, setting up significant detection programs in selected locations, vaccination of those that could be exposed, and expenditures to essentially sanitize areas with exposures are prominent illustrations. The financial cost of these actions is substantial and there may be some human-health related costs such as increasing the chances of drug-resistant species and public disenchantment with repeated warnings that could lead to unwillingness to respond to a real event.

Risk assessment could play a much more powerful role if better data were available and if some of the models described in the chapter were wedded to more realistic scenarios. Without these steps, the burden falls on risk managers who are likely to respond in ways that are as protective as possible, irrespective of the immediate and near term costs and benefits. Meanwhile ongoing efforts to prepare first responders and the public are crucial to reduce morbidity, mortality, and economic impacts, even if preparedness is a costly overreaction in some places unless it contributes to building public health infrastructure.

At the end of this chapter readers should be able to answer the following seven questions:

1. What are the reasons why some biological agents are considered more hazardous than others?
2. What are common mechanisms that lead to anthrax?
3. Why is anthrax a major concern?
4. What level of exposure to anthrax spores is considered likely to lead to a serious exposure by risk assessors?
5. Based on actions taken after the postal attack, what level of exposure is considered tolerable by risk managers?
6. Why were the postal attacks in 2001 and the CDC and DOD mailings of anthrax of such concern to government officials?
7. What are the major risk options available to risk managers who deal with agents like anthrax, and how do these vary by agent and location?

References

Advisory Committee on Immunization Practices (ACIP). (2010) Use of anthrax vaccine in the United States: recommendations of the Advisory Committee on Immunization Practices, 2009. www.cdc.gov/mmwr/preview/mmwrhtml/rr5906a1.htm. Accessed February 10, 2015.

Associated Press. (2005) Hamilton, N.J., post office reopens after anthrax attacks. USA Today. March 14, 2005. http://usatoday30.usatoday.com/news/nation/2005-03-14-anthrax-clarnup_x.htm. Accessed May 7, 2015.

Barnett D, Thompson C, Errett N, Semon N, Anderson M, Ferrell J, Freiheit J, Hudson R, Koch M, McKee M, Mejia-Echeverry A, Spitzer J, Balicer R, Links J. (2012) Determinants of emergency response willingness in the local public health workforce by jurisdictional and scenario patterns: a cross-sectional survey. BMC Public Health. 12;12:164. www.biomedcentral.com/1471-2458/12/164. Accessed June 6, 2015.

Block S. (2001) The growing threat of biological weapons. American Scientist. 89, 1, 128–137.

Brachman P, Plotkin S, Bumford F, Atchison M. (1960) An epidemic of inhalation anthrax: the first in the 20th century II. Epidemiology. American Journal of Hygiene. 72, 6–23.

Carus S. (2002) Bioterrorism and biocrimes: the illicit use of biological agents since 1900. Amsterdam: Fredonia.

Centers for Disease Control and Prevention. (2013a). Preparation and planning for bioterrorism emergencies. www.bt.cdc.gov/bioterrorism/prep.asp. Accessed September 1, 2014.

Centers for Disease Control and Prevention. (2013b) A history of anthrax. www.cdc.gov/anthrax/history/index.html. Accessed February 10, 2015.

Centers for Disease Control and Prevention. (2013c) Cities readiness initiative. www.cdc.gov/phpr/stockpile/cri/index.htm. Accessed September 1, 2014.

Centers for Disease Control and Prevention. (2014). Report on the potential exposure to Anthrax. July 11, 2014. www.cdc.gov/about/pdf/lab-safety/Final_Anthrax_Report.pdf

Centers for Disease Control and Prevention. (2015a) Botulism. www.cdc.gov/nczved/divisions.dfbmd/diseases/botulism. Accessed May 15, 2015.

Centers for Disease Control and Prevention. (2015b) Plague. www.cdc.gov/plague. Accessed May 15, 2015.

Centers for Disease Control and Prevention. (2015c) Smallpox disease overview www.bt.cdc.gov/agent/smallpox/overview/disease-facts.asp. Accessed May 15, 2015.

Centers for Disease Control and Prevention. (2015d) Tularemia. www.cdc.gov/Tularemia. Accessed May 15, 2015.

Centers for Disease Control and Prevention. (2015e) Viral hemorrhagic fevers www.cdc.gov/ncidod/dvrd/spb/mnpages/dispages/vhf.htm. Accessed May 15, 2015.

Centers for Disease Control and Prevention. (2015f). Anthrax www.cdc.gov/anthrax/bioterrorism/cdc-action.html. accessed February 10, 2015.

Centers for Disease Control and Prevention. (2015g) Bioterrorism preparedness and response. http://emergency.cdc.gov/bioterrorism. Accessed May 4, 2016.

Centers for Disease Control and Prevention. (2015h) People with certain jobs. www.cdc.gov/anthrax/risk/occupational.html. Accessed February 10, 2015.

Cheng K, Crary D, Ray J, Safta C. (2013) Structural models used in real-time biosurveillance outbreak detection and outbreak curve isolation from noisy background morbidity levels. *Journal of the American Medical Informatics Association.* 20, 3, 435–440.

Cherkasskiy B. (1999) A national register of historic and contemporary anthrax foci. *Journal of Applied Microbiology.* 87, 192–195.

Coen B, Nadler E. (2009). *Dead silence – fear and terror on the anthrax trail.* Berkeley, CA: Counterpoint Press.

Cohen M, Whalen T. (2007) Implications of low level human exposure to reparable *B. anthracis. Applied Biosafety.* 12, 2, 109–115.

Cole L. (2009) *The anthrax letters, a bioterrorism expert investigates the attacks that shocked America – case closed?* New York: Skyhorse Publishing.

Coleman M, Thran B, Morse S, Hugh-Jones M, Massulik S. (2008) Inhalation anthrax: doses, response and risk analysis. *Biosecurity and Bioterrorism: Biodefenese Strategy, Practice, and Science.* 6, 2, 147–159.

Cymet T, Kerkvliet G. (2004) What is the true number of victims of the postal anthrax attack of 2001? *The Journal of the American Osteopathic Association.* 104, 11, 452. PMID 15602039. www.experts.scival.com. Accessed June 5, 2015.

Duffy E. (2011) A decade on, legacy of anthrax lingers in Mercer County and beyond. *The Times of Trenton.* www.nj.com/mercer/index.ssf/2011/10/after_a_decade_legacy_t.html. Accessed May 7, 2015.

Eitzen E, Takafuji E. (1997) *Historical overview of biological warfare, military medicine: medical aspects of chemical and biological warfare.* Washington, D.C.: Office of the Surgeon General, Department of the Army.

Federal Bureau of Investigation. (2001) Amerithrax or anthrax investigation. www.fbi.gov/about-us/history/famous-case/anthrax-amerihrax. Accessed May 15, 2015.

Federal Emergency Management Agency. (2007). National preparedness guidelines. www.fema.gov/pdf/emergency/nrf/National_Preparedness_Guidelines.pdf. Accessed September 1, 2014.

Fowler R, Sanders G, Bravata D, Nouri B, Gastwirth J, Peterson D, Broker A, Garber A, Owens D. (2005) Cost-effectiveness of defending against bioterrorism: a comparison of vaccination and antibiotic prophylaxis against anthrax. *Annals of Internal Medicine.* 142, 601–610.

Franco C, Bouri N. (2010) Environmental decontamination following a large-scale bioterrorism attack: federal progress and remaining gaps. *Biosecurity and Bioterrorism.* 8, 2, 107–117.

Frieden T. (2014) Review of anthrax lab incident. www.edu.gov/washington/testimony/2014/t20140716.htm. Accessed February 10, 2015.

GAO. (2004a) Better guidance is needed to ensure an appropriate response to anthrax contamination. GAO-04-239. www.gao.gov/cgi-bin/getrpt?GAO-04-239. Accessed June 9, 2015.

GAO. (2004b) Public health response to anthrax incidents of 2001. GAO-04-152. www.gao.gov/cgi-bin/getrpt?GAO-04-152. Accessed June 9, 2015.

Graysmith R. (2003) *Amerithrax: the hunt for the anthrax killer.* Berkeley CA: Berkeley Books.

Grundmann O. (2014). The current state of bioterrorist attack surveillance and preparedness in the U.S. *Risk Management and Health Care Policy.* 7, 177–187.

Harnden T. (2001) Building the case against Iraq. *The Daily Telegraph* (London). October 26. www.freerepublic.com/focus/fr/557137/posts. Accessed June 4, 2015.

Hennigan W. (2015) Anthrax: as many as 51 labs in 17 states, 3 countries, received live samples. www.latimes.com/nation/nationnow/la-na-pentagon-anthrax-2015-20150603-story.html. Accessed June 8, 2015.

Hong T, Gurian P, Ward N. (2010) Setting risk-informed environmental standards for bacillus anthracis spores. *Risk Analysis.* 30, 10, 1602–1622.

Institute of Medicine Committee on Smallpox Vaccination Program I. (2003) *Review of the Centers for Disease Control and Prevention's smallpox vaccination program implementation: letter report 2.* Washington, D.C.: National Academies Press.

Ishibashi H, Jolivet J, Kelly S. (2001) Bacillus anthracis. www.columbia.edu/cu/.../ BacillusAntracis.ppt. Accessed June 9, 2015.

Jernigan D, Raghunathan P, Bell B, Brechner R, Bresnitz E, Butler J, Cetron M, Cohen M, Doyle T, Fischer M, Greene C, Griffith K, Guarner J, Hadler J, Hayslett J, Meyer R, Petersen L, Phillips M, Pinner R, Popovic T, Quinn C, Reefhuis J, Reissman D, Rosenstein N, Schuchat A, Shieh W-J, Siegal L, Swerdlow D, Tenover F, Traeger M, Ward J, Weisfuse I, Wiersma S, Yeskey K, Zaki S, Ashford D, Perkins B, Ostroff S, Hughes J, Fleming D, Koplan J, Gerberding J, and the National Anthrax Epidemiologic Investigation Team. (2002) Investigation of bioterrorism-related anthrax, United States, 2001: Epidemiologic findings. *Emerging Infectious Disease Journal.* 8, 10, wwwnc.cdc.gov/eid/article/8/10/02-0353_article. Accessed May 15, 2015.

Johnston W. (2007) Review of fall 2001 anthrax bioattacks. www.johnstonarchive.net/ terrorism/anthrax.html. Accessed May 15, 2015.

Lamothe D. (2015) Pentagon: live anthrax inadvertently distributed by army laboratory. www.washingtonpost.com/news/checkpoint/wp/2015/05/27/pentagon-army-laboratory-inadvertently-. Accessed May 28, 2015.

Lesperance A, Stein S, Upton J, Toomey C. (2011). Challenges in disposing of anthrax waste. *Biosecurity and Bioterrorism.* 9, 3, 310–314.

Marr J, Malloy C. (1996) An epidemiologic analysis of the ten plagues of Egypt. *Caeduceus.* 12, 1, 7–24.

Meselson M, Guillemin J, Hugh-Jones M, Langmuir A, Popova I, Shelokov, Yampolskaya O. (1994) The Sverdlovsk anthrax outbred of 1979. *Science.* 266, 1202–1208.

Milanovich F. (1998) Reducing the threat of biological weapons. *Science and Technology Review.* June, 4–9, https://str.llnl.gov/str/pdfs/06_98.pdf. Accessed June 2, 2015.

National Public Radio. (2001) History of biological warfare. www.npr.org/news/ specials/response/anthrax/features/2001/oct/011018.bioterrorism. Accessed June 13, 2015.

Office of Laboratory Services, Bureau of Public Health, CDC. (2015) CDC category list of biological diseases. www.wvdhhr.org/labservices. Accessed December 18, 2015.

Pollard W. (2003) Public perceptions of information sources concerning bioterrorism before and after anthrax attacks: an analysis of national survey data. *Journal of Health Communication.* 8, 93–103.

Preston R. (1995) *The hot zone*. New York: Random House.

Preston R. (2003) *The demon in the freezer*. New York: Random House.

Raber E, Hibbard W, Greenwalt R. (2011) The national framework and consequence management guidance following a biological attack. *Biosecurity and Bioterrorism*. 9, 3, 271–279.

Reuters (2015) U.S. base shipped live anthrax to 19 states plus D.C.: Pentagon. www.reuters.com/article/2015/06/08us-usa-military-anthrax-idUSKBN0OO2ER 20150608. Accessed June 8, 2015.

Rotz L, Khan A, Lillibridge S, Ostroff S, Hughes J. (2002) Public health assessment of potential biological terrorism agents. *Emerging Infectious Diseases*. 8, 2, 225–230.

Sarasin P. (2006) *Anthrax: bioterror as fact and fantasy*. Cambridge, MA: Harvard University Press.

Sparks B, Associates for Biblical Research (2007) Did anthrax plague the Egyptians? http://www.biblearchaelogy.org/post/2007/10/17/Did-Anthrax-plague-the-Egyptians.aspx. Accessed May 8, 2015.

Starr B. (2015) Live anthrax inadvertently shipped by U.S. military. www.cnn.com/2015/05/27/politics/live-antrhax-us-military-sent-inadvertently. Accessed May 28, 2015.

Toor A. (2015) Pentagon accidentally sent live anthrax samples to labs via FedEx. www.tjeverge.com/2015/5/28/86765007/live-anthrax-samples-per. Accessed May 29, 2015.

Toth D, Gundiapalli A, Schell W, Bulmahn K, Walton T, Woods C, Coghill C, Gallegos F, Samor M, Adler F. (2013) Quantitative models of the dose-response and time course of inhalational anthrax in humans. *PLOS Pathogens*. 9, 8, 1–18, e1003555. www.plospathogens.org. Accessed May 12, 2015.

Tucker J. (1999) Historical trends related to bioterrorism: an empirical analysis. *Emerging Infectious Diseases*. 5, 4, 498–504.

Tyshenko M. (2007) Management of natural and bioterrorism induced pandemics. *Bioethics*. 21, 7, 364–369.

Wagner M, Moore A, Aryel R. (2006) *Handbook of biosurveillance*. San Diego, CA: Academic Press

Wein L, Craft D, Kaplan E. (2003) Emergency response to an anthrax attack. *Proceedings of the National Academy of Sciences*. 100, 7, 4346–4351.

White House. (2004) President Bush signs Project Bioshield Act of 2004. Whitehouse.gov. georgewbush-whitehouse.archives.gov/news/releases/2004/07/20040721-2.html. Accessed May 14, 2015.

Willman D. (2011) *The mirage man: Bruce Ivins, the anthrax attacks, and America's rush to war*. New York: Bantam Books.

Wood JP, Blair M. (2009) Development and field testing of a mobile chlorine dioxide generation system for the decontamination of buildings contaminated with Bacillus anthracis. *Journal of Hazardous Materials*. 164, 2–3, 1460–1467.

Woods M. (2000) Anthrax translates into doom. *The Toledo Blade*, February 15, 2000. http://rense.com/health3/anthrax.htm. Accessed May 12, 2015.

Ziskin L, Harris D. (2007) State health policy for terrorism preparedness. *American Journal of Public Health*. 97, 9, 1583–1588.

PART III

Supplements

9

RISK ANALYSIS AND DISASTER SCIENCE FICTION

Introduction

Fiction allows us to temporarily climb out of a real world that all too often seems mundane and unpleasant. Disaster science fiction takes us to events and locations that may never exist, adds emotionally disturbing horrors, introduces individuals and groups that are caricatures of good and evil, courage and cowardice, and brilliance and stupidity. Once a semester, I give undergraduate students passages from a few of the books and movies described in this chapter, and then we connect the passages to the science we know, highlighting the areas of overlap and places where writer creativity replaces reality. The students enjoy the exercise, sometimes as much as I do. A few times I have given them an assignment of reading a disaster sci-fi book or watching a movie and writing a short essay about it.

For risk analysts, a good science fiction novel and movie should not only be entertaining and mind stretching, but also provoke us with challenging hazard events, memorable images of human and ecological damage, captivating albeit not necessarily effective risk management solutions, and unacceptable economic and political consequences. Movies have the additional attributes of stirring images and sounds, which may be what people remember more than the plot, which I think too often can be shallow.

The chapter is divided into three parts. I begin with a review of some sci-fi books. Some of the text from the book section was originally published in *Risk Analysis, An International Journal* as an essay (Greenberg 2011). I received many positive comments from colleagues who recommended that I expand it to movies. Movies are where most of our students encounter disaster sci-fi. The third section of the chapter lists common characteristics that I have observed in disaster science fiction, including an unflattering characterization of how scientists are characterized in nearly every movie.

Several caveats are in order. There are thousands of disaster sci-fi books and I make no pretense to have read or seen any more than a small set of them. Some categories of disaster sci-fi are not represented here. For example, I have no airplane or train crash movies, chemicals destroying parts of the world, nor do I emphasize end-of-the-world nuclear war movies like *On the Beach* (Kramer 1959) and *The Sum of All Fears* (Neufeld 2002). These come too close to work that I have done and make me too uncomfortable to write about them as fiction.

An alternative option for organizing this chapter was to use one of the many lists of "best" or most read or watched disaster sci-fi. However, after reading some of these reviews, I rejected the idea because I did not necessarily agree with the rankings. Indeed in some cases, several of the highest rated movies would be on my worst movie list. Nor do I believe that more dollars earned equals more interesting disaster sci-fi. Hence, I used my own experiences, which I supplemented with those of colleagues, friends, and relatives. Indeed, what I hope to accomplish in this chapter is for you, the reader, to read or view some disaster sci-fi and react to it from analytical and affect perspectives, forming your own assessments, not adopting mine or critics'.

Disaster science fiction books: a sample

I am impatient with disaster sci-fi novels. If they annoy or bore me, I stop reading them. I read all of those featured here from cover to cover, several more than once. *The Last Gasp* by Trevor Hoyle (1983) is my risk analysis disaster science fiction book standard of excellence. Published in 1983, when President Ronald Reagan decided to challenge the Soviets by introducing the Strategic Defense Initiative (SDI) and escalating the arms race to overtax the Soviet economy, the book is grounded in events of that era and even tries to include some risk science, albeit in bizarre ways.

Trevor Hoyle creates Gavin Chase, a British marine biologist, whose research shows that pollution and industrial oxygen consumption have irrevocably destroyed the world's oxygen supply. When Chase and his colleagues attempt to alert government officials, they learn of a secret U.S.-Soviet plan to launch an "environmental war" to exterminate three-fourths of the population with a dioxin-bearing virus. This book has bizarre and intriguing events, catastrophic consequences, and solutions ranging only in the degree of pain inflicted on the Earth's inhabitants. What I liked about this book is that it was engaging, forcing me to think about what was happening in the world Hoyle had created, and what, if anything, could really save such a degraded world.

If you like reading about natural hazard events, Stephen Baxter's (2008) *Flood* is a good choice. The story is about submarine seismic activity that just about destroys human civilization. The image of Mount Everest covered by water in 2052 still sticks with me. In fact, I spent a few hours trying to figure out if it was possible to cover Mount Everest with water, if it remained at its current elevation. The common element of these two books is that they stimulated me into thinking about alternative realities.

Whitley Strieber and James Kunetka's (1987) *Nature's End* was equally challenging. Set in the year 2025, which seems right around the corner, with the world near the stage of environmental collapse, one solution is the deliberate extermination of a third of the world's population. The book speaks to issues of resource use, dependence on technology, and the obvious all too apparent presence of have and have not populations. To place this fiction in perspective, I recommend Paul Collier's (2007) book, *The Bottom Billion*, and Paul Sabin's recent fascinating book *The Bet* (2013), which compares the views of Paul Ehrlich, sometimes referred to as the disaster prophet scientist, with those of the late Julian Simon. These two scholars debated vociferously and sometimes acrimoniously over these issues, with Ehrlich's views finding their path into the policies of President Carter and Simon's into President Reagan's. Chapter 7 of this book has some of that same tone, but not nearly to the level of these two protagonists.

If you like politically oriented satirical disaster sci-fi, I recommend Kim Stanley Robinson's (2004) *Forty Signs of Rain*, which tells a story of a frustrated National Science Foundation employee and her stay-at-home husband (who is also an environmental activist consultant).

This pair, along with some Buddhists concerned about inundation of their own lands, devise interesting risk management options but largely fail to persuade disinterested and incompetent elected officials or their staff. The latter are the target of satirical comments, some of which are really funny. The theme of incompetent and uncaring government officials is common in disaster sci-fi, especially in the movies.

For stimulating risk-related dialogue about computer-related hazards, I recommend Sean McMullen's (1999) *Souls in the Great Machine*. A global event called "Greatwinter" eliminates our standard technologies, including computers and everything else electronic. Instead, we rely on human power (walking, biking), and especially wind. Enter a young woman, Zavora Cyberline (she's also a gunslinger), who decides to build a computer. She cannot build what we have today because old satellites from the previous technological era sense and then destroy any electric-powered machines. So she resorts to the public library, paper, and even to people who do calculations the old fashioned way. The biggest risk, however, is a "Call," an unexplained force that periodically summons people to walk southwest to their destruction. Unfortunately, old fashioned risk management does not seem to solve this risk management dilemma.

In fact, after reading *Souls in the Great Machine*, I felt that I needed to be transported to Emerald City to ask the Wizard of Oz to save the world.

A disaster sci-fi review has to have something about nuclear war. My favorite of this genre is Walter Miller's 1960) *A Canticle for Leibowitz*. This award winner depicts the aftermath of a nuclear war, beginning 600 years after the twentieth century. An abbey founded by a Jewish engineer Isaac Leibowitz (he converted to Catholicism) has saved and hidden a great deal of accumulated knowledge because in response to the nuclear holocaust, books were destroyed and literate people were summarily killed. Centuries later, the world is on the brink of nuclear war again.

The book presents graphic stories of the ecological impacts of nuclear war, as opposed to only human ones, and Miller creates story lines and characters that tell this painful story with real insights and a meaningful discussion of the roles of church and state.

In terms of fantasy, Scalzi's (2009) edited book *Metratropolist* offers five post-disaster stories about how urban-centered civilization changes after globalization and global warming drive all the world's economies to failure. Each chapter is about a different vision of this post economic collapse. Jay Lake's is about "Cascadiopolis" (Portland to Vancouver) where people live in a communal existence in the forest and whatever science they develop is shared without cost. Corporations, opposed to free technology, spy on the commune in order to gain new technologies. Tobias Buckell's "Stochasti-City," which is what remains of Detroit, depends on individual initiative and chance meetings and events. Good and bad things can happen to you depending where you are at any moment, truly probabilistic risk assessment without computers. More entrepreneurial post-motor Detroit residents turn to activities like trying to turn a skyscraper into a farm. Elizabeth Bear's story is about another part of Detroit where everything is recycled. Everyone shares the limited goods they have, and they live a communal life. Scalzi's chapter is about a new St. Louis, where everybody works (or is sent out of town), with their jobs determined by testing. Some of these jobs are less than the best, even for the politically privileged. My favorite story is Karl Schroeder's creation of a set of cyber cities where people's interactions are not governed by the need for their physical presence. I cannot possibly do justice to these authors; their creativity is impressive. These authors stimulated my imagination and were a temporary escape from the real world of hazards and risks. Scalzi's edited book is one of my favorites. After reading this set of five stories, I would not have blinked at a story that argued that the Earth is really flat.

Auler's (2010) *Twilight's Ashes* gave me a headache. The story begins in 635,039 A.D. The world is in a new Ice Age, and the few humans left are facing creatures that are hunting down and destroying humans. The hero Jebden Gale lives in a village near Saskatoone (in today's Canada) in an ice sheet with 200-foot sheer cliffs. The first two chapters were fascinating, describing hard to imagine environments, including compelling images of massive creatures with long blond manes attacking people and other post-human period creatures killing people in Rome (the sixth of eight cities to be conquered). Once I got past the first two chapters, it became a chore to follow Jebden migrating south, trying to forge relationships with other human settlements. Auler has a way with words, but the book slows down – too much mysticism, too many prophecies, too many gods of all kinds, too many languages, names, symbolism, and even a new calendar – and the book made me feel like I was back in high school reading Chaucer for the first time. I would have been happier with a 200-page rather than 450-page version of *Twilight's Ashes*.

Overall, with rare exception, these disaster sci-fi books depict smart scientists frustrated by inflexible government, greedy corporations, and now and then the evil scientist. The main characters are involved in romantic episodes. The language is written to induce interest, most often through horror, and the authors present countless struggles to survive and create, and to live in communal-like settings where investments, bank accounts, and the accoutrements of capitalism do not matter. And since what humans do seems to almost always fail, there are mystics, magicians, and other forces that bring the planet back from disaster, well at least sometimes.

Movies

There are so many categories of disaster sci-fi movies that I had to impose some classification and organization on them. I begin with large bodies crashing into the Earth and conclude with natural hazards.

Heavenly bodies collide with the Earth

Deep Impact (Brown, Zanuck 1998) is a multi-layered story about the near extermination of human civilization by a 7-mile-wide comet. One of the heroes is a smart teenager who happens to be an amateur astronomer. The teenager discovers a dangerous comet and alerts a professional astronomer. Unfortunately, the astronomer dies in a car accident before he can alert authorities. The teenage boy, his family and beloved girlfriend is one layer of the story. A second is about forgiveness, and is told by a television journalist for MSNBC who while investigating a possible scandal involving a cabinet officer learns that the United States government is aware of the oncoming hazard and has built an underground refuge for a million people. Her strained relationship with her father and her courage and willingness to sacrifice her life are a second layer of the story.

Without the further divulging additional subplots, this story is one of the better representations of what might actually happen. The United States government is not portrayed as incompetent and trying to ignore the risk. The President, played by Morgan Freeman, is aware of the hazard and is cooperating with Russia to build a ship that can intercept and destroy the comet. The United States and other nations have implemented plans to save people and elements of the environment (Noah's Ark idea). When the first attempt to destroy the object fails, the President announces it publicly and communicates forthrightly with the public throughout the stressing hazard event. After the comet breaks into two parts, he tells them approximately where the two bodies will strike the Earth and the overall impact. Both scientists and government officials behave as I would expect them to, that is, they act professionally and do what they need to do to prevent the impact and to be resilient in the event their plan fails. They communicate with each other throughout the process. Yes, of course there are multi-love stories, sacrifice, and many tear-jerking tales embedded in his film. However I enjoyed the fact that government did what they could do in the face of global elimination threat. The group trying to save the Earth was not brilliant, nor did they flash big muscles, but they were gritty and strategic.

Armageddon, (Bruckheimer, Hurd, Bay 1998) released during the same year with the same general plot is notably different. The U.S. government only has 18 days' notice that an asteroid the size of Texas is heading toward the Earth. Government's response is to try to send up experts to destroy the asteroid. They recruit a group of oil drilling experts who will land on the asteroid and destroy it with nuclear weapons. Government officials are not portrayed as the overly bright (a kind way of stating how they were portrayed), including military commanders and the astronaut commander of the mission who looked like and acted like the vice-principal of one of my public schools who always seemed more interested in following rules than solving problems. Thank goodness that the oil rig experts are headed by none other than Bruce Willis, his crew, including Ben Affleck, and they are assisted by a Russian astronaut who was piloting the space station, which is the jumping off point for the attack on the asteroid.

Except for Willis and his crew who managed to make mistakes but through courage, intuition, grittiness and luck, almost everyone else comes across as incompetent. For example *somehow no one* knew about this rogue meteor until 18 days before it would hit the Earth. The Russian astronaut fixes mechanical failures in the spaceship by hitting and kicking it, which of course restores the ship's functions. Watching Willis and his crew bumbling and fumbling on an asteroid approaching the Earth was hard to take seriously and reminded me of a 1957 movie *Outer Space Jitters* (White 1957), starring the Three Stooges, who confronted a threat to civilization in outer space in a way that only they could manage, or I should say mismanage to a successful ending.

Nevertheless, despite my preference, I was not surprised to learn that *Armageddon* was a bigger box-office hit than *Deep Impact*. *Deep Impact* is a too thoughtful, and it is a humorless and stressful film that portrayed people in roles that they would likely play in life, whereas *Armageddon* is a story of a bunch of cowboys trying to save the Earth. In the end, my friends liked *Armageddon* more than *Deep Impact*. Bruce Willis and Ben Affleck using their instincts and doggedness proved to be a better story than Robert Duvall and Morgan Freeman using their brains.

These two 1998 stories are both entertaining, yet there have been others. Foremost amongst these is *When Worlds Collide* (Pal 1951). Until *Deep Impact* and *Armageddon* were released, this post-World War II movie was my favorite of the worlds collide genre. The essence of the story is about the soon to occur collision between the Earth and a star. Recognizing that this eventuality could not be prevented, a group of smart scientists try to persuade government to act before the eight months they have to save the human race. Their case is made before the United Nations (created in 1945), which is persuaded by mainstream scientists to reject the catastrophe argument (again, the stubborn rigid scientist and engineer.) Hence, the hero scientists and entrepreneurs work together to build a spaceship that will be launched from the Earth heading toward a place where humans and animal species might be able to build a new home. This now 65-year-old story movie is more like *Deep Impact* than it is like *Armageddon,* which for me is a plus.

For those that want to see violence and greed, this movie has more than its share, as well as the usual tender moments and people who sacrifice their lives for others.

Alien invaders

In April 1951, I saw a terrifying black-and-white movie, *The Thing from Another World*, (Lasker 1951), which my friends and I called the "Thing." The "Thing" was played by James Arness who starred in the television Western *Gunsmoke* for 20 years (the longest playing television show in history). Arness played a markedly different role as the Thing. A flying saucer crashes near the North Pole, and soldiers recover a massive frozen body. Unfortunately they warm it, which causes the massive humanoid-shaped figure to revive, whereupon it is shot at and then attacked by dogs. It flees into the frozen blackness of the North Pole, but soldiers recover its arm. Scientists discover that it is a plant and they obtain seedlings, which they grow. The wounded humanoid returns with a vengeance, battling the military and demonstrating intelligence. Ignoring attempts by a physician/scientist to reason with it, the soldiers kill the plant creature. Even though this was a black-and-white movie, the *Thing* has some spectacular photos, especially when the Thing is caught and being killed by arcs of electricity; I still remember them.

The *Thing from Another World* was made between World War II and the commencement of the Korean War. Sentiment is clearly pro-soldiers and anti-scientist. *Time* magazine named the *Thing* the best sci-fi movie of the 1950s. It certainly was the scariest movie I saw until the *Birds* came along. My friends and I had a different view of plants after we saw the *Thing* movie. I am sure that we were not the only little boys who thought the plant creatures would return. For those that are interested in plants, I suggest *The Day of the Triffids* (Pitcher 1962) as another alien plant invasion, in this case by plants that look to me like big asparagus plants that can walk and kill people that are easy targets because they have been blinded by a meteor shower. Thank goodness that the triffids cannot handle salt water, or humans would have been plant food (see ending of *War of the Worlds* below).

A few months after the *Thing* appeared in movie theaters and scared me, *The Day the Earth Stood Still* (Blaustein 1951) appeared in the movies with a markedly different message about alien invaders. A flying saucer lands in Washington, D.C. A humanoid emerges from it. That humanoid, unlike the massive figure of James Arness or the walking triffids, seems less imposing. Nevertheless, trigger-happy soldiers, of course, shoot the humanoid, whereupon a giant robot emerges from the flying saucer and destroys all the soldiers' weapons. The injured humanoid, Klaatu, is taken to the hospital and while recovering tells the U.S. President's staff that he needs to speak with the world's leaders. He is rebuffed by government leaders but wise senior scientists meet with him. In order to gain their undivided attention, Klaatu cuts off electricity everywhere, except for aircraft in the skies, hospitals and in other cases where health and safety would be sacrificed. Nevertheless he is shot by frightened people and appears to die in the end, before leaving, However, Klaatu emerges and tells the scientist that if the Earth takes their nuclear weapons into outer space, then the Earth will be destroyed.

Reviewers, critics, and the writers noticed that Klaatu had certain attributes of Jesus Christ. He offers earthlings a chance for life; he is misunderstood and is killed; he appears to rise from the dead; and he gives his name as John Carpenter (J.C.).

The contrast between the two 1951 movies is striking. The first says trust the generals that won World War II and were in the Korean War, and the second suggests that bigger and better bombs and guns are not the solution.

Many more interesting alien invasion stories are available. Before I was born, *Flash Gordon* (MacRae 1936), a serialized show starring Buster Crabbe, a handsome gold medalist in the 1932 Olympics, and Charles Middleton as the infamous Ming the Merciless, Emperor of the Planet Mongol, was an alien invasion favorite. Ming the Merciless seeks to poison everyone on Earth. The movie hero was Flash Gordon, but I thought the real hero was Dr. Alexis Zarkov who looked like a scientist and kept devising technologies that would allow Flash to save the world. Full length Flash Gordon movies have appeared with much more realistic looking rocket ships but with less engaging Emperor Mings and Dr. Zharkovs. The latter surely would have been a risk analyst today; a nerd trying to save people using his intellect.

The Star Wars movies, especially *The Empire Strikes Back* (Kurtz 1980) remind me of the Flash Gordon episodes. Both have evil leaders, heroic young men, beautiful young heroines, and a mixture of science and magic. Indeed, George Lucas, who wrote The *Empire Strikes Back* acknowledged that Flash Gordon was the inspiration for the Star War series.

The *Man from Planet X* (Pollexfen and Wisberg 1951) is another 1951 movie featuring an alien invasion, good and bad scientists, and a military solution. This movie has a really scary looking space invader who looks like a human compressed by immense pressure encased in a space suit that looks like something that an underwater diver of that era would have worn. The invader in *Man from Planet X* was even more frightening looking than James Arness as the "Thing." In fact, I think the *Man from Planet X* was far scarier than the creatures in the *Predator* (Gordon 1987), even including the lizards that fought with the predators.

Fast-forward from the 1950s to 1996 and the release of *Independence Day* (Devlin 1996). Days before United States Independence Day on July 4, a massive flying saucer locates over Washington D.C. along with dozens of smaller flying sources (each 15 miles in diameter (24 km)) that deploy over major U.S. and other world cities. A scientist discovers that the aliens are planning a coordinated attack not peaceful foreign relations. He learns that the aliens are like locusts and will kill everyone and pillage the planet of all of its resources. Working together, the scientist and the military planners build a computer virus, which drops the alien ships' protective screens, and then the military pilots destroy them.

This is a remarkable movie for several reasons. One is that it introduces old hazards in a new form – massive spaceships that can coordinate an attack on the world, led by an even more massive command ship. But the world responds with science and military coordination and use of common assets, which is so rare in disaster sci-fi movies and novels which normally depict scientists and/or military as incompetents. To be sure the ultimate hero who sacrifices his life was a Vietnam veteran pilot who has been flying a crop duster. Somehow he manages to learn how to fly the F/A-18 Hornet fighter plane for the final attack. Other than that improbability, the film has the proper people playing the kinds of roles that they would play. The movie was number 1 in the box offices for 1996 and won awards for visual effects and sound.

Starship Troopers (Davison, Marshall 1997) is a combination of alien invasion and bugs, in this case large ones not those in the following section. In the twenty-third century, the Buenos Aires region is destroyed by an asteroid launched by the Arachnids, or so-called "bugs." This militaristic movie, reminiscent of the 1940s and early 1950s, features efforts by the good guys and gals to capture a so-called "brain bug" so that they can devise a strategy to beat the bugs. The bugs in this movie range from tiny mouse-size creatures to some that are the size of dinosaurs and breathe fire, and have devised the capacity to launch weapons that shoot down large space ships. Several more in this series have appeared during the last 15 years, and there will be more because arachnids are scary looking. The real hero is a soldier with a square jaw and strong muscles, not a thinker, who makes it through multiple wars with the bugs and looks every bit the role of the heroic soldier.

My last alien invasion movie is *War of the Worlds* (Pal 1953). This initial movie and various newer ones are based on H.G. Wells's 1898 novel. Wells, like many, was intrigued by the idea that Mars is inhabited and would eventually invade the Earth. In his book, spaceships crash land all over the Earth, and Martian war machines that look like giant manta rays use heat rays, energy weapons, as well as poison gas to destroy human civilization.

On October 30, 1938 the day before Halloween, Orson Welles broadcast a radio show that terrified some Americans. Supposedly breaking into a regular radio show, Americans were led to believe that a Martian spaceship had landed in New Jersey (West Windsor) about 60 miles from New York City and 22 miles from where I live). At various times in the broadcast, reporters broke in with updates of people being killed, mostly by poison gas. My parents loved Orson Welles' shows and told me that they knew it was not real. However I had a recording of the broadcast, and I would have been terrified if I had not known that it was a spoof. Some listeners were so scared that they needed medical treatment. Welles was both praised and severely criticized.

The first movie about Mars invades the Earth was released in 1953, with Gene Barry playing one lead. He played Dr. Clayton Forrester who had worked on the Manhattan nuclear weapons project. Dr. Forester and friends are fishing when a meteor-like structure crash lands nearby. Marines surround and then are routed by the Martians' superior weapons and held off by force fields. A local minister approaches the spaceship with goodwill signs but is killed. A bomber drops a nuclear weapon on the Martian spaceships, but the weapons cannot penetrate the force field. As the battle emerges, Dr. Forester and other scientists at Pacific Tech in Los Angeles determine that the Martians are vulnerable. But the Martians are winning, until the climactic scene when survivors are huddling and praying. That salvation comes when the Martian ships fall out of the sky. Apparently, luckily for humans, the Martians were vulnerable to the Earth's bacteria and viruses.

The 1953 version is somewhat different from the H.G. Wells novel, as are the subsequent versions, including one in 2005, starring Tom Cruise. The *War of the Worlds* visuals and sound effects are amazing, and the opportunity for making a lot of money and winning awards are too obvious for a future generation of directors/writers like George Pal and Steven Spielberg to not revisit. There will be more versions of this movie, and I expect one will feature cyber war. A smart Martian risk analyst would advocate that technology as part of their war strategy.

Killer birds, bees, and larger species

I begin with five of my favorites. *The Birds* (Hitchcock 1963) is an Alfred Hitchcock thriller. The story is about birds attacking residents of Bodega Bay, California. The movie begins as a typical boy meets girl. That plot quickly changes when chickens, gulls, and nasty crows mass and attack people in the street, including breaking through windows and attacking people in their homes and stores. The movie ends neither with the death of all the people or all the killer birds. Instead it ends with a few survivors leaving town and birds massing.

Birds attacking people is unusual enough. Birds perching on trees ready to pounce escalates the uncomfortable uncertain feelings left by this movie. I do not expect birds to attack me, but the special effects, including bird sounds, bodies with no eyes, even without today's enhanced capabilities, sent shivers up my spine and the spines of my friends. *The Birds* is classic. The special effects were nominated for an Academy award, and Hitchcock received an award for the film.

Hitchcock's team created incredibly powerful emotional stimuli. What had been a mundane subject – bird behavior – suddenly became a subject of considerable discussion for at least a month or two, I remember scanning the trees for birds after the movie. *The Birds*, in short, is one of the scariest movies I've ever seen.

If you are afraid of bees, maybe you should not see the *Swarm* (Allen 1978), or at lease watch it with someone else. I remember watching it with two of my friends and one of them twice jumped out of her seat. I read the reviews of *The Swarm* and was surprised that there were some strong negative reviews. Nevertheless, I liked it because it includes other environmental hazards. Briefly, a swarm of bees attacks people in Marysville, Texas, killing almost everyone and killing the pilots of two helicopters sent to investigate the attack. A general orders survivors to be evacuated by train. However, the bees attacked the train killing people. The swarm is headed toward Houston, Texas when a doctor/scientist drops what he calls eco-friendly bombs on the bees, which fails to stop them. The swarm then attacks a nuclear power plant, killing the staff, destroying the plant, and everyone in the area. The risk increases as the swarm continues to move toward Houston, but the general and the doctor, come up and implement a plan to get the swarm to move out to sea and set it on fire.

The Swarm is not a stellar movie. However, the subject is fascinating and the cast includes Michael Caine, Katherine Ross, Richard Widmark, Richard Chamberlain, Olivia de Havilland, Ben Johnson, Lee Grant, José Ferrer, Fred MacMurray, Patty Duke, Henry Fonda and Cameron Mitchell. This is a prominent cast for any movie, much less a disaster movie. Despite this cast, the movie did not win any awards. The story is not well developed especially from a scientific point of view. Given what we know about the challenges of maintaining bees, competition among them and other species, I suspect someone can and will write a better swarm movie in the not-too-distant future.

Arachnophobia (Kennedy snd Vane 1990) is funnier than it should be, given the topic. The film begins with an entomologist searching the Amazon Forest for new arachnids and insects. He succeeds in capturing a new spider that turns out to have a deadly bite. Through a series of all too human mistakes, the spider ends up in the United States in a small California town. The spider bites a crow which had snatched it for food, killing the crow and dropping the spider near a barn where it takes up residence mating with a local spider and producing another hundred spiders with a lethal bite. After the nest is discovered, residents attempt to destroy it. The town exterminator, played by comedian John Goodman, manages to introduce some laughter into a battle between people and spiders. Of course there is a smart young town doctor, but as usual, his warnings of doom are ignored until the situation gets desperate. Spiders scare many people. We know a lot about them and good scientists could have made this movie and *The Swarm* better movies, or at least less silly.

Rise of the Planet of the Apes (Chernin *et al.* 2011) presents a different kind of human risk story. A biotechnology scientist is testing a viral-based drug, which is intended to cure Alzheimer's disease and chimpanzees are chosen as the test animals. The test is successful, dramatically increasing the intelligence of one chimp named "Bright Eyes." But Bright Eyes is killed when she behaves inappropriately toward an abusive human. The plot is that she had given birth, and the baby called "Caesar" is saved and he grows into a leader of the species. Imprisoned for attacking a man who was abusing his human master, Caesar eventually escapes freeing other imprisoned chimps, apes, and gorillas, in the process, killing his prison guard and speaking English, a shocking part of the movie.

Caesar administers the wonder drug to apes, gorillas which quickly raises their mental capacity. They escape into the Redwood forest in California and prepare to defend themselves against humans who surely will hunt them down. The film ends with an interesting twist. Caesar's abusive human neighbor, who happens to be an airline pilot, is sick with a deadly virus that he will spread around the world killing the human population. *Rise of the Planet of the Apes* is one of a series of humans versus apes movies, and there will continue to be more because of their popularity. The underlying message is humans trigger hazards that they cannot control.

The last of my five animals turning on human stories is *Godzilla* (Tull *et al.* 2014), another human-caused or enhanced hazard. Like the planet of the apes movies, the 2014 Godzilla film is one in a series, beginning with a nuclear explosion in 1954. Forty-five years later, a Japanese nuclear power plant experiences tremors. These tremors turn out to be caused by a massive winged creature that kills everyone in the nuclear power plant and releases a radioactive plume causing the area to be quarantined. A United States Navy fleet approaches the area with orders to find the Massive Unidentified Terrestrial Organism (MUTO) that caused the damage. Film viewers learn that the MUTO and Godzilla are natural enemies. MUTO attacks Hawaii, and in turn is attacked by Godzilla, causing a tsunami in Honolulu. A second MUTO devastates Las Vegas, and flies to meet the first MUTO with which it will mate in the San Francisco area.

The United States initially plans to destroy these creatures with nuclear weapons, but the creatures devour one of the weapons and the second one is seized by the first MUTO. The MUTOs build a nest in the Chinatown area of San Francisco. Indeed, San Francisco, I believe, wins the award as the most disaster-abused city, albeit music lovers will recall that it was the site for Richard Rodgers and Oscar Hammerstein's (1958) *Flower Drum Song*.

For lovers of Godzilla, he engages the two MUTOs, and the MUTO nest is destroyed. The nuclear weapon is taken out to sea. Godzilla leaves and is saluted by San Francisco residents as a savior of the city. But was he? Literally yes, but figuratively no. My interpretation is that Godzilla represents a living tornado able to drop out of the sky or emerge from the water as a reminder that nature can devastate human populations, especially when humans create conditions that increase their vulnerability. For me, Godzilla does not represent a large house pet willing to surrender his life to protect his master. Some people prefer the 1998 version, or even the original 1950 version, which many older movie viewers remember.

Human technology run amuck

Humans are frequently blamed as creating the disasters in sci-fi movies, typically because of their incompetence and greed. Two of my favorites first appeared in 1972 and 1974, respectively. The *Poseidon Adventure* (Allen 1972) is about greed. SS *Poseidon*, a luxury liner, modeled on the *Queen Mary*, crosses the Atlantic Ocean from New York City to Greece. The ship on its last voyage needs more work and ballast, but the greedy company manager orders them to leave. Unfortunately an underground earthquake occurs sending a tsunami toward the ship and then capsizing it. Some survivors are clever enough to use a Christmas tree to climb toward the hull. Others are not and die. Others die when the ships technologies fail. Some brave passengers sacrifice their lives for others; only six survived.

With Gene Hackman, Ernest Borgnine, Red Buttons, Shelley Winters, Roddy McDowall, and Leslie Nielsen in the cast, and with John Williams as the music composer (*Jaws, Towering Inferno, Star Wars, Superman, E.T., Indiana Jones, Jurassic Park*, etc.) the movie became a classic winning multiple awards for acting and music. Based on the novel the *Poseidon Adventure* by Paul Gallico, the movie was remade, most recently in 2006, and it will probably be remade in the not-too-distant future given its box-office success.

With some of the same key contributors as the *Poseidon Adventure*, the *Towering Inferno* (Allen 1974) is again about a disaster caused by greed and exacerbated by incompetence. With Steve McQueen and Paul Newman as the co-leads, and including Fred Astaire, the plot revolves around the opening of the world's tallest building: 138 storeys. Before the opening, initial tests showed a small electrical problem. During the building opening ceremony, a bad fire breaks out killing some people and trapping others. After many attempts, the San Francisco Deputy Fire Chief makes the tough decision to demolish the water tanks, which would put out the fire but kill people. The anti-greed and incompetence messages are similar to those in the *Poseidon Adventure*.

Nearly every example in this chapter is about the United States, especially California. Here is an exception. In 1961 a Soviet nuclear submarine the K-19 was sent on a special mission to surface at the North Pole and simulate firing a nuclear missile. *K-19: the Widow Maker* (Bigelow 2002) is about this misadventure. Starring Harrison Ford and Liam Neeson, the mission starts badly, the reactor officer is fired and the medical officer is killed. The K-19 does break the surface and conducts its simulated launch. However, ice damages its communication system and a pipe with reactor cooling water leaks. The Soviet fleet cannot be contacted for help. Furthermore the backup cooling pipes were not installed. Men are sent to repair the system. However the wrong protective suits were brought on board. Many die from radiation exposure. An American destroyer offers help, and their offer is declined. In the end, 28 men died of radiation exposure. An epilogue film includes fascinating comments from the captain and members of the crew who survived and were still alive.

Strictly speaking, K-19 is not a sci-fi movie because it is based on a real event. The movie's dramatic tale challenged the idea that nuclear powered ships are safe. Nuclear power has been a major part of disaster sci-fi, and Three Mile Island, Chernobyl, and Fukushima-Dachaii continue to be a major sources for sci-fi writers and for movies like *The China Syndrome* (Douglas 1979), which was released immediately before Three Mile Island occurred. Hopefully, at some point, science fiction writers will try to capture reality about nuclear materials more than they have in the past. But, perhaps, I am being entirely unrealistic. I enjoyed the K-19 movie, and many of the Soviet naval survivors described it as being relatively realistic. Yet K-19 was far from a box-office success. I am not sure why but perhaps writing a sci-fi thriller without substantial deviation from reasonably expectable events is boring for many movie audiences.

A case in hand is global climate change, represented by *The Day After Tomorrow* (Emmerich 2004). The movie shows that humans have abused the Earth and caused a new Ice Age. Scientists try but fail to persuade their government that a rapid freeze is occurring. By the time government is ready to act, three enormous storms appear over Canada, Scotland and Siberia. New York City streets flood, and a good guy scientist tries to reach his son in New York City. By the time he arrives, the main New York City public library on 42nd Street, where this author has spent many hours, is buried beneath snow. The outside temperature is close to -100 degrees celsius. In order to survive, people trapped in the public library burn books for heat and take food from the vending machines.

There's nothing subtle about this movie. United States government officials and many scientists are portrayed as fools, and our collective greed has done us in. The less obvious message is the historical reversal of the Northern Hemisphere's domination of the Southern Hemisphere (see Chapter 7). After the northern hemisphere freezes over, astronauts look out of their space ship and comment that the air appears to be cleaner than ever. The U.S. President and other residents of America have moved to Mexico and other parts of the southern hemisphere. It is hard to believe that such a change would occur without considerable angst on the part of those living in the southern hemisphere. Also, scientists rightfully panned this movie because an Ice Age would not appear overnight. The images were impressive; viewing the northern hemisphere from outer space as one large white area and seeing the public library buried in deep snow were powerful graphic images, which I assume is what was intended by the writers and directors. After watching *The Day After Tomorrow,* I admitted to myself that watching actual global climate change take place is a little bit like watching paint dry, unless you happen to be in one of those areas experiencing stronger temperature, precipitation and winds than normal. The process had to be accelerated to get the public's attention.

Microbes and humans

Disaster sci-fi writers have explored what would happen if humans inadvertently triggered a catastrophe by creating microbes that threated all humans. *Outbreak* (Katz *et al.* 1995) is a movie about a fictional outbreak of an-Ebola like strain in a small California town. A deadly virus is discovered in the African jungle in the late 1960s. United States Army officers take blood from victims of the Motaba virus in order to build a weapon of mass destruction. The virus is carried to California by a white monkey that was smuggled into the United States. The infected monkey bites the smuggler and infects another monkey. The smuggler, his girlfriend, and others die as a result of the hemorrhagic fever, while the monkey escapes into the woods.

The threat magnifies enormously because the virus mutates and can be spread like influenza. Cedar Creek, California, is quarantined by the U.S. Army. The main hero, Colonel Sam Daniels (Dustin Hoffman) learns that the Army has a vaccine and is keeping it secret. Trying to contain the outbreak and protect their secret mission, the Army prepares to bomb Cedar Creek. Meanwhile Colonel Daniels, after much effort, captures the white monkey, and he is able to mix antibodies from the monkey with a previously secret vaccine. But before saving the world, Daniels and his coworker have to stop a bomber on its way to destroy Cedar Creek. Of course, they are successful. And the unethical Army officers are arrested, and the newly developed vaccines administered to save the town. The movie moves at a frantic pace, making the event seen even more frightening than it is portrayed to be.

A powerful image in the film is a computer map of the United States that shows deaths from the virus, and it changes very quickly from isolated clusters to extinction. When the screen turned red, anyone watching the movie probably felt a little sick. One risk management issue is could the CDC, which is portrayed in a positive light, react fast enough to stop the kind of immediately devastating threat portrayed in this movie. I doubt it. Second would the United States government really kill everyone in the town in order to contain such a virus?

This film scared many of my younger undergraduates; everyone dying seemingly overnight and Americans being bombed by the U.S. military are not common thoughts. It is one of the most popular films we have discussed in class.

I Am Legend (Goldsman *et al.* 2007) is about a United States Army virologist played by Will Smith who lives near Washington Square Park in New York City (near New York University). The vibrant area is largely desolate and Smith believes himself to be the sole survivor of a genetically modified measles virus that was supposed to cure cancer. Instead it killed 90 percent of the population, and the remaining 10 percent responded to the infection by mutating into "Dark Seekers" that cannot tolerate sunlight. Colonel Smith lives with his dog, tries to avoid the Dark Seekers, and is exploring possible treatment to the virus, which he tests on a captive Dark Seeker.

Colonel Smith finds a woman and boy that were not affected. However he has been followed by the Dark Seekers who attack his sanctuary, and he kills himself and the Dark Seekers in order to protect his vaccine. The woman and young boy leave the next morning with a vaccine and turn it over to a colony of survivors.

Will Smith's character played multiple roles in the movie, and he seems to be the poster actor for disaster movies. In this one, he had to survive, find a reason to live, and to try to find a cure. The visuals were striking, for example, a destroyed Brooklyn Bridge, a short distance away from where I worked as a teenager. The scientific elements were less believable; it does not have a lot to do with scientific method. It mostly has to do with one man's struggle to survive and to help the human race survive.

I end this section with my favorite microbes movie and book, *The Andromeda Strain* (Wise 1971). The plot is that a satellite picks up an extraterrestrial organism that dissolves plastic and otherwise wreaks havoc on human technology and humans. What I like about this story is that scientists play important roles in figuring out the risk consequences and in risk management. I will not say any more because in the ending is uncertain and I do not want to give it away for those of you that have not read the book or watched the movie. This is a good one for risk analysts.

Natural disasters

Avalanches, earthquakes, lightning strikes that cause fires, floods, hurricanes, Nor'easters and other storms, mudslides and tsunamis all qualify as natural hazards.

As a collective, I consider natural hazards sci-fi to be the worst disaster sci-fi movies. It is too much of a stretch for me to believe that we do not have warnings of events, that if there is a warning it is ignored by elected officials, that their managers are idiots, and that the public has no ability to understand the threat and respond to instructions from credible first responders and political leaders. My experience is that with rare exceptions we have some idea of where and when there will be a problem, (although the exact time and location remain difficult to forecast). Elected officials, in my experience, do not ignore hazard events, and you get to see them in a way that is different from their normal political posturing photo appearances. Also, contrary to the panic stricken public, most people follow advisories, instructions for evacuation when these come from credible elected officials and first responders. Many members of the public are themselves prepared and offer assistance to friends.

I really do not have a lot of patience with the overwhelming majority of these natural hazard movies, irrespective of whether the natural hazard is a tornado, mudslide, tidal wave, or earthquake. We know a great deal about natural hazards, unlike invasions from Mars and giant blobs covering city streets, and hence movies should try to mimic what might actually happen, as opposed to having everyone's lives depend upon a twenty-first century super hero. The recent movie *San Andreas* (Flynn *et al.* 2015) is illustrative, with the usual powerful death and destruction views, romance, heroism, and a good cast, but not much else to offer, including little scientific understanding.

An exception is the movie *Twister* (Bryce 1996). I enjoyed it. In addition to the romantic elements, the movie featured two scientists experimenting with devices intended to extract data from inside tornadoes. After multiple failures entailing scenes of dead people and cows, as well as destroyed automobiles and houses, their monitoring device which seems like a Rube Goldberg contraption actually worked. Maybe I was desperate but this movie at least had some people who were competent and were trying to do something.

Lessons learned

I make no pretense to be a sci-fi novel or movie critic. Nevertheless, here, only partly offered tongue-in-cheek, are some of the overall observations I have made by reading scores of disaster novels and watching at least an equal number of movies:

Risk analysis

- Risk assessment and risk informed decision-making are rarely part of disaster sci-fi. With some exceptions, deliberative thinking and planning appear to conflict with the intent of most writers to emphasize the common sense (whatever that is), courage and fighting skills of attractive, well groomed, adult males who try to save the world, sometimes aided by magic and luck.

Occasionally, the heroes are aided by attractive young females but more often than not the women scream, cry, and need to be rescued by the heroes.

Context

- Audiences want romance, powerful male actors, strong images, and sounds of death and destruction of buildings and bridges;
- Strong acting can compensate for weak plots, especially if the acting is accompanied by outstanding images and sounds;
- Disaster science fiction is set in political, social, physical and temporal environments, and movies and books mimic that context, even if they are set in the twenty-second and twenty-third centuries; and
- Color has replaced black and white in movies. However, *The Birds, The Man from Planet X, The Thing from Another World,* and some of the most frightening movies were in black and white. *The Day of the Triffids* looks black and white, despite the fact that it is in color. Black and white and all the shades of gray allow a more dreamlike quality to emerge on the screen. Stay tuned for a rebirth of black and white.

People

- The public is shown to be anything but helpful during a disaster. They are too busy panicking, confronting authority instead of following directions, and their irrational behavior complicates the efforts of the heroes trying to save them. While heroes fight to save them, much of the public turns from panic to fatalism. Public preparedness and reasoned thinking does not seem to be a major feature of disaster sci-fi;
- Animals are represented as instinctively aware that something bad is about to happen, albeit there is some data to support that characterization for some animals;
- Elected officials typically are portrayed as narcissistic, so preoccupied with themselves, that they are clueless about risk and their staff are too worried about their jobs and prerogatives to inform their bosses;
- Depending upon the date of the movie, senior military commanders are painted as preferring to shoot first and ask questions later;
- Scientists, with a few exceptions, are portrayed as too old, rigid, and/or eccentric to save the world. Not only do they lack muscles, but they lack common sense. If anyone with a science background is reliable, it is likely to be a local physician who also happens to be young, attractive and male;
- Human curiosity and greed are depicted as out of control leading to destruction of everyone and everything on Earth; and
- California's population is portrayed as experiencing an inordinate share of hazard events. Surely it is the disaster sci-fi capital of the world?

What did Chapter 9 explain about risk analysis? Summary and learning objectives

Disaster sci-fi writers', directors' and producers' jobs depend on attracting audiences that buy tickets, products and tell their friends to do the same. Audiences' collective emotions are stimulated by an arsenal of powerful tools: physically and mentally powerful and attractive heroes and heroines; striking visual images; music that stays in the mind after the show; and plots that resonate with public values. The heroes' and heroines' roles are enhanced by people that play stereotypical roles, for example, the ill-informed and self-absorbed elected official, the war mongering general, the greedy businessman, the nerdy scientist, and so on. Masters of print and the screen may secretly wish that they did not distort reality, but they do what they must do to stimulate audiences' emotions and earn themselves unimaginably high payments. See Figure 9.1 for a characterization of stereotypical roles.

I recommend that every reader of this chapter read a disaster sci-fi book and/or view at least one movie, and then answer the following seven questions:

1. What story are the authors trying to tell, that is, what is their takeaway message?
2. How is the story told to the audience? What tools are used to tell the story?
3. What are key political, social and environmental issues at the time the story was written, and how are they reflected in the message?

FIGURE 9.1 Cartoon of risk analysts

4. On a scale of 1 to 10, where 1 = not at all realistic in terms of information, and 10=extremely realistic, how realistic is this disaster sci-fi story?
5. What parts, if any, of the plot are most faithful to what we know about the subject?
6. Could the story have been as interesting if inaccurate information were presented more realistically?
7. What role do women, soldiers, elected officials, and scientists play in telling the story?

References

Allen I (producer), Neame R (director). (1972) *The Poseidon Adventure*. United States, 20th Century Fox.

Allen I (producer), Guillermin J (director). (1974) *The Towering Inferno*. United States, 20th Century Fox.

Allen I (producer), Allen I (director). (1978) *The swarm*. United States, Warner Brothers.

Auler I. (2010) *Twilight's ashes*. Bloomington, IN: iUniverse Press.

Baxter S. (2008) *Flood*. London: Gollancz.

Bigelow K (producer), Bigelow K (director). (2002) *K-19: The widowmaker*. United States, Intermedia Films.

Blaustein J (producer), Wise R (director). (1951) *The day the Earth stood still*. United States, 20th Century Fox.

Brown D, Zanuck R (producers), Leder M (director). (1998) *Deep impact*. United States, Paramount Pictures.

Bruckheimer J, Hurd GA, Bay M (producers), Bay M (director). (1998) *Armageddon*. United States, Touchstone Pictures.

Bryce I, Crichton M, Kennedy K (producers), de Bont J (director). (1996) *Twister*. United States, Warner Brothers.

Chernin P, Clark D, Jaffa R, Silver A. (producers), Wyatt R (director). (2011) *Rise of the planet of the apes*. United States, 20th Century Fox.

Collier P. (2007) *The bottom billion: why the poorest countries are failing and what can be done about it*. New York: Oxford University Press.

Davison J, Marshall A (producers), Verhoeven P (director). (1997) *Starship troopers*. United States, TriStar Pictures.

Devlin D (producer), Emmerich R (director). (1996) *Independence day*. United States, 20th Century Fox.

Douglas M (producer), Bridges J (director). (1979) *The China syndrome*. United States, Columbia Pictures.

Emmerich R, Gordon M (producers), Emmerich R (director). (2004) *The day after tomorrow*. United States, 20th Century Fox.

Flynn B, Garcia H, Vinson T (producers), Peyton B (director). (2015) *San Andreas*. United States, Warner Brothers.

Goldsman A, Lassiter J, Heyman D, Moritz N (producers), Lawrence F (director). (2007) *I am legend*. New York, Warner Brothers.

Gordon L, Silver J, Davis J (producers), McTiernan J (director). (1987) *Predator*. United States, 20th Century Fox.

Greenberg M. (2011) Book review essay: risk analysis and science fiction. *Risk Analysis*. 31, 6, 1033–1035.

Hitchcock A (producer and director). (1963) *The birds*. United States, Universal Pictures.

Hoyle T. (1983) *The last gasp: the rise and fall of the American gas chamber*. New York: Crown.

Katz G, Kopleson A, Kopleson A, Petersen W (producers), Petersen W (director). (1995) *Outbreak*. United States, Warner Brothers.

Kennedy K, Vane R (producers), Marshall F (director). (1990) *Arachnophobia*. United States, Buena Vista Pictures.

Kramer S (producer and director). (1959) *On the beach*. United States, United Artists.

Kurtz G (producer), Kershner I (director). (1980). *The empire strikes back,* United States, 20th Century Fox.

Lasker E (producer), Nyby C (director). (1951) *The thing from another world*. United States, RKO Radio Pictures.

MacRae H (producer), Stephani F (director). (1936) *Flash Gordon*. Serial. United States, Universal Pictures.

McMullen S. (1999) *Souls in the great machine*. New York: Tom Doherty.

Miller W Jr. (1960) *A canticle for Leibowitz*. New York: Crown.

Neufeld M (producer), Alden Robinson P (director). (2002) *The sum of all fears*. United States, Paramount Pictures.

Pal G (producer), Maite R (director). (1951) *When worlds collide*. United States, Paramount Pictures.

Pal G (producer), Haskin BR (director). (1953) *The war of the worlds,* United States, Paramount Pictures.

Pitcher G, Yordan P (producers), Sekely S (director). (1962) *Day of the triffids*. United Kingdom, Rank Organisation and Allied Artists.

Pollexfen J, Wisberg A (producers), Ulmer E. (1951) *The man from planet X*. United States, United Artists.

Robinson K. (2004) *Forty signs of rain*. New York: Bantam.

Rodgers R, Hammerstein O. (1958) *The flower drum song*. New York: Schubert Theater.

Sabin P. (2013) *The bet*. New Haven, CN: Yale University Press.

Scalzi J (ed). (2009) *Metatropolis*. Burton, MI: Subterranean Press.

Strieber W, Kunetka J. (1987) *Nature's end: the consequences of the twentieth century*. New York: Harper Collins.

Tull T, Jashni J, Parent M, Rogers M. (producers), Edwards G (director). (2014) *Godzilla*. United States, Warner Brothers.

White J. (producer and director). (1957) *Outer space jitters*. United States, Columbia Pictures.

Wise R (producer), Wise R (director). (1971) *Andromeda strain*. United States, Universal Pictures.

10

RISK ANALYSIS ONLINE AND ON PAPER

Introduction

Compared to my students, I am a novice using online sources. I asked them and several colleagues for advice about an online chapter. Their advice was not to bore readers with an encyclopedic introduction to 100+ web sites because they can already find sites. Nor did they want me to copy screens from web tools and then explain those screens; they said they could figure out information on screens. They urged me to point out key web sites and describe their use as well as their limitations. Accepting the advice, I have chosen, with a few exceptions, to focus on U.S. federal government websites and tools that can be used in homes, neighborhoods, and classrooms. Lastly, at the end of each section, I added up to five other websites to consult, which include many international ones.

In regard to risk analysis on paper, the challenge was to choose several journals and a small number of books for follow-up. At the end of the chapter, I suggest two risk analysis journals and ten risk analysis books. Please recognize that I could have added ten times as many, but listened to my students and resisted the temptation.

The web sites discussed below have a similar style:

- A cover page with an A–Z search engine;
- History of the organization; and
- News, and other highlights.

Searches are more efficient when the reader is specific about what s/he wants to find. For example, earlier this year, I wanted to read about falcons in New Jersey. I started with the word falcon on the U.S. EPA website, and I found a reference to a refinery in Texas, a school district in Colorado, a foam manufacturing company, and other irrelevant leads. When I typed in falcon, bird, and New Jersey, I found what I needed.

The United States Environmental Protection Agency: human and environmental health

The EPA website is like a large department store for human and ecological health information. The home page connects to environmental news, laws and regulations, EPA's history, and the A–Z search engine. The EPA website also connects to EPA's comprehensive guidelines for risk assessment and management, for example, reproductive toxicity risk, ecological risk, carcinogens, neurotoxicity, Superfund and others. I often consult these guidelines before I look for articles and texts.

One of EPA's most important online information tools is the *Integrated Risk Information System (IRIS),* which provides toxicity information about numerous substances. The simplest way to use *IRIS* is to pick a substance and look it up in *IRIS.* The reader will find an *IRIS* summary and citations to the basic science supporting the summary. While I always start with *IRIS,* I do not end with it. Some of the entries are supported by a great deal of data. Others are not. Much of the data were compiled during the 1980s and early 1990s and may not have been updated. You can subscribe to an IRIS newsletter, which will alert you to updates.

After *IRIS* I search the National Library of Medicine's *International Toxicity Estimates for Risk (ITER),* which contains data from CDC, ATSDR, Canada, IARC, other government and various independent parties.

In regard to mapping tools, EPA has some interesting new ones. Mapping tools are helpful to illuminate where possible hazards are located, but the user has to be careful because they may lead to misleading risk perceptions. One problem is how information is displayed. Certain colors (red, orange, yellow) increase risk perceptions and others (blue, green) reduce risk perceptions. Spatial distortion is a second problem. Choropleth maps, for example, fill polygons with data, but the population may live in only a tiny part of the polygon. Imagine a map of age-adjusted cancer rates in a large rural area that has high cancer rates compared to the nation as a whole. Typically, high rates are displayed in red or orange. Reds, oranges and yellow colors are likely to lead people who only look at the maps to believe that the entire area has high cancer rates when most of the areas may have no occupants. A city may have the same cancer rate, but the problem looks less imposing to the viewer because of the presentation of the data. This is only one of many reasons that I suggest that readers not take mapped information at face value (Tyner 2015).

With these caveats noted, EPA has some good mapping-based tools that are accompanied by explanations that need to be read by users. *MyEnvironment* and *Environmental Justice Screen* are two interesting ones. If you go to the EPA site and ask for *MyEnvironment,* it will guide you to a tool that allows you to see a great deal of collected information on a map. The easiest way of doing it is to enter your 5-digit zip code. The map will show locations where there have been:

- Toxic releases to the air and water;
- If there are eight-hour ozone and fine particulate standard issues;
- Direct emissions into rivers, including toxic releases;
- EPA water monitors and U.S. Geological Survey real-time water gauging stations;
- Emergency incidents; and
- Superfund sites (CERCLIS), and brownfields.

MyEnvironment also provides names of community groups in the area; cancer risk, infant mortality rates, and low birth weight rates for areas where those rates have been calculated. All of this information is explained in accompanying text.

I put in my zip code area and found that my zip code area violates the eight-hour ozone standard. The ozone standard is commonly violated during the summer along the entire northeast corridor from Washington, D.C. to Boston, Massachusetts. Clean summer air anywhere in this area historically called "megalopolis" by French geographer Jean Gottmann (1961) is an annual summer challenge. Ozone is a regional risk issue.

In regard to land information, one set of mapped data are superfund sites (CERCLIS). The word Superfund site scares people. But the sites listed as Superfund (CERCLIS) do not necessarily pose any immediate threat of fire, explosion, or any other present or near-term threat. It is easy to confuse the entire Superfund list with the National Priority List (NPL), which is a selective list of more dangerous sites. The explanation is found in the data base, but I worry that people will not understand the difference. Likewise, the data base lacks information on slightly to somewhat contaminated brownfield sites that I know exist.

The package has a good number of Toxic Release Inventory (TRI) emitters. But what does it mean to live in an area with toxic air emissions? Answers to these and other questions are in the *MyNeighborhood* site and other EPA reports, but the explanations are not intuitively obvious without background. When I worked on the data base that later became TRI, one of our major concerns was that people would jump to conclusions that high TRI values means a dangerous area and no TRI emissions means a safe one. I would not draw that conclusion.

EPA's *EJScreen* uses much of the same data as *My Neighborhood* and adds additional layers. *EJScreen* is a tool for those that want to compare different places in the United States. If I type in my area code, I will learn the following:

- How many people live in the area;
- Population density;
- Demographic attributes of the people living in the area, including per capita income; education, language, age, sex; and
- Housing units built before 1950 (older housing is a signal for houses with lead paint).

The data are typically a few years old, but that should not pose a major problem.

The most interesting layers in *EJScreen* are comparisons of the environmental indicators in the area designated by the user with the state of as a whole and the nation. The program produces a bar chart, and offers the data in a spreadsheet. My community is relatively low compared to the state and the nation for all the following indicators:

- NPL proximity;
- TSDF proximity (treatment, storage, and disposal facility of hazardous waste);
- Lead paint;
- Traffic proximity; and
- Fine particulates.

My zip code area is 50 percent of the national and 52 percent of the state level for ozone. In other words, the average person in my zip code has an EJ score greater than half of the national and state population with regard to ozone. On the other hand, the lead paint indicator is only 10 percent of the national one. According to the package my area code is 37 percent minority, which in my community are Asian, Hispanic, and Black (non-Hispanic) in that order.

Chapter 5 used Chester City, Pennsylvania as an illustration. *EJscreen* allows you to put a polygon around your area of interest. I drew one around the area of Chester that was the focus of the EJ Title VI-based law suit. According to *EJScreen*, 90 percent of the population in that area is minority, nearly all of it Black. The environmental indicators for that area of Chester are 90 percent–100 percent for every human health and environmental indicator, which is not a surprise. *EJScreen* allows me to see that Chester was and remains an area of environmental justice concern.

While EJScreen is interesting, it is not clear what 90 –100 percent or even 50 percent means in regard to human health risk. For answers to that question, risk assessment is needed, and for an evaluation of the options to deal with the risk, we need risk management. The bar charts should not lead readers to assume that an area is absolutely high or low in risk, only relatively high or low in indicators that may be associated with risk.

Overall, if you are willing to commit about 45 minutes to read the *EJScreen* manual, then you can do environmental justice comparisons of where you live, your friends, and relatives live, but I reiterate that you must not take the results at face value. In my case, I inserted the area codes for the area where I was born in the South Bronx, and other places where I lived. The numbers made sense as a qualitative indicator. But I did not take them as face value, nor should you.

I recommend the following additional five websites for review:

Environment Canada;
European Environmental Agency;
Ministry of Environmental Protection of the People's Republic of China;

Natural Resources Defense Council; and
United Nations Environment Programme

Centers for Disease Control and Prevention: human health

CDC.gov has many of the attributes of the EPA site. The home page allows you to read articles about protecting children against hazards, what to do in response to floods, and many other human health risk issues. The CDC site will lead you to the CDC newsroom, messages from the CDC Director, sections about CDC science, and the history of CDC. One important source to be reached through the site is the *Morbidity and Mortality Weekly Report* (MMWR), which contains important public health news and summaries of studies, and CDC's "outbreaks" section, which on October 8, 2015, when I was writing this chapter, reported a *Salmonella* Poona problem with cucumbers that already had led to four deaths, 150 hospitalizations, and 732 cases in 35 states. I had not been aware of this outbreak.

"*The Built Environment*," which includes elements from a variety of other tools, is relatively new. The built environment includes buildings, homes, parks, roads, sidewalks, transit, utilities that influence walking, biking, and overall human health and safety. I estimate that this software package could be the basis of a class project involving six to 12 students. I have not used this is class because it came out in July 2015 (www.cdc.gov/nccdphp/dch/built-environment-assessment), which meant I could not arrange to test it in class. The project I conceive of would involve evaluating the following:

- Roads;
- Curbs;
- Ramps;
- Intersections;
- Traffic control systems;
- Attributes of walking paths;
- Safety, aesthetics and amenities (e.g., fountains, bicycle racks, gardens, trees); and
- Access to grocery and others stores.

The tool asks for signs of physical and social disorder in the environment. The user can add more questions, a good feature. It can be applied to any urban, suburban or rural place.

Ideally, students with backgrounds in health, engineering, law, planning/architecture, and any number of social sciences would work together. I personally tried it out on a busy street about four blocks from my office, which I have perceived to be dangerous for walkers and bikers. After using the tool on both sides of the street, I am persuaded that my intuitive evaluation was correct. But now I know more about the basis of my assessment. The time allotted to cross the street is not long enough. They have installed new curbs that are fine during the day but become tripping hazards at night, and they moved the walking-bicycle crossing about 10 feet, which makes it more difficult for drivers to see people or bikers crossing the street.

Users need to read the manual because there is some technical language, such as different kinds of curbs and other physical features. They need to see for themselves how well the infrastructure is maintained, about building setbacks and heights of buildings. It asks surveyors to rate the streets for bikeability, to indicate food-related land uses, to indicate if there are government buildings, warehouses, factories, abandoned buildings, as well as schools, pools, parks, golf courses and other land uses.

One of the appendices has photos to illustrate some of the terminology. Surveyors code both sides of the street and all the street corners. Most of the scores are 0 or 1; a few are more complex and are coded 0, 1, 2, or 0–6. At the end of the formal walk through, the user needs to note other issues not on the survey forms. For example, I am really annoyed by the number of drivers on two street corners that make turns while using their cell phones, and drivers pull into the path where riders and bikers walk, requiring people and bikers to go in front or behind cars and trucks waiting for the signal to turn to green.

At the end of the *Built Environment* exercise, the group will have amassed a lot of information about an area as small as a block and as large a neighborhood or small community. The best application is to do an assessment in cooperation with a town and send a report to the town and to the state Department of Transportation. I can readily see this tool used as part of a health impact assessment.

CDC has many other interesting tools that relate to its larger health-care agenda. For example, some U.S. States are more able that others to estimate health costs and allocate their health-care budgets than others. Version 2 of its *Chronic Disease Cost Calculator* (CDC 2013) provides a tool for estimating the cost of arthritis, asthma, cancer, cardiovascular diseases, depression and diabetes. States can add their own information, and states without the data can use defaults. Like many of the tools being built, this one walks the user through multiple windows and provides estimates of costs for managing these diseases. The authors are clear about the ability to adjust estimates with local data and the implications of not doing that. If your work includes health-care outcome costs, this may be the most important tool mentioned in this chapter. I was impressed by the tool, and yet concerned by the many assumptions in the tool, which of course is no different from many of our methods for estimating toxicity and cancer.

I recommend the five following additional websites for review:

American Medical Association;
American Public Health Association;
Children's Environmental Health Network;
National Cancer Institute; and
World Health Organization.

Partners to track influenza

Many people know that heart disease, cancer, and stroke are the major causes of death in urban nations. The combination of influenza and pneumonia ranks ninth as a cause of death in the United States, and ranks fifth among the population over 65 years old. The risk is primarily a winter one. Senior citizens like me now get flu and pneumonia vaccinations.

For many years, the death and illness rates have been collected by the federal government and later published. Reports of new strains of the virus are reported in the *MMWR*, for example, when the H1N1 pandemic occurred in 2009. Recently, a website was created by Boston Children's Hospital, the American Public Health Association, and Skoll Global Threats Fund to track the spread of flu and offer suggestions. After reading this section, I suggest that every reader of this chapter type http://flunearyou.org and consider participating in this interesting disease surveillance exercise. The website and mobile application allows the public to report their health information every week. The data are incorporated into a data base that is mapped on Google and available to the participants. The weekly probe will ask if you have had a

- Fever;
- Headache;
- Diarrhea;
- Fatigue;
- Nausea or vomiting;
- Cough;
- Sore throat;
- Body aches, chills/night sweats; and
- Shortness of breath.

It takes about 30 seconds to fill out and submit. Every week the report updates the reader on how many have reported flu-like symptoms. Flunearyou is not only a simple and valuable surveillance tool, but it also signals a clear trend to surveillance via the web. We can use it to get real-time data on people's reactions to serious storms, tornadoes and other serious natural hazard events.

I recommend the following sites for more information about influenza:

National Institute of Allergy and Infectious Diseases;
U.S. Centers for Disease Control and Prevention; and
World Health Organization (weekly epidemiological record) and global influenza program.

Agency for Toxic Substances and Disease Registry (ATSDR): hazardous waste

In response to concern about cancers caused by hazardous waste sites across the United States (see Chapters 2 and 3), the Comprehensive Environmental Response and Liability Act of 1980 (CERCLA, or Superfund) charged the U.S. EPA with overseeing remediation and enforcement of actions needed to protect human health and the environment. In 1985, ATSDR was created within the Department of Health and Human Services to focus on human health assessments at National Priority List (NPL) sites. ATSDR shares a director with CDC and some administrative functions. ATSDR's guidance documents on environmental data needs for environmental assessments published in the mid-1990s have been replaced by more comprehensive documents, but stands as an excellent introduction on how to conduct a health risk assessment. Its year 2005 Guidance Manual for ATSDR Public Health Assessments and toxicological profile data base are used by many of us. Also, ATSDR maintains registries for the World Trade Center terrorist attack, ALS (Lou Gehrig Disease), and tremolite asbestos.

ATSDR initially concentrated on National Priority List (NPL) superfund sites. However, as these have been remediated and managed, ATSDR turned its attention to brownfield sites, which are less dangerous facilities numbering in the tens of thousands across the United States. ATSDR's (2014) *Brownfield/Land Reuse Health Initiative* is intended to allow local and state health officials, developers, regulators, and environmental science experts to build a data base that can be used to estimate human health effects before redevelopment begins. The form asks users to input quantitative and qualitative data about the site, including the following:

* Past, current and potential future uses;
* The surrounding community; and
* Land uses, such as schools, homes and other facilities hosting seniors and children.

You can list very specific information, for example, if the site tends to attract children and pets.

Some of the site information is detailed including size, soil and structural information about the site, institutional controls (e.g., land use, fencing, security), and lists of violations known to have occurred. The user can enter potential future land uses, as well as historical and existing land uses. The package is not complicated, and different users working together can enter information.

Users are asked to indicate exposure scenarios (soil, water, air, food).

The software package produces inhalation and ingestion exposure results for land-use scenarios. The outputs are exposures with 95 percent confidence limits, and the program assesses the quality of the data.

The package can be used by a group of students with access to data about a brownfield site, by a government agency/developer, or by a combination of all of these. For students this tool requires Microsoft Access. If would suggest inviting a speaker who has used the package.

I recommend the following additional websites for follow-up:

International Agency for Research on Cancer;
Occupational Health and Safety Administration with the U.S. Department of Labor;
Toxics Action Center;
United States Department of Transportation; and
United States Environmental Protection Agency.

U.S. Department of Agriculture (DOA), U.S. Department of Commerce (DOC), and U.S. Army Corps of Engineers (CoE): climate change

The USDA, USDOC, and the CoE are among the oldest U.S. government agencies. However, they are not included here because of age, but because they are major sources of information about climate extremes. You may wonder why climate change is in the DOC, which focuses on growing the U.S. economy. The Weather Bureau was transferred to Commerce from the Department of Agriculture in 1940. The National Oceanic and Atmospheric Administration (NOAA) was created in DOC in 1970 because of the important role of weather in the economy. NOAA's role in Commerce, indeed DOC's existence has been called into question in recent years by both political parties. An option is to replace it with a DOC that concentrates on trade and exports. NOAA would go to the Department of Interior. This transfer or something else like it may happen. But as of the writing of the book, NOAA is part of the Department of Commerce.

I call your attention to NOAA's U.S. *Climate Resilience Toolkit* because it is a readable effort to explain resilience and provide a framework to develop an implementable land-use plan. It walks the reader through five steps:

- Identifying the problem;
- Determining vulnerabilities;
- Investigating options;
- Evaluating risks and costs; and
- Taking action.

Each step is accompanied by suggestions of where to look for data and references, how to work with stakeholders, and prompts. A course can be built around this tool, and the results would be valuable to local governments. The *Climate Resilience Toolkit* (National Oceanic and Atmospheric Administration 2015) comes with mapping capability and reading materials.

The USDA's role in climate is based on the influence of weather on agriculture. Currently, the website publishes "drought disaster updates," including maps showing the serious droughts, press releases on drought and USDA responses to drought, and fact sheets about the USDA's programs.

USDA is increasing collaboration with NOAA and the Department of Interior. Some of their joint tools are really interesting, for example, *ForWarn* and *CropScape*. *ForWarn*, released in July 2012, by the U.S. Forest Service allows users to track changes in forests due to storms, fires and droughts (collaboration with the National Aeronautics and Space Administration). The maps are based on satellite flights every eight days. Assuming that clouds are not blocking views, the user observes what is happening on the ground with relatively little delay.

For those of us who can recall seeing maps of large areas of their country showing the location of crops and then being tested on that crop in a geography class, CropScape is an amazing set of tools that allows users to see land at 30-meter resolution. Users can see the impacts of floods, droughts, hail storms and other events dating back to almost two decades.

The Department of Defense is a massive organization that includes the U.S. Army Corps of Engineers (CoE), which can be traced back to 1775. One of CoE's official duties is shore protection against waves, erosion, and inundation. Toward that end, the CoE's *Beach-fx* software package should be appealing to risk analysts (Rogers, Jacobson, Gravens 2009; Gravens, Males, Moser 2007). The tool runs on a desktop computer, is based on an event-based life cycle simulation that uses a Monte Carlo tool simulator, and has good GIS displays. *Beach-fx* uses meteorological, coastal engineering and economic data and models. I like the fact that as a user I can define the storm seasons at the site, and each plausible storm event takes place within that season. I live in New Jersey, and we had a Nor'easter and were fortunate to avoid a serious tropical storm (Joaquim) within a week of each other in early October 2015. *Beach-fx* is an advancement beyond what has been used in the past, which was more cumbersome to use and had a less visual set of tools that relied on central tendencies and proportions rather than user-supplied data focused on specific locations and incidents.

Based on the record of events, the computer users a Poisson distribution to estimate the number of different types of storms that are expected in the season. Then the model randomly selects that many storms and randomly selects a time when the storm will occur. The location is specific but the beach is generalized as are the attributes of the waves in regard to height, water elevation, and other attributes. The package has a model that estimates the response of beaches (already stored in the data base) and the Monte Carlo simulator selects the response that is the closest fit to beach of interest. An economic component computes costs and benefits of the various options available to the decision-makers. The user is able to edit input data and then rerun the models. Outputs include tabular and graphic views of the data. The CoE does not claim that the model is without limitations, and it continues to invest in working on it. I predict that this package will be tried by many who do coastal planning and engineering.

I recommend the following additional websites for follow-up:

European Climate Change Programme;
National Aeronautics and Space Administration for Climate Kids;
Pew Center on Global Climate Change;
U.S. Environmental Protection Agency; and
World Meteorological Organization (United Nations).

U.S. Department of Homeland Security (DHS): natural hazards and cyber security

The DHS is an amalgam of previously existing federal agencies, created in 2002 as one response to the September 11 terrorist attacks on the U.S. DHS contains the U.S.'s immigration and border protection, transportation security, and coast guard functions. The U.S. Secret Service, which protects government officials sits within DHS, and DHS houses the Federal Emergency Management Agency (FEMA). DHS is charged with protecting the U.S. and its territories from terrorist attacks, and responding to both human and natural hazard events.

The Federal Emergency Management Association's (FEMA) *HAZUS* methodology is a relatively simple and widely used tool that estimates potential economic losses from earthquakes, floods, and coastal surges. The package estimates an area's exposure to these hazard events and multipliers calculated by the federal government to estimate losses to structures, the local economy, and associated social impacts. After completing a set of calculations, the user can alter some variables and obtain estimates of the benefits and costs of building levees, elevating property, adding shelters and other options.

HAZUS is on the DHS-FEMA website. The mapping tool requires ArcGIS software, which may be a problem for some potential users. The economic models are not as sophisticated as those featured in Chapter 6, yet they provide initial economic estimates. FEMA has been investing in the models to make them more realistic. For example, the U.S. flood insurance program pays out claims on the basis of depreciated value. The *HAZUS* flood model includes that feature. *HAZUS* has many users who are willing to share what they have learned through a user's group and individually. *HAZUS* does not fit some situations, which we learned when we tried to apply it in New Jersey as an advisory tool. *HAZUS* can be used by someone without a degree in economics, but the results would be easier to understand if one was available. Before using *HAZUS*, I strongly advise contacting someone who has used it for advice.

Cyber, or computer security, is about protecting hardware and software systems from theft and damage. This means limiting access to hardware and intercepting codes that could disrupt a system. I assume that everyone reading this book has suffered from a cyber-attack. In the United States, cyber security is divided among the U.S. Department of Homeland Security, the Federal Bureau of Investigation, the Department of Justice, the Cyber Command within the Department of Defense, and the Federal Communication Commission. Each of these has a website. I periodically examine the FBI site to check on cyber-crimes, and I receive reports from them that summarize major recent attempts to commit cyber-crimes. For example, a recent FBI memo warned that the new credit cards are less vulnerable than the old ones, but the new chip cards are also vulnerable (Foxworth 2015; U.S. Department of Homeland Security 2015a).

In regard to cyber security tools, the U.S. Department of Homeland Security (2015b) offers a mobile security card for smart phone owners, which I suggest that my students and friends use. It is a simple list of seven suggestions, accompanied by additional information:

- Use strong passwords;
- Keep software up to date;
- Disable remote connectivity;
- Be careful what you post and when;
- Guard your mobile device;
- Know your apps; and
- Know the available resources.

Another DHS effort aims at business. A recent DHS (United States Department of Homeland Security 2015c) report advises business and other organizations to:

- Invest in physical and cyber risk management products and plans;
- Educate employees about critical infrastructure security and resilience;
- Plan for business continuity;
- Share threat and incident information;
- Report suspicious activity; and
- Prepare for all hazards at home and at work.

Digging deeper, DHS has proactive and reactive subgroups that deal with cyber and other homeland security threats. DHS has established university-based centers of excellence that produce products that are available for such areas as visualization, explosives, zoonotic and animal diseases, food protection, and many others. The case study in Chapter 6 was developed as part of the DHS National Transportation Security Center of Excellence with additional support from the Defense Department. I strongly recommend that readers of this book with an interest in high-level risk analysis issues in cyber and other homeland security issues consult the DHS website. The universities that belong to the consortium have their own websites with explanations of what they do and copies of papers and reports.

DHS's Cyber Security Division has actively been trying to engage organizations to increase their security. For example, the *Cyber Security Evaluation Tool (CSET)* is intended to help organizations protect their cyber assets. It allows users to determine the status of their systems based on industry-standard recommendations and actions. Users assess their status and identify vulnerabilities. Users, in fact, can request onsite training. The first step is to provide information about the organization to DHS so that you can receive the detailed materials.

I recommend the following additional websites for follow-up:

European Network and Information Security Agency;
European Space Agency for Natural Disasters for Kids;
Natural Hazards Center at University of Colorado;
United Nations Office for Disaster Risk Reduction; and
U.S. Federal Bureau of Investigation.

U.S. Department of Energy: energy conservation and nuclear materials

The U.S. Department of Energy essentially is three agencies in one department. The name suggests that the focus is on energy research, which is true of the part of the DOE that concentrates on new science and energy conservation. When someone asks me for suggestions about home energy upgrades, I send them to the Department of Energy's (2015) *Energy Saver Guide* (energy.gov/energysaver/downloads/energy-saver-guide), which features tips on specific items, and in essence, suggests home owners do the following:

- Have energy audits;
- Find the right contractor; and
- Consider options, including air sealing, resetting water heaters, add attic and wall installation, and replace inefficient refrigerators, water heaters, furnaces and other appliances.

The last time I used this guide and hired an energy expert to do an audit, I ended up adding insulation in the front of my home (built in 1913), which has reduced heating costs and cut down on drafts. The guide and the expert helped me set priorities (Knaub 2013).

The DOE's Office of Energy Efficiency and Renewable Energy has multiple software packages that allow companies to examine their energy footprint, performance of their energy operations, and staff that can be reached for advice. I suggest that business managers consult this site before making expensive investments.

Another one of DOE's groups, Environmental Management (EM) has the responsibility for managing the nuclear weapons legacy. The United States has spent over $150 billion managing this legacy and is expected to spend at least $200 billion during the next 60 years at 16 sites (U.S. Department of Energy 2014; Omnibus 2015). With an annual budget of $5–$6 billion, the Environmental Management (EM) group within DOE is a source of considerable debate, especially in the host states. Readers with an interest in this evolving risk assessment and management story should consult the DOE's EM website, which will guide you to other online sources.

The National Nuclear Security Administration (NNSA) is responsible for building, maintaining, and securing the U.S. nuclear weapon stockpile, and is the third part of the DOE. NNSA does not get much attention but it is vital to consult if you are interested in nuclear proliferation, how the U.S. is making decisions about configuring its nuclear weapon stockpile. I also suggest consulting the Arms Control Association's web site to keep up to date on nuclear risk.

The U.S. Nuclear Regulatory Commission (USNRC) and the U.S. Defense Nuclear Facility Safety Board (DNFSB) are independent bodies that oversee commercial nuclear energy and the nuclear weapon legacy, respectively. These websites are important to consult periodically. Overall, the DOE is an agency that eventually might be broken apart and reassigned to different federal departments. In the short run, each of its three components has a critical role in risk analysis and each of the three groups has online sites to be consulted.

I recommend the following additional websites for follow-up:

Arms Control Association;
Energy Star Kids Website;
United Nations Office for Disarmament Affairs:
U.S. Defense Nuclear Facility Safety Board; and
U.S. Nuclear Regulatory Commission;

Department of Interior: ecological and cultural assets

The U.S. Department of Interior (DOI) is charged with protecting and enhancing the U.S's natural and cultural resources. DOI is responsible for huge national parks, such as the Grand Canyon, and for historical facilities such as Ellis Island and the Statue of Liberty in New York and New Jersey where many immigrants entered the United States in the early twentieth century. DOI's website allows the user to quickly find something about their own area. DOI also offers tools that ecological risk assessors will find valuable, starting with the *Ecological Site Inventory* Tool (Habich E. 2001).

I recommend the following additional online sites:

Ecology Games Organization;
Ecology Global Network;
Ecological Society of America;
Institute for Global Communications for EcoNEt; and
Natural Resources Defense Council.

U.S. Department of Transportation (DOT)

The DOT has a broad expanse of responsibility with risk-related challenges. Given reliance on automobile traffic in the United States, it will not come as a surprise that DOT has tools that measure road safety, traffic loads, highway design and maintenance, performance, and many others. Nor should it surprise anyone to see quite a few tools on risk assessment and management, including some that focus on project risks and financial assessment.

A report by ICF (2000) lays out a framework for assessing and managing the transport of hazardous materials. The flow of assessment and management is consistent with what has been described elsewhere in this book. Another relatively old but valuable tool is U.S. Department of Transportation's (1998) *Critical Management Incident Guidelines*, which goes into considerable detail about how a transit critical incident can be assessed and managed in a risk analysis framework. While these documents have been superseded, the logic is valuable for anyone interested in these areas of risk analysis. The U.S. faces major transportation challenges, but these are small compared to those of China and India, and hence I have included reference to their websites.

I recommend the following five additional websites for follow-up:

European Road Safety Observatory;
Ministry of Road Transport and Highways Government of India;
Ministry of Transportation of the People's Republic of China;
Transport–EU Commission; and
U.S. Department of Homeland Security.

Journals and books

Online access is already essential and will only become more so. Yet, it is important not to forget standard paper sources, many of which are also available electronically.

With regard to journals, there are quite a few that touch on risk analysis. I recommend the following two:

* *Risk Analysis, An International Journal*, which is published monthly and the SRA's website provides access to special virtual issues, book reviews, profiles of leading risk analysis scholars, a newsletter and other assets.
* *Journal of Risk Research,* published ten times a year, is a second very strong journal read by many academic and practitioners of risk analysis.

With regard to books, there are dozens with value. I list and comment on the main target audience for the following ten:

Banerjee A, Duflo E. (2011) *Poverty and risk: a review of poor economics, a radical rethinking of the way to fight global poverty.* The best book I have found that tries to understand the relationships between poverty and risk analysis.
Cox LA, Jr. (2013) *Improving risk analysis.* A must for experts interested in cause and effect in risk analysis and modeling.
Garrick BJ. (2008) *Quantifying and controlling catastrophic risk.* Garrick is one of the great thinkers in the field of risk analysis. This book is for those interested in risk analysis of catastrophes.
Haimes Y. (2016) *Risk modeling, assessment, and management.* 4th edition. A must for engineers

and operations research experts that covers a massive amount of the interface of risk analysis and systems engineering.

Loftstedt R. (2008) *Risk management in post-trust societies.* An important book for those that need to understand the significance of communicating about risk.

Renn O. (2008) *Risk governance: coping with uncertainty in a complex work.* A must for those interested in the underpinnings of risk management decisions.

Robson M, Toscano T, eds. (2007) *Risk assessment for environmental health.* A great reference for those interested in risk assessment targeted to specific groups at risk.

Rosa E, Renn O, McCright A. (2015) *The risk society revisited: social theory and risk governance.* A marvelous book for those with an interest in key social theorists in Europe and the United States and how Marx, Durkheim and Weber, and more recent theorists have influenced risk analysis.

Silver N. (2012) *The signal and the noise: why so many predictions fail – but some don't.* Trying to explain probability is a challenge. This book does a great job of explaining probability and why it is important.

Slovic P. (2010) *The feeling of risk.* My students' favorite risk analysis book. Required reading for those working on the social and psychological underpinnings of risk.

What did Chapter 10 explain about risk analysis? Summary and learning objectives

This chapter has described ten U.S. departments and agencies, as well as one other website that are high priority for risk analysis. It added more than 40 other websites for follow-up. The chapter focused on almost 20 tools, which range from simple checklists to complex data bases backed by mapping and simulation capabilities. These represent a selected sample of what is already available, and inevitably there will be more sites and many more tools. Despite the official-looking maps, charts, and tables, I strongly advise readers to be careful about what they accept at face value. Many government sites are carefully monitored and checked for accuracy, but not all are constantly updated, and many non-government websites need to be upgraded and examined for quality. I used several EPA tools to illustrate my concern about not taking information at face value, especially when it appears as charts or maps. I added two suggested journals that focus entirely on risk analysis and ten other books for follow-up.

At the end of this chapter, readers should be able to answer the following seven questions:

1. What are some of the websites that should be consulted for risk analyses sources?
2. Which one or two are the most appealing to you? Why?
3. What tool would you most likely consult? Why?
4. How would you find information about a possible chemical hazard online?
5. Why should you be concerned about using data from online tools? How can you prevent errors?
6. What concerns should you have in using mapping tools?
7. Which of the ten books listed near the end of the chapter are you most likely to consult first? Why?

References

Agency for Toxic Substances and Disease Registry (ATSDR). (2014) ATSDR Brownfield and Land Reuse Site Tool, www.atsdr.cdc.gov/sites/brownfields/site_inventory.html. Accessed June 12, 2015.

Banerjee A, Duflo E. (2011) *Poverty and risk: a review of poor economics, a radical rethinking of the way to fight global poverty*. New York: Public Affairs Books.

Centers for Disease Control and Prevention. (2013) Chronic disease cost calculator. November, version 2. Prepared for CDC by Research Triangle Institute. www.cdc.gov/chronicdisese/calcuator. Accessed October 10, 2015.

Cox, LS, Jr. (2013) *Improving risk analysis*. New York: Springer.

Foxworth D. (2015) FBI warns that new credit cards may be vulnerable to exploitation by fraudsters. www.fbi.gov/sandiego/press-releases/2015/fbi-warns-that-new-credit-cards-may-be vulnerable-to-exploitation-by-fraudsters. Accessed October 16, 2015.

Garrick, BJ. (2008) *Quantifying and controlling catastrophic risk*. Cambridge, MA: Academic Press.

Gottmann J. (1961) *Megalopolis: the urbanized Northeastern seaboard of the United States*. New York: Twentieth Century Fund.

Gravens M, Males R, Moser D. (2007) Beach-*fx*: Monte Carlo life-cycle simulation model for estimating shore protection project evolution and cost benefit analyses. *Shore & Beach*. 75, 1, 12–19.

Habich E. (2001) *Ecological site inventory: inventory and monitoring*, technical reference 1734–7. Bureau of Land Management. www.blm.gov/nstc/library/pdf/1734-7.pdf. Accessed October 15, 2015.

Haimes Y. (2016) *Risk modeling, assessment, and management*. 4th edition. Hoboken, NJ: John Wiley & Sons, Inc.

ICF. (2000) *Risk management framework for hazardous materials transportation*. Prepared for Department of Transportation. www.phmas.dot.gov/pv_obj-cache/pv_obj_id_70A8CFBAD414F1C9492C144390D69E082F9D0200/filename/risk_framework.pdf. Accessed October 20, 2015.

Knaub R. (2013) *Living comfortably: a consumer's guide to home energy upgrades*. www.energy.gov/articles/living-comfortably-consumers-guide-to-home-energy-upgrades. Accessed October 21, 2015.

Loftstedt R. (2008) *Risk management in post-trust societies*. New York: Earthscan.

National Centers for Chronic Disease Prevention and Health Promotion, CDC. (2015) *The built environment, an assessment tool and manual*. July 12, www.cdc.gov/nccdphp/dch/built-environment-assessment. Accessed August 15, 2015.

National Oceanic and Atmospheric Administration. (2015) *U.S. climate resilience toolkit*. https://tookit.climate.gov. Accessed October 10, 2015.

Omnibus Risk Review Committee. (2015) A review of the use of risk-informed management in the cleanup program for former defense nuclear sites, report presented to Appropriations Committee of U.S. House of Representatives and U.S. Senate, Nashville, TN, Vanderbilt University, August.

Renn O. (2008) *Risk governance: coping with uncertainty in a complex world*. New York: Earthscan.

Robson M, Toscano T, eds. (2007) *Risk assessment for environmental health*. Hoboken, NJ: John Wiley & Sons, Inc.

Rogers C, Jacobson K, Gravens M. (2009) *Beach-fx user's manual: Version 1.0*. ERDC/CHL SR-09-6. Washington, D.C., U.S. Army Corps of Engineers.

Rosa, E, Renn O, McCright A. (2015) *The risk society revisited: social theory and risk governance*.

Philadelphia, PA: Temple University Press.

Silver N. (2012) *The signal and the noise: why so many predictions fail – but some don't.* London: Penguin Books.

Slovic P. (2010) *The feeling of risk.* New York: Earthscan.

Tyner J. (2015) *The world of maps.* New York: Guilford Press.

U.S. Department of Agriculture. (2015) *CropScape.* http://nassgeodata.gmu.edu/CropScape/. Accessed October 8, 2015.

U.S. Department of Agriculture, U.S. Forest Service. (2012) *ForWarn.* www.fs.usda.gov/ccrc/tools.forwarn. Accessed October 8, 2015.

U.S. Department of Energy. (2014) *Department of Energy FY 2015 Congressional Budget Request Environmental Management,* DOE/CF-0100 Volume 5. http://energy.gov/sites/prod/files/2014/12/f19/EM_FY2015_Congressional_Budget_Request.pdf. Accessed May 7, 2015.

U.S. Department of Homeland Security. (2015a) *CSET downloads.* www.us-cert.gov/forms/csetiso. Accessed October 14, 2015.

U.S. Department of Homeland Security. (2015b) *Mobile security tip card.* www.dhs.gov/stopthinkconnect. Accessed October 16, 2015.

U.S. Department of Homeland Security. (2015c) *Critical infrastructure security.* www.dhs.gov/topic/critical-nfrastructure-security. Accessed October 16, 2015.

U.S. Department of Transportation (1998) *Critical incident management guidelines.* FTA-MA-26-7009-98-1. http://fta.dot,gov/documents/critical_incident_management. guidelines.pdf. Accessed October 2-0, 2015.

11
EXTERNALLY IMPOSED CHALLENGES FOR RISK ANALYSIS

Introduction

The history of risk analysis as a formal field shows interdisciplinary-oriented scientists collaborating to increase knowledge within specialty areas and to build linkages among them in order to help society understand and manage threats to the public and environment. Looking forward, and admittedly without a crystal ball or clairvoyance, I feel confident that the community of risk scientists will press on with these objectives. Elsewhere, my colleagues and I have written about the future of risk assessment (Greenberg *et al.* 2015), focusing on issues that are briefly reviewed in Chapter 2 and I believe are resolvable without sacrificing the scientific integrity of the field. What I am saying is that I believe that issues that are controllable by risk analysis professionals will be worked through, not always to the optimum benefit of the public as a whole, but at least human health and ecological scientific information will be at or close to the core of decision-making rather than driven out to the margins.

In this final brief chapter, I describe my deep concern about two trends that were briefly touched on in a 2011 editorial (Greenberg 2011) and are largely not controllable by risk analysts. Elsewhere I have written a short paper that overlaps some of the themes in this chapter for a public health audience (Greenberg 2014a).

Globalization of risk

Measured by transportation of ideas, people, goods and services, and problems, the world is globalizing. Here are several issues that follow from or are exacerbated by the increasing and more rapid integration of the world's economies spurred by technology.

Time and secrecy pressures

The number of new chemical, physical, and biological products has been exponentially increasing. I read cybercrime reports and speak with involved parties, and there is unmistakable pressure to quickly move products from discovery to markets, and to provide as little information about the product as possible to protect investments. Can the economic value of new products be protected against criminal elements so that those who invested will benefit and hence be willing to continue to invest in new products, and at the same time provide sufficient time for thorough review? Arguably, the U.S., EU and international organizations can keep up with global product development, but it becomes a greater challenge if time is constrained and access to the substance and product is limited by fear of theft.

What about those parts of the world that lack scientific expertise and resources? It is unrealistic to expect every nation, state, province and local government to build capacity to evaluate technologies and new products, or even to keep track of what the federal governments that do have capacity are finding. My state, New Jersey, for example, has three highly motivated state-funded scientists who work for the state assessing new chemicals, and it is hard for them to keep up with requests. Some entities have no one. The state commissioner of environmental protection asked the state science advisory board to review the literature and comment on the microbeads threat. New Jersey has the resources to at least assess the literature, but many others do not have people to read and understand it.

Microbeads are only one example. Every day there are questions about new products and technologies, for example, fracking and organisms that have been genetically modified. These products and technologies may save people from starvation, lower the price of energy, and have important positive benefits. The human and environmental health verdicts on these and so many new technologies are uncertain, and may not be known be for a generation or more. In the meantime, how can governments make risk management decisions that are risk-informed rather than be solely based on values and perceptions of business and government managers? Scientists have no hope of doing proper assessments without sufficient time and access to information.

Shrinking spatial buffers

For many centuries, we relied on space to protect us against hazardous emissions. Multi-national and multi-state events such as Chernobyl, the Gulf of Mexico and many other oil spills, global climate change, international shipments of products emitting toxins at high concentrations, sick people carrying disease agents across the globe illustrate that we cannot rely on space as a buffer.

Some of the most vulnerable places in the world lack the scientific and organizational capacity to understand risk data and implement policies to protect their populations and assets, even if they wanted to. Diffusing information about environmental and occupational health risks and their management across political jurisdictions has become essential. An early example of this was about response to industrial accidents along the Danube River (Federal Ministry 2011). There is need for many more agreements that will require cooperation among parties that do not necessarily have a history of cooperation; indeed, many have an antagonistic history that will need to be overcome.

Loss of trust in authority

Increasing pressure is being directed at risk analysts to know what events are going to happen, when are they going to happen, and what can be done about them. The group of worldwide risk analysts has brought this expectation upon ourselves by demonstrating that we can use simulation models, laboratory and other methods to better understand and sometimes prevent risk and be resilient when an event occurs. Risk analysts have become the science equivalents of the International Federation of Red Cross and Red Crescent Societies, that is, expected to respond without error and with efficiency to hazard events. Over the course of my career I have seen expectations rise much faster than our ability to successfully predict, even with large increases in the capacity of computers and expansion of some data sets. Unfortunately, every reader of this book knows that estimating the location, time, and size of a single event is highly uncertain. Even the best scientists and their best models cannot know where a plume of a hazard will go without knowing the kinds of information described in the Chapter 6 case study. When predictions fail, reputations decline, financial and political support shrink, and scientists may even be prosecuted (BBC 2012).

In some places, science has become part of the conflict over what values should prevail in regard to local and global hazards. For example, in the United States, the EPA has been accused of practicing "secret science" in order to justify regulations and other government interventions. Such science, some argue, should not be permitted to be used unless all the data are made public. The other side of this debate is that much of the key raw data contain identifiers and are not permitted to be made public under U.S. laws. A great deal has been written about this debate, and scientists are the losers because the manner in which both sides present their arguments is not easy to understand (Cama 2015; Environmental Defense Fund 2014; Leber 2014; Union of Concerned Scientists 2014). Coping with rising expectations and use of science as part of value-driven arguments will be daunting challenges in our globalizing risk world.

Mortality has declined across much of the globe, and that change is associated with economic development and investments to protect human health and safety. Logically this set of facts should increase trust in the governments and private enterprise, as well as science. Yet detractors counter with facts that over a billion people mostly in Africa, south Asia, and South America should not necessarily expect to live longer and have higher quality lives (Collier 2007). Their water supply is far from their locations and/or dubious quality. They have no sewage system, and their food supply and their lives in general are precarious. How can we expect these people to trust authority?

In regard to major hazard events, the *Guardian* (Provost 2011) summarized the ten worst disasters from 2000 to 2011, observing that these impacted every continent, killed well over a half million people, injured many more and destroyed many billions of dollars of property, and left many homeless and in helpless conditions, especially the disadvantaged. While it is true that the media exaggerate risk, and it is easy to blame them, there is a deep reservoir of public concern that governmental agencies cannot and private concerns will not protect them against hazards.

Even in places without eminent threats to the basic needs of life, risk surveys show considerable fear and distrust of authorities that extend to risk managers (Greenberg 2014b). I have tried to imagine circumstances under which trust would increase, and cannot imagine those circumstances in the current globalizing environment.

Shrinking human resources for risk analysis

Do more with less

I have heard the mantra to do more with less attributed to Benjamin Franklin who said "so by diligence shall we do more with less perplexity" (Sparks 1836). But I do not interpret Franklin's statement as do more with less. Commentators typically understand Franklin's expression to mean that better results will follow from hard focused work and simplification.

The modern meaning seems to have originated during World War II when millions of workers were in military service. I hear those four words everywhere, including from national, state and local governments, businesses and not-for-profits like my state university (Jaffe-Walt 2009). The twenty-first-century justification is that taxpayers do not want to pay higher taxes, and stockholders want higher profits. This means that we need to reduce the number of employees that want good salaries, health care, vacation and other benefits. The unspoken take-a-way is that that you do more with less, or your jobs go elsewhere.

Older employees, typically with higher salaries and benefits, are the primary target group for force reduction. I have heard it argued that they are less up to date with current information, lack the on-the-job focus of their replacements, and are blocking the upward mobility of more valuable younger employees. Data suggest that many of the older employees are leaving with buy-outs and their institutional memories, including high-risk industries where the industry is trying to replace them with mixed success, such as the nuclear industry (O'Shea 2012; Whyte, Greene 2006; Simonovska, von Estorff 2013; Peralta 2014). A great deal has been written about skill shortages in key industries such as chemicals, nuclear, construction and others where the risk to workers and the public can be substantial. Loss of institutional knowledge and essential skills is a stressful challenge for those who recognize the importance of the sixth risk analysis question relating to organizational capacity.

Rely more on communication devices

The expectation is that communication devices, more data bases, and high-speed computers allow smart and young people and a few older colleagues to access information and each other across the globe. The kinds of tools illustrated in Chapter 10 presumably will allow the remaining employees to do the work, and the highly skilled workers will be better prepared than those they replaced. These money-saving and selective workforce reductions may work for some workplaces. But they are a concern where hazardous materials and activities are in place.

When there is a serious event, post-event analysis sometimes will tell us that the employees were intoxicated, on drugs, or too tired. Other times, we will learn that the event was caused by the loss of personnel who knew how to maintain and update the equipment, lack of training and institutional memory of how to respond to signals of a failure. Blame will be assigned, and government and business will allocate resources to address these until public furor subsides, as illustrated by responses to the Gulf Oil spill in 2010 and Hurricane Sandy in 2012; only two among too many events that follow this pattern. I do not believe that all the key steps to markedly reduce the consequences of these two events have been taken. Solving a problem in the short-run that leads the public to believe that the problem has been fixed is a good short-term political strategy but bad long-term public policy that may lead to bigger risk-related wounds and loss of trust.

One partial solution is to have older staff train their younger replacements and then retire. I have no systematic data on this replacement process, but anecdotal information from the chemical, manufacturing and construction industries, and from personal contacts suggest the early retirements are accelerating and leaving little time for on-the-job transition. My concern increases when I do not see ongoing investments in employees. Some governments do not allow their employees to attend conferences. While webinars are a good way of learning, they are not a substitute for face-to-face training for critical staff working on hazard issues. Loss of institutional memory and skimping on training are bad decisions when engineered systems are controlling hazards.

Risk analysis responses

I have worked with risk analysis professionals for decades, and I expect that they will be motivated and resilient in the face of the globalization of risk and diminishing resources. First, I expect more reliance on communication tools that allow us to connect to colleagues across the globe (Kaku 2011). This is easier said than done because not everyone communicates in the same language, nor do they use the same equipment. Some may face political restrictions on accessing colleagues and information in other places. Nevertheless, I am confident that these obstacles can be overcome.

A second challenge is the need for more interdisciplinary training. This need collides with the fact that expertise has historically been measured by peers in the context of narrow specialties. I tell our new non-tenured faculty to become one of the ten best known experts in a specific area before spreading out to the larger system. But each set of specialists should learn the basics of the issue so that they can work with each other, in other words, tap into a larger pool of experts. After clearing the expert hurdle, some scientists are likely going to want to spend more of their time on the broader issues. It is these interdisciplinary trained scientists who will be able to advise elected officials and their staff, and the media. Some will face the challenge of explaining risk results to audiences with little patience for what seems to them to be at best waffling and at worst deception with numbers.

A serious intellectual challenge, perhaps the most serious one, is understanding uncertainty in all its forms (Cox 2012; Renn 2008; Weick, Sutcliffe 2007). Ruth Mack (1971) characterized uncertainty as omnipresent, elusive and complex (see also John Dewey 1929). Chapters 2–8 identified a continuum of risk-related issues from well-defined outcomes and well-defined agents to those that have broad outcomes and many agents. An example of the first is cancer and a single agent of concern. For these types of problems, the set of quantitative risk assessment and decision tools, such as multi-attribute utility theory, cost-benefit analysis, Monte Carlo modelling, Bayesian methods, and statistical testing have worked. Scientists use sensitivity analysis, uncertainty factors, and decision heuristics to measure the consequences of these uncertainty challenges.

At the other end of the continuum is a large geographical area that needs to make choices about how to reuse an area devastated by floods. The outcomes are human health and safety, jobs and taxes, and social interactions, and the agents are natural hazards that are not going to be stopped and humans, even if the humans think that they can tame nature. These kinds of broadly defined policy issues call for various forms of participation and deliberation, negotiations, use of scenarios and charrettes to solicit public perception, values and preferences, and maps that allow overlaying of different kinds of attributes. Health impact analysis can be a valuable tool in these cases. Uncertainty in these cases can be overwhelming, and analysts even if they think that they understand preferred public outcomes may find that human preferences are unstable. Hence, analysts must continuously scan and monitor and be able to adapt to changing human preferences and be resilient to natural and powerful anthropogenic hazards.

Whatever the specific risk issue, progress on understanding and narrowing uncertainty is needed in five areas:

1. Increase the accuracy of measurements, whether they are of environment or people;
2. Increase replications of important studies and as much as possible fill in data gaps in historical measurements;
3. Update models based on historical data so that they reflect current conditions;
4. Increase clarity about what are direct and indirect causes and effects, as well as identify and explain spurious relationships; and
5. Increase certainty about how to communicate and interact with decision-

makers and the publics, including accounting for randomness in space and time.

What did Chapter 11 explain about risk analysis? Summary and learning objectives

The trends toward globalizing risk and fewer resources in the context of increasingly complex risk-related challenges means more political and economic pressure on risk scientists, engineers and managers to promptly and unerringly assess threats and then manage them. This pressure in its worst form could distort the fundamental processes that legitimate risk scientists use to inform decisions and compromise protection of human health and the environment. Yet, this same pressure is an opportunity to improve risk analysis in ways that will help build more effective decision-making processes that are more risk-informed.

At the end of this chapter readers should be able to answer the following five questions:

1. How does globalization pose a challenge to risk analysis?
2. How do threats of criminal activity, including cybercrime, the inability to rely on space to protect populations against hazard events, and loss of trust in authority complicate risk analysis?
3. How do shrinking resources for protecting human health and the environment pose a challenge to risk analysis?
4. How do loss of senior experts and reliance on online data bases and communication devices complicate risk analysis?
5. What actions can risk analysts take in response to these externally imposed trends?

References

BBC News, Europe. (2012) L'Aquila quake: Italy scientists guilty of manslaughter. www.bbc.com/news/world-eurpose-20025626. Accessed May 13, 2014.

Cama T. (2015) GOP Attacks EPA on "Secret science." http://thehill.com/policy/energy-environment/233714-gop-attacks-epa-on-secret-science. Accessed May 5, 2016.

Collier P. (2007) *The bottom billion*. New York, Oxford University Press.

Cox L. (2012) Confronting deep uncertainties in risk analysis. *Risk Analysis*. 32, 1, 1607–1629.

Dewey J. (1929) *The quest for certainty: a study of the relation of knowledge and action*. Gifford Lectures 1929. New York, Minton Balch & Company.

Environmental Defense Fund. (2014) EPA's climate change protections under attack. www..edf.org/climate-epa-greenhouse-gas-litigation. Accessed January 18, 2015.

Federal Ministry for the Environment. (2011) Nature conservation and nuclear safety, hazard crisis and management in the Danube delta, www.unece.org/fileadmin/DAM/env/teia/doc/AP/Danube_Delta_project/Danube-Layout-EXEC-EN-.pdf. Accessed June 26, 2014.

Greenberg M. (2011) Time to worry: whither risk analysis and the compression of government funding in the United States? *Risk Analysis*. 31, 3, 344, 2011.

Greenberg M. (2014a) Insidious trends and social/environmental justice: public health's challenge for responding to hazard events, *American Journal of Public Health*, 104, 1, 1802–1805.

Greenberg M. (2014b) Energy policy and research: the underappreciation of trust. *Energy Research and Social Science*. 1, 152–160. http://elsevier.thomsondigital.com/ERSS_28/215C7602E7181759EFCC1FF4F17A3B67

Greenberg M, Goldstein B, Anderson E, Dourson M, Landis W, North D. (2015) Whither risk assessment: new challenges and opportunities a third of a century after the Red Book. *Risk Analysis*. 35, 11, 1959–1968.

Jaffe-Walt C. (2009) Workplace refrain: do more with less. February 26. www.npr./template/story.php?.storyID=101177718. Accessed October 28, 2015.

Kaku M. (2011) *Physics of the future*. New York: Anchor Books.

Leber R. (2014) The five battlefronts in Republicans' war on the EPA. *New Republic*. www.newrepublic.com/article/120228/what-expect-gop-war-epa. Accessed January 15, 2015.

Mack R. (1971) *Planning on uncertainty: decision making in business and government administration*. New York, Wiley Interscience.

O'Shea P. (2012) Navy and nuclear industry sign deal to fight workers shortage. *Times On Line*. September 4, 2012. www.timesonline.com/news/business/navy-and-nuclear-indsutry-sign-deal-to-fight. Accessed June 26, 2014.

Peralta K. (2014) U.S. manufacturers say skills gap could compromise competitiveness. *U.S. News & World Report*. www.usnews.com/news/articles/2014/05/07/u.s.-manufacturers-say-skills-gap-could-compromise-competitiveness. Accessed November 3, 2015.

Provost C. (2011) A decade of disasters – get the key data. www.theguardian.com/global-development/datablog/2011/mar/18/world-disasters-earthquake-data. Accessed November 4, 2015.

Renn O. (2008) Risk governance: coping with uncertainty in a complex world. Sterling, VA: Earthscan.

Simonovska V, von Estorff U. (2013) Shortage of qualified EU nuclear personnel. Nuclear Engineering International. April 24, 2013. http://neimaganzie.com/features/featureshortage-of-qualified-eu-nuclear-personnel. Accessed May 14, 2014.

Sparks J. (1836) The works of Benjamin Franklin. 2, 92–103. www.swarthmore.edu/socsci/bdorsey1/4docs/52-fra.html. Accessed October 25, 2011.

Union of Concerned Scientists. (2014) The truth behind the bogus attacks on EPA. www.ucsusa.org/publications/got-science/2014/got-science-may-2014.html#.VdTPIViko. Accessed January 2015, 2015.

Weick K, Sutcliffe K. (2007) *Managing the unexpected: resilient performance in an age of uncertainty*, 2nd edition. New York, John Wiley & Sons, Inc.

Whyte D, Greene S. (2006) The skilled workforce shortage. National Center for Construction Education and Research. White Paper. www.nccer.org/uploads/fileLibrary/research/SkilledWorkforceCrisis.pdf. Accessed June 26, 2014.

INDEX

Van Burkalow, Anastasia 213
Varga *et al.* 143
Velthuis, A. and Mourits, M. 78
viral disease 51
viruses 237
volcanic eruptions 233
Vorosmarty, C. and Sahagian, D. 204, 205
Vorosmarty *et al.* 204, 215–17
Vos *et al.* 79
vulnerability 3, 5, 27, 41–4, 53, 75–6, 90–3,
    110, 121, 146, 155, 183, 194, 196, 13,
    220, 222, 224–5, 227, 269–70, 292, 300

War of the Worlds (Pal) 269–70
Warren County 139
WASH-740 7
WASH-1400 7
Waste Isolation Pilot Plant 69
waste management 66–73
waste sites 33–9, 67; US 139, 139–41
water: underground pollution 34; *see also*
    freshwater resources
water footprint 208
water mining 205
water quality 22; problems with 87
water resources 86; demand for 87; Durban
    219–24; Mexico 204; scarcity 204; *see
    also* freshwater resources
water resources modelling 211–13
water supply: competing priorities for 86;
    dead pigs 81–2; leaks 87; politics of 87

Weather Bureau 289
Weibull model 25
weighting responses 6
weight of evidence (WOE) 50–1
Wein *et al.* 55, 249
Weinstein, Judge Jack 23
Wells, H.G. 269–70
Wertheimer, N. and Leeper, E. 45
West Valley PRA 31, 32–3
When Worlds Collide (Pal) 266
White House: Office of Management and
    Budget (OMB) 71
WHO (World Health Organization): food
    safety facts 39
Williams *et al.* 127
Williams, H.P. 145
Wilson, M. and Schwarzman, M. 63–4
winter precipitation 207
Wise, R. 275
Wolf *et al.* 204
Woods, Michael 234
World Health Day 39
World Trade Center 184
World War I: chemical weapons 106, 108;
    mountain warfare 106

X-rays 29

Yellow River 214
Yonkers Raceway 43